Hans Küng: New Horizons for Faith and Thought

Hans Küng

New Horizons for Faith and Thought

Edited by Karl-Josef Kuschel and Hermann Häring

CONTINUUM • NEW YORK

1993

The Continuum Publishing Company
370 Lexington Avenue
New York, NY 10017

Printed in Great Britain

ISBN 0-8264-0593-2

LC 93-072968

Contents

V   Dialogue with Judaism

VI   World Religions

Preface

Few German-speaking Catholic theologians can have attracted as much attention in the English-speaking world as the Swiss theologian Hans Küng, who since 1960 has taught at the German University of Tübingen. To begin with, Küng's influence, especially in the United States and Great Britain, was beyond doubt connected with a particular moment in history: the Second Vatican Council. Hans Küng had the good fortune to be alive and at the right theological place at a moment in modern church history when the Catholic church began to reassess its theological foundations for the first time since the Reformation. Pope John XXIII had announced the Council in 1959; the very next year saw the publication of Hans Küng's book *Konzil und Wiedervereinigung*, which many people at the time regarded as something like a programme for the Council. So it is no wonder that it was not so much Hans Küng's first book, his highly theological, academic work on the doctrine of justification in Karl Barth, as his second book, which at a stroke made this young priest and theologian known especially in the English-speaking world. The book appeared in translation a year after the German edition, in 1961, in Britain under the title *The Council and Reunion* and in the USA under the title *The Council, Reform and Reunion*. Küng's lecture tours through the English-speaking world also contributed to making his name more than others a symbol for a thoroughgoing reform of Catholicism.

Since then Hans Küng has consistently continued to go his own way: the present book contains a wealth of interpretations of that way and critical commentaries on it. With amazing creativity he has made his quite specific contribution to almost all the great fields of systematic and ecumenical theology. The structure of the book, the German edition of which first appeared on Küng's sixty-fifth birthday, 19 March 1993, is based on these fields: ecclesiology; catholicity; ecumenicity; christology and the doctrine of God; Judaism; and the world religions. At first glance these may seem disparate areas, but those who know Küng's theology will recognize a consistent progress here.

The course of Hans Küng's thought can be described as an ever-widening theological incorporation of increasingly complex fields of thought, without his ever abandoning the centre of his own faith. This immediately suggests the image of concentric circles. The centre is and remains a convinced being a Christian, reflection on the significance of Christian existence in today's world. Around this centre, in the 1960s Küng first drew a circle of ecclesiological and ecumenical renewal. In the 1970s he decisively broke out of this, first with questions to Christianity generally, the question of Jesus as the Christ and the question of God in the face of the challenge of historical criticism and modern atheism. In the 1980s a third circle was added, the circle of world ecumenism, dialogue with the non-Christian religions and the question of a world ethic. Here – for all the changes in detail – Küng's basic theological insights have remained remarkably constant. His fundamental theological conception has been less influenced by fashion than that of other theologians, even though the issues which he has been able to bring to public attention have been highly topical and have had a high degree of popular attraction. However, if one reviews his career, a constancy of conviction and coherence of theological theorizing are unmistakable. We hope that this book communicates something of that to its readers.

For the German language edition we invited a large number of theologians especially from the English-speaking world to enter into critical dialogue with Hans Küng. We are grateful to all those who accepted our invitation. We did not plan, nor did we produce, a celebratory volume for Hans Küng's birthday, but rather a book which would be a critical companion to and comment on a theologian's work in process. The German original has been abbreviated for the English-language edition by the exclusion of articles which are of less relevance for English-speaking readers.

We hope that this book contributes not only towards making Hans Küng's theology more 'popular' but also towards a real understanding of it: by showing its power of conviction, its decisions in terms of method and historical criteria, its strengths and weaknesses, its limitations and its riches – in short, by its quite specific perspective on being a Christian in today's world – and bearing witness to Christ in as credible a way as possible.

Those in search of a complete bibliography of all Hans Küng's works are referred to the original German edition of this book. The select bibliography contains details of all his *books* and of all other material available in English. Dates of Hans Küng's books given in the text refer to the German original; because of the presence of the bibliography, references to books and articles in the notes are given in short form.

Tübingen and Nijmegen, August 1993

Karl-Josef Kuschel

Hermann Häring

The Aim of This Book

In 1965, the then members of the Institute for Ecumenical Research in Tübingen produced a 'Festschrift' for its founder and director. Twenty-nine pages long, and with an edition of twenty-three copies, it was produced more as a joke than anything else. It had no scholarly pretensions. Of course Hans Küng was spoken of on every page, and the picture which emerged from these contributions will be no surprise. There was the active boy from Sursee, the successful chaplain in youth pastoral work, and the dynamic organizer. There was talk of the battle-tried 'racer' (on a bicycle, be it noted) and of the 'blonde infant prodigy' who had taken on Karl Barth at such an early stage. A woman author already gave an account of the hospitality of the Küng home and a woman bookseller reported how well his books sold. His native Sursee near Lucerne had as much of a place as Rome, to which the 'zealous Council *peritus*' had been returning regularly since 1962, and where for the first time he found the limits to his stamina.

There was as yet hardly any mention of the critic of the church, but there was mention of the reformer and the unpopular son of his church, if the reader was knowledgeable and acute enough even then to decipher the allusions to '399/57i' (the number of Küng's dossier at the Vatican Congregation of Faith). At the same time one could admire a photograph of Küng the world traveller – as yet without a motive, but with good foresight: he was then already deeply interested in Asian cultures.

Hans Küng, born in 1928, whose book *Justification* appeared in 1957 and caused a great stir, who was given a chair in the Tübingen Theological Faculty in 1960, who in 1964 opened the Institute where this account began, and whose director he has remained to the present day, has of course gone many different ways in all these years. He has researched and taught, raised questions which go deeper and deeper, and opened up new horizons which extend wider and wider. He has composed resolutions and withdrawn into study; he has ploughed through complexes of strictly theological problems, and kept in contact with politics and literature, with music and economics. People have admired him and been very hard on him. 'At the pulse of the time' has been his slogan, and for that very reason he has kept returning to the one message of Jesus Christ. He has been discriminated against by churchmen who have claimed that he is no longer a Catholic because he has stubbornly recalled the great Catholic tradition. 'In Deed' was the title of the early

Festchrift, and for him already at that time this meant study and writing. His fluent style has been and is praised, but only intimates know how often and tenaciously he polishes each paragraph. Commitment has always had to be thought through and given a foundation.

Thirty years of theology

From this perspective, over the years Hans Küng has changed as little as his Institute, which still welcomes the visitor with a creaking wooden floor and cedar panelling. The basic features have remained. The index number mentioned above similarly runs through Küng's biography, just as Tübingen has become the place for his life's work. And just as the Institute for Ecumenical Research still remains the basis of his creative activity, so he still goes on the offensive in promoting the renewal of the church – along the lines of the Second Vatican Council.

And yet over thirty years almost everything has changed. Just as the Institute is bursting at the seams – filled to the roof with studies, books and archives, so the scope of its leader's action has continually expanded in the course of years. At the same time there is crisis, breaking off and new beginning everywhere. And just as banishment from the theological faculty could not rob Hans Küng of his home at the University of Tübingen, so in retrospect all the breaks and new beginnings have proved to be the resumption and continuation of earlier lines. The reason for this is that while the theologian Küng has been occupied with many things, he has always kept to his last. In the course of his years as a theologian he has not just chosen the themes which bring the most publicity – as many people unknowingly suppose – but has followed a consistent course. Certainly he has recognized the signs of the time, but these have been the problems of 'eternity': the questions of ecumenism and reform within Catholicism, and the quest for a new response on the part of Christian faith; the question of God, which moves countless people, and the dialogue with world-views and world religions. Here Küng has worked out his positions in critical discussion with the major philosophical and theological approaches and sought relevance in a constant critical discussion with scripture and the rules of a scientifically responsible theory. Consequently Hans Küng has primarily expressed himself, not in articles, interviews or racy statements, but in usually long and demanding books. Only his compulsion for clarity of thought and transparency of language have been able to guarantee his constant international presence.

Only in this way could he succeed in continually extending the horizon of his faith and thought. He became a specialist in many things without ever dwelling on one particular point. Even the merciless strategy of his opponents in the Vatican could not pin the role of heretic on him in specific ecclesiological questions. For a long time now it has been impossible to catch Küng out over questions of church ministry and papal infallibility. Anyone who wants to catch up with him must take the trouble to follow him theologically at the same tempo. So for Küng, a constant widening of horizons proved the best way of showing how immovable his opponents were and how bent they were on ecclesiastical self-preservation.

In the collection *Hans Küng – His Way and Work* (1978), the editors provided relevant information on Küng's person, and on the themes, aims and results of the focal points of his research. In *Gegenentwürfe* (1988) we presented 'Twenty-Four Resumés of a Different Kind of Theology'. Here we offered illustrations of a hermeneutic of conflict, indispensable to any theology today which is committed to the church and at the same time open to the world. Of course this book had a great deal to do with Hans Küng's own theology. However, we did not want to celebrate him in an undetached way, but to set his concerns in the wider context of a history of theology which to a large extent was and is still governed by critically committed theologians, men and women. Each in their time stimulated theological thought and paid for their contribution with controversies which were forced on them and often proved hopeless, with harsh criticism, discrimination and public condemnation, with excommunication or banishment, sometimes even with death. Here, too, it is as impossible to deny that they too could go wrong and sometimes get entangled in the guilt of being self-opinionated and violent, as to deny that the church owes a great deal in particular to a theology which crosses frontiers.

A workbook

On Hans Küng's sixty-fifth birthday, it is now time to offer a workbook which is comprehensively devoted to his career, his work and his influence. Even now this is not to be the usual kind of 'Festschrift', a congratulatory volume, but it is not to be a series of contributions put together at random either. We invited the authors, as we invite our readers, to an intellectual journey which is both demanding and enjoyable. Its destinations are the main stages of Küng's theology. The journey should be undertaken sympathetically, but knowledgeably and quite critically. It should lead to deeper acquaintance and critical discussion of substantive issues, but above all to taking issues further and to constructive criticism. This critical attitude is expressed in many contributions, and the editors know all too well that particularly in certain disputed questions Hans Küng does not share the positions of the authors brought together here. However, their contributions in particular can show that a critical discussion of specific theological questions and mutual respect within a generally Catholic framework are not exclusive. So the criticism expressed here and presented with respect could become the model for a discussion within the church which is both decisive and fair.

This book therefore simply seeks to shed light on Küng's work. His theology has never been provincial, but in all its phases has presented, and still presents, the important and comprehensive themes of a contemporary faith. So the book also serves as a committed illustration of the strengths and weaknesses, the actual state of a Catholic, an ecumenical, a world-wide Christian theology. Is that to put the claim too high? Do the editors want to claim that here a position is being adopted on all issues, that here a kind of universal theology has been established which in mediaeval fashion has the answers to all the questions? That certainly cannot be the case. No theology any longer offers the answer to all the questions, as far as possible equipped with many footnotes and the whole range of academic equipment. Political theology and the theology of hope, liberation theologies and other outlines of an emancipatory thought, have increasingly recognized that only a committed theology concentrated on the centre, a theology reacting openly to anxieties and hopes, a theology which resolutely attacks the mechanisms of ideology and oppression, can hope for a future. In our view, Hans Küng has one such theology, which works in a concentrated and academically responsible way, reacts openly to human questions, and at the same time is ready to uncover the oppressive mechanisms of ideologies and power-politics, even at the cost of his own disciplining. Certainly this is not the only place where good theology can be learned, but the theology discussed here programmatically opens up new horizons of faith and thought.

But what is the state of a Catholic, ecumenical, world-wide Christian theology? On the one hand it has simply to take up the great tradition of the Christian faith, the biblical writings and the messianic remembrance of Jesus of Nazareth. It is clear from many contributions how hard Hans Küng has worked for that. On the other hand, such a theology must engage far more than before in dialogue with non-Christian world-views, the cultures and religions of humankind, and examine their effect. So this book also seeks to call attention to the *effects* of Küng's theology in different countries, among the adherents to other religions and representatives of our society, of science, economics and politics. Of course this aim could only be achieved fragmentarily, and this is an aspect which the English edition can illustrate even less, but it was important for us to make a start. From these contributions it becomes clear that despite all the warnings against secularization and pluralization, despite all the complaints about diffusion of identity and irrelevance, Christian theology need not degenerate into the hobby of a few specialists. Irrelevant speculations will not make it a hot-house. The voice of theology will be heard more than ever if it raises the urgent question of God and unconditional trust, ultimate meaning and the common values of humankind.

We have learned, have had to learn, modesty. We have no right to foist our theology on Christians on other continents. Nor can we force the other religions on to the one-way street of Western categories before we enter into a dialogue, presenting ourselves as victors before the conversation has really begun. But that does not mean that we should conceal our own positions, make our Christian convictions negotiable or wait to see how things actually go. No, we are convincing and will be heard precisely when we begin the dialogue with our own strong convictions. Theology and Christian faith, too, are in love with success and should hope to have an effect. That this is possible is clear from many pages of this workbook.

Seven topics

To provide information about Küng's theology, information about the state of a worldwide Christian theology, information about possible effects on countries, religions and societies: this workbook aims to serve these three purposes. How are these aims to be achieved? We shall be moving in seven steps or, better, in seven concentric circles. Küng's theology has drawn and still draws on the seed-bed of his own church, in which – much to the sorrow of some of his opponents – he has put down viable roots. The first group of themes in this workbook (I: Church) is concerned with questions of the image of the church, with the problems and insuperable obstacles of a consistent reform of the church, against the background of Küng's early works. To see how theoretical and practical problems, hermeneutics and political strategy, the discussion of infallibility and action in the church today, conciliar traditions and present-day pluralism all overlap is as instructive as the search for a common ground in which assent to and criticism of Hans Küng come together.

The second group of topics takes us further, to the question whether and to what degree Küng's thought is Catholic (II: Catholicity). That this simple question can open up whole fields of debate over the relationship between Catholicity and ecumenical thought, scriptural exegesis and dogma, rational faith and theological method, is simply the consequence of the church's lofty claim to this title of honour. Only those can be truly Catholic – and thus span the world – who can justify their claim equally before scripture and the great church tradition, before the researches and questions of reason, and before the great existential human questions. Already in his early years Hans Küng made it clear that this cannot come about without the virtue of theological truthfulness. So in this group of topics, too, we are concerned not only with Hans Küng's personal Catholicity but also with the question how far a truly Christian theology corresponds to the demands of a Catholic form of thought.

This almost automatically leads to the contributions to the third, even wider, group of themes (III: The Ecumenical World). The subject of the debate is the classical ecumenical theology with which Hans Küng's work began and which is illuminated particularly from a Protestant perspective. Of course here there has to be a contribution on justification in faith. Here at the latest it becomes evident that over the last decades ecumenical theology has gone beyond its classical bounds. Latin America also has a say. These are model perspectives, and perhaps also a first answer to the question where the true friends of a Christian theology which is open to the world are to be found: wherever there is a struggle for a human face for humankind and wherever knowledge of an ultimate mystery is not suppressed, independently of the limits of cultures, continents or world-views.

The Christian tradition, supported by age-old religious experiences and by the biblical scriptures, has always given a clear name to this mystery. 'God' stands for that indispensable and at the same time inexpressible factor which both permeates and at the same time transcends our reality. But in the Christian tradition it has been given a human and at the same time a messianic name. It is often overlooked that the questions of God and Christ have always been at the centre of Hans Küng's thought. So the four contributions in Part IV are devoted to christology and the doctrine of God.

It is for readers of the book to decide whether here the group of themes is extended or brought back to its centre. What is certain is that dialogue with Judaism and the other world religions (Parts V and VI) have to take their bearings by these two themes. Only because our God is a God of all human beings and only because in Jesus Christ human honour has been rescued may we track the truth of faith, together with those of other religions who are in search of God, without becoming untrue to ourselves. For Hans Küng this conviction has even become sharper over the last decade. We would be untrue to the Christian tradition if we did not seek dialogue with the other religions and thus together approached the great human questions of peace and justice. So we must be particularly grateful to the non-Christian authors in this book, the Jews, the Muslims and the Buddhists, for having sought and carried on dialogue with Hans Küng.

This group of topics opens up, finally, on a wide range of 'influences', only a few of which could be included in Part VII of the English edition. In the original there were contributions from Italy, Switzerland, Czechoslovakia and Hungary as well. The book ends with a bibliography of Hans Küng's main works.

This workbook is devoted to the theology of Hans Küng, but it derives its force from the commitment of its authors. We express our thanks here to all of them, without mentioning them by name. We are particularly fortunate in the contribution of some non-theologians, who in this way have done a service not only to Hans Küng but also to the cause of Christian theology. We are well aware of the enjoyment with which many colleagues have worked on this book, and in so doing have shown Hans Küng their friendship. However, the overall plan and the requirements of the publisher imposed limits on us which we cannot exceed. So we would ask all those who did not receive an invitation to contribute not to see this as a rejection.

A call for rehabilitation

We editors, then, have called this volume a workbook and have given it three aims: an analysis of Hans Küng's theology, a description of the state of a world-wide Christian theology, and a reflection of its effects in a variety of language areas. But a workbook, too, commended for discussion and study, can have a public effect. If enlightenment lives up to its meaning, it leads to relevant action, to a clarification of the situation and a humanization of relations. An appendix with three documents rounds off the volume. These three documents have not been chosen without a purpose. They indicate that Küng's relationship to Rome still needs a more subtle clarification. The Küng cause has not only been fought in public; rather, Küng himself and respected theologians who are above suspicion have kept approaching Rome in confidence with a request that the unjustified measures against Hans Küng should be withdrawn. In so doing they have expressed their conviction that – for all the criticism of details – Küng's theology is Catholic to the core and that the critical discussion with him should be carried on in the context of a legitimate Catholic pluralism.

As is well known, however, with the express assent of the present pope, in December 1979 the Roman Congregation of Faith denied Hans Küng the right to teach as a Catholic theologian. And yet, thank God and without detriment to a legitimate Petrine service in the church – in the twentieth century, too, Rome cannot go it alone in deciding what is Catholic and what is not. Rather, this volume shows that even Küng's critics want to fight out their dispute with him within Catholic theology. A variety of contributions point out urgently the Catholicity of Küng's theology. Read first the discussions here by Pesch, Tracy and Koch. Then, secondly, read Küng's response to the pope of 20 December 1979 (Document 1 in the appendix) in which Küng, literally at the last minute, made an extreme attempt to clarify his understanding of himself as a Catholic theologian – a text which, it should be noted, was acknowledged positively by Walter Kasper, then Professor of Dogmatic Theology at Tübingen, who was also involved in the discussion process at the time. Thirdly, read the dramatic letter of Karl Rahner and other Catholic theologians (Document 3), which expresses the conviction that 'Küng's inner disposition' justifies 'hope for agreement' and that there are 'substantive matters' between Küng and Rome which 'have not yet been clarified in every respect' and 'which cannot wait to be pursued further only after a "submission" on Küng's part'. We are of the opinion that the theological content of these documents has not been sufficiently explored and that therefore the opening of a new dialogue between Küng and the *magisterium* (without any preconditions) would be justified.

For we are convinced that even after thirteen years, Rome's step has no theological or legal legitimacy. When his *missio* was withdrawn, Hans Küng was granted neither the usual legal norms which are also recognized by Rome nor even a legal hearing in Germany. Furthermore, no orderly proceedings were held either in Rome or in Germany, above all in matters of christology, which on the church side were linked with the question of infallibility. It is time to clear up this legally untenable situation in a fair and ordered way. So we recall the 'Appeal' of our colleagues Norbert Greinacher and Herbert Haag from 1980 (Document 3) which already at that time indicated the pastoral, theological, ecumenical, political, church-historical and procedural dimensions of the 'Küng case'.

However, the present volume also clearly makes a second point: Küng's criticism of the present form of the official church and especially of an exaggerated claim on the part of the church's *magisterium* and leadership pales when set alongside the scope and richness of all the other themes which he has opened up for discussion, worked on intensively or brought to a solution. Once again we recall the great themes of ecumenism, of being a Christian and belief in God, of dialogue with the religious and non-religious world-views, the Christian stimuli in topical questions of our time and commitment to a world ethic. Unmistakably, it is critical figures like Küng in particular who have made it possible again for countless people to remain or become Christians or even Catholics; in particular, it is theologians like Küng who are open to the world who are again commanding respect for theology and the faith by the standards of a science which argues in a matter-of-fact way; it is Christians like Küng, ready for dialogue and ready to learn, who are gaining a worldwide hearing with Jews and Muslims, with Buddhists and the representatives of Hindu and Chinese religions. Here at last we have the practice of what evangelization must mean on the threshold of the twenty-first century, both within and outside the church.

In view of his influence, it is absurd to want to deny this defender and servant of Catholic faith his Catholicity by orders from the supreme source – without discussion, without a hearing, without an argument which is even half fair. It is even more absurd, in view of the present religious situation in the world on the one hand and Küng's theological development on the other, to maintain this position in the year 1993. We think that a revision is necessary. It is time to rehabilitate Hans Küng as a Catholic theologian. So we end with a request for 'reparation' which the great old ecumenist of Catholic theology, Professor Heinrich Fries, already made publicly in October 1992 at a conference of the Catholic Academy in Bavaria, when Hans Küng was allowed to speak again there for the first time since the withdrawal of his licence: 'Is the Catholic church so narrow that it cannot tolerate a man like Küng, or is it so rich that it can dispense with him?' In the meantime other theologians have taken up this demand (Catholic News Agency, Bonn, 25 October 1992). This would also be an encouraging ecumenical signal to the churches of the Reformation, one of whose leading churches, the Evangelical Church of the Union, bestowed its 'Karl Barth Prize' on Hans Küng on 1 December 1992 for his ecumenical services.

Many Christians have meanwhile come to believe that Rome has definitively given up any readiness to listen to its critics. All appeals are interpreted as anti-Roman feelings, all warnings as signs of hatred or a lack of faith. We cannot and will not be content with such a diagnosis. But we also see that new convictions have become established throughout the Catholic world church, so that the great questions and objections to Hans Küng, especially in German-speaking dioceses, can no longer be dismissed as exaggerations. Anyone with eyes to see can see that the discussion within the church has fundamentally hardened, that the crisis in church ministry has intensified, that ecumenism is paralysed. But even Hans Küng's criticism of the present leadership of the church may not be used as an excuse for refusing to enter into dialogue. In the end – as Küng himself keeps stressing – it arises out of a love for the church.

So we gladly take up the appeals made by many people in this book for the rehabilitation of Hans Küng and suggest the following:

In consideration of the fact,
– that even after many years Rome has not been able sufficiently to substantiate its charge that Hans Küng cannot be considered a 'Catholic' theologian,
– that the universal conviction of Hans Küng's Catholicity has not declined but rather increased in the awareness of committed Christians,
– that Hans Küng along with others has remained or once again become a symbolic figure of reform along the lines of the Second Vatican Council,
– that even critics of Hans Küng's position do not deny him Catholicity,
– that Hans Küng has performed inestimable service for the development of Catholic theology and the credibility of Christian faith,
– that with his condemnation the aims, convictions and attitudes of many committed Catholic Christians have also been condemned,
in view
– of the changed spiritual situation, especially of the Catholic church in Germany,
– of the developments in method and substance within Catholic theology which are documented here,
– especially of the progress of the discussion of the theological positions attributed to Küng in both the Catholic sphere and that of Christian ecumenism,
– of the many resolutions, proposals and requests, made both publicly and in confidence,

we request the Bishop of Rottenburg-Stuttgart to initiate proceedings for the revision of the measures which were taken against Hans Küng by his predecessor in December 1979 under strong pressure from Rome. Such a measure would not only undo a historical injustice but also give a sign of the consistent renewal of the church in the spirit of the Second Vatican Council.

The editors and other distinguished theological colleagues are ready to support the bishop in implementing this enterprise.

Nijmegen/Tübingen, January 1993
The Editors

I Church

Otto Hermann Pesch

The Infallibility of the Papal *Magisterium*: Unresolved Problems and Future Perspectives

1. Twenty years after: a mixed result

In 1970, precisely at the centenary of the First Vatican Council (1869/70), Hans Küng published his book entitled *Infallible? An Inquiry*. This sparked off a debate, with speech and counter-speech, with direct references and indirect allusions, which still has not ended.[1] But as early as 1977, August Bernhard Hasler in his book *Pius IX, Papal Infallibility and the First Vatican Council*, already had to lament the complete ineffectiveness of the discussion over Hans Küng's book.[2] That is of course quite correct, in that one would speak of a 'result' only if the exercise of the papal *magisterium*, in its self-understanding and practice, or at least in its theology, had completely swung round into following Hans Küng's line. That was not to be expected. However, if we take 'result' in a less rigorous way, the 'Küng debate' has in fact had considerable effects.

The much-quoted declaration of the Congregation of Faith, *Mysterium Ecclesiae* of 1973, which without mentioning Küng's name is clearly a 'Küng declaration', is the first official church document which hesitantly but clearly concedes the historical contextuality of dogmatic formulations and grants that as a result the wording of a decision by the church's *magisterium* does not express what is meant equally well at all times.[3] The disputed 1990 instruction of the same Congregation 'on the ecclesial vocation of the theologian' has not withdrawn this, but confirmed it once again.[4] As for theology, it can at least be stated that apart from some unteachable ultra-conservatives, even those theologians who in no way agree with what Hans Küng says and how he expresses it, and who are guarding their tongues and expressing themselves as cautiously as possible in presenting the doctrine of the infallibility of the papal *magisterium*, stress above all the reciprocal connection between the papal *magisterium* and the sense of faith among believers in order to exclude any idea of a rule of the pope over the faith of Christians.[5] At all events, all Catholic Christians have meanwhile become aware that in a modern world which sees freedom of questioning and of expressing opinions as a basic human right, the understanding of the infallibility of the papal *magisterium* and the practice of leadership founded on it is the decisive factor as to whether the church can still remain credible as a true witness to the gospel. That certainly could not be the case if obedience to the word of God, captivity of thought in obedience to Christ (II Cor. 10.5), in fact had to be identified with the unconditional and literally unquestioning acceptance of doctrinal statements from the desk of an authority in the Roman Curia. And if that is not a 'result', what is?

Yet now, even more than fifteen years ago, Hasler's lament is right in a deeper, indeed bizarre sense. Precisely what Hans Küng sought to prevent seems to have happened: (Catholic) theologians and Christians no longer consider the question of the infallibility of the papal *magisterium* a topic for discussion, and no longer take heed of the subtle distinctions and connections which go with it, between 'ordinary' and 'extraordinary', 'authentic' and 'infallible' doctrinal proclamation by the pope, between 'active' and 'passive' infallibility, and so on. They get furious over detailed arguments and series of arguments with which 'Rome' wants to keep the faithful on course or bring them back on course on disputed questions – eschatology, sexual ethics, the ordination of women, means of communication, etc., but they no longer take seriously the basis on which all this is played out. To put it in a rather unguarded way: the theme of an 'infallible' or even a 'binding' *magisterium* is as it were no longer on the table, and now people are simply scandalized by the stubborn 'ideologists' holding the reins of power in Rome and elsewhere who cannot be moved to a better insight and who have lost contact with the real consciousness of Catholic Christianity in the modern world generally and its consciousness of faith in particular. So anyone, even among Christians, who approaches these thoroughly controversial questions from other perspectives or works through them with other arguments is left perplexed at the fact that 'Rome' seeks to maintain an untenable argument by the use of means of power and reprisals which affect people's careers. All that is then left is protest and resistance, since 'the Pope is doing something which does not pertain to his office'.[6]

The most expressive evidence for this bizarre situation, in which the substantive arguments in statements of the *magisterium* are discussed but no questions are asked any longer about the formal basis for its legitimation, is the development – if one cares to call it such – of the Roman statements on family planning, birth control and contraception since 1988 and the reactions of the church public to them. In the unspeakable statement of the head of the Papal Institute for Marriage and the Family, Carlo Caffara, to the (carefully chosen) International Congress of Moral Theologians in Rome on the twentieth anniversary of the encyclical *Humanae vitae*, there is the explicit argument: anyone who disputes the doctrine of *Humanae vitae* disputes the existence of any church *magisterium*.[7] This only emphasizes what Pope Paul VI himself makes clear at the end of the said encyclical when he points out that Catholic priests, theologians and Christians owe obedience to the doctrine put forward in the encyclical not only and principally because of the reasons put forward in it, but because of the support of the Holy Spirit which is promised to the *magisterium* even in statements about questions of the natural order.[8]

However, Pope John Paul II went beyond this statement in his address to the same International Congress of Moral Theologians given on 12 November 1988, once again by asserting that the doctrine of the encyclical *Humanae vitae* is not just 'a doctrine invented by human beings; rather, it is inscribed on the nature of the human person by the creative hand of God *and endorsed by him in revelation*. To put it in question therefore amounts to refusing God himself the obedience of our understanding. It means that we prefer the light of our reason to the light of the divine wisdom ...' (no. 3). 'Here we touch on a central point of the Christian doctrine of God and man. Note that what is put in question here if one rejects this doctrine is the notion of God's very holiness' (no. 5).[9]

However, the church public and especially the theologians, where they are not *a priori* on the side of papal teaching, do not react to this over-clear demonstration that the pope here is appealing beyond all substantive arguments to his *magisterium* and his competence to expound revelation by making the infallibility of papal teaching a theme for discussion but with the comment already indicated and clearly taken to be beyond question, that here the pope is going beyond the competence of his office and attempting to impose a personal or a Roman scholastic theological view of Christianity as a 'doctrine of the church'. The discussion then goes straight on to substantive counter-arguments on the matter at issue.[10] Even the Nestor of Catholic moral theology, Bernhard Häring, argues in his dramatic letter to the pope following the Roman Congress, which meanwhile has been publicly documented, not by questioning the claim to magisterial competence but by expressing the expectation that in the question under dispute exceptional circumstances can be envisaged in which forbearance is in place.[11] In the case of Bernhard Häring it cannot be assumed that 'tactical' considerations are involved in respect of what one can 'expect of the pope' and what one cannot. That makes the line of his argument all the more striking.

So that is the bizarre situation a good twenty years after Küng's book: the more the intellectual church public concerns itself with substantive questions and no longer with the special status of a statement by the *magisterium*, the more 'Rome' stresses its magisterial competence as a global legitimation for its statements. But the more Rome repeats this position with increasingly 'steep' arguments, the less impressed the public is, and gets on with the matters of the day. And that is also why the opposing parties continually fail to hear what each other is saying. The scandalized theologians and Christians do not understand why even the most pertinent arguments simply do not penetrate to the Roman Curia, while the Curia's representatives think that they do not even have to consider these arguments, since they start *a priori* from a false view of the church's *magisterium*.

If there is to be a way forward here – certainly not in the short term, but the first steps might be taken – then there is no getting round the question of the competence of the church's *magisterium* and the character of its binding nature. That is why the new edition of Hans Küng's book also bears the subtitle: 'An *unresolved* question' (my italics). In the Foreword Küng's colleague Herbert Haag pleads, almost begs, for the question at last to be taken up again. His remarks should not be misundertood as being simply a plea for justice at last to be done to Hans Küng and for his question to be seen to be as important as it is. The necessity is an intrinsic one. For there can only be latent and indeed already the beginnings of open schism if large groups (still, time and again) in the church unconditionally take up and follow every word from Rome and at least inwardly excommunicate all those who contradict them, while equally large (and ever larger) groups in the church have gradually already stopped listening when anything is uttered from Rome. And as if this intrinsic pressure were not enough, at the latest since the 1990 Instruction of the Congregation of Faith 'on the ecclesial vocation of the theologian', it has indisputably intensified. Here it is insisted with a clarity which cannot be overlooked or interpreted away that all Catholic Christians and theologians owe inward and outward obedience not only to the defined doctrine of the church, i.e. to dogmatic decisions, but also to the 'authentic', 'ordinary' doctrinal proclamation of the pope, and along with that obedience and submission to the curial authorities who are working with him. None of this, of course, is new; it is there almost word for word in the new *Codex Juris Canonici*.[12] And yet, above all in connection with the oath of loyalty which is required of all in church office and all theologians,[13] there is a clear recollection that the debate about the infallibility of the papal *magisterium* is still in its beginnings, because it is still not allowed by Rome; and indeed the fact that it is not allowed is evidently to be stated firmly once again in connection with the expected encyclical on moral theology, regardless of the consequences to be expected.

This situation and such reasons make it a matter of urgency that the theme of 'infallibility' should not in any way be banished to 'ecclesiological oblivion' – that would be just 'ecclesiological repression'. Since, for the reasons mentioned above, a generation of theologians now growing up runs the risk of not having been confronted with the full seriousness of the question, it is necessary first of all to remember what is at issue in this debate (2 below). Then – passing over the details of the discussion, which can be read elsewhere –[14] it is important to look at the dimensions of the problem to be worked on, including those which Hans Küng himself did not discuss so intensively (3 below). Brief reflections on possible first steps in the present desperate situation will form a conclusion (4 below).

2. What is at issue

(i) Küng's 'enquiry' [15]

According to the Foreword to his book, Küng sees his 'Enquiry' occasioned by the deep and widespread disappointment that five years after the Council the great upsurge of renewal in the Catholic church seemed to have ebbed away and that instead of this, resignation was already beginning to spread on all sides (even then!). I personally know that he was also prompted by the deepening impression, which moreover was then confirmed by the facts,[16] that for prudential reasons, the centenary of the First Vatican Council would be kept quiet about. Now this at least Küng was able to prevent. At any rate, Küng made the attitude of the Roman Curia and the pope (Paul VI) personally in his teaching and church leadership responsible for this resignation. Küng had already taken up a position on the question of the theological foundation for papal authority *in leadership*, the primacy of jurisdiction, in his book *The Church*; he had discussed criteria for the exercise of authority in church leadership and thus, as was soon to emerge, provoked the beginning of church reactions which ended in 1979 with the 'Küng case'.[17] In terms of content the 1970 book sought to supplement the earlier book by investigating the primacy of the pope in *doctrine*.

Over and above this, Küng was moved by the baneful consequences of the doctrine of the papal primacy in doctrine which robbed the church of its credibility, as had become clear two years earlier through the encyclical *Humanae vitae*: Pope Paul VI had not deleted anything from this and, as is well known and has already been mentioned, John Paul II stressed this at every available opportunity as if this were in fact the central question of Christian faith. So Küng begins with the theological problems of this encyclical and first of all shows why, on existing theological presuppositions, the Pope could not have adopted any other position.

Understandably, this approach in Küng's book was much criticized, since he made it more difficult for the interpreters of the papal encyclical, including bishops, first of all to reassure shocked Catholic Christians with the formal argument that an encyclical was not an infallible doctrine but one in principle open to revision, so that the discussion could and must go on – as is well known, this was indeed the tenor of the bold 'Königstein Declaration' of the German Conference of Bishops.[18] Küng argued in the following way: the Second Vatican Council still stated that the infallible teaching of Christ comprises not only doctrines presented by a council or a pope alone speaking *ex cathedra*, but also those which all bishops, though separated in space, have clearly taught always and everywhere in accord with the pope.[19] Now in fact there are only a few doctrines of the church – in this case in the sphere of moral theology – which have demonstrably been put forward so clearly up to the

Second Vatican Council as the doctrine that any 'artificial' contraception is a mortal sin and therefore deserving of eternal damnation.[20] Granted, the justifications given for this doctrine have varied in history, and the central arguments of the encyclical *Humanae vitae* are recent. Nevertheless, a change in this doctrine would have meant the concession that the Holy Spirit had left the church in error on such an important question for around two thousand years; indeed, even worse, that at the same time it had been granted to the Protestant churches, which at a world conference in 1929 declared that contraception even with so-called artificial means was permissible, and had refused its support to Pope Pius XI two years later in the encyclical *Casti connubii*.[21]

This was the very argument of the minority opinion of the papal commission which was appointed after the Council to examine this question. Paul VI was faced with the alternative of either keeping to the old teaching or putting the infallibility of his *magisterium* and the *magisterium* of the church generally in question. The statements of both Vatican Councils prevented him from making a decision in the latter direction. Now in accord with the wide response of the church public, and not only among theologians, for Küng it is clear that the teaching of *Humanae vitae* is an error of the church's *magisterium* and therefore is not binding church doctrine. But according to the teaching of the First and Second Vatican Councils that is impossible. So for Küng, the question necessarily arises whether the dogma of the First Vatican Council (1869–70), which was repeated word for word by the Second Vatican Council, namely that particular doctrinal statements of the church and especially of the Bishop of Rome, presented under conditions which are laid down quite precisely, are infallibly true in themselves and *a priori*, and not on the basis of the assent of the church,[22] is correct or whether it is not itself an error. Küng affirms this *enquiry* in the form of a disputation thesis: the dogma of the First Vatican Council is in fact an error. He puts forward the following grounds for this – which according to the rule of a disputation must be refuted by the representative of the opposite view.

1. Vatican I does not produce any tenable evidence for its doctrine from scripture or tradition which can be recognized as binding by the whole church. On the contrary, the evidence from scripture – which Küng examines in detail – says something quite different from what the Council wants to prove with it, and the evidence from the tradition goes back directly or indirectly to the Decretals of Pseudo-Isidore, that notorious collection of forged conciliar and papal decrees from the ninth century which were already partly doubted in the Middle Ages and were finally unmasked in the seventeenth century as a forgery, though they were nevertheless still sometimes regarded as authentic shortly before the First Vatican Council.

2. The doctrine of the Catholic tradition is simply that the church *as a whole* is indestructible and as a whole remains in the truth. There is no mention in the tradition of the infallibity of holders of a particular office.

3. The First Vatican Council starts from the presupposition that the church can be guaranteed to abide in the truth only if it can express itself in infallible statements. This presupposition as such was not discussed at all at the Council. However, it is logically included in the doctrine that the pope can make such infallible statements. The question is whether a doctrine can be binding if its logical presupposition is not only unclear but not even evident because of its lack of clarity.

4. The Second Vatican Council merely repeated the doctrine of the First and did not discuss whether the doctrine of 1869/70 was either in accord with scripture or had a basis in tradition. Instead of this it even extended it by the explicit doctrine that the 'ordinary *magisterium*' of the episcopate was infallible in the circumstances already indicated.

Küng's final conclusion is that a doctrine which has so little foundation in scripture and tradition and moreover has to cope with so many contradictory facts in the history of theology and dogma – the encyclical *Humanae vitae* is indeed only the latest example of 'errors' by the *magisterium* – cannot be binding on the church. In this sharp thesis Küng can still escape a formal contradiction of the two councils: strictly speaking, he is not attacking the *result* of the councils but the *presupposition* of the result which is included in it and which was not discussed at the councils, namely that the church can only abide in the truth if there is somewhere the possibility of infallible statements. Küng also gives a Solomonic answer to the question whether the First Vatican Council 'erred': 'It would be better to say that it was blind to the basic problems. Instead of coming to grips with them, it passed them by.'[23] But what the Council has not stated explicitly cannot be contradicted formally.

Utterly in the spirit of the disputation which he intends, moreover, he opens the book with a saying from Augustine's famous work *De Trinitate*: 'Where the reader is as certain as I am, let him go on with me; where he hesitates, let him ask me; where he recognizes himself to be in error, let him return to me; where he recognizes me to be so, let him call me back.'[24]

(ii) Küng's own answer

And what is Küng's own answer to his own question? He equally rejects both the traditional Protestant doctrine, which attributes infallibility 'only to Holy Scripture', and the doctrine of the Orthodox churches that only the ecumenical councils are infallible, because they basically get into the same difficulties that also underlie papal formulations of doctrine, above all the basic difficulty whether the abiding of the church in the truth in any event depends on guaranteed infallible principles. Küng's own thesis is that despite erroneous doctrines in detail, the church is nevertheless maintained in the truth *as a whole*. The church certainly has to make statements – it cannot make its faith clear without human language. And in some circumstances it even has to make *polemical*, delimiting, 'defining' statements which exclude counter-statements – in particular when it is important at a quite specific historical moment to safeguard the confession of the church against anti-confessions, to mark off belief from superstition. And Küng declares explicitly that the leadership of the church has the authority to make such statements.

However, *binding* statements are rather different from *infallible* statements. If one takes the word in the strictest sense, only God is infallible. So in accordance with clear facts of the history of the church and of dogma, the abiding of the church in truth must be described in such a way that errors can occur in matters of detail – errors which are possibly detected only after a lengthy period – and that the most solemn statement of a council may not be above critical inquiry. The formulation of the faith in concrete, individual statements is a task which is never completed. Or to put it another way – in view of the problem of language (which will be taken up once again later): the truth in which the church abides and is maintained by the Holy Spirit is to be distinguished from the truth of statements in which that truth expresses itself: these can be erroneous, or at least become erroneous, at a later period, because notoriously they have been understood wrongly, and yet the church can abide in the truth which it intends to state and interpret even in such erroneous statements.

If in this process the church is always kept in the truth, although this does not exclude propositional errors, that means that the abiding of the church in the truth is not a matter which could be demonstrated by a historical examination of church doctrine with a view to a unity which always remains the same. Moreover, such an examination would always have to be subject to the proviso that even statements that the examiner still endorsed at the time of the examination could later prove to be an error. So the statement that the church is always maintained in truth, even through all individual errors, is a statement that can only be made by faith. And with such a statement, faith is simply saying that even in substantial errors the church fundamentally remains the church of Jesus Christ and must not be afraid of being separated from its Lord in knowledge and action by any human mistakes.

3. Problems old and new

(i) The still disputed interpretation

Anyone who reads the dogma of infallibility will even now still first of all pause on the closing statement, that the definitions of the Bishop of Rome are 'unchangeable of themselves, and not on the basis of the consensus of the church' (*ex sese, non autem ex consensu ecclesiae ... irreformabiles*). Indeed not only non-Christians and non-Catholics, but also countless Catholic Christians, cannot conceive how an individual could have the possibility of declaring particular statements, *human* statements, to be binding in such a way that nothing can be altered in them in the future. The strong minority which put a brake on the First Vatican Council until the last day could not prevent this formulation, which moreover was only inserted at the last minute.

After that, anyone who did not and does not want to go the way of Johann Ignaz von Döllinger and later the Old Catholic church and nevertheless did not simply want to turn a deaf ear to such absolutist claims because of an ungracious feeling of scepticism or inner resistance, had to and of course has to pay careful attention to where the text of the dogma itself sets clear limits to the infallible authority of the papal *magisterium*.[25] Moreover these limits can be made out clearly: the immutability of the papal definitions which is claimed applies only

– in explicitly *ex cathedra* decisions which are characterized as such;
– in disputed questions with reference to faith and moral norms, and nowhere else;
– moreover, it is only sure of being preserved from error by the power of the Holy Spirit, and does not have the guarantee of being the best and unsurpassable formulation of the question for all times.

To these limits which are already laid down in the dogma itself are to be added others which are not in the text but which follow clearly from the wider context and from the history of the origin of the dogma. The 'absolutist' formulation which has been cited was demonstrably meant to exclude the idea that papal decisions *ex cathedra* needed later ratification by the church or a body representing the church in order to be implemented – the fear of such old tendencies from the time of conciliarism and Gallicanism had not yet died out among many fathers at the Council. Moreover, the authority to made a decision *ex cathedra* applies to the pope only *qua* supreme bishop of the whole church – it is an authority *in* and *for* the church, but not *over against* the church, as though the pope himself were here not a part it. That is also explicitly excluded by the formulation that in *ex cathedra* decisions the pope enjoys that infallibility with which Christ has endowed *the church* in faith. Furthermore, the minority had its way with the famous 'historical preface' according to which in the exercise of their *magisterium* popes always needed the help of the bishops at councils and synods – which can now be understood and evaluated normatively against the notion of an absolutist praxis of the *magisterium*. The extension of the infallibility of the church's *magisterium* to the 'ordinary *magisterium*' of the pope if there is unanimous agreement with the world episcopate,[26] which the Second Vatican Council spoke of, confirms like a distant echo what the 1870 minority had already wanted to put on paper and indeed probably would have done had it been possible to continue the council: the incorporation of the papal *magisterium* into the collegial *magisterium* of the bishops.

And finally, scholars have also been able to take into account the general 'political climate' at the time: the oppression of Catholics in many laicist or Protestant states, the idea of sovereignty, the philosophy of the state which also had its effects on the understanding of leadership in the church, and the spiritual authority of the papacy which had been strengthened again after the confusions of the French Revolution, the Napoleonic era and the wars of liberation.[27] Even conservative Catholic theologians who were indubitably loyal to the pope did not neglect at that time to mark carefully the limits of the 1870 definition and made no small contribution towards reassuring public opinion inside and outside the church.[28]

Along this line the conviction could develop that in 1870, fundamentally the minority at the council who were concerned to put a brake on things, to set limits to papal omnipotence, and already at that time were moving towards something like the 'collegiality' of the bishops with the pope, had their way over essential concerns. True, scholastic dogmatism did not allow itself the slightest word of criticism. How could it, after the shock of the dispute over 'modernism' at the beginning of the century had once again made it clear for decades that questions about the historicity of the church and the historical conditioning of its form at that time were unacceptable unless the questions aimed at working out the continuous progress towards its present highest form. Still, even scholastic dogmatism stressed the explicit limits to the dogma of primacy and had its routine explanations for the disruptive historical factors.

As I have already indicated, church history was somewhat bolder, above all in the prelude to and context of the Second Vatican Council. Moreover, in the course of an ecumenical dialogue which was becoming more intensive the theme of 'papal primacy' could not of course be bracketted off – indeed in the end Pius XII had deliberately taken into account the burden that would be placed on this dialogue when in 1950 he in fact for the first time claimed the infallibility of his *magisterium* promised him by the First Vatican Council with the dogma of the bodily assumption of Mary into heaven.

Nevertheless, it remained as it were the ground-bass of the defenders over against the critics of the First Vatican Council that there was no ground for anxiety about the freedom of theological research and questioning, since the limits of the dogma had been drawn so narrowly that no 'accident' could happen, and a papal intervention with dogmatic binding character was to be expected only rarely, and then in a dramatic emergency for the church. Moreover the problems remained a matter for theologians – 'church folk' were untouched by it and essentially found that everything was in order over the papacy.

Regardless of how one judges Hans Küng's book on infallibilty, it is indisputably his merit to have made people world-wide sensitive to the fact that the 'minimalist' interpretation of the dogma of primacy along the line of the 1870 minority, which is firmly rooted in professional theology, could be a trivialization. The way in which he begins his book with the situation created by the encyclical *Humanae vitae* has often been criticized as an inappropriate approach to the problems. However, the opposite is the case. Here Küng, by bringing out the connection between the infallible *ordinary magisterium* of the bishops and the popes, endorsed at the Second Vatican Council, and the papal *ex cathedra* decisions, on an existential question which affects all Catholics, makes it necessary for the problem of magisterial infallibility as such to be treated as a specific theme in the interest not only of theologians, but now also of all Catholics in the world, since all can be affected by it. The outcome thus clarified now looks like this: if there is such a thing as an infallibility of the church's *magisterium*, then by the nature of the case the limits are wider than people have so far persuaded themselves that they are, and papal *ex cathedra* decisions with what in fact are very narrow limits are then only a special case which does not embrace the whole set of problems.

In the subsequent world-wide discussion the contentiousness of the correct interpretation of the First Vatican Council, historically and subsequently also substantively, emerged all over again. In the face of Küng's arguments some withdrew with reasons old and new to the established, minimalistic, reassuring interpretation of the professional theologians; others, challenged by Küng, began to develop new thoughts on the topic of the 'infallible *magisterium*'. The one who went furthest in respect of both a minimalizing interpretation and new ideas, against Küng and beyond Küng, was the Dutch theologian and pupil of Edward Schillebeeckx, Anton Houtepen, in his book on *Infallibility and Hermeneutics*.[29] He summed up his thesis like this: 'The dogmatic definition of Vatican I on the infallible magisterial statements of the pope did not intend to dogmatize the dogma or to lay down the immutability of dogmatic formulas, but on the contrary sought to demonstrate that the content of the Christian gospel must constantly be described again carefully and authoritatively in the church.'[30] As a result of the prehistory of Vatican I the concept shifted from the mediaeval sense of the word 'infallible' as meaning the reliability and faithfulness of God and the 'inerrancy' of the church in faith to denote the supreme authority of the Bishop of Rome, against which there could be no appeal to a yet higher authority. Consequently that also applied to his decision as arbiter in doctrine. The openness of the history of the formulation of faith is protected as in a dialectical covering by the fact that the pope is bound in his 'irrevocable' decisions only by scripture and tradition, not by church law, the decisions of his predecessors or his own earlier decisions. However, under what it felt to be threats from philosophy and the process of secularization in the nineteenth century, the council was only concerned with the question *who* has the last decision in a particular case, and not with the hermeneutical problems of continuity in the ongoing development of the proclamation of faith. Houtepen attacks Hans Küng for focussing the problem on 'infallible statements', something which the council did not mean in this way, but he agrees with Hans Küng that the council did not reflect on the fundamental hermeneutical problems of the dogma of primacy.

A few years later the split in the discussion was repeated over the book by August Bernhard Hasler already mentioned.[31] However, Hasler had a simple and disarming argument for all minimalistic interpretations: if these were right, then the bishops in the minority should not have left, but should have rejoiced![32] And he explicitly objects, against Houtepen, that the subsequent history of the subjection of the minority bishops actively brought about by Rome refutes the thesis that the papal doctrinal decisions were only legally unassailable and not theologicaly irreformable. According to Hasler the doctrinal decisions of the pope are not infallible because they are legally irrefutable, but irrefutable because they are infallible.

(ii) The grey zone of the implementation of doctrinal decisions

However, at one point Houtepen has drawn attention to a problem which, if I am right, has not been sufficiently illuminated in the Küng discussion: the connection of the dogma of infallibility with the wider dogma of the primacy of papal jurisdiction, indeed its dependence on it.[33] This can already be seen without any knowledge of the prehistory, simply from a closer reading of the text of the dogmatic constitution *Pastor aeternus*. The comprehensive dogmatic statement is that of the universal primacy of leadership of the Bishop of Rome which is derived from the foundation of his office by Christ. One consequence of this – within the given limits – is the infallibility of the papal *magisterium* in doctrinal decisions which are ultimately binding. Therefore these decisions, i.e. the 'doctrinal statements' which follow the famous colon, as revealed and therefore to be held, are not 'infallible' but, as the text explicitly says, 'irreformable' – it is the authority which decrees them that is 'infallible'.

However, what happens here is more than just a legal shift in the concept of 'infallible'. Rather, simply out of a concern to clarify the competence of decisions within the church, faith is turned into obedience to the legally binding decisions of the leadership of the church. Moderate Catholic dogmatics in particular confirms this in the years after 1870 in calling for 'inward and outward obedience' to the binding '*ex cathedra* statement' in the form of a law.[34] So Houtepen is once again on the right lines when as a continuation of the discussion he asks that there shall be no restriction to the 'question of the historical continuity of the *confession* articulated by the *church*', but attention to 'the deeper question of the continuity of the *event of faith* in the *community of faith*, namely the question whether and how the community of faith may accept and experience that in its thought, language *and action* it stands in line with what from of old has been indicated in the Jewish-Christian tradition with parables and metaphors as "the plan of God" and "the cause of Jesus".[35]

Subsequent Roman curial practice and the episcopal praxis which followed it in many places drew other conclusions from this legalistic codification of the understanding of faith. Indeed the duty of ecclesiastical obedience extends further than the realm of dogmatic definitions in the strict sense, and the legal competence of the church's office of leadership effectively extends beyond the decreeing of doctrinal decisions. Magisterial positions can be expressed, if not already in the form of laws, at least in the form of legally binding instructions. They then have consequences which can be implemented with ecclesiastical or constitutional means – and there is no appeal against them. So the papal exercise of *magisterium* does not *need* even formally to speak *ex cathedra*. It can simply prevent contradiction by the normal legal efficiency of its standpoints. The strict limits in the dogma of 1870 can in this way become extremely elastic, and the legalization of the understanding of faith just depicted contains an almost irresistible temptation to extend them further and further.

In this connection it is of course quite conclusive that for the successors of Pius IX and their collaborators it seems inconceivable that the work of theology, not to mention the experience of faith and life among believers, could have some constructive, critical, stimulating, warning influence on the statements of the *magisterium*.[36] In fact – unfortunately, but sometimes also to the good fortune of the church – things can be quite different. Even popes have studied theology sometime, somewhere, and both before and after their elections have been open to the influence of theologians and even wise non-theologians who are critical of their time. But in theory the interpretation in faith of the message of faith is entrusted *solely* to the *magisterium*, first of all to the pope as Peter's successor and the representative of Christ, and that not only relates to the strict doctrine of faith and morals but embraces all areas of knowledge and action which overlap or even touch on the sphere of faith. Therefore the church *magisterium* throughout its sphere is formally and substantively the intrinsic norm of theological work and indeed the next and universal norm of truth. In a word, theology can only be done by 'delegation'. The *magisterium* delegates its teaching function to theologians; these do not teach by virtue of their own right or their own scientific insight. Rather, they hold an auxiliary office for the real teachers of the church, and it is their task to demonstrate *how* – not *that*! – the proclamation of the *magisterium* is contained in the sources of revelation in precisely the sense in which it is made.

This concept has reached two high-points in recent times. One is the 'encyclical paragraph' in Pius XII's encyclical *Humani generis* of 1950,[37] according to which the theologians may no longer discuss a previously open question if the pope has taken a position on it in an encyclical – a prescription which, had it been followed, would have prevented the Second Vatican

Council – and the instruction already mentioned 'on the ecclesial vocation of the theologian' and the oath of loyalty newly introduced in connection with it, which commits those in office and theologians to hold firm in inward and outward obedience even to 'authentic' teaching of the papal *magisterium* which has not been defined.[38] Strictly speaking, this goes even further than the 'encyclical paragraph' in *Humani generis* and if carried through consistently would inevitably have prevented any progress in theological knowledge, in so far as it made a criticism of previous 'authentic' teaching inevitable.

In short, in complete contradiction to parts of professional theology, in official church praxis a *maximalist* intepretation of the First Vatican Council has imposed itself and persisted down to the present day. Statements of the Second Vatican Council running counter to this – about the participation of the whole people of God in the prophetic ministry of Christ, about the inerrancy of the church which expresses itself in the sense of faith of all believers, and about the part played by theology in the preparation of the church's proclamation of doctrine – [39] have not changed that.

The consequence was and is an oppressive grey zone in which doctrinal decisions are made, teaching is disciplined by administrative decisions which are as unassailable as the supreme office of leadership of the church is generally, and thus in fact equip themselves with this office – truly a 'maximalist' interpretation of Vatican I, in the face of which the deep sigh can already be uttered: if only Rome would keep to the *First* Vatican Council! Today it should really be taken for granted that if a theologian working conscientiously and passionately is accused of something so monstrous as a knowing and deliberate or even only unperceived deviation from binding church doctrine, i.e. ultimately from that by which the church stands or falls, then there must first be the most careful examination, using every measure of caution required by experience of the inadequacy of human verdicts, with the granting of any legal protection which protects the weaker from the powerful. It should have been taken for granted that permission to teach would be withdrawn from theologians only when according to all the strict procedural rules which are provided in such a case they were to be condemned as heretics. As is well known, the facts are different. One need only look over the 'famous' condemnations of this century: *de facto*, *one* theologian has always condemned, or caused another to be condemned and/or required his submission, by going through administrative procedures on the basis of the possibilities which accrued to him under church law – from Alfred Loisy to Marie-Dominique Chenu and Yves Congar, from Henri de Lubac to Charles Curran and Leonardo Boff. Hardly ever was there tangible, manifest heresy against which the faithful really had to be warned. And in no case had a legitimate condemnation for heresy preceded this – all the reports of previous extensive 'examinations', in some cases lasting for years, do not conceal this. And as is well known, all this took place and still takes place in forms which have contempt for human courtesy and a human style of doing things, not to mention the criteria of Christian solidarity. It is left to the the successors to the judges then to see to rehabilitation – not always, but sometimes, even leading to a cardinal's hat for the former deviant. And then in some circumstaces they make the mistakes of their predecessors all over again.

Now we must not be unrealistic. I am not thinking of asking that, as in the time of the early church, only councils or at least synods should condemn Christans for heresy. There may and must be less expensive procedures in the present-day world church. And of course such a process of disciplining teaching – the need for which cannot be dismissed – also has a technical and administrative side. But in that case the rules of procedure must be much stricter, so that the grey zone of the maximalist exercise of office is illuminated and made clear. Where, if not here, could the collegiality of the bishops also have proved itself outside the council? Where, if not here, could the synod of bishops meeting every five years do good service? Moreover my utopia would be a kind of 'church constitutional court' to which even a pope had to be responsible, regardless of his competence in ultimately binding decisions, in respect of legitimate procedures in decisions on conflicts of teaching. Such a court, conversely, would constantly have to examine whether the law and practice of the church are in accord with its truly binding teaching, for example with the concessions of the Second Vatican Council. For given all the experience, no one in the church may feel sure that they will not fall victim to the temptation of the misuse of power, and no one in the church is obliged, over-hastily, before all other possibilities are exhausted, to leave such misuse of power to God's judgment alone. If the issue is one as decisive as the freedom of the word of faith in the midst of the people of God, the grey zone of doctrinal discipline as we now experience it almost daily is not only a scandal but testimony against the gospel.

(iii) Infallibility and language

The discussion so far is adequate evidence of how 'unresolved' Hans Küng's 'enquiry' still is, despite the truly tremendous effects that it has had. No one requires and expects 'Rome' imperceptibly, simply to elevate Hans Küng's theses to church doctrine – and indeed that would be contrary to the intentions of his book. However, 'Rome' shares the responsibility for the fact that the 'enquiry' is still 'unresolved', that there the debate itself, in so far as it does not repudiate Küng, is regarded as a sign of heresy and therefore as inadmissible. The points which follow therefore do not open up any new dimensions of the discussion but simply mention quite briefly some perspectives which were already expressed basically in the first round of the discussion but which have been reinforced in the meantime.

Like all other doctrinal decisions, papal doctrinal decisions are *propositions*, linguistic expressions. As such – and this is not just an insight of present-day linguistic philosophy – they not only convey 'right content' but have effects, effects in thought and understanding and effects in action. The effects in action are tangible. Magisterial statements – as has indeed just been recalled – are almost immediately both inclusive and exclusive: they are inclusive to the degree that they make clear who 'belong', and exclusive in that they make clear who, in the view of those who formulate them, *do not* belong and what the conditions for renewed belonging are. There is no need to stress that both the inclusion and the exclusion can be positively necessary in the interest of a clear proclamation of what the gospel and faith are about, but can also have negatively fatal consequences, if spiritual power is misused here.

But we do not need to think that far at this point. The linguistic problem has already been discussed once, very thoroughly, in direct connection with the appearance of Küng's book, in the hard discussion between Hans Küng and Karl Rahner.[40] In the debate over infallibility the great Karl Rahner, to whom Catholic theology in this century owes so many brave new beginnings, could never get rid of the idea that the truth of a statement ultimately consists in its unchanging *correctness*, i.e. in the way in which it matches the content that it expresses. This matching can be disturbed, and indeed is most of the time. Since any human statement is shaped by human knowledge, it is burdened with finitude, inadequacy, the possibility of misunderstanding, and indeed the threat of error. However, all this does not yet make it a *real* error, an *untrue* statement. Moreover, like all linguistic statements it can be pushed through with particular ideological, philosophical and sociological presuppositions, formulated unhappily and thus robbed of its force, be misused – but one must not and may not for that reason ever call it erroneous. Rather, the way in which the statement is loaded and vitiated is a constant challenge to interpret it better. Therefore such a statement can indeed be 'infallible', to be understood with the complete Yes of faith, and at the same time nevertheless need infinite criticism.[41] Thus Rahner believes that he can answer Küng's question and refute his thesis: the dogma of infallibility does not require more than assent that an ultimately binding expression of church teaching preserves its truth, even if it is infinitely in need of interpretation for the reasons cited.

Over against this Küng maintains that the *truth* of a statement, at any rate of a statement of faith, is not its correctness, which can be examined at any time, but its *power to disclose right life* – in our case, lived in accordance with the gospel. To put it another way: the truth of a statement is real only as *concrete* truth. Only by the concrete use of a statement does it emerge whether it is true or false – though theoretically and in the abstract it may be right. Now in so far as the proclamation of the church is expressed in statements, it cannot in principle cover in a 'telling' way all concrete situations in which the gospel is to be communicated literally. So the claim to be able to formulate infallible statements of faith which are guaranteed *a priori* is incompatible with the essence of church doctrinal formulations generally.

For Rahner, for example the following statement is infallibly true: 'The dignity of every individual is to be respected and every individual is to be loved as one's neighbour.' Küng concedes that this statement is of course true to the degree that it expresses an obligatory basic human and Christian attitude. But after that the problem begins. The important thing is where and how this statement has and maintains an effect on decisions in everyday life. The statement is true, for example, when an American pastor uses it to protect a poor black from the financial exploitation of a white. It is false when someone wants to use it to back up white exploitation – and is so although it continues to remain true as an expression of an obligatory basic attitude.

Here Küng begins from the quite natural presupposition that statements of church doctrinal proclamation, and in particular those which are claimed as ultimately binding, as 'irreformable', in fact *mean* to have an effect on the thought and action of believers. To want to avoid the problems connected with this by retreating to an everlasting but abstract rightness beyond their actual function and intended effect is in fact to condemn official church doctrinal proclamation to sterility: all the more thoroughly, the more binding the form in which they are expressed. That could not and cannot be the way out of the problems. So on the one hand the discussion has continued along Rahner's line, and on the other the whole meaninglessness of such an attempt at evasion has been disclosed. One example of this is the friendly dispute in 1980 between Albert Keller and Bernhard Lohse on the scope of the 1870 definition of infallibility.[42] Using all the instruments of modern linguistic philosophy, Keller wants to demonstrate not only that to speak of 'infallible statements' is 'sloppy' in terms of linguistic philosophy but that the question of papal infallibility is 'in fact of little significance for the belief of Christians', above all 'because the true statements guaranteed by infallibility could also be misunderstood'. Keller then wants to take the question further by an energetic attempt to work out the otherness of the act of faith in comparison to mere acceptance of statements. This is to be approved warmly. And yet in the face of the destruction of the 1870 dogma by linguistic analysis – which does not go into the long and partly baneful prehistory and sequel – the dry question which his opponent Lohse puts in return seems correct: 'Does not such a thesis represent a much sharper questioning of the dogma of infallibility than that offered by Küng, who at least does the First Vatican Council the honour of taking it seriously?'[43]

If it is certainly true that only a dogma which is not misunderstood really helps faith, but that the danger of misunderstanding can never be banished once and for all; and if it is similarly certainly true that the imperative interpretation of dogma already begins with the translation of the original text, though *every* interpretation of dogma must be carefully distinguished from the statement itself, which alone can claim infallible binding character,[44] then I can certainly say quite rightly that a dogma is *de facto* ineffective in the linguistic state in which it is promulgated. But it does not help to defend the dogma of 1870 reassuringly with this ineffectiveness, because at that time and on its presuppositions an effect was intended and indeed – in another way – was and is in fact aimed at. So an approach from linguistic analysis does not offer a real way out of the problems; however, it does also help to explain the blindness to the basic problems among council fathers of the First Vatican Council that Küng and Houtepen each complain about, each in his own way.

4. Statements of faith and moral norms

Before the appearance of Hans Küng'a book, up to and including the encyclical *Humanae vitae*, in all detailed critical discussion the principle held that magisterial decisions in questions of moral life are in principle to be evaluated in the same way as decisions in questions of faith. The question whether there is not an essential difference here, with the consequence that even a positive answer to the question of the possibility of infallible statements *of faith* does not yet settle the other question, whether there could also be infallible moral *norms*, is a question which, as far as I can see, was first raised directly in the framework of the debate over Hans Küng.[45] The distinctive character of moral action, which is only moral action when it is performed with responsible insight into the moral significance of the action in question, excludes a *blind* obedience without insight which possibly might still be taken into account in assent to statements of faith – one might think, say, of statements about the triune God or about the resurrection of Jesus.

But that opens up a quite new set of problems, and in some instances the old problem-fields expand. The definition made by the First Vatican Council simply sets questions of faith and questions of morals side by side, as if they were about the same things, and the claim to be able to make infallible decisions is related equally to both. Now it is still clear from the text of *Humanae vitae* – from the appeal to the support of the Holy Spirit – that the representatives of the *magisterium* did not make the distinction mentioned above between (possible) infallible statements of faith and (impossible) infallible norms, and the latest developments described at the beginning make it clear that this distinction is still not being made. It might just be mentioned in passing that behind this is the still unfinished dispute between theologians over a so-called deontological or teleological grounding of ethical norms.[46] More important is the observation which needs to be made in precisely this connection that in the question of the exercise of the *magisterium* there are today *de facto* only two fields of conflict which are publicly effective and which therefore provoke both protest and resignation. On the one hand there are the conflicts over the understanding of the church and its ministry, where the new theological beginnings complained about give the impression through the content of their theses or through direct demands that they affect traditional and established structures of the exercise of power in the office of leadership. I have indicated how this is dealt with, and how little credibility this procedure has, particularly with respect to what people want to sustain and protect. The other field of conflict covers questions of Christian ethics, i.e. questions which, in the view of leading theologians, have no prospect of being answered by 'infallible norms'. On the other hand, and this is shown specifically by the case of *Humanae vitae*, it is precisely over ethical questions in the past and present that there is most obviously a 'collegial' consensus between the bishops of the world church and the pope: in short the classical case of an 'infallible decision of the ordinary *magisterium*'.

Again no reference back to unassailable abstractions is any help here. The 'enquiry' whether the claim to be in possession of 'infallible' competence is right cannot be avoided. However, we are not without significant help in that from recent years. In the meantime it has been demonstrated in exemplary problem areas – from freedom of religion to social teaching – that the proclamation of doctrine by the 'ordinary *magisterium*' which today emphasizes precisely what is regarded as valid in the light of faith, which fifty years earlier was the view of an opposition in the church which was attacked harshly.[47] Should that not make us cautious in all conflicts? The encyclical *Humanae vitae* appeared in 1968. What will we think about it in the year 2018?

Ironically, the number fifty plays an important role in another connection. According to a rule of thumb among church historians which has been verified by experience the reception of a council takes fifty years. A few years ago Walter Kasper noted that the reception of the Second Vatican Council, which in the view of many pessimists was being betrayed by the official church, had only just begun.[48] The Second Vatican Council ended in 1965. Will the church of the year 2015 at least have begun to become the church of the Second Vatican Council? Is it possible that in this connection, in recent years the problems of the reception of official statements of the church are beginning to become the theme of the decade?[49]

4. Steps into the future

(i) The function of the magisterium

The editors wanted me to help to keep in mind the discussion on the infallibility of the papal *magisterium* prompted by Hans Küng and also to present it as an unresolved problem to the rising generation of theologians who were not around at the time of this discussion. Because of the limited space available, and for the sake of clarity, that has necessarily led to sharp statements which, were there a possibility of greater length, could have been toned down by suitable qualifications. I also know from many sources of the secret suffering in office of many episcopal chancelleries and in much-abused 'Rome'. And as in fact even the most urgent problems cannot be resolved at a stroke, and a real solution in accordance with the gospel cannot yet be communicated to all Catholics in the world overnight, the conscience of all those involved has to be respected, even when other verdicts are arrived at than one's own. It should be stated quite firmly that one-sided attributions of guilt are furthest from my mind.

It is even less possible for me to develop my own ideas for solving unresolved problems at this point than it is to offer qualifications. In outline and always somewhat aphoristically I have done this in various ways in connection with the Küng debate and in other contexts.[50] Moreover, in later statements Hans Küng himself has developed his remarks in *Infallible?*, and others have followed him in an attempt to give a deeper answer to the question of what kind of a truth it is in which one can abide, though there is the possibility of errors of detail in the statements in which this truth is expressed. Quite certainly it will be a truth which does not amount to a set of propositions, even 'correct' propositions. Or, if one wants to put it that way, it will not be theoretical but existential truth – a truth which shapes the self-understanding and fulfilment of my existence as one human being among others. Quite certainly it will not be a truth which can be imposed on me from outside as a law to be followed, but rather will be one which shows itself to be truth in my concrete life, in both its experiences of happiness and its crises. Therefore it will be as incapable of completion before death as my life is still incomplete. Precisely for that reason it is a truth which can be expressed in an incalculable wealth of forms of expression, because the people in whose lives this truth is to show itself are incalculably different. Nevertheless, it is a truth which is not only my truth but a truth which can be communicated to all, which was already there before me and will be there after me. It is thus a truth which is universally valid – otherwise it would not be truth – although this universal validity can always be grasped only in individual cases.

It is no help, or it is only the beginning of an answer (though the all-important beginning), if we say that this truth is not a proposition, a theory, a doctrine, but a person – God as communicated in Jesus Christ. For in the closer 'description' of this person – already in the interpretation of the term 'person' – the making of images, conceptions and concepts which claim individual and yet universal validity came and come first. Not to mention the misuse and betrayal which have similarly always crept in here in thought and praxis.

I cannot go into any of this more deeply here. But I would just like to hint briefly at one thought, not stopping here to consider whether it has not already been brought out sufficiently in the discussion. However, I think I can see that it has remained unilluminated, although both theoretically and practically it could help to solve the problem. The problem of the basis of abiding in the truth despite possibly erroneous statements in no way rules out a church *magisterium*. However, this *magisterium* takes on a different function from that traditionally attributed to it.

First of all, the '*magisterium*' is fundamentally not an authority with an address in Rome which can be given out, nor is it the official duty of someone in office or a group of those in office, but an 'office' of the whole church. The church as a whole owes the *world* a binding testimony of its belief in the gospel: that is its teaching 'office'. Though I cannot go into detail here, I would venture to remark that this basic sense of *magisterium* can be given good foundations in the New Testament and the history of theology. Now of course testimony to the gospel has to be 'co-ordinated'. With the bearing of witness 'the world' must also be told who is giving false witness and what the world should *not* follow in its questions about the gospel. In this way, i.e. as a derivation of the basic meaning of '*magisterium*', the office of teaching also becomes a function within the church, in the end and after many further steps, which are taken not least in the course of historical development, and also an authority in which and through which this function within the church is pre-eminently exercised. What precise function can this 'teachng office' in the narrowest sense have in the co-ordination of the church's witness to the world and its advancement?

In the light of the Second Vatican Council's doctrine of the priesthood of all believers and the participation of the whole people of God in the prophetic office of Christ – i.e. in its testimony to God's irrevocable forgiving concern for human beings and the world – a thesis about the special task of the church's ministry has found assent today which states the following: the essential task of church office in the exercise of its task of proclamation is to co-ordinate and moderate dialogue and cooperation between the charisms in the church and to keep this going as a blessing for all.[51] A dialogue, a collaboration, always involves the distribution of various roles, whether this is planned or simply happens. And clearly the aim of such dialogue and collaboration is necessarily for the community, the church, to give an answer to the constantly new questions of the time which accords with the situation and the gospel. In other words, the aim of such dialogue and such collabora-tion must necessarily be to lead the community, the church, on a good way for the future, in which the good message of God's concern for men and women in Jesus Christ can reach people, raising them up, comforting them, guiding them and if need be also criticizing them, as it has reached believers now. It is in the nature of things that the pressure towards new, hitherto unconceived-of considerations, towards changes and creative new developments, towards the overcoming of all anxiety about losing the warm nest of the traditional, is dominant – at any rate in a living community. What greater temptation is there than that of regarding only what is conceivable and illuminating for the moment and for the imminent future as the concrete perspective on the gospel which is now valid? If one gives way to this temptation, then in fact there can be a break with tradition and the message of faith can be identified with the signs of the time – the worst disaster that can happen to the church, and in some phases of church history one which is quite obvious, at least in retrospect.

It is in precisely this context that a '*magisterium*' of the church in the narrower sense of the word has its indispensable function, not to say 'its role'. In the process of the constantly ongoing dialogue of faith about the gospel it has to see that there is also real listening – and that people do not give way to that temptation. It would accord well with a Catholic view of the church's *magisterium* if it were combined with a fundamental scepticism about a particular present, to the degree that a single era, a single period, cannot have the capacity or be in a position to express the whole wealth of the gospel. Only a 'memory of the church', which always contains more than the individual believer or even the individual group in the church can bring to concrete life, can preserve the old treasure from being squandered. For the same reason the *magisterium* also has every right by its very nature also to be 'conservative'. It watches over the dialogue of believers not only with the gospel in its original form, viz., with the Bible, but also with the history of the interpretation of the gospel in the church: in short, with tradition. Because faith does not begin with us, and because it was not us, but already our mothers and fathers, who were wise in the faith, it is good for the living exposition of the gospel in the thought and life of the contemporary church if it also as it were puts spokes in the wheels from tradition. Assurance of the continuity of present-day thought and action with the 'cause of Jesus' can only further that. And it can and may release the whole pastoral and theological passion of a person, a theologian, to serve the faith of the church on its pilgrim way into God's future in such a 'role'.

However, this understanding of the function of the *magisterium* does not tolerate just *any* style of its exercise. That opens up the question of 'first steps' in the direction at least of a practical answer to the unresolved problems of the *magisterium*. I can only give a few headings here.

(ii) First steps

The exercising of the *magisterium* can take place appropriately only in *dialogue*. For the guidance of a dialogue among people who have equally received the Holy Spirit necessarily excludes any compulsion and any prohibition of thought, and the moderator of the dialogue is not exempt from the rules of the dialogue.

Those responsible must give any contentious discussion which has begun more time than it has had previously to achieve clarification on the basis of the subject matter, and they must use official interventions only as a last resort – as a rule of thumb, at the earliest after twice as much time as has previously elapsed before, as experience has shown, such interventions have taken place in recent decades.

There must not be condemnations if it is not clear beyond a shadow of doubt that there is heresy and that believers are being led astray. That is not the case simply if the person in office who is summoned to judgment personally as a theologian 'no longer goes along with' the disputed theological doctrine – it is precisely at that point that the duty to relativize oneself begins. There must be more courage to leave a controversial question temporarily open if agreement has not been reached, with confidence in the future – as moreover has also often happened in the history of the councils.

Anyone who becomes involved in a conflict with the church authorities over doctrine must be able to rely firmly on a legal and fair procedure which safeguards personal honour and dignity. The protection of church law must not fail at the very point where it must protect the weaker ones against the mighty.

If a measure of disciplining has become unavoidable, it too must be carried out in a style which corresponds to what is seemly in dealings between adults. Famous proceedings in recent decades, not to mention unknown ones, only allow us to conclude that there are substantial human failings here. Is it so eccentric to imagine someone holding office in the church, who is fully justified in disciplining a fellow-Christian legally for particular doctrinal statements, opening the decision with a request to the person concerned to excuse him because on the basis of his office he sees himself bound by conscience to do what he would have preferred for all the world to avoid?

Such dialogical exercise of the *magisterium*, which does not allow itself to become aggressiveness, even in a serious conflict, will become all the more significant in the future, the more the church continues and extends towards being a world church in the way which began at the Second Vatican Council. For this way involves – and here again we can only have headings[52] – ongoing de-doctrinalization of faith and theology (the fundamental theological aspect of the problem), ongoing de-Romanizing of the form of the church (the ecumenical aspect of the problem), progressive de-Europeanizing (the aspect of the contextuality of faith and theology) – not to mention the as yet unforeseeable consequences of an intensification of dialogue with the non-Christian religions, to which Hans Küng has so notably devoted all his theological passion in recent years. Who could seriously continue to believe that it is possible to safeguard the clarity of Christian identity, to help these problems of a coming world church, by a style of doctrinal discipline and disciplining which bears within it the scars of the centuries and especially the second millennium of Western church history, and owes its focus, which still continues to have an oppressive effect today, to an unrepeatable special situation of Catholic Christianity in the nineteenth century?

(iii) A summary in twelve theses

In the summer semester of 1981, in connection with the 'Küng case', along with my Protestant colleague Traugott Koch I held a systematic theological seminar on the topic 'Does the church need a supreme *magisterium*?' The final theses which I presented to the seminar at that time are a summary of the previous comments and indicate some further perspectives which could not be discussed here.[53] So I shall leave the theses in the form in which they were presented at that time – though today I would express some of them differently and occasionally would also want to qualify their substance somewhat. With this hitherto unpublished text, which in the framework of my work is also a bit of the history of the 'Küng case', I send Hans Küng my greetings on his sixty-fifth birthday. I wish him, and his colleagues, continued good health and physical and psychological stamina in exercising his specific charisma in the service of the gospel. For me there has never been any doubt that, even in the midst of the disputes, indeed in the midst of all human, all-too-human personal controversies which such a dispute tends to involve even among the saints, Hans Küng has been and is a loyal witness to the gospel, which countless people have come to love again through his service as a theologian. The theses presented on 24 June 1981 run:

1. 'History makes free'; i.e., where theories run into dead ends, a look at history opens up not only back doors, but double doors.
2. In the history of the formation and formulation of the Christian conviction and 'doctrine' of faith, things have never, either before or after Vatican I, gone as they should have done according to the dogma of the infallibility of the papal *magisterium*; the course of events has been precisely similar to the way in which doctrinal difficulties are played out and a consensus is arrived at in the Protestant church and in Protestant theology. To be specific, Catholics have (or take) their free space; Protestants have, *de facto* and often even *de iure*, their 'teaching discipline'. That the extent of both can be regulated by 'measures' of church power does not refute the thesis but confirms it.
3. The real problem of Vatican I is not the way in which it gives competence to the pope nor even the linguistic presupposition mentioned by Hans

Küng of the existence and necessity of infallible statements but the identification of the concept of faith, i.e. its reinterpretation as obedience due to the church. For the definitions proclaimed by the pope are not infallible (it is the office that is infallible when they are decreed) but unalterable, i.e. legally unassailable, obliging every Catholic Christian to inward and outward obedience.

4. Catholic theology and the Catholic consciousness of faith have gone beyond this legalized concept of faith, just as the constellation of problems which brought it about – partly understandable, partly indeed justified – has disappeared.

5. The abiding positive impulse of Vatican I – which both produced the Council and also strengthened it – was its stress on the continuity of the proclamation of faith with history and tradition. Protestant theology underestimates this impulse, so that after the end of a pre-critical and naive *sola scriptura* – it is tossed around, without a focus, between a church of professors, a church with its own (historically late) confession and a revivalist church with no criteria at all.

6. Just as it is the task of the office of 'leadership' to co-ordinate gifts of grace (charisms) in the community and to bring them into fruitful interplay (as W. Kasper puts it), so it is the task of the *magisterium* (whoever may hold it) to see that there is serious dialogue with the tradition. In this sense the *magisterium* is always 'conservative' – and rightly so – and sceptical about a particular present in so far as it tends to regard as the truth of the gospel only what can illuminate the presuppositions for understanding current in an age. The church needs such a *magisterium*.

7. Such a *magisterium* (whether supreme or lower) need not be infallible, since it would need to be infallible only if it had to present unalterable propositions for the obedience of faith.

8. The statements of the *magisterium* must correspond to the nature of faith and its structural vulnerability: in other words, the *magisterium* must protect the uncertain from the certain and not vice versa.

9. An uncompromisingly clear reference by the *magisterium* to the cause of the gospel is not a flat 'statement of the truth' but encouragement and recollection, an invitation to a faith which is free of domination, and a deliberate helpless waiting on the work of the Word.

10. The proclamation of the *magisterium* is not a one-way street but is done in dialogue and also in dispute, between experiences in history and in the present which have abiding and in each instance personal truth.

11. The *magisterium* should also take public 'measures', but only through the Word. In cases of doubt, it should support the helplessness of the petitioner (see Paul)!

12. This definition of the function of the *magisterium* cannot be justified by exegesis, but it can be justified biblically to the degree that the origin of the

Bible itself is due to a process of the exercising of office of precisely the kind that is described here.

Notes

1. H. Küng, *Infallible?*. The new German edition of 1989 contains a preface by Herbert Haag and further material by Hans Küng: his preface to August B. Hasler, *Wie der Papst unfehlbar wurde*, Munich 1979, and *The Church Maintained in Truth*. The most important surveys and discussion volumes are: H. Küng, 'A Short Balance-Sheet of the Debate on Infallibility', *Concilium* 9/3, 1973, 129–36 (cf. also 117–28); id., 'Eine Bilanz der Unfehlbarkeitsdebatte', in H. Küng (ed.), *Fehlbar?*, 307–524 (with documentation and bibliography); K. Rahner (ed.), *Zum Problem Unfehlbarkeit. Antworten auf die Anfrage von Hans Küng*, Freiburg im Breisgau 1971; Arbeitgemeinschaft ökumenischer Universitätsinstitute (ed.), *Papsttum als ökumenische Frage*, Munich and Mainz 1979; M. Seckler (ed.), *Lehramt und Theologie. Unnötiger Konflikt oder heilsame Spannung?*, Düsseldorf 1981; W. Kern (ed.), *Die Theologie und das Lehramt*, Freiburg im Breisgau 1982. I myself have contributed to this debate three times directly and once indirectly: O.H. Pesch, 'Vom Bleiben der Kirche in der Wahrheit. Ein Rekollektionsvortrag, zugleich ein Beitrag zu der aktuellen "Anfrage" von Küng', *Klerusblatt* 51, 1971, 5, 64–67; 'Unfehlbarkeit im Disput. Ein Streit zwischen Karl Rahner und Hans Küng', *Wort und Antwort* 12, 1971, 82–88; 'Bilanz der Diskussion um die vatikanische Primats- und Unfehlbarkeitsdefinition', in *Papsttum als ökumenische Frage* (see above), 159–211, printed with extended bibliography in id., *Dogmatik im Fragment. Gesammelte Studien*, Mainz 1987, 206–52 (this is the edition which I shall quote); 'Kirchliche Lehrformulierung und persönlicher Glaubensvollzug', in H. Küng (ed.), *Fehlbar?*, 249–79, reprinted in *Dogmatik im Fragment*, 266–91. There are extensive references to further important contributions above all in my 'Bilanz'. For the present situation see now Herbert Haag's preface to the extended new edition.

2. Cf. A.B. Hasler, *Pius IX. Päpstliche Unfehlbarkeit und 1. Vatikanisches Konzil. Dogmatisierung und Durchsetzung einer Ideologie*, Stuttgart 1977, x, 537. Hasler's other book, mentioned in n.1, is so to speak the 'popular edition' of this great investigation. It immediately sparked off a new round of lively discussion. Details in Pesch, 'Bilanz' (n.1), 236–8. At the same time as Hans Küng, in 1971 Ulrich Horst ventured some bold steps forward on the basis of the fundamental theology of his time and ecumenical dialogue in *Umstrittene Fragen der Ekklesiologie*, Regensburg 1971, see 119–69 for Vatican I; and in the subsequent period blank areas in the prehistory of the dogma of primacy began to be filled in with a series of articles on the ecclesiology of the Thomistic school. In connection with the debate on Hasler his books, which are indispensable to the prehistory of Vatican I, were revised, enlarged and continued: *Papst-Konzil-Unfehlbarkeit. Die Ekklesiologie der Summenkommentare von Cajetan bis Billuart*, Mainz 1978; *Unfehlbarkeit und Geschichte. Studien zur Unfehlbarkeitsdiskussion von Melchior Cano bis zum*

I. Vatikanischen Konzil, Mainz 1982; *Zwischen Konziliarismus und Reformation. Studien zur Ekklesiologie im Dominikanerorden,* Rome 1985.

3. Original text in *AAS* 65, 1973, 396–408. For interpretation cf. K. Rahner, *'Mysterium Ecclesiae'.* On the Declaration made by the Congregation for the Doctrine of the Faith on the Doctrine of the Church', *Theological Investigations* 17, 139–55: 149–54.

4. Cf. Congregation for the Doctrine of the Faith, Instruction on the Ecclesial Vocation of the Theologian, nos 10, 24(!), 30.

5. Cf. by way of example Deutsche Bischofskonferenz (ed.). *Katholischer Erwachsenenkatechismus. Das Glaubensbekenntnis der Kirche,* Kevelaer etc. 1985, 301–6; and now M. Kehl, *Die Kirche. Eine katholische Ekklesiologie,* Würzburg 1992, 356–66.

6. Thus the 'Cologne Declaration' of 6 January 1989.

7. This reference is based on B. Häring, 'Lehramt und pastorale Verantwortung', in *Zur Debatte. Themen der Katholischen Akademie in Bayern* 19, 1989, no.2, 7–15: 7f., where Häring in turn quotes from the manuscript of Mgr Caffara which was distributed at the Congress.

8. *Humanae vitae* 28.

9. Cf. *Osservatore Romano,* 25 November 1989.

10. Cf. e.g. F. Böckle, *'Humanae vitae* als Prüfstein des Wahren Glaubens? Zur kirchenpolitischen Dimension moraltheologische Fragen', *Stimmen der Zeit* 208, 1990, 3–16; D. Mieth, *Geburtenregelung. Ein Konflikt in der katholischen Kirche,* Mainz 1990. R. Schwager, 'Kirchliches Lehramt und Theologie', *Zeitschrift für katholische Theologie* 111, 1989, 163–82, on *Humanae vitae,* 178, is a refreshing exception.

11. Cf. B. Häring, *Meine Erfahrung mit der Kirche. Einleitung und Fragen von G. Licheri,* Freiburg im Breisgau 1989, 225–31.

12. Cf. CIC, canon 218 and 752–4.

13. G. Thils and T. Schneider, *Glaubensbekenntnis und Treueid, Klarstellungen zu den 'neuen' römischen Formeln für kirchliche Amtsträger,* Mainz 1990.

14. See n.1.

15. Cf. my contribution of the time (now out of print), *Unfehlbarkeit im Disput* (cf. n.1), which I follow here. I do not have to retract anything that I said then.

16. At the symposium of the Arbeitsgemeinschaft ökumenischer Universitätsinstitute, documented in *Papsttum als ökumenische Frage* (see n.1), Yves Congar told me that nothing officially was done on the initiative of Rome towards a centenary celebration, any more than for the fiftieth anniversary in 1920: cf. Pesch, 'Bilanz', 213–16.

17. Cf. H. Küng, 'Die Kirche. Dokumentation des Konflikts', in W. Jens (ed.), *Um nichts als die Wahrheit. Deutsche Bischofskonferenz contra Hans Küng. Eine Dokumentation,* Munich 1978; N. Greinacher and H. Haag, *Der Fall Küng. Eine Dokumentation,* Munich 1980; Sekretariat der Deutschen Bischofskonferenz (ed.), *Zum Entzug der kirchlichen Lehrbefugnis Professor Dr. Hans Küngs. Gemeinsames Kanzelwort der deutschen Bischöfe,* Die Deutschen Bischöfe 25, Bonn, 7 January 1980.

18. The 'Königstein Declaration' is 'Wort der deutschen Bischöfe zur seelsorglichen Lage nach dem Erscheinen der Enzyklika "Humanae vitae"', and 'Verlautbarung

nach Abschluss der ausserordentlichen Vollversammlung der Deutschen Bischofskonferenz am 29./30. August 1968'. Anyone who wants to remind themselves of
the turbulent discussion which broke out then should consult: F. Oertel (ed.),
*Erstes Echo auf Humanae vitae. Dokumentation wichtiger Stellungnahmen zur umstrit-
tenen Enzyklika über die Geburtenkontrolle*, Essen 1968; F. Böckle and C. Holenstein
(eds.), *Die Enzyklika in der Diskussion. Eine orientierende Dokumentation*, Zurich
1968 (both Königstein texts are printed in Oertle, and the statement by the
German bishops in Böckle and Holenstein); H. Fries, *Argernis und Widerspruch.
Christentum und Kirche im Spiegel gegenwärtiger Kritik*, Würzburg ²1968, 175–90;
A. Görres (ed.), *Ehe in Gewissensfreiheit*, Mainz 1969; O.H. Pesch, 'Über die
Verbindlichkeit päpstlicher Enzykliken. Dogmatische Überlegungen zur Ehe-
Enzyklika Papst Pauls VI (1968)', now in *Dogmatik in Fragment* (n.1), 253–65.
19. Vatican II, Constitution on the Church, no. 25.2.
20. Cf. J.T. Noonan, *Birth Control*, Cambridge, Mass. ²1967.
21. Cf. DS 3700–3724, here especially 3715–18.
22. Cf. DS 3074; Vatican II, Constitution on the Church, nos. 18, 25.3.
23. Küng, *Infallible?*, 124.
24. *De Trinitate* I, 2, 5.
25. Fine examples of this concern are: H. Fries, 'Was heisst Unfehlbarkeit des
Papstes?' (1968), in id., *Glaube und Kirche auf dem Prüfstand. Versuche einer
Orientierung*, Munich 1970, 180–206; id., *Fundamentaltheologie*, Graz 1985, 480–
96; U. Horst, *Umstrittene Fragen* (n.2); P. Knauer, *Der Glaube kommt vom Hören*,
Frankfurt am Main ²1982, 252–70, 354–66.
26. See above, II, 1.
27. Cf. above all H.J. Pottmeyer, *Unfehlbarkeit und Souveränität. Die päpstliche Unfehlbarkeit im System der ultramontanen Ekklesiologie des 19. Jahrhunderts*, Mainz
1975.
28. Thus above all M.J. Scheeben, *Handbuch der katholischen Dogmatik* 1 (= M.J.
Scheeben, *Gesammelte Schriften*, ed. J. Höfer, Vol.III), Freiburg im Breisgau 1948,
231–41, also 211–31. There are detailed comments on this and what follows in
Pesch, 'Bilanz' (n.1), 208–13, 221–38.
29. Cf. A. Houtepen, *Onfeilbaarheid en Hermeneutiek. De betekenis van het infallibilitas-
concept op Vaticanum I*, Bruges 1973; cf. also id., 'A Hundred Years after Vatican I',
Concilium 9/3, 1973, 117–28, which includes a summary of the thesis of the book.
Houtepen personally told me that this promptly landed him in a conflict over
doctrine with Rome, but of course nothing came of it.
30. Ibid., 374.
31. Cf. Hasler, *Pius IX* (n.2).
32. Cf. ibid., 474–84, 527f.
33. Ibid., 528.
34. Cf. Scheeben, *Handbuch* (n.28).
35. Ibid., 377.
36. Cf. M. Seckler, 'Die Theologie als kirchliche Wissenschaft nach Pius XII und
Paul VI', in *TQ* 149, 1969, 209–34, also reprinted in id., *Im Spannungsfeld von
Wissenschaft und Kirche. Theologie als schöpferische Auslegung der Wirklichkeit*, Freiburg im Breisgau 1980, 62–4.

37. DS 3885.

38. See n.4, and above all no.23 – this brazen demand was not lifted even by the subsequent honest concerns to go into the difficulties of a dissent caused by both personalities and the subject-matter. For the oath of loyalty see Thils and Schneider (n.13).

39. Vatican II, Constitution on the Church, no. 12; Constitution on Revelation, no. 12,5.

40. Cf. K. Rahner, 'Kritik an Hans Küng. Zur Frage der Unfehlbarkeit theologischer Sätze', *Stimmen der Zeit* 188, 1970, 361–77; also H. Küng, 'Im Interesse der Sache. Antwort an Karl Rahner', *Stimmen der Zeit* 189, 1971, 43–64, 105–22, also reprinted in H. Küng (ed.), *Fehlbar?*; also K. Rahner 'Replik. Bemerkungen zu: Hans Küng, Im Interesse der Sache', *Stimmen der Zeit* 189, 1971, 145–60.

41. Cf. also K. Rahner, 'Theologie und Lehramt', *Stimmen der Zeit* 198, 1980, 363–75; also already id., 'Magisterium and Theology', in *Theological Investigations* 18, New York and London 1984, 54–73; H. Fries and K. Rahner, *Einigung der Kirchen = reale Möglichkeit*, Freiburg im Breisgau 1983, extended special edition ²1986, 35–53.

42. Cf. A. Keller, 'Die Tragweite der Unfehlbarkeitsfrage', *Stimmen der Zeit* 198, 1980, 147–58; B. Lohse, 'Die Tragweite der Unfehlbarkeitsfrage. Bemerkungen zu dem Aufsatz von Albert Keller SJ', ibid., 405–12; also in turn A. Keller, 'Verbindliche Glaubensaussage und Unfehlbarkeitsdogma. Zu den Anregungen von Bernhard Lohse', ibid., 413–20.

43. Lohse, ibid., 410.

44. Thus Rahner, 'Theologie und Lehramt' (n.41), 369f.

45. Cf. F. Böckle, 'Unfehlbare Normen?', in H. Küng (ed.), *Fehlbar?* (see n.1), 280–304; cf. also Böckle's article mentioned in n.10.

46. In addition to the articles mentioned and in a critical response to the discussion, F. Böckle, *Fundamentalmoral*, Munich 1977, 306–19.

47. Cf. the illuminating investigation by J.R. Dionne, *The Papacy and the Church. A Study of Praxis and Reception in Ecumenical Perspective*, New York 1987.

48. Cf. W. Kasper, 'The Continuing Challenge of the Second Vatican Council', in id., *Theology and Church*, London and New York 1989, 166–76, here 167.

49. Cf. W. Beinert, 'Rezeption. Bedeutung für Leben und Lehre der Kirche', *Catholica* 44, 1990, 91–118; id. (ed.), *Glaube als Zustimmung*, Freiburg im Breisgau 1991; D. Wiederkehr (ed.), *Wie geschieht Tradition?*, Freiburg im Breisgau 1991; id. (ed.), *Sensus fidei = Consensus fidelium*, Freiburg im Breisgau 1993 (forthcoming). H. Fischer, 'Rezeption in ihrer Bedeutung für Leben und Lehre der Kirche. Vorläufige Erwägungen zu einem undeutlichen Begriff', *Zeitschrift für Theologie und Kirche* 87, 1990, 100–23, is critical, from a Protestant perspective, of the lack of clarity of the term.

50. See the works listed in n.1 and *Unsicherheit und Glaube. Zur Frage nach dem Halt im Glauben*, Zurich 1981, esp. 50–69; '"Der mitgehende Anfang". Die Bedeutung von Bibel und Bibelauslegung für Glaube und Theologie', in H.J. Fabry et al., *Bibel und Bibelauslegung. Das immer neue Bemühen um die Botschaft Gottes*, Regensburg 1993 (in preparation).

51. Cf. as one example to serve for all, the articles by W. Kasper, 'A New Dogmatic

Outlook on the Priestly Ministry', *Concilium* 5/3, 1969, 12–18; 'Die Funktion des Priesters in der Kirche' (1969), in id., *Glaube und Geschichte*, Mainz 1970, 371–87; 'Amt und Gemeinde', ibid., 388–414. Cf. also the unconventional, bold reflections by P. Wess, *Ihr seid alle Geschwister. Gemeinde und Priester*, Mainz 1983, 86–119 – wrongly ignored in the discussion, although they were developed as a fundamental criticism of the debate of the professionals.

52. Cf. in rather more detail O.H. Pesch, 'Ökumenische Kirchlichkeit der Theologie. Einige Überlegungen zum theologischen Alltag', in P. Neuner and H. Wagner (eds.), *In Verantwortung für den Glauben. Beiträge zur Fundamentaltheologie und Ökumenik. Für Heinrich Fries*, Freiburg im Breisgau 1992, 293–318, esp. 300–6.

53. The theses presented by Traugott Koch became the basis of his article 'Die Freiheit der Wahrheit und die Notwendigkeit eines kirchenleitenden Lehramtes in der evangelischen Kirche', *Zeitschrift für Theologie und Kirche* 82, 1985, 231–50. If one compares with this the two articles by Karl Rahner listed in n. 41 and the article by Karl Lehmann, 'Zum Verhältnis zwischen kirchlichem Amt und Theologie', in M. Seckler et al. (ed.), *Begegnung. Beiträge zu einer Hermeneutik des theologischen Gesprächs (FS Fries zum 60. Geburtstag)*, Graz 1972, 415–30, one can understand that the observance of some basic, predominantly human, rules of the game presupposes that the problem of *'magisterium* and theology' need not prove so hopeless an ecumenical problem as it commonly appears.

Norbert Greinacher

Cui bono? What is the Use of Public Statements by Theologians and Whom do they Benefit?

In his speech on behalf of Roscius Amerinus,[1] Cicero (106–43 BCE) several times raised the question 'Whom does it benefit?'. In this speech he quotes a remark by Lucius Cassius, who was censor in the year 125 BCE and in murder trials pressed the judges to investigate whom the death of the murdered person benefited.

For whose benefit is theology done? And in particular, whom do public statements by theologians benefit and whom do they harm? These are the questions to be investigated here.

1. *Early conflicts in Tübingen*

Christian theology represents the attempt, to be undertaken over and over again, to reflect on Christian faith: 'Be always ready to give an account of the faith which is in you' (I Peter 3.5). In this reflection, theology is always governed by two poles. One pole of Christian theology is God's communication of himself in the history of Israel, in the history of Jesus of Nazareth, in the history of humankind generally, and in the history of Christianity in particular. The second pole of Christian theology contains our present-day world of experience.[2] For Christian theology, however, this reflection has a practical purpose. It is not primarily concerned with 'seeing the essence' of God and the world; Christian theology cannot allow itself to give answers to questions which interest no one but theologians. In discipleship of Jesus Christ Christian theology must be concerned to reflect on human beings, their happiness and salvation, and commit itself to a 'human earth'.

Because this is the case, Christian theology has continually attempted to carry on its affairs in *public*: 'What I say to you in the darkness speak of in clear day, and what people whisper in your ear proclaim from the rooftops' (Matt. 10.27), Jesus admonishes his disciples. After the Ascension the apostles constantly teach publicly in the temple in Jerusalem. When summoned to speak before the high priests, Peter replies, 'We must obey God rather than men' (Acts 5). Paul bore witness to the Christian message before the critical public of the Areopagus in Athens (Acts 17).

The public character of the practice of theology also takes on a *political dimension* if we do not lose sight of the original meaning of the term politics. *Ta politika* denotes what concerns citizens, the state, the public good, the community, the state. It cannot seriously be doubted that central contents of the Christian message like peace, salvation, justice, freedom, brotherliness and sisterliness relate to the common good and are to that extent political.

It is evident that as a result, in the history of theology theological work has constantly taken place before the public eye and has constantly had political consequences; often enough, too, theological statements have been misused ideologically in the service of a particular interest. Here the political dimension of theology has always had two aspects. First, theology is directed outwards, to 'secular' politics. A fascinating example of this is the public theological disputation carried on in 1550 and 1551 at the royal court in Valladolid, Spain, partly in the presence of the Spanish king, between Dr Juan Gines de Sepúlveda and Fr Bartolomé de Las Casas. The main question was: 'Is the King of Spain allowed to wage war against the Indians – before the faith is presented to them – in order to subject them to his rule, so that then he can instruct them more easily in the faith?'[3]

Secondly, the political dimension of theology is directed inwards: at the form and structure of the church itself. A terrible example of this is the work by Dionysius the Areopagite from the fifth/sixth century, *The Celestial Hierarchies*,[4] in which the author seeks to justify the hierarchical structure of the church as a divine ordinance with the help of Neoplatonic arguments.

However, here by way of example I shall also recall how the professors of the Catholic Theological Faculty in Ellwangen (1812–1817) and later (after 1817) in Tübingen constantly attempted to perceive this public and political dimension of their theological work anew *and therefore* continually came into conflict both with the state institutions and the church government.[5]

In 1815, Johann Sebastian Drey was condemned for his work on auricular confession. Two years later Pope Pius VII admonished the Vicar General of Ellwangen, Karl Fürst von Hohenlohe-Waldenburg, to pay better heed to the teaching of his professors. Andreas Benedikt Feilmoser, who came to Tübingen in 1820, had already had difficulties with the episcopal ordinariate in Brixen and with the nunciature in Vienna during his Innsbruck years. So for some time his call to Tübingen had been in question. In 1821 the Vicar General of Rottenburg, Johann Baptist Keller, felt the need to send an admonitory pastoral letter to the editors of the *Theologische Quartalschrift*. The specific occasion for this admonition was primarily a discussion in the journal. Johann Baptist Hirscher had – anonymously – criticized the attitude of the official church on the question of priestly celibacy in a review. The pastoral letter states, among other things:

> Not only the direction which various articles in this periodical are taking, but above all the article in the fourth issue for the year 1820, which contains

two reviews of works for and against the celibacy of Catholic clergy on pp.637–670, has made a deep impression and caused offence to a large number of the clergy entrusted to our paternal supervision, especially the outline of the career of Catholic clergy contained on pages 640–649. As a result of this the clergy see themselves stripped before the public eye in a manner which in no way seems compatible with the dignity of this state and which at least to this extent and generalization we confidently believe in no way to correspond with reality. Moreover we were surprised to find in it even accusations against those in authority in the church, and responsibility being laid at their door, to the effect that, as is said on p.663, 'they do not take this question into serious consideration, though it cannot be unknown to the editor that this cannot be a matter for the few churchwardens who still remain or individuals among them, and general discussion and assemblies of churchwardens cannot take place at present'.[6]

Some time later Johann Adam Möhler was barred from taking up a professorial chair in Bonn by the Archbishop of Cologne, August Graf Spiegel, because of his book *Unity in the Church or the Principle of Catholicism, in the Spirit of the Church Fathers of the First Three Centuries.*[7] Johann Baptist Hirscher, who went to Freiburg in 1837, had great difficulty in demonstrating his orthodoxy in subsequent years. All proposals to make him senior pastor or coadjutor of a German diocese were rejected by Rome. In 1848 a complaint reached the nunciature in Munich about heretical statements by the Munich moral theologian Josef Gehringer. The attacks on the theology of Johann Evangelist Kuhn after 1856 led some years later to formal proceedings before the Holy Office.

In 1870 the former Tübingen church historian Karl Josef von Hefele was one of the minority leaders at Vatican I, and among the resolute opponents of papal infallibility. In a letter from Rome to Stuttgart dated 7 March 1870 he wrote:

So I stated in today's session with Cardinal Rauscher that I did not submit to a mere majority decision in matters of faith. I declared this with all possible solemnity and heard many bishops echo, 'Nor I, nor I.' What will follow when I and others protest against the new dogma is clear, but I will not stand as a hypocrite before the world, come what may. I already envisaged this possibility when I accepted election (as a bishop). Better lose everything than lose honour and a good conscience.

And a letter of his from Rome to Stuttgart, dated 13 July 1870, reads:

It is said that when the pope proclaims the dogma, he wants every bishop to be given two documents to sign: 1. that he believes in infallibility, and 2. that he recognizes that the Council was completely free. I cannot sign either document, even if they excommunicate me.[8]

As early as 1863, Johannes Joseph Ignaz Döllinger, the professor of church history, took the initiative and invited the Catholic scholars of Germany, Austria and Switzerland to a 'gathering of Catholic scholars' in Munich. In his opening address on 'The Past and Present of Theology', which has rightly been called a declaration of the rights of theologians (Goyau), Döllinger called for complete freedom of movement for theologians in spheres which were not directly concerned with dogmatic questions of faith: 'This freedom is as indispensable to the discipline as air to breathe is to the body.' Just as the Israelites had both prophecy and the priestly hierarchy at the same time, so too there must be an extraordinary power in the church alongside the regular authority: public opinion.

Pope Pius X reacted to this congress with a letter to the Archbishop of Munich in which he regretted that a gathering of theologians had taken place without a licence from the hierarchy, though 'it is its task to guide and supervise theology'.

In answer to the clerical and authoritarian Roman tendencies which were articulated in the Catholic church after the triumph of Ultramontanism under Pope Pius X (1846–1878), at the end of the nineteenth century and in the first decade of the twentieth, a movement developed in the German Catholic church which has been called 'Catholicism of the Present', 'Critical Catholicism' (sic!) or 'Reform Catholicism'. This movement brought together liberal elements, opponents to the centralist Roman church government, heirs of the efforts at reform in the sphere of the liturgy, opponents of compulsory celibacy, opponents of political Catholicism, etc. They were represented above all by Franz Xaver Kraus, Hermann Schell and Albert Ehrhard. The Roman Curia responded to this and similar efforts in France, England and Italy with the terrible decree *Lamentabili* and the encyclical *Pascendi* (1907), and the authoritarian imposition of the anti-modernist oath (1910).

This particular discussion about reform, centred on 'Reform Catholicism', also alienated the Catholic Theological Faculty of the University of Tübingen from Bishop Paul Wilhelm von Keppler. It is against this background that disciplinary proceedings against the dogmatic theologian Wilhelm Koch (1874–1955) are also to be seen: they began in 1912 and four years later compelled him to leave his chair and the university.[9]

Karl Färber has recorded his recollections of Wilhelm Koch in a disturbing way.[10] Färber, later editor of the journal *Christlicher Sonntag* (later *Christ in der Gegenwart*), belonged to the course which came to study theology in Tübingen in 1907, the year of the encyclical *Pascendi* and the Syllabus *Lamentabili*. Bishop Keppler of Rottenburg gave the following reason for his instruction to the Ministry of State to dismiss Koch, dated 29 August 1912: 'What makes Professor Koch unsuitable for the exercise of this teaching office, and the root cause of all his individual errors, is the general tenor of his spirit and his spiritual attitude to the church and the teaching authority of the church.'[11] These statements stand in marked contrast to the recollections of Karl Färber.

Another professor of the Catholic Theological Faculty of the University of Tübingen was in permanent conflict with the teaching authority of the church: Karl Adam (1876–1966).

The archepiscopal ordinariate in Munich had opened canonical proceedings against the young theologian Karl Adam – he was a junior lecturer in Munich from 1908 to 1917 – because of his statements on the historicity of church dogma. Faced with the threat of suspension, Adam already began to look round for new work: he hovered between activity in the Old Catholic church and the study of medicine. Then unexpectedly things took a lucky turn: Crown Prince Rupprecht, both of whose sons were receiving religious instruction from Karl Adam, made it known to the church authorities that the Bavarian crown did not desire church measures against Adam. That led to an immediate stop to proceedings. On 1 August 1932 the Holy Office decreed that Adam's book *The Spirit of Catholicism* should be withdrawn from sale (along with all foreign translations) and that the author was obliged in future to submit all works with a religious or dogmatic content to an *auctoritas superior Ecclesiastica* before they appeared. However, this and many other measures against him did not prevent Karl Adam from immediately declaring himself ready to submit unconditionally, 'not only with obedience but with delight'.[12]

In respect of the split among Christians he wrote:

> *Nostra culpa, nostra maxima culpa*! And we theologians are above all the guilty ones. For we have cast what divides us in hard and rigid forms and thus made the split permanent. So it is above all our duty and responsibility to make our contribution to restoring the old unity. And it seems to me that Tübingen in particular is the place where the efforts for unity must take root and flourish.[13]

Against the background of these historical developments, the conflict between Hans Küng and the church authorities does not seem to be qualitatively anything new, though it is all the more scandalous for Hans Küng the human being, Christian priest and theologian.[14] Is it not high time that those holding office in church government studied the history of theology and learned from it? No one nowadays would seriously describe the views of Johann Baptist Hirscher, Johann Sebastian Drey, Joseph Döllinger, Wilhelm Koch or Karl Adam – to mention just these – as un-Christian or un-Catholic. But must such conflicts really always be ended with the instruments of denunciation, refusal of the *nihil obstat*, withdrawal of the licence to teach, and indeed suspension? Is it purely utopian to hope that the present and future conflict in the Christian church between theologians on the one hand and church officials on the other will be solved by dialogue and critical discussion?[15]

2. Public statements by Catholic theologians since the end of the Second Vatican Council (1965)

The following list makes no claim to completeness.[16] Nor does it include the numerous statements by Catholic initiative groups like the 'Committee for Christian Rights', the 'Church from Below' Initiative, the 'Association of Catholic Solidarity Groups', etc. Here I have simply attempted to survey to some degree the number and the most important content of public statements by Catholic theologians.

1. For the freedom of theology

This statement was signed at the end of 1968 by 1322 theologians from all over the world.[17] The central statement runs: 'The freedom won by the Second Vatican Council for theologians and theology in the service of the church must not be endangered again today.' The specific demand made was orderly procedure in the case of a conflict. In response to this declaration, the Roman Congregation of Faith issued a procedural order which takes up some of the requests presented, but the most important of them are still ignored.

2. The election of bishops

The editors of the Tübingen journal *Theologische Quartalschrift* circulated the following proposal in 1969: 'In future the period of office for residing bishops should be eight years. A re-election or prolongation of this period of office is to be possible only by way of exception, for objective external reasons which lie in the church-political situation ... The election of a bishop by a larger body seems unconditionally desirable because of the significance of the episcopal office and the need for a living contact with the diocese, and is an integral element of the proposal for a limitation of the period of office.'[18] This proposal by the professors of the Tübingen Catholic Theological Faculty was also signed by Joseph Ratzinger, who was at that time one of their number.

3. For the Viri probati

The Conference of German-Speaking Pastoral Theologians unanimously passed a resolution at their conference held between 2 and 5 January 1970 which stated, among other things: 'It is the unanimous view of the conference that the leadership of the communities in principle is part of the unrestricted service of the ordained presbyter, particularly including the celebration of the eucharist. As pastoral theologians we feel obliged to ask the bishops in our language-area to see to it that each community has an ordained president, even if this president has other work or is married. Therefore we call on the bishops urgently to take the necessary steps to alter those regulations of church law which stand in the way.'[19] This resolution was explicitly endorsed by the same conference in 1972.

4. For a rethinking of the duty of celibacy

On 6 February 1970, eighty-four Catholic professors of theology in the German-language area made an appeal to their bishops: 'We therefore call on our bishops, in accordance with the co-responsibility for the whole church again endorsed at Vatican II, as individuals and through their conferences to intercede publicly in Rome for the long-overdue discussion which has often been asked for on this question (viz. compulsory celibacy).'[20] This declaration was signed by, among others, Walter Kasper, who was at that time a professor of theology in Münster.

5. Against resignation in the church

In the 1972 declaration it is stated: 'So the credibility of the Catholic church, which at the beginning of the pontificate of Paul VI was perhaps higher than it had ever been in the last 500 years, has sunk to a disturbing degree. Many people are suffering over the church. Resignation is spreading ... It is, rather, the church system itself which has remained far behind the times in its development and still betrays numerous features of a princely absolutism: pope and bishops as in fact sole rulers of the church who combine legislative, executive and judiciary functions.' This declaration was signed by thirty-three theologians, including Walter Kasper, then a professor of theology, and Hermann-Joseph Vogt.[21]

6. Declaration on a 'basic law of the Catholic church'

In view of the danger, then threatening, of a centralistically determined and authoritatian basic law of the Catholic church, in 1977 more than 200 signatories warned against the dogmatizing of church law and the legalizing of dogma. 'With this basic law the church would fall even further behind the awareness of law in our world, which is wholly due to its Christian roots.'[22]

7. The right of the community to its priests

In a joint leading article, the editorial board of the journal *Diakonia* – also in 1977 – stated that in the church there was something like a binding basic norm which for all its historical and social conditioning was removed from human intervention because it arose out of the very substance of Christianity, the statements of the New Testament and the traditions of the church that had been handed down, namely the right of the community to its own ordained leader.[23]

8. The pope we need

With a view to the imminent papal election after the death of Pope Paul VI, ten theologians of a great variety of nationalities put forward their views on the pope the church needs.[24]

9. For a pope of the poor and oppressed of this world

To provide an opposite emphasis to that in the appeal mentioned under no. 8, Karl Rahner and Johann Baptist Metz wrote an 'Open Letter to the German Cardinals'.[25]

10. Statement on Puebla

In connection with the Third General Assembly of the Latin American Conference of Bishops which took place in Puebla in 1978, the members of the *Concilium* Foundation made a statement.[26] It said, among other things: 'Because of all this we have noted with indigation and horror how those who within and outside Latin America profit from the damnable social conditions there have reacted by cruelly suppressing any effort to establish a more just social order. The answer to the longing for a life of human dignity was imprisonment, torture and death. Among those who suffered this fate were many Christians – peasants, bishops, workers, students and priests – who were concerned to preach the gospel from the standpoint of the poor. This is the price that any prophetic action has to pay ... And what is perhaps the greatest scandal in all this is the fact that this oppressive power is exercised by governments which claim to be Christian and thus to be defending what they regard as values of the Western world and of Christianity.'

11. Statement on the pastoral regulation on admitting remarried divorced persons to the sacraments

The committee of the Conference of German-speaking Pastoral Theologians made an extended statement in 1979 on the question of the admission to the sacraments of divorced persons who had remarried.[27] Among other things this statement said: 'Whether in individual cases remarried divorced persons may be admitted to the sacraments cannot be answered without the conscious decision of those involved.'

12. Statement by the editorial board of Concilium *on the proceedings of the Congregation of Faith against Jacques Pohier and Edward Schillebeeckx* [28]

The statement from 1979 says, among other things: 'On the basis of all these objections ... the signatories are of the opinion that in the case of their colleague Edward Schillebeeckx the authorities of the church, who make a "public" stand on human rights, must themselves respect the exercise of these rights within the church.' This statement was signed by thirty theologians, all members of the editorial board of *Concilium*.

13. Statement by the editorial board of Concilium *on the 'Küng case'*

On the occasion of the withdrawal of the church's licence to teach from Hans Küng in December 1979 the editorial board of *Concilium* made the following statement: 'We, directors of the international theological journal *Concilium*, see no reasonable ground why our colleague Hans Küng should no longer be regarded as a Catholic theologian. We therefore wish to press for a revision of the condemnation. Moreover we call on the church's mode of proceedings finally to take into account human rights which apply universally.' [29]

14. Statement by the professors of the Catholic Faculty of Theology in the University of Tübingen

On 18 December 1979 all the professors of the Catholic Faculty of Theology – including Walter Kasper, who was also a professor at that time – made the following statement: 'We have heard on the radio, from simultaneous statements by the nunciature and the German Conference of Bishops, that our colleague Professor Dr Hans Küng has had the church's licence to teach withdrawn by the Bishop of Rottenburg, on the basis of a decision of the papal Congregation of Faith dated 15 December 1979. We are deeply disturbed by this decisive step by the Congregation of Faith and by the way in which the move has been made in a concerted action. We are horrified at the prospect of yet unforeseeable consequences. We see serious dangers to the credibility of the church in present-day society and the freedom of theology in research and teaching.' [30]

15. Statement by seven professors of the Catholic Faculty of Theology in the University of Tübingen: 'Church Struggle with the Help of Theology? Against the Total Confrontation in Catholicism'

The statement by seven professors dated 5 February 1980 made the political decision that Hans Küng could no longer remain a member of the Catholic Faculty of Theology. This statement said, among other things: 'However, the continued existence of the theological faculties is now in danger, not only from outside but increasingly also from within. Anyone who allows or wishes a theologian without a *missio canonica* to have long-term membership of a theological faculty undermines its academic status and its guarantee under the law of constitution and concordat.'[31]

16. Open letter from Catholic college professors in the Federal Republic of Germany to the Catholic theological faculties or departments in the Federal Republic of Germany

On 8 February 1980 ninety professors from various faculties of various German universities published an open letter which said among other things: 'The change in the world in which we live on the one hand and the rigid maintaining by the church of formulations of faith which have been shaped by past eras on the other lead to a split consciousness. So increasing discontent is driving many Christians at all levels to a helpless distance from church and faith. It is also becoming increasingly difficult for us academic teachers, too, to explain our ties to the church to colleagues and students.'[32]

17. Letter of 145 professors and lecturers in Catholic theology in the Federal Republic of Germany to Cardinal Höffner

The first signatories to this letter were Professors Alfons Auer of Tübingen, Heinrich Fries of Munich and Bernhard Welte of Freiburg. The letter said, among other things; 'In order to do duty to its work as a discipline, theology must be able to make unlimited use of the freedom to employ all viable methods in research into and exposition of the faith ... With the 1968 declaration on "The Freedom of Theologians and Theology", signed by 1360 theologians, we emphasize that "this freedom (represents) a heavy responsibility for us theologians, not to endanger the authentic unity and the true peace of the church and all its members ..." We must emphatically point out the far-reaching consequences that any limitation of the freedom of theology must necesarily have. The most recent development gives the impression that in the eyes of the bishops the face of theology has changed considerably compared to the time of the Council, despite some statements to the contrary ... With great concern we see the gulf which is opening up here. It would be a disaster if this represented the beginning of a process which went back behind what was achieved by the Second Vatican Council and the responsible work of theologians over decades.'[33]

18. Six questions to Pope John Paul II

On the occasion of the first visit of Pope John Paul II to the Federal Republic of Germany in 1980, 135 Christians and 25 church groups from the Federal Republic wrote a letter to him. This said, among other things: 'Today 2.3

billion people – more than half the population of the earth – must get by on an average annual income of less than 600 DM, and 800 million of them live in absolute poverty ... Are you prepared to revise the church teaching on birth control so that responsibility for the means to be used and the number of children is left to the conscience of parents themselves, which was the position of the former papal study commission and the Königstein Declaration of the German Conference of Bishops?'[34]

19. Trusting the power of truth

The meeting of the Association of German-language Catholic Dogmatic and Fundamental Theologians held in January 1981 passed almost unanimously a resolution which among other things said: 'Here on the foundation of the one faith of the church there can and must be different schools and trends ... conflicts between the church's *magisterium* and individual theologians are always possible and in some circumstances necessary for the truth ... But as the truth seeks to convince of itself, it is to be expected of the church *magisterium* that it presents such decisions by way of argument and here trusts more in the power of truth and the force of argument than in administrative measures which do not do away with open questions but can do serious damage to the credibility of the church.'[35]

20. Public letter to Pope John Paul II on the 'Küng case'

The 1981 letter of Norbert Greinacher and Herbert Haag, professors in the Catholic Faculty of Theology in the University of Tübingen, states, among other things; 'In the past you have had several conversations with Archbishop Lefebvre, even on 15 December 1979, the very day that you approved the decree of the Congregation of Faith against Hans Küng, and again after that. Many people in our church are therefore asking: is it just that you should single out a suspended bishop with your readiness for conversation and refuse this to Hans Küng, who has urgently asked for such conversation several times as a Catholic priest, which he still is with full rights. Holy Father, you will soon be making a visit to Switzerland, Hans Küng's homeland, in which the proceedings against him have provoked a particularly large number of protests with thousands of signatures. We therefore appeal once again to you: clarify matters with Hans Küng before you set out on this journey.'[36] The authors received no answer to this open letter.

21. The threat to the new ways in the church

With a dateline of 7 June 1984 the theologians of *Concilium* gathered in Nijmegen published a statement on the new attacks on the theology of liberation. The statement said, among other things: 'We certainly do not claim to possess the truth, and we are well aware that we are only one voice among others, though this is a church voice through and through ... We declare our resolute solidarity with the liberation movements and their theology. We protest against the suspicions and unjust criticisms which are levelled against them. We are firmly convinced that these movements have to do with the future of the church, with the advent of the kingdom of God and the judgment of God on the world.'[37]

22. Tübingen professors on disarmament

The wide-ranging initiatives on disarmament on the part of Mikhail Gorbachev were initially regarded with much scepticism: the anxiety that they were merely tricks, deceptive tactical manoeuvres by a Soviet empire which was still striving for world domination, was hard to overcome. In this situation, in a joint declaration dated 5 May 1987, 131 professors of the University of Tübingen took up Gorbachev's proposal to introduce a double-zero solution for nuclear weapons in Europe: 'We call upon the Bundestag and the Federal Government to support the Soviet and North American interest in a double-zero solution for nuclear weapons in Europe. Even after the implementation of such a double-zero solution, fears would be unjustified that Europe's security would be more endangered in the future.'[38] The signatories included not only Hans Küng and the initiator, Norbert Greinacher, but also three members of the Catholic Theological Faculty.

23. Statement of the Association of German-Language Catholic Dogmatic and Fundamental Theologians on the practice of giving the nihil obstat on appointments to chairs

Serious events in this sphere give occasion for deep concern, as the statement stresses. The *nihil obstat* has often been refused without those concerned being accused of specific deviations from Catholic teaching and without the mode of proceedings leading to the refusal having been made clear. 'Both are likely to provoke uncertainty, mistrust and offence not only among those concerned but also in the colleges and among the public generally.'[39]

24. Remaining in dialogue with Drewermann

At a conference in Erfurt on 4 June 1988 the Committee of the Conference of German-speaking Pastoral Theologians passed a resolution on the Drewermann case. The resolution said, among other things: 'The committee sees the style of the controversy with and around Eugen Drewermann as a touchstone for the readiness for dialogue and openness and the capacity to sustain tension called for by the Council. Without these virtues the church would lose its credibility.'[40]

25 Resolution of the Committee of the Conference of German-speaking Pastoral Theologians on suspect developments within the Catholic church

This 1988 resolution begins with the following statements:

'We observe with anxiety and concern that:
– laity may no longer preach at the eucharist;
– in appointments to theological chairs the right of the church authorities to object has been abused to intimidate theologians and make theology uniform;
– in the occupation of episcopal sees the independence of the local churches is infringed and degraded so that they become branches of the Roman central office.'[41]

26. Church unity is being put at risk!

Under the dateline of 16 November 1988 the five Catholic practical theologians Ottmar Fuchs of Bamberg, Norbert Greinacher of Tübingen, Leo Karrer of Fribourg in Switzerland, Norbert Mette of Münster/Paderborn and Hermann Steinkamp of Münster made a statement on the problem of the nomination of bishops.[42] This statement says among other things: 'There can no longer be any doubt that the Pope and the Roman Curia are engaged in church politics with the nomination of bishops. They are using this policy once again to reverse the opening up of the church which manifestly began during and after the Second Vatican Council and are taking the Catholic church back into a ghetto ... In view of the clear statements of the biblical traditions, in recollection of the old democratic customs in church history and against the background of a society which is in process of fundamental democratization, the present-day Roman practice of nominating bishops represents a structural heresy which not only puts the credibility of the church seriously in question but also puts church unity at risk.'

27. Against Incapacitation – Towards an open Catholicity. The Cologne Declaration

The Cologne Declaration of January 1989 probably found the greatest response world-wide. Three problem areas which most oppress theologians were touched on at the beginning of this declaration:

'1. The Roman Curia is aggressively pursuing a strategy of filling episcopal

sees throughout the world unilaterally, without regard for the proposals of
the local churches and without respect for their due rights.
2. Throughout the world, qualified theologians are in many cases being
refused permission to teach by the church. This is a significant and
dangerous interference in the freedom of research and teaching and in the
dialogical structure of theological knowledge which the Second Vatican
Council stressed at many points. The granting of the church's licence to
teach is being abused as an instrument of discipline.
3. We are witnessing a highly questionable theological attempt to make
illegitimate and excessive use of the magisterial as well as the judiciary
competence of the papacy.'

The statement ends: 'If the pope does what does not pertain to his office, he
cannot call for obedience in the name of Catholicism. In that case he must
expect opposition.'[43]

This statement, which was initiated by the Tübingen theologians Norbert
Greinacher and Dietmar Mieth and a group of first signatories, was signed by
162 Catholic professors of theology in the German-speaking world and the
Netherlands. Similar statements followed in Belgium, France, Spain, Italy,
Brazil and the United States. In addition the declaration was signed in the
Netherlands by about 17,000 and in the Federal Republic of Germany by
around 16,000 pastors and laity and about 100 Catholic groups.

*28. Open letter on developments in the politics of the churches and schools by
Italian theologians and intellectuals*

This 1989 letter mentions 'discontent at particular actions on the part of the
central church authority in the educational, disciplinary and institutional
sphere'.[44]

*29. Letter of the Fifth Plenary Assembly of the Brazilian Association of
Theologians*

The question of the nomination of bishops is also one of the main points in this
paper – similarly approved in 1989. The theologians complain very urgently at
the changes to the overall situation of the church in the country.[45]

30. For freedom in the church. Tübingen Declaration of 12 July 1990

The thirty theologians who were signatories, above all from German-speaking
countries, see themselves threatened by the Roman Congregation of Faith's
Instruction 'On the Ecclesial Vocation of the Theologian' and oppose any

form of 'inquisition, however subtle'. The teachers of the church may not be gagged by compulsory measures, but must have the right to proclaim the Word, whether the Vatican likes it or not.[46]

31. Resolution of the Association of German-speaking Catholic Dogmatic and Fundamental Theologians on the Roman Congregation of Faith's Instruction 'On the Ecclesial Vocation of the Theologian'

At their conference at the end of September 1990 the Association of German-speaking Catholic Dogmatic and Fundamental Theologians passed a resolution on the Roman Congregation of Faith's 'Instruction on the Ecclesial Vocation of the Theologian'. In it, among other things, the view is put forward 'that the document does not do justice to essential aspects of the task of academic theology, its relation to the *magisterium*, to the proclamation of Christian faith in our time, and to the proper understanding of church community'.[47]

32. 'Do not quench the Spirit'

This saying of Paul's was the title of the 'Washington Declaration' with which at the end of 1990 more than 400 North American Catholic theologians made a critical contribution to the discussion of the church situation in the USA and Canada and of a variety of disputed questions of recent years in the church as a whole.[48]

33. Lucerne statement against the 'Sell-out of the Second Vatican Council'

The 'Lucerne statement' of March 1991 carries the slogan, 'We cannot and may not keep silent'. The statement was signed by about 12,000 church workers, both full-time and honorary, throughout Europe. The statement says, among other things: 'We are working towards a church which first of all takes human rights seriously in its own ranks ... We are working towards a church in which women have full and equal rights and participation in decision-making processes. We are working towards a church in which the sense of faith of all believers is an essential element in the process of the church's discovery of truth ... We are working towards a church which deals humanely and fairly with conflicts that arise, not with the means of power but in the spirit of the gospel. We are working towards a church in which the Bishop of Rome's Petrine service is exercised in such a style and with such claims as to be able to build bridges between the various local churches and theologies ... We are resolved to make the vision of a church of brothers and sisters, liberating and free from anxiety, as far as we can a reality through our work. We will not be diverted from the course of church renewal.'[49]

34. Petition of five pastoral theologians from Switzerland and the Federal Republic of Germany to the Members of the 'Eighth Ordinary Plenary Assembly of the Synod of Bishops'

In connection with the Synod of Bishops concerned with the problem of the formation of priests, which was due to begin in Rome on 30 September 1990, the five pastoral theologians Ottmar Fuchs of Bamberg, Norbert Greinacher of Tübingen, Leo Karrer of Fribourg in Switzerland, Norbert Mette of Münster and Paderborn, and Hermann Steinkamp of Münster sent a petition to the synod dated 17 September 1990. This said, among other things: 'The New Canon Law (1983) ends with the statement *salus animarum qua est in ecclesia suprema semper lex esse debet*. Freely translated, this means that human salvation is always the supreme law for the church. If this important norm is to be realized in the praxis of the church, in view of the devastating lack of priests world-wide, decisive changes must be made to the regulations of canon law about the offices of the church, and above all priestly office, in the shortest possible time.'[50]

35. Statement of the Committee of the Conference of German-speaking Pastoral Theologians to the 1990 Synod of Bishops

This statement says, among other things: 'The "structural sin" of the church, its desire to clarify questions of substance at an administrative level, through economic pressure and a deliberate policy of focusing on individuals, calls for individual and ecclesial conversion to responsible dialogue and a pluriformity guided by the Spirit, if it is to be in accord with the demands of Jesus and the expectations of the people of God. If the 1990 Synod of Bishops is not imprisoned in anxiety, but accepts in trust the charisms in the people, we can have a well-founded hope for the development of pastoral ministries and thus for the church in present social conditions.'[51]

36. Towards a church which has a future

A declaration dated 16 December by five Catholic practical theologians (Ottmar Fuchs, Norbert Greinacher, Leo Karrer, Norbert Mette and Hermann Steinkampf) on the crisis of pastoral care caused by the lack of priests said, among other things: 'The pastoral emergency in the Catholic church calls for courage to undertake wide-ranging reforms.... In the medium and long term the concern must be to produce forms of community leadership which correspond to local pastoral needs. Conditions for admission to ordination imposed hitherto must be made secondary to this ... In all this the ordination of women and men (as priests) will further rather than restrict the universal priestly calling of the faithful.'[52]

37. A re-evaluation of the unity of the church endangered by Opus Dei

With a dateline of 30 November 1991 the committee of the Conference of German-language Pastoral Theologians passed a resolution on the impending beatification of the founder of Opus Dei, Monsignore José Maria Escrivá de Balaguer.[53] The resolution stated, among other things: 'The future of society and Christianity essentially depends on how far it proves possible in the sphere of the church to recognize human dignity, a capacity for tolerance and dialogue, justice and the capacity for reconciliation as Christian values, and realize them as Christian virtues. We regard as a disturbing decision, and one which is dangerous for the church both politically and pastorally, the endorsement and sacralization by the beatification of its initiator of a type of thought and action so characterized by polarization and exclusion ... It is our impression that the beatification of the founder of Opus Dei encourages a dubious and obscure force in the church and neglects pastoral care for the unity in plurality.' In the meantime the beatification of Escrivá de Balaguer has gone ahead.

3. Cui bono? A critical survey

Confronted with these efforts by Catholic theologians to obtain more freedom in the church – and there have been others – one is inevitably reminded of the beginning of the book of Koheleth: 'Vanity, vanity, said the preacher, all is vanity. What advantage does a man have from all his possessions for which he labours under the sun?' (1.2f.). A survey of the history of theology in the nineteenth and twentieth centuries, above all in the German-language sphere – depicted here very fragmentarily – suggests a dialogue between the deaf. Has one partner ever listened to the other? Let us just take the example of compulsory celibacy. For a good 170 years in Tübingen and elsewhere there has been talk of the unconditional pastoral necessity of abolishing the canon law requirement of obligatory celibacy.[54] So far, nothing has changed. It really looks as if those who at present hold office in the church have learned nothing from the conflicts between the theological teachers and their predecessors in the nineteenth and twentieth centuries. The conflicts are played out according to the selfsame ritualized mechanisms which were already in use at the beginning of the ninenteenth century.

An eloquent example of this is the Instruction of the Vatican Congregation of Faith 'On the Ecclesial Vocation of the Theologian', which a mere three years ago provoked alongside many other protests the Tübingen statement 'For Freedom in the Church' (cf. no. 30 above) and a Resolution of the Association of German-speaking Dogmatic and Fundamental Theologians (cf. no.31). If the text of this instruction – the very classification 'instruction' is treacherous – sounds indisputably anachronistic for people of the late twentieth century, at the same time it is terrifying testimony to the realities of the Catholic church.[55]

First of all, positively, the emphasis on 'collaboration between theologians and the *magisterium*'[56] is to be maintained. Theology is accorded the utmost significance for the life of the church, indeed for the whole of humankind, when it is stressed: 'Theology has importance for the Church in every age, so that it can respond to the plan of God "who desires all men to be saved and to come to the knowledge of the truth" (I Tim. 2.4)'.[57]

At the same time, however, theology is authoritatively deprived of air to breathe. The language and style alone are deeply humiliating: above all the extension of the teaching competence of the Roman *magisterium* with divine support to make statements without giving an infallible definition and without making a 'definitive' statement[58] is devastating in content and breaks with every tradition of the church. The First Vatican Council, which has already caused so much disaster for the church, is left far behind, with incalculable consequences for faith in the gospel. Moreover the 'Collaborative Relations' (the heading of section IV.A) of theologians and *magisterium* in particular is taken to absurd extremes by Section IV.B, 'The Problem of Dissent', which immediately follows. To pick out just one of many portentous statements here too: dissent, i.e. the 'attitudes of general ... opposition to the *magisterium* of the church' – formulated, moreover, personally in the instruction, like for example 'the devil' – is described as being highly dangerous particularly if it extends 'its influence to the point of shaping a common opinion',[59] in other words to where theology must turn in ongoing processes of research if it is to be true to its duty.

If we survey the now twenty-five years of publications by theologians since the Second Vatican Council, three statements have taken on special significance: 'For the Freedom of Theology' (1986, cf. no. 1); the statement 'Against Resignation in the Church' of 1972 (no. 5); and the 'Cologne Declaration ('Against Incapacitation – For an Open Catholicity') of January 1989 (no. 27).

To be noted critically is the problem that most of these declarations seem above all to speak 'in their own cause'. In other words, one could ask whether they are not too concerned with the freedom of theology and do not forget other far more important problems. This should be considered. From a defensive position their main concern is to protect themselves against actual or threatened interventions by the Roman *magisterium* in theological research and the fullness of power which Rome claims for itself in theological questions, to criticize, and to insist on alterations to what goes on within the church and church structures. Theologians are concerned for fair human dealings in cases of conflict, i.e. social norms which can be demonstrated publicly and are universally valid. Here they are in danger of coming to terms with a system which high-handedly reserves to itself the possibility of destroying controversial argumentative discoveries of theological truth. These statements by theologians represent something like desperate self-defence against the power of Rome.

On the other hand, on the positive side it must be noted that they encourage or perhaps even stimulate a process of consciousness in respect of more plurality, more freedom, specifically within the church. Something like an internal church public has been created which first made possible a public discussion of controversial standpoints. Many Christians felt that the statements, most recently and above all the Cologne Declaration, were a real liberation, a longed-for light in a church heaven that was getting increasingly dark. That is also a sign that many Catholic Christians have understood that the theologians are not just concerned for their freedom, but that their freedom also implies the freedom of all church members.

Ultimately the fundamental issue is whether the church will develop into an anachronistic religous sect or whether it will refuse to give up confronting the gospel of Jesus Christ with the *today* of life and world, living *today* with men and women as a church with its liberating traditions. As long as there are groups of Catholic Christian men and women who are energetically fighting for the freedom of the children of God, we must not give up hope. But on the other hand it is also the case that as long as such statements are necessary, this freedom has still not come within our grasp, and it is important also to see how more and more people are turning their backs on the church and fundamentalism is gaining ground within the church.

In the statements quoted above, however, the whole dilemma of Catholic theology is clear. Is not an almost impossible contradiction evident here to non-Catholics? On the one hand the decisive plea for emancipation from Rome, and on the other side a constantly sad gaze towards Rome, hoping against all experience? Self-critically it has to be granted that here one can see a remarkable emancipated tutelage, a rejection of absolutist authorities which goes with excessive respect for these authorities.

Twenty-five years of public statements by Catholic theologians 'against': against the refusal to allow theology and theologians to come of age, against the procedures of the Congregation of Faith, against the destruction of liberation theology, against the obscure way in which the *nihil obstat* is given, against a reactionary basic law of the Catholic church, against betrayal of the Second Vatican Council, against the new encyclical on morals, against authoritarian nominations of bishops, against ... How long should this, how long must this, go on? Will teachers of theology twenty-five years from now have to wear themselves out pleading for fundamental natural rights for all Catholic Christians before finally – and then probably too late – constructive theological work 'for' becomes possible?

I have a dream: what if a new Tübingen Declaration were formulated, which broke with the fixation on Rome and said that after more than twenty years of this kind of experience one had to agree that the Roman *magisterium* was utterly incapable of dialogue? I try to imagine a text with a wording like this:

> The Roman *magisterium*, especially the Roman Congregation of Faith, can no longer be taken seriously, as above all the Instruction on the Ecclesial Vocation of the Theologian has recently shown. As long as the Church of Rome does not remedy its terrifying failure to heed the message of Jesus of Nazareth as a result of its fixation on maintaining domination within the church, and in so doing increasingly distances itself from the faithful, we theologians think it beneath our dignity to engage in argument with such declarations. To do justice to our own responsibility as teachers of Catholic theology, in the footsteps of Jesus of Nazareth we would like ultimately to put our work once again at the service of urgent substantive questions for which people seek answers. We warmly invite our church leaders in Rome also to make their contribution, so that a common, fruitful search can be got under way.

Notes

1. 31.86.
2. Cf. H. Küng, 'Auf dem Weg zu einem neuen Grundkonsens in der katholischen Theologie? Zum "Zwischenbericht" von Edward Schillebeeckx', *Theologische Quartalschrift Tübingen* 159, 1979, 272–85.
3. Cf. L. Hanke, *All Mankind is One. A Study of the Disputation between Bartolomé de Las Casas and Juan Gins de Sepulveda in 1550 on the Intellectual and Religious Capacity of the American Indians*, Illinois 1974.
4. English translation by J. Parker, Oxford and London 1897–99.
5. What follows is based above all on the admirable studies by my colleague R. Reinhardt: R. Reinhardt (ed.), *Tübinger Theologie und ihre Theologen. Quellen und Forschungen zur Geschichte der Katholisch-Theologischen Fakultät Tübingen*, Tübingen 1976; id., 'Die Katholisch-Theologische Fakultät im 19. Jahrhundert. Fakten und Phasen ihrer Entwicklung', in G. Schwaiger (ed.), *Kirche und Theologie im 19. Jahrhundert. Referate und Berichte des Arbeitskreises Katholische Theologie*, Göttingen 1975, 55–87; *Theologische Quartalschrift Tübingen* 150, 1970, 1 (jubilee issue on professors of the Tübingen Catholic Faculty of Theology).
6. Quoted from *Theologische Quartalschrift Tübingen* 150, 1970, 174.
7. *Die Einheit in der Kirche oder das Prinzip des Katholizismus, dargestellt in Geist der Kirchenväter der ersten drei Jahrhunderte*, Tübingen 1825.
8. On the basis of copies which my colleague Joachim Köhler kindly put at my disposal.
9. Cf. M. Seckler, *Theologie vor Gericht*, Contubernium 3, Tübingen 1972.
10. 'Erinnerungen an W. Koch', *Theologische Quartalschrift Tübingen* 150, 1970, 102–15.
11. Ibid., 115.
12. Cf. A. Auer, 'Karl Adam', *Theologische Quartalschrift Tübingen* 150, 1970, 131–40.

13. Ibid., 143.
14. Cf. above all W. Jens (ed.), *Um nichts als die Wahrheit. Deutsche Bischofskonferenz contra Hans Küng*, Munich 1978; N. Greinacher and H. Haag (eds.), *Der Fall Küng. Eine Dokumentation*, Munich 1980.
15. Indeed the point has gradually been reached when as a professor in the Catholic Theological Faculty of the University of Tübingen one can no longer make a public stand if one does not want to become a victim of church sanctions. At any rate, I can point out that Bishop Walter Kasper, who was professor in the Catholic Theological Faculty of the University of Tübingen from 1970 to 1989, pointed out to me in a letter of 2 January 1991 that my thesis on the 'democratization of the church' (*Theologische Quartalschrift Tübingen* 179, 1990, 253–66) was 'in contradiction to binding Catholic teaching'. Kasper also wrote to me: 'I do not think that the positions expressed are appropriate for the education of future priests and pastoral workers.' The conflict has meanwhile been settled.
16. I would be very interested in corrections and further information. It is worth mentioning in passing that the Spanish journal *Palabra* has published in its number 285 of March 1989 a 'Ranking de los Habituales de la Protesta'. I was fascinated to see that I come third on the list after Hans Küng and Johann Baptist Metz!
17. First published in the *Frankfurter Allgemeine Zeitung* of 17 December 1968, and later in H. Küng, *Reforming the Church Today*, 177–80.
18. *Theologische Quartalschrift Tübingen* 149, 1969, 111–15.
19. Quoted from *Publik-Forum*, 1 April 1977, 15f.
20. Ibid., 16.
21. First published in *Publik-Forum*, 24 March 1972, and later in H. Küng, *Reforming the Church Today*, 181–6.
22. Published in *Publik-Forum, Kein Grundgesetz der Kirche ohne Zustimmung der Christen. Text des Entwurfs und Kritische Bemerkungen von J.G. Gerhartz, W. Kasper and J. Neumann*, Munich 1977, 89–92.
23. *Diakonia* 8, 1977, 217–21.
24. First published in *Süddeutsche Zeitung*, 14/15 August 1978.
25. First published in *Süddeutsche Zeitung*, 16 August 1978.
26. *Concilium* 14, 1978, 563–75 (these statements, see also nn. 28, 29, 31, 37, do not seem to have been published in the English edition).
27. *Pastoraltheologische Informationen* 8, August 1979, 104–11.
28. *Concilium* 15, 1979, 693f.
29. *Concilium* 16, 1980, 153.
30. Quoted from N. Greinacher and H. Haag (eds.), *Der Fall Küng. Eine Dokumentation*, Munich 1980, 100f.
31. First published in the *Frankfurter Allgemeine Zeitung* of 5 February 1980; later published in N. Greinacher and H. Haag (eds.), *Der Fall Küng*, 235–44. Walter Jens produced a four-line poem (*Schwäbische Tagblatt*, 7 February 1980): 'In fear they've cooked it up; if only they had kept quiet! Then no one would ever have discovered the difference between the Göttingen and Tübingen Seven' [the 'Göttingen Seven' are professors who protested against state authority for political reasons].
32. First published in the *Frankfurter Rundschau* of 8 February 1980; later published in N. Greinacher and H. Haag (eds.), *Der Fall Küng*, 233f.

33. First published in *Deutsche Tagespost*, 12 February 1980; later published in N. Greinacher and H. Haag (eds.), *Der Fall Küng*, 249–53.
34. First published in *Süddeutsche Zeitung*, 11 November 1980.
35. Wording in *Publik-Forum*, 6 February 1981.
36. First published in *Publik-Forum*, 15 May 1981. Also in W. Kern (ed.), *Die Theologie und das Lehramt*, Freiburg 1982, 234–7.
37. *Concilium* 20, 1984, 359f.
38. The 'Statement by 131 Professors of the Eberhard-Karls-University of Tübingen on the Double-zero Solution' – four further signatures came in late – was sent directly to Chancellor Kohl, Foreign Minister Genscher and the party leaders of parties represented in the Bundestag, and also published in the *Süddeutsche Zeitung* of 6 May 1987.
39. Cf. *Herder-Korrespondenz* 42, 1988, 540.
40. *Pastoraltheologische Informationen*, Heft 1, 1988, 261–3.
41. *Pastoraltheologische Informationen*, Heft 2, 1988, 365.
42. First published in *Frankfurter Rundschau*, 19 November 1988, and later in *Pastoraltheologische Informationen*, Heft 2, 1988, 366–78. The preface to the publication of this statement in *Pastoraltheologische Informationen* states: 'The Committee of the Conference of German-language Theologians welcomes the fact that five colleagues from the conference have made a statement on an urgent problem, shares their concerns and thinks it right that the full wording of the statement should be documented.'
43. Published in many places by the media, and later in H. Küng, *Reforming the Church Today*, 187–91.
44. Cf. *Herder-Korrespondenz* 43, 1989, 285.
45. First publication in Europe, *Il regno*, 16 July 1989; cf. *Herder-Korrespondenz* 43, 1989, 386.
46. First published in *Süddeutsche Zeitung*, 13 July 1990.
47. Cf. *Herder-Korrespondenz* 44, 1990, 542.
48. First published in *Catholic News Service*, 13 February 1990; cf. *Herder-Korrespondenz* 45, 1991, 66–8.
49. *Publik-Forum*, 23 March 1991.
50. Unpublished. There was no reply to the petition.
51. *Pastoraltheologische Informationen*, Heft 1, 1990, 263–7.
52. First published in *Frankfurter Rundschau*, 7 January 1992, and later in O. Fuchs et al., *Der pastorale Notstand. Notwendige Reformen für eine zukunftsfähige Kirche*, Düsseldorf 1992, 112–26.
53. *Pastoraltheologische Informationen*, Heft 1, 1992, 314f.
54. Cf. *Theologische Quartalschrift Tübingen* 172, 1992, 1 (the subject of this issue was 'Viri probati').
55. I am here using the text published by Sekretariat der Deutschen Bischofskonferenz (ed.), *Theologie und Kirche. Dokumentation*, Arbeitshilfen 86, 31 March 1991, 104–25.
56. No. 22; cf. also no. 6, pp.40,42.
57. No. 1.
58. Cf. no. 23.
59. No. 34.

Peter Hebblethwaite

Between Lucerne and Krakow: European Pluralism and the *Magisterium*

'Catholic theology exists in Europe only in the plural: and it is to be hoped that this will also continue to be the case in the future.'[1] Walter Lesch is here stating what he considers to be a truism. The 'plurality' of theology in Europe had been brought home to him by the first meeting of the European Society for Catholic Theology held at Hohenheim, Stuttgart on 5–9 April 1992, at which Hans Küng made a fleeting appearance in the group discussing 'world religions'.

Jozef Tischner, reliably reported to be 'close to Pope John Paul', shocked some by the vehemence of his attack on 'Western' theology. It allegedly 'ignored the reality of evil', encouraged Neo-Thomist compromises with Marxism, and borrowed too much from the Naziphile Martin Heidegger. These 'errors' had spread to Latin America and spawned 'liberation theology'.

Now before we indignantly set about refuting Tischer, we have to try to understand the mind-set which lies behind his comments. That mind-set was on display at an earlier theological conference in which Central and East European theologians met at Lublin on 11–15 August 1991. Tischner was again an important figure, declaring that 'in the Eastern part of the continent the witnesses to the faith are not theologians but martyrs'. The Czech theologian Otto Madr, who spent fifteen years in jail, remarked: 'In the famous *Handbuch der Pastoraltheologie* I found no word throughout its more than 3,000 pages about the Church under persecution.'[2]

In defence of the *Handbuch der Pastoraltheologie*, one can no doubt say that it was not intended for persecuted churches. But Madr would reply – or Nosowski replies on his behalf – that within living memory the church in Germany had known Nazi persecution and that just as Jewish theologians have to work 'after the *shoah*', so all European theologians have to 'come to terms' with the reality of concentration camps and Gulags. It is another version of the Tischer thesis: the West cannot, or at any rate does not, cope with the monstrous evil that has marked the twentieth century.[3]

'Overcome evil with good' is the message from the East. 'Western' theologians, so runs the story, are preoccupied, indeed obsessed, with contraception, women's ordination and ecclesiological questions. They stand condemned as intolerably superficial. Now there is a strong element of moral blackmail in this position. Who could be so craven as to argue with the witness of the martyrs?

But there are other ways of looking at the Lublin conference. It undoubtedly had the seal of official papal approval. The proof is that on 6 December 1991, Stanislaw Nagy, Professor of Fundamental Theology at the Catholic University of Lublin, reported on the conference to the special Synod on Europe at considerable length. Nagy's witness is important because he was one of the organizers of the conference. Nagy admits – but the admission is a boast – that they were at the stage of witness rather than theological reflection on the witness. 'This created,' he said, 'a climate of almost biblical narratives of salvation history emerging from the apocalyptic darkness of the the system of hatred and organized struggle directed against God and man.'[4] What had happened was 'an anthropological catastrophe', 'the Calvary of the church', and 'total enslavement cynically realized in the name of liberty and pushed to the very limit of unimaginable cruelty'.[5]

Once again, the Western theologian is disarmed in advance, crushed beneath the experience of martydom and suffering. Yet Nagy's rhetoric does not reflect the truth of the Polish situation in the 1970s and 1980s. The Polish church, far from being 'totally enslaved', grew in influence, if not power. In this period there were far more martyrs in Latin America than in Poland. Poland had one martyr, Fr Jerzy Pospielusko, and his killers were brought to trial and sentenced by the Communist regime. That is more than can be said of the thousands of 'disappeared ones' of Latin America whose anonymous murderers went scot-free. And throughout this period the Catholic University of Lublin continued to exist and indeed flourish. If one wants an example of 'total enslavement', then the Ukrainian Catholic church provides a better case of 'Calvary'.

I am not trying to minimize the sufferings of the church in Poland, merely to disengage them from Nagy's rhetorical inflation. And my witness to this is Karol Wojtyla in 1972. He has no doubt forgotten this encounter but I have not. I was visiting Krakow and my Polish friends urged me to see their Archbishop. He was much subtler than Cardinal Stefan Wyszyński, they said. Both had just issued pastoral letters on St Stanislaw. For Wyszyński he was simply an heroic bishop who had dared to denounce the iniquities of the king. The moral lesson was obvious: St Stanislaw was the patron of bishops who heroically denounced evil rulers.

Wojtyla's pastoral letter reached the same conclusion, but he allowed for some ambiguity: he conceded that some nineteenth-century historians thought that Stanislaw was 'asking for trouble' and that a more prudent man would not have courted martyrdom so assiduously. Since precisely the same point had been made about Thomas of Canterbury, a near contemporary of Stanislaw, this interested me greatly.[6] So I went along and was granted an hour from 5 p.m.

I spent the afternoon preparing myself. But when I arrived he asked all the questions. What was I doing in Poland? Whom had I seen? What did they say? Why was I sponsored by Pax? I explained that I was in Poland, for the fifth time, to try to understand the church there and to explain it to English-speaking readers. He pursued his interrogation. I had nothing in my notebook. Then, with five minutes to go, he said (we were speaking French):

If you want to explain the church in Poland you must understand two things. First, we are not a 'church of silence'. You cannot call us a 'church of silence' given that we have eleven thousand pulpits from which the gospel is proclaimed every Sunday morning

Second, we are not a 'persecuted' church. We were indeed persecuted in the period of Stalinism, but that is no longer so. *Nous sommes une église harcelée*, harassed and impeded in every way, unable to get paper for our publications and to build churches as we would wish, but that is not the same as persecution.

He blessed me and I departed.

It was only when he became Pope that I realized the full import of this conversation. The Cardinal Archbishop of Krakow was distancing himself from the Primate, Cardinal Stefan Wyszyński. For Wyszyński's constant theme was that the Polish church was a persecuted church of silence. Indeed, he once bitterly remarked at a press conference in Rome that 'They call us the church of silence, but in Rome I find the church of the deaf.' But the upshot of this memory is simply this: the melodramatic and apocalyptic picture of Communism as absolute evil and the Polish church as utterly oppressed propounded by Nagy in 1991 was not endorsed by Karol Wojtyla in 1972.

The Czechs, who did suffer more oppression than the Poles because of the failure of the Prague spring of 1968, have a different view from Nagy in any case. At a fringe meeting during the Euro-Synod organised by Pax Christi, Fr Tomas Halik, now secretary of the Czech Bishops Conference, made a remarkable statement:

I dreaded coming here because I was afraid that our churches of Central and East Europe would be patronized and patted on the head, over-whelmed with anxious pity, killed with kindness. Fortunately this did not happen.

But something worse happened. We came here and were treated as heroes and models for the universal church. It was mostly right-wing movements that did this, which have been a powerful influence here.

Some were heroes, of course; but there were cowards too who ran away. You should neither idealize us nor underestimate yourselves. So for example we are a poor church – but that does not mean that we have the true spirit of poverty. Once we get our hands on wealth, we may be just be as greedy and grasping as anyone in the West.

The attempt by the right wing to build up the suffering church as the one true church is dangerous. The left wing caricatures us in another way as the place where married men and even women were clandestinely ordained to the priestly ministry.

But the main distortion comes from the right. The fact that we have no theology, for example, does not mean that we have the true faith or are paragons of orthodoxy: it just means that we have no theology. But we cannot do without theology – reflection on faith.[7]

That seems to me considerably more true, more helpful and more hopeful for European theology than Nagy's apocalyptic rhetoric.

Moreover, there was another witness at the Lublin conference who cannot be accused of 'underestimating the power of evil'. Lothar Ullrich is professor in Erfurt in the former DDR. He turned his inability to travel to the West to good account, gaining a good knowledge of the theological scene in Poland, Hungary and Czechoslovakia.

His account brings out very clearly the subordination of theology to the episcopate. The Rector of the Catholic University of Lublin, Stanislaw Wielgus, who issued the invitations, is also *'praeses Commissionis Episcopatus Polonia pro Doctrina Catholica'*. Bishops presided over all the liturgies, and were given a privileged place in the debates. 'So the unity of University and episcopate was stressed quite clearly, as was also evident in the daily worship and during the sessions of the Congress, especially on the opening day and at the meeting with the Pope on the last day of the conference in Czestochowa.'[8]

Now one could call this a difference of theological style and defend it on grounds of pluralism were it not for two disquieting facts. First, there were 'Western' theologians present at this meeting, but they came exclusively from the International Institute of Philosophy in Lichtenstein. Professor Rocco Buttiglione, of Communion and Liberation, indeed, reported to the Congress on an 'international Symposium' under the direction of Professor Tadeusz Styczen, the presumed author of the encyclical on moral matters, *Splendor veritatis*. The symposium was sponsored by the 'John Paul II Institute' and, by some remarkable co-incidence, happened to take place immediately before the Lublin meeting, which meant the Lichtensteiner were on hand.

Buttiglione's report on conscience and moral norms included an attack on the positions taken by the Bonn moral theologian Franz Böckle. After various protests, the Buttiglione statement was declared to be 'not part of the Congress' and will not be included in its *Acta*.[9]

That was gratifying. But there remained the problem of the Congress 'Declaration'. This document, of unknown origin, was read out to the Congress, who thus heard about it for the first time, and approved it 'by acclamation'. Ullrich remained seated while all about applauded a text which said that the greatest danger for the future was 'a radical liberal ideology'.

Ullrich went to the microphone and said that this procedure was inadmissable. Nowhere in the world did congresses accept as their 'message' texts they had neither discussed nor amended. These were Communist methods. Stunned silence. A Polish colleague shook Ullrich's hand as he returned to his place and said, 'Well done, Lothar.'[10]

Ullrich ends his article by recalling that Western theologians are so often exhorted not to make 'our Western thought simply the criterion'. But what that really means, he concludes, is this: 'We must note that what we encounter there is a mixture of episcopal and professional theology, in other words, to use Thomas Aquinas's terms, there the *cathedra pastoralis* and the *cathedra magistralis* are not as separate as in our sphere of theology.'[11]

We come now to the centre of this discussion. European theology is plural, or it does not exist. Yet in Central and Eastern Europe, *magisterium* is singular. It is most commonly referred to as *the magisterium* as though there were only one form of *magisterium*, the episcopal or (in fact) papal *magisterium*. The distinct, characteristic theological *magisterium* is swallowed up and therefore disappears into the maw of the papal *magisterium*. I will maintain that this 'doctrine' (or *theologoumenon*) is characteristic of the pontificate of Pope John Paul II. It was not found in the pontificate of Paul VI. And this difference between the two popes of the late twentieth century explains why Hans Küng, though frequently criticized under Paul VI, had to wait until the pontificate of of John Paul II to be 'condemned'.

In September 1966 Pope Paul VI gave his most important speech about the relationship of theologians and the *magisterium*. The occasion was a Congress in the Domus Mariae to study, or rather to celebrate, the theology of Vatican II. Though Hans Küng was not invited, most of the great names were there – Karl Rahner ('The Multiple Presence of Christ in the Church'), Edward Schillebeeckx ('The Church as Sacrament'), Yves Congar ('Catholicity as the Foundation of the Church's Dialogue with the World'), and John Courtney Murray ('Religious Liberty and Ecumenism'). The theologians who had been under a cloud in the 1950s, and had then emerged as *periti* at the Council, now came to savour their Roman triumph.

That was one sign of the changing role of theologians in the church. Another was the presence of Karl Barth, now very aged, who tottered up the aisle to immense applause, sustained by his equally fragile wife. Invited to the Council by the Secretariat for Christian Unity as a 'personal Observer' (a new category), Barth responded with a slim volume *Ad limina Apostolorum*, in which he commented generously though not uncritically on the conciliar texts.[12] He said that if Hans Küng's interpretation of his doctrine of 'justification' was right, then the entire Reformation reposed upon a mistake. So Küng was 'present in his absence'.

How would Pope Paul react to the new role assigned to theologians? His

address on Saturday, 1 October 1966, was the most substantial treatment he
ever gave to the relationship between the *magisterium* and theologians. It fell
into two contrasting parts.

First he rehearsed familiar ground. The *magisterium* and theology are both
subject to the Word of God, to divine revelation. Pope Paul alluded, to, but did
not quote, the passage in the dogmatic constitution, *Dei verbum*, which says
that 'the *magisterium* is not above the Word of God, but serves it, teaching only
what is handed on'.[13] Indeed his reminder that Vatican I taught that the
magisterium was 'proximate and universal norm of the indefectible truth of
revelation'[14] could be considered a qualification, though not a retraction, of
Dei verbum. A reference to the 1950 encyclical *Humani generis*, which had
silenced many of the theologians he was addressing, seemed unnecessary.

But having reassured the right wing, Paul proceeded to make some more
constructive remarks. Theologians, he said, have a double responsibility,
towards the *magisterium* and towards the people of God. They are the
intermediaries between the faithful and the teaching authority of pope and
bishops. Their service to the *magisterium* and to the faithful is to articulate and
render 'reasonable' Catholic faith. They communicate upwards and downwards; the theologian is a go-between:

> Theologians are, as it were, mediators between the faith of the Church and
> the *magisterium*. They are attentive to the living faith of Christian com-
> munities, their truth, their accents, their problems, the initiatives that the
> Holy Spirit arouses in the People of God – *quid Spiritus dicat ecclesiis* (what
> the Spirit is saying to the Churches).[15]

This was novel. For pre-conciliar theology had spoken as though the *magisterium* (the *ecclesia docens*) plucked its teaching from mid-air, while the faithful
(the *ecclesia discens*) had only to receive it passively.

Instead of opposition between the *magisterium* and theologians which had
prevailed in the past, Paul proposed 'communion' in a common task:

> For it is theology that shapes the understanding and the minds of pastors ...
> and without theology the *magisterium* would lack the essential instruments
> on which to compose the symphony which should pervade the whole
> community so that it learns to live and think according to the mind of Jesus
> Christ.[16]

No modern pope had spoken in this way before. It remained to find a way of
giving practical, administrative expression to this healthy way of stating the
relationship between theologians and the *magisterium*.

Paul's answer came on 29 April 1969, during a consistory in which he
created the greatest number of cardinals ever made on a single day, thirty-five,
who included Jean Daniélou and Michele Pellegrino. He announced that,
according to the *votum* or desire of the 1967 Synod, he was setting up an

International Theological Commission (ITC) of thirty members. They would come from various parts of the world, and continue the healthy experience of the Council. On the crucial question – their relationship with the Congregation for the Doctrine of the Faith (CDF) – Paul restricted himself to the remark that the new body would take its place 'alongside' those theologians whom the CDF already used as consultors, who were to be thanked for their admirable work (*illis Theologiae cultoribus, quorum consilium Congregatio pro Doctrinae Fidei utitur ... haec nova se adiunget Commissio*).[17] The only reason, he explained, why there had been so much delay in setting up the ITC, was the need to consult with so many people.

That was true. But it was not the whole truth. The CDF under Ottaviani would never have accepted the ITC because its very existence cast doubt on its own theological competence. The 'reformed' CDF, now in the charge of the Croatian Franjo Seper, accepted the new body because the Holy Father wanted it. It then proceeded to try to neutralize it. But this was not immediately apparent. Anyway the appointment of the Louvain scholar and 'renaissance man', Mgr Charles Moeller, as Secretary of the CDF, was a good sign.

The history of the ITC remains to be written. Did anyone argue for the inclusion of Hans Küng? Any list of the thirty top theologians of the Catholic church at that date would have to have included him. The chosen thirty included Henri de Lubac, Yves Congar, Joseph Ratzinger, Karl Rahner, Bernard Lonergan, who had been silenced in the 1950s, as well as younger theologians like Joseph Ratzinger who had contributed to the Council. It was a fair-minded list, representative theologically and geographically (though there were no Africans and no Latin Americans). But just as significant as the exclusion of Hans Küng was the inclusion of the 'other' Swiss theologian, Hans Urs von Balthasar.

Von Balthasar had hitherto played no role in international church life. He was not a *peritus* at Vatican II. To judge by his later criticisms of the Council, he would have chafed under its 'committee theology'. He believed that its theological weakness was that it neglected the 'hierarchy of problems', devoting itself to the shallows of 'second-order' questions summed up under the slogan *aggiornamento* instead of launching into the deep waters of Father, Son and Holy Spirit. He wanted to set the *absolute* claim of Christ against the reductionist Christ who was little more than 'the man for others'. Meantime, he pursued his own *oeuvre*.[18]

So when in 1969 he emerged from Basel and began to play a role in international church-political life, the ITC provided him not exactly with a platform but with a position of back-stairs influence that he exploited to the full. For example he was a member of the ITC's sub-commission which prepared a document on priestly ministry written in view of the 1971 Synod.[19]

Hans Küng is taken to task, specifically and by name, for a passage in *The Church* which distinguishes between two types of structure in the early church:

the distinctively Pauline type, which was 'charismatic', and the 'Palestinian', which stressed rather the presbyterate and the conferring of the power of order through the imposition of hands. The following passage is quoted:

> In Corinth there were neither *episkopoi* nor presbyters nor ordinations but, apart from the authority of the apostle, only a spontaneous manifestation of charisms. Despite this, according to the testimony of Paul himself, the Church at Corinth was a community provided with everything that was necessary, equipped with the preaching of the word, baptism, the celebration of the Lord's supper, and other ministries.[20]

Küng's position is said to derive from 'the Bultmannian school'. It is severely dealt with in the six theses or propositions which conclude the ITC treatment. Thesis five is directed against Küng:

> Though one must acknowledge a certain development in the structures of the early Church, one cannot maintain that some Churches – the Pauline ones – had a purely charismatic constitution, in contrast with the ministerial constitution of other Churches. For in the primitive Church there is no opposition but rather complementarity between the freedom of the Spirit in dispensing his gifts and the existence of a ministerial structure.[21]

Von Balthasar's six theses then appeared in almost identical form in Cardinal Joseph Hoeffner's *relatio* to the Synod on Priestly Ministry.

Whatever one thinks about priestly ministry, the point is that this is what made Küng a 'target'. The argument was not only about the New Testament doctrine of ministry: it was about the uses to which it might be put in 1971. Pat to the purpose came Küng's booklet, *Why Priests?*, which has a section on 'Charism and Institution', where we read:

> A basic and direct 'officialization' of charism is contrary to the New Testament ... Where the human qualities of leadership are lacking; where there is no ability for dialogue, communication, organization; where human knowledge, initiative, imagination and a will to lead are absent; and *where there is no trace of the liberating spirit of Christ, despite all institutional claims, there is no genuine ministry and no true leadership.*[22]

One can say – with hindsight – that Küng's increasingly vigorous critique of Pope John Paul II in the 1980s and 1990s derives from the application of this same charismatic criterion to church leadership.

Besides priestly ministry, the Synod of 1971 had another theme, justice in the world. Perhaps unwisely, the 'progressives' at the Synod devoted most of their attention to justice, which might be said to have taken over the 'Latin American' agenda. Some of its conclusions would have had a bearing on the treatment of theologians, and therefore of Hans Küng.

Thus: 'While the Church is bound to give witness to justice, she recognizes that anyone who ventures to speak to people about justice must first be just in their eyes.... Within the Church rights must be preserved.'[23] However, the impact of this was somewhat blunted by its vagueness and the fact that the *Nova agendi ratio in doctrinarum examine* had been officially approved on 15 January of that same year 1971. Since it represented 'progress' of some sort on what went before, it was hardly likely to be changed again so soon.

In any case, von Balthasar, acting through Cardinal Joseph Hoeffner as *relator* of Cologne, displayed no interest in the justice theme. This group concentrated on the priestly ministry where their main aim, successfully achieved, was to change the title. One advocate of this change was Cardinal Karol Wojtyla, who declared that what he wished to say was contained in the 'ten theses that Cardinal Höffner has so brilliantly expounded in his *relatio*'.[24] To start from the nature of *ministry* itself was to suggest that there were all sorts of ministries in the church of which the *priestly* ministry was only one example; alongside it were lay ministries, diaconal ministries, catechetical ministries and so on (later systematized in *Ministeria quaedam*). This fitted the formula, 'one mission, many ministries'.

For Karol Wojtyla this approach dissolved the uniqueness of the priestly ministry into the general priesthood of the laity. The uniqueness could be brought out, and the difference of essence and not merely degree restored to it, by substituting the term 'ministerial priesthood'. With his speeches at the 1971 Synod, Karol Wojtyla for the first time began to play a role on the international stage of the church, became an elected member of the Synod Council and *relator* for the Synod of 1975 on evangelization. That was his launch-pad for the papacy. But that is not our concern here.

Also in 1971 Cardinal Karol Wojtyla addressed the Polish Theological Association on 'Theology and Theologians in the Post-conciliar Church'.[25] The entire lecture is taken up with the question of the relationship of theologians and the *magisterium*. This was hardly a very live problem in the Poland of the 1970s, yet with Wojtyla it was already an obsession. The Council, he explained, had been the model of fruitful collaboration between theologians and bishops. But that phase was over. And since then the relationship had soured. The proper task of theologians was to 'guard, defend and teach the sacred deposit of revelation' in close association with the bishops and in strict subordination to them. The function of theologians is purely 'consultative' – Vatican-speak for 'they may not decide anything'. He quoted with approval a remark of Cardinal Franco Šeper, Prefect of the CDF, warning against 'making the Word of God an instrument for forcing one's own opinions'.

Theologians should not be allowed to usurp the teaching function in the church. It belonged uniquely to the pope and the bishops. There would have been no need to say all this unless certain theologians – unnamed – were believed to be sowing doubt in the minds of the faithful on such fundamental doctrines as christology, the Trinity, the real presence of Christ in the eucharist and the indissolubility of marriage. It may be possible to question some of the traditional formulations of faith, but never at the expense of the substance of revealed doctrine. He maintained that post-conciliar theologians had not respected this principle. They had succumbed to pressures from outside the church which had led them into 'false irenicism', 'humanism' and even 'secularism'. Happily, he concluded, Poland was on the whole free from such disastrous tendencies.

'Certain circles, especially the West,' he said, regard Polish theology as 'conservative'. Well, was it? He distinguished between a mere clinging to the past (Marcel Lefebvre?) and 'an honest relationship to the deposit of faith and respect for the *magisterium*'. He regretted that because of linguistic isolation, Poland imported more theology than it exported. He thought that another imbalance that should be corrected.

There had been a proposal for a Polish-language edition of *Concilium*, but this was rejected on the grounds that Polish theologians were all linguists capable of reading it in the already available languages. That bluff was called, however, in 1972 when *Communio* appeared and had a Polish edition from the outset. It was founded by Hans Urs von Balthasar, Henri de Lubac and Joseph Ratzinger, and Cardinal Wojtyla was an enthusiastic supporter from the outset. On its twentieth anniversary in 1992 he praised it extravagantly. Cardinal Stefan Wyszyński used to say that 'We need a Polish theology for Poland, written from the standpoint of the East, for a community living in the East.' What he really meant, commented a Polish theologian, was that 'progressive' theology (for which read *Concilium*) had emptied the churches of Holland and France and was not now going to be allowed to do the same in Poland. Andrzej Zuberbier accurately described the Polish theological scene in 1974:

> Polish theology flows quietly by, some might say monotonously by. There are no problems, no conflicts of views, no noisy proclamations. If a discussion takes place at all, it happens within the narrow circle of those involved. Theology does not have the function which it has in the West, where it is critical of the whole activity of the church.[26]

On the surface, at least, Polish theology has not changed since then, as the 1991 Lublin conference bears witness.

All these events from 1971 onwards emphasized the role of the *magisterium* and diminished the role of theologians in its formation. Only the first part of the dialectic sketched by Pope Paul in his 1966 address was retained. Thus oppositions were sharpened. What was an avoidable rift grew into an un-bridgeable gulf.

While Karol Wojtyla was 'reinforcing' the *magisterium*, von Balthasar's tone was increasingly polemical, reaching its culmination in his 1974 book on the *Anti-Römisches Affekt*. Criticism of 'the structures of the Church' is dismissed as 'incurably romantic', being based on Renan's simplified rosy 'gospel' and a Marxist critique of society which 'hopes to establish that evangelical paradise by "changing the structures" (a new mythical-magical spell)'.[27] None of this, of course, applied specifically or exclusively to H. Küng. But by now another factor entered the situation: publicity. The Twelve Theses of the International Theological Commission of 1976, 'On the Relationship between the Ecclesiastical *Magisterium* and Theology', allude to this problem, without offering any solution.[28]

Thus the battle-lines of the future were drawn up in the 1970s. Not only did Karol Wojtyla not change on becoming pope – that is self-evident: but he was able to make up for lost time, and repair the weaknesses, as he saw them, of Paul VI. He is nothing if not consistent. His entire pontificate has developed the attitudes displayed in the 1971 lecture. The 1991 instruction *On the Ecclesial Vocation of the Theologian* works it out in detail, treating theologians with suspicion, expecting them to be infected with 'the critical spirit' and charging them with setting up a 'parallel *magisterium*'.

In December 1979 the instruction withdrawing H. Küng's licence to teach as a Catholic theologian said he had departed from the teaching of the *magisterium* on infallibility and, more grievously, displayed 'a contempt for the *magisterium* of the Church' on other questions, '*exempli gratia* those teachings which pertain to the consubstantiality with the Father, and to the Blessed Virgin Mary'. This was a vague, barrel-scraping charge, with no attempt to produce evidence. The comment of Hans Urs von Balthasar confirmed what everyone knew: Küng had long been in his sights:

> John Paul II is safeguarding nothing less than the fundamental substance of Catholic faith. No one can deny that this was urgent after years of dogmatic, moral and liturgical permissiveness ... Perhaps it is inevitable that the Pope should give the impression of Hercules cleaning out the Augean stables.[29]

This is a slur on the memory of Paul VI. And that a theologian should compare the work of his fellow theologians to the contents of the Augean stables marks a new low in theological controversy. Little has changed since 1980, Küng's Swiss resolution being equal to Polish determination: the conflict is in the end about how the relationship of theologians and the *magisterium* is to be conceived.

It is not a new conflict, and may be a necessary tension. John Henry Newman gave much thought to this question. In the final chapter of his *Apologia Pro Vita Sua*, published in 1865, he regarded it as self-evident that theological development should come from outside Rome, while Rome had an essentially 'conservative' function:

It is individuals, and not the Holy See, that have taken the initiative, and given the lead to the Catholic mind, in theological enquiry. Indeed, it is one of the reproaches urged against the Roman Church that it has originated nothing, and has only served as a sort of *remora* or break in the development of doctrine.[30]

In the Middle Ages originality and diversity came from the different schools associated with the universities, with Rome exercising the function of judge or umpire.

In the nineteenth century – Newman thought – the catholicity of the church would be expressed by not allowing any one European nation to prevail theologically:

It is a great idea to introduce Latin civilization into America, and to improve the Catholics there by the energy of French devotedness; but I trust that all races will have a place in the Church, and assuredly I think that the loss of the English, not to say the German, element in its composition has been a most serious misfortune.[31]

No doubt Newman was thinking of the French missionary societies which made an enormous contribution the the expansion of the church in the nineteenth century.

But implicit in his remarks is some view of national character in Europe as an enrichment: ultimately traceable back to Herder, this theme contributed greatly to the nationalism which marked the nineteenth century, notably among the nations which made up the Austro-Hungarian Empire. In Poland romanticism combined with messianism to produce a particularly vivid sense of national identity and mission.

But none of these European type-casting theories pays attention to Switzerland. One author, indeed, while strongly wishing to assert the existence of an *Austrian* national consciousness as distinct from a pan-German one, dismisses Switzerland in a single sentence: 'Thus Switzerland has almost certainly cut herself off from the main currents of intellectual and artistic life of Europe by the rigid restrictions which she has imposed upon the employment of aliens within her borders.'[32]

Even if that be true – and it seems to me very sweeping – Hans Küng, as a Swiss who has for the most part worked outside Switzerland, cannot be accused of any form of intellectual isolationism. Perhaps the Swiss contribution to the theological symphony of Europe is to speak out boldly, with that courage or *parrhesia* of which Acts speaks.

Exactly the same spirit animated the 'dissidents' of Central and Eastern Europe throughout the long years of travail. The British writer, Timothy Garton Ash, in answer to the question 'How could the dissidents of Eastern

Europe hope against hope, where did they find the courage?' quotes these lines from Schiller's *Wilhelm Tell*:

No, the tyrant's power has a limit,
when the oppressed can nowhere find justice
and the burden becomes intolerable.
Then he reaches up to heaven with confident boldness
and draws down from there his eternal rights
which hang above as everlasting and indestructible
as the stars themselves.[33]

Notes

1. Walter Lesch, 'Katholische Theologie in Europa', *Orientierung* 56.9, 15 May 1992, 101.
2. Both quotations come from Zbigniew Nosowski, 'Theology after the Gulag', *The Tablet*, 30 May 1992, 670.
3. This charge is particularly inapplicable to H. Küng, who sets the 'Holocaust' in the context of other twentieth-century acts of genocide from 'the murder of the Armenians by the Turks to the Pol Pot massacres in Cambodia. In particular Stalin's mass murders, long ignored or relativized by many on the left, must not be passed over in silence' (*Judaism*, 225).
4. *Synodus Episcoporum, Bolletino* 18, p.3.
5. Ibid.
6. See T.S. Eliot's play *Murder in the Cathedral*. Karol Wojtyla was interested in the theatre and wrote theatre criticism in *Tygodnik Powszechny*. Some of his articles appear in Karol Wojtyla, *The Collected Plays and Writings on Theatre*, ed. Bodeslaw Taborski, Berkeley 1987, especially 371–95. Though he concentrates on the Polish classics, he has a very 'European' view of the theatre, discussing Shakespeare productions and adaptation of Dante for the stage.
7. This is a reconstruction based on my notes at the time. I can vouch for its authenticity, though I do understand that Tomas Halik was not very happy that I should have published part of it in *The Tablet*: 'A Sermon from the Synod', 21/28 December 1991, 1563.
8. Lothar Ullrich, 'Zur Theologie in Europa', *Europäische Theologie*, 1991.2, 78.
9. Ibid., 87f.
10. Ibid., 87.
11. Ibid., 89. Ullrich adds: 'It seems to me that Bohemian theology in particular could have an important bridge function here. Prague is in the middle of Europe!' The quotation I gave above from Tomas Halik would confirm this judgment. Mikhail Gorbachev chose to make his first speech on 'Our Common European Home' in Prague on the same grounds: it is in the middle of Europe.
12. Karl Barth, *Ad Limina Apostolorum*, Zurich 1967. For Paul VI, who remembered

Barth's attack on the Roman Catholic church in Amsterdam at the foundation of the WCC in 1948, this was proof of a remarkable transformation.

13. *Dei verbum*, 10.

14. *Insegnamenti*, 1966, 451.

15. *Insegnamenti*, 1966, 452–3. I have translated *theologia* as theologians to make the remarks less abstract.

16. Ibid., 453.

17. *Insegnamenti*, 1969, 255.

18. Von Balthasar made these remarks in *Zwei Plädoyer* (1972), a book I have been unable to trace. It consists of two lectures – the other by Joseph Ratzinger, on the theme 'Why I am Still a Christian'.

19. *International Theological Commission: Texts and Documents* 1969–1985, ed. Michael Sharkey, San Francisco 1989.

20. H. Küng, *The Church*, 442.

21. Ibid., 87.

22. H. Küng, *Why Priests?*, 65 (my italics).

23. *The Christian Faith*, ed. J. Neuner SJ and J. Dupuis SJ, no. 2162.

24. *Karol Wojtyla e il sinodo dei Vescovi*, Vatican City 1980, 171.

25. *Teologia i theologowie w Kosiele Posborowym*, presented by Robert Modras in *Commonweal*, 14 September 1979, 493–5. See also Henryk Nowacki, 'La teologia nella Chiesa postconciliare', in *Studi in honorem Caroli Wojtyla*, Vol. 56, 1979, 239–60.

26. 'What Polish Theology is Like', *Wiez*, December 1974.

27. H. Urs von Balthasar, *The Office of Peter and the Structure of the Church*, San Francisco 1986, 35.

28. 'Today, in case of conflict, "publicity" often intervenes between Magisterium and theologians. Thus pressure is applied, tactical moves are considered, etc., in all of which the "atmosphere" of dialogue is lost. The authenticity of the dialogue is thus reduced. Facts of this sort constitute a new situation, which certainly deserves further consideration', *International Theological Commission* (n.19), 143. Karl Lehmann was the author of this thesis.

29. Quoted in P. Hebblethwaite, *The New Inquisition? Schillebeeckx and Küng*, London 1980, 99.

30. John Henry Newman, *Apologia pro Vita Sua*, London 1900, 265.

31. Ibid., 269.

32. Barry Smith, 'The Production of Ideas; Notes on Austrian Intellectual History from Bolzano to Wittgenstein', in *Structure and Gestalt. Philosophy and Literature in Austro-Hungary and Her Successor States*, ed. Barry Smith, Amsterdam 1981, 227.

33. *Wilhelm Tell*, Act Two, Scene Two, lines 1275–81.

II   Catholicity

David Tracy

Truthfulness in Catholic Theology

1. Introduction: the range of truthfulness

Among Hans Küng's many contributions to Catholic theology, his insistence
on truthfulness at all times and for all issues demands further methodological
attention.[1] Küng's directness of speech and style, the democratic ethos and
empirical sensibility in his thought and argument, have always appealed
strongly to his many admirers in North America. Moreover, Küng's belief that
all serious Christian theology should be ecumenical, free, and critical correctly assures his Swiss evangelical Catholicism a ready audience throughout
the world.[2]

Küng's catholicity of spirit and achievement is clear. His present cross-
cultural and inter-religious interests have united with his earlier inner-
Christian ecumenism to produce a unique form of evangelical Catholic
theology which persuades by its intellectual clarity and its ethical honesty. His
theology is catholic in the best senses of the word: inclusive of all; respectful of
the whole tradition in all its plurality; grounded in genuine community; open
to the use of philosophy and all expressions of reason; sacramental in religious
sensibility and analogical in theological language and vision. Küng's theology
is just as clearly evangelical: centred on Jesus Christ as Word of God;
prophetic and thereby also ethical and political in spirit; grounded in the whole
tradition but just as insistent that the tradition always be judged by the gospel
of Jesus Christ. Paul Tillich (in many ways Küng's real predecessor in
theology despite the more direct influence of Karl Barth) argued that all
serious Christian theology should include what Tillich named Catholic
substance and Protestant principle. Despite the gains of the inner-Christian
ecumenical movement (to which Küng has contributed so importantly), there
are still too few contemporary Christian theologians today (whether Protestant, Catholic, or Orthodox) who are both genuinely evangelical and deeply
catholic. Hans Küng is one of the few great exceptions. His theology is both
catholic and evangelical. As an evangelical Catholic theologian, he shows a
way forward for all serious Christian theology today.

Küng's intrinsic interest in and generosity towards other cultures as
different and other and thereby enriching has significantly expanded his
original fine Swiss sense of the importance of cross-cultural experiences to a
genuinely global perspective. Moreover, Küng's evangelical Catholic theology

also has opened to the demands and promise of theological inter-religious dialogue. Küng's works in this latter area include not only the erudite studies of other religious traditions (like his recent study of Judaism) but also his careful, probing analyses of the challenge of the other great religious traditions for his own Christian (more exactly evangelical Catholic) theology.[3] Perhaps only a Christian theology which was, from the very beginning, religiously ecumenical and, as Swiss,[4] empirically cross-cultural could become the kind of genuinely global Christian theology at present so badly needed.

All of these unusual accomplishments are clear and solid gains for all Catholic and Christian ecumenical theology. And yet pervading all these achievements with firmness, clarity, and consistency is perhaps Hans Küng's greatest contribution to all Catholic theology: his relentless insistence on truthfulness as the virtue most needed in Catholic theology. Küng's acknowledged love of the Catholic tradition is clear. But that love never allows him (as it still does too many Catholic theologians) to ignore consciously or unconsciously the profound and non-reducible pluralism of the tradition and the equally profound ambiguities in the tradition.[5] Küng insists that all Catholic theologians must face that pluralism without yielding to the peculiarly Catholic temptation of finding and inventing sanguine harmonizations. He also insists that all Catholic theologians face the deep ambiguities of the tradition with the courage always necessary to be truthful, especially about those persons and realities one deeply loves and fundamentally trusts.[6]

As Küng's important works have clarified, only a truthful Catholic theology can aid our Catholic community: truthful about our former and present errors; truthful about the importance of historical context for understanding both scripture and doctrine; truthful about the systemic distortions (clericalism, triumphalism, classism, racism, imperialism and sexism, etc.) of our often deeply damaged tradition; truthful about the difficulties that different paradigms of theology make for mutual understanding in the ambiguous, pluralistic and often conflictual history of theology.[7] Let it be said with the clarity and directness of Hans Küng's own style: no theologian, Catholic or Protestant, has practised or reflected upon the importance of truthfulness, that singularly necessary theological virtue, as well as Hans Küng. Every theologian is in Küng's debt for this exceptional achievement. In the remainder of this contribution, I should like to reflect further on this Küngian criterion of truthfulness in order to try to clarify its more exact character as a criterion for all theology. I shall also raise some critical questions on its possible future uses by Küng himself.

2. Criteria of Christian appropriateness: truthfulness and historical-critical methods

Like so many progressive Catholic theologians, Hans Küng has developed what can be named a revised correlational method for contemporary theology.[8] Indeed, Küng has developed, in the context of his erudite and brilliant works on the nature of paradigm-changes in the history of theology, a quite specific method. Küng's method 'correlates' what he calls two 'constants'. The first constant (the 'horizon') is 'our present-day world of experience with all its ambivalence, contingency and changeableness'. The second constant ('the basic norm') is 'the Jewish-Christian tradition which in the final analysis is based on the Christian message, the Gospel of Jesus Christ'.[9] It is surely not insignificant that, in Küng's formulation of a revisionary correlational method, he names the first experiential constant 'the horizon' and the second christocentric constant 'the basic norm'.[10] There are, moreover, several interesting possibilities and puzzles of meaning in Küng's careful use of language for naming the basic character of each constant: either as 'horizon' or as 'basic norm'.

For present purposes, however, I wish to analyse a narrower issue: In my judgment, in Küng's critical development of the kinds of analysis needed for interpreting and analysing each 'constant', it is a criterion of 'truthfulness' that seems to play the central role. Such, at least, is my hypothesis for interpreting Küng's proposal for a revisionary correlational method for Christian ecumenical theology. I shall now test that reading.

First the 'basic norm': the 'Jewish-Christian tradition which is the final analysis is based on the Christian message, the Gospel of Jesus Christ'. It is fascinating to note here the basic consistency in Küng's use, *mutatis mutandis*, of this norm: from his earliest works on justification and ecclesiology through his famous debates over a 'canon within the canon' with Ernst Käsemann and Hermann Diem through his exchanges with Karl Rahner and Hans Urs von Balthasar (among others), through his fullest development of criteria for this 'basic norm' in *On Being A Christian* and in his ground-breaking works on paradigm-changes in theology, to his recent development of analogous criteria of appropriateness or identity ('origin and/or authenticity') for interpreting the other great religious traditions.

Besides this basic consistency amidst different formulations of the norm over the years there have also been subtle shifts in Küng's various formulations. Basically, however, the same christocentric criterion holds – as does the very Catholic affirmation of the 'tradition' united to Küng's own insistence on the need for 'truthfulness' in clarifying how this criterion can best work in relationship to the tradition. What Hans Küng insists upon (in contrast to, for example, Hans Urs von Balthasar)[11] is the need to develop historical-critical criteria to locate, clarify and formulate the exact meanings of 'the Jewish-

Christian tradition which in the final analysis is based on the Christian message, the Gospel of Jesus Christ'. As far as I can see, Küng's insistence upon the importance of 'historical-critical exegesis' for a revised 'historical-critical' correlational theology is principally in order to correct the errors and distortions which are also clearly present in the tradition's interpretations of 'the Gospel of Jesus Christ'. In more strictly theological terms, Küng's turn to and use of historical-critical exegesis is warranted by the New Testament insistence that the scriptural apostolic texts witness to Jesus Christ and are to be judged by the Word of Jesus Christ (and not vice versa). To assure a properly theological interpretation in our period, therefore, demands that the theologian make use of that method developed in the modern period which is best able to assure, on modern scholarly and ethical ground, the truthfulness of historical interpretation: viz. historical-critical methods.

Like Van Harvey in his famous study of the clash between an 'ethics of belief' and an 'ethics of historical reason' for all serious modern Christian theology,[12] Hans Küng, from the very beginning of this theological work to the present, has insisted that theologians employ historical-critical exegesis (i.e. on scriptural exegesis, doctrinal exegesis and church history) in order to assure the scholarly accuracy and truthfulness of their historical claims. It is also interesting to observe that for Küng as for Harvey and, before both of them, Troeltsch, the demands of what Küng names the second constant of theology (the modern 'horizon') enters into the criterion of truthfulness for interpreting not only modernity but the 'basic norm' of theology itself. Clearly this move is made principally in order to clarify the historical truthfulness of any contemporary theological interpretation of 'the Jewish-Christian tradition' based on 'the Christian message, the Gospel of Jesus Christ', in modern scholarly and thereby ethical terms.

There are persuasive reasons for the use of this historical-critical criterion. First, there is the need, in disputed historical matters, for the use, not of traditional authorities (clearly a *petitio principii* in the dispute) but of historical-critical methods with their relatively neutral ability to assess strictly historical claims. Second, there are very good reasons (as Küng's many detailed studies of particular historical misuses of scripture, doctrine and church history demonstrate) for some extra-traditional criteria for assessing historical claims in dispute.

As his formulation of this constant of 'tradition' as a 'basic norm' shows, Küng is also clear that the 'central message' of the 'Gospel of Jesus Christ' is fundamentally grounded in personal faith in Jesus Christ as that faith is mediated in word and sacrament, and, therefore, by the tradition.[13] But that fundamental or *constitutive* grounding of the interpretation of this normative constant of theology also needs the kind of corrective now available through historical-critical exegesis. Otherwise, how could a Christian theologian sort out the good, the bad and the downright awful interpretations which the 'tradition' (from the New Testament to the present) has handed down as interpretations? If my interpretation of Küng's complex position is correct, then I hope he may also accept the following friendly correction of some of his formulations:[14] viz. the results of historical-critical exegesis (e.g. on the 'historical Jesus') can and should prove corrective to all interpretations of the tradition; but historical-critical exegesis cannot be *constitutive* theologically for the strictly theological interpretations of 'the Jewish-Christian tradition and the central message of the Gospel of Jesus Christ'.

Historical-critical methods (like such other methods as ideology-critique, womanist and feminist theology and genealogical methods)[15] are corrective to, but hermeneutically not constitutive of, all properly theological interpretations of scripture. I have defended this claim elsewhere on general hermeneutical grounds and on Christian theological grounds.[16] Here I simply cite it for its theological import: viz. *yes* to Küng's insistence on the importance of historical-critical method for truthfulness (the role of all the great modern correctives); *no* if this method (or any other) is allowed to constitute the truth of the central Christian theological claims for Jesus Christ. The latter, as Küng's longer formulation of the second constant (the 'basic norm') suggests, is constituted by the gift of faith in Jesus Christ as mediated through word and sacrament (and thereby the tradition). Why, otherwise, would one employ the complex Küngian formulation, 'the Jewish-Christian tradition which in the final analysis is based on the Christian message, the Gospel of Jesus Christ'? At the same time, the Catholic tradition, like all traditions, is both pluralistic and ambiguous and needs the help of any corrective available. Moreover, the Catholic tradition theologically, on its own prophetic and, therefore, self-correcting grounds must be open to all the correctives available (especially, but not solely, from historical-critical methods in the modern period).

For myself, theologically the Catholic tradition is the principal mediation of the constitutive personal and communal faith of the contemporary Christian faith in Jesus Christ. The primary Christian confession, after all, is 'We believe *in* Jesus Christ *with* the apostles'.[17] Hans Küng's important reformulations of how this Christian confession can function truthfully for a historically conscious age, viz. by becoming the 'basic norm' corrected by historical-critical exegesis, is one of the great contributions to a truthful Catholic theology in our day. If Küng could accept my reformulation of some of his earlier formulations, I believe that his position would be strengthened in terms of both general hermeneutical principles and of the specific Christian theological principles implicit in his own 'basic norm' for theology. Moreover, Küng's suggestive work elsewhere on the subtle relationships of religion and literature as well as religion and music surely could be complemented by further work on the literary genres of the New Testament as hermeneutically productive of the meaning and truth disclosed by those grounding texts.[18] Otherwise it is puzzling, I think, to find so sensitive a literally-critical

interpreter of contemporary literature so silent on the hermeneutically productive character of the narratives, symbols and doctrines and other genres of
the tradition and styles of individual theology. But this latter move to literary
hermeneutics of the Bible and tradition will occur only with the explicitness
and systematic thoroughness that we have all come to expect of the theology of
Hans Küng after he reformulates and perhaps rethinks his position on the
important but limited, i.e. corrective, role of historical-critical methods in his
general theological hermeneutics and his reformulations on 'norm' and
'horizons' for a revised correlational method for all Christian ecumenical
theology.

3. *Truthfulness and truth in philosophy and theology*

To summarize my interpretation of Küng's criteria of assessment for the 'first
constant': the fundamental truth of the Christian belief in Jesus Christ is
theologically grounded in the gift/grace of the faith of an individual Christian
and/or the Christian community *in* Jesus as the Christ. Since that Christian
faith in Jesus Christ is also a faith *with* the apostles, it follows that the
fundamental mediation of any personal Christian faith in Jesus Christ is
through word and sacrament and, therefore, through tradition and church
(i.e., *with* the apostolic canonical writings and with the apostolic tradition).
However, there are other factors to consider: Christianity clearly involves
explicitly historical claims (viz. a belief in Jesus of Nazareth, not merely in a
Christ-symbol); second, there is also a pluralism even in the apostolic
canonical witnesses of the New Testament; third, there are obvious and
sometimes profound ambiguities in the tradition's interpretations of the
historical facts about Jesus and the church (e.g. the traditional claim of the
'institution' of the sacraments by Jesus or the claims of the presence of an
'infallible interpreter' as distinct from the whole church's indefectibility in
spite of errors). All three of these realities demand some further external
criterion for assessing truthfulness. For Hans Küng such a further, external
criterion is provided principally by historical-critical exegesis acting as a
fundamental corrective of all erroneous historical claims and helping to
expose all unconscious distortions. Thus one can spot and help to remove
any of those systemic, unconscious distortions (imperialism, racism, triumphalism, clericalism, sexism, antisemitism, classism, Eurocentrism, etc.) in
the tradition's interpretations of the Gospel of Jesus Christ. In sum, historical-
critical methods are one great modern expression of a more general
phenomenon: the need for some external criteria not to constitute the truth of
Christian belief in Jesus Christ, nor to replace the fundamental mediation of
the tradition, but to correct the tradition's interpretations whenever necessary.

As noted above, modern criteria of intelligibility and ethical honesty impel most modern theologians to use historical-critical exegesis of both scripture and tradition. At the same time, Hans Küng also develops these criteria in new and important ways, as is shown by the expanded range of his interests in more recent works: for example, his proposals in relationship to other religious traditions show how Christian problems in the interpretation of its own basic scriptural norm may illuminate the analogous debates in the other traditions (i.e. their analogue to a canon for establishing authenticity or self-identity).[19]

A further question occurs. What happens to Küng's other criteria for assessing religious claims to truth on relatively external grounds in his theological work? As demonstrated most clearly in his magisterial work, *Does God Exist?*, Hans Küng holds philosophically to a position of 'critical rationality' that opposes both rationalism and fidelism.[20] He argues (in a modern reformulation of a traditional Catholic theological distinction between 'reasonableness' and 'proof') that one cannot strictly 'prove' God's existence (or non-existence). However, the modern enquirer can show how belief in God is an entirely reasonable belief grounded in a reasonable trust in reality itself. This firm position of 'critical rationality' (which Küng further refines, but happily never rejects, in his later analyses of a post-modern paradigm) provides both criteria of truthfulness (viz. the honest admission of our inability either to prove or disprove the existence of God) and criteria of truth (viz. the epistemological principle of critical rationality linked to the existential-empirical principle of a fundamental trust in reality).

Moreover, Küng provides further methodological reflections on the question of truth when he turns to the question 'Is There One True Religion? An Essay in Establishing Ecumenical Criteria'.[21] This important programmatic essay, issued in the midst of Küng's amazing and ongoing study of the other great religious traditions in depth and in detail, is revelatory. I believe that his more recent work on interreligious dialogue and on traditions other than Christianity also shows how central the criterion of truthfulness has always been for Hans Küng.

The great promise of Hans Küng's developing position on inter-religious dialogue from the viewpoint of contemporary ecumenical Christian theology is clear. More than any theologian (including those who take a far more 'pluralistic' position than his),[22] Hans Küng consistently develops ethical criteria of humane-ness as relatively 'external' and relatively 'neutral' ways to assess the truth-claims of the great religions. Küng's basic argument is both subtle and persuasive. In so far as the religions promise, in varying ways, true humanity to their participants, they are thereby open, on their own terms, to criteria for assessing the truth of those claims to true humanity by assessing the truthfulness of the claims to achieve a humane, good life in terms of fundamental ethical criteria.[23]

The promise of Küng's position is in the subtlety of the argument, viz., in Küng's way of showing how, in the singular case of religion with its claim to provide its participants with true humanity, the truth of that claim must involve ethical-political truthfulness – i.e. on whether the religion does or does not provide the 'good life' for its participants. The puzzle is this: why, in this important essay on criteria for inter-religious dialogue, does Küng say so little else about the further criteria that may also be needed?

What, for example, is the role of the 'critical rationality' and the 'existential trust' which Küng had earlier developed for his analysis of the central referential claim to truth of the monotheistic religions, viz., the reality of God? What, as a second example, does Küng think of hermeneutical models of truth as primordially manifestation (Gadamer-Ricoeur) or disclosure-concealment (Heidegger)?[24] Are they not useful for interpreting religious claims to the manifestation-disclosure of Ultimate Reality? Surely it is puzzling to find silence on those further criteria for truth in an article devoted to the topic unless, perhaps, the author had somehow decided that the analysis of ethical-political truthfulness provides not merely necessary but sufficient criteria for assessing the truth-claims of the religions.

This American reader of Hans Küng's complex work on criteria for truth in theology cannot avoid the temptation to suggest that what may otherwise seem a relatively minor interpretation by Küng is actually very revelatory of both the promise and the puzzles of his position in truth cited above. I refer to Küng's interpretation of the criteria of assessment of American pragmatism, especially of William James.

'In this century it was above all the Americans Charles Sanders Peirce, William James, and John Dewey who proposed a pragmatic solution to the quest for truth. In looking at the truth of religion, pragmatism simply asks how a religion, on the whole, "works", what practical consequences it has, what its actual value is for the shaping of one's personal existence and life together in society – in history, here and now.

No one could deny that such a concept of the function and utility of religion contains much that is right. In religion don't theory and practice overflow into one another? Doesn't there have to be practical proof of what a religion 'is good for', in keeping with the words of Scripture, 'By their fruits you shall know them'?

The question is only, can truth be simply equated with usability? Can the truth of a religion be reduced to usefulness, helpfulness, and the satisfaction of needs? Can it be sacrificed in case of emergency to tactical necessity, or even surrendered to commercial or political exploitation? And might not a religion that is seldom practised still be true? Might not a programme that is for ever being violated nevertheless make sense? Might not a message that finds little or no faith still be a good one?

In any case we need to reflect here whether there is not a deeper understanding of pragmatism than its utilitarian variety reveals, a pragmatism that is not a mere reduction of religion to practical reality, but its reconnection to the practice of a truly good life. Still in any case the questions arise: By what criteria should such complex phenomena as the major religions be judged? Should we characterize the effects over millennia of Buddhism in Asia or Catholicism in Europe as good or bad? Don't all contemporary religions have their credit and debit sides? And doesn't such a way of looking at things continually seduce the observer into comparing the high ideals of one's own religion with the more lowly reality of the others; for example, comparing real Hinduism or real Islam with ideal Christianity?

Thus the question 'What is the true religion?' must be returned to those who asked it. Back in the very beginning of his classic treatment of the *Varieties of Religious Experience* (1902) James argued that a usable criterion for judging authentic religion was not only the 'ethical test' but – along with immediate certainty – the 'philosophically demonstrable reasonableness.' But what does 'philosophically demonstrable reasonableness' mean in this context? Evidently, for all one's orientation to praxis there is no getting around the question of truth.[25]

The main reason why this long quotation is fascinating to an American reader is that Küng seems to suggest that American pragmatism is a question of pure functional utility. This clearly is not true of Peirce, nor, to be fair, even of James, at least in James' more careful moments – especially those moments when James treated religion – as Küng himself acknowledges with some puzzlement! My point is not as chauvinist as it may first appear. For although I am convinced that here at least, Küng misreads American pragmatism's epistemological and ethical-political claims, my principal point is cross-cultural and not dependent on the debate over how to interpret pragmatism.[26]

The fact is, as William James saw clearly in *The Varieties of Religious Experience*, religion is the kind of phenomenon which demands both pragmatic and other than pragmatic criteria for assessment of meaning and truth.[27] To be sure, religion does demand ethical-political criteria of assessment on religion's own grounds. Compare, here, James' fascinating ethical-political analysis of those he names 'saints' with Küng's more subtle but analogous argument cited above on why religion as religion demands ethical-political criteria of assessment.

Religion, as James saw, also involves explicitly cognitive claims demanding further modes of assessment (for James this is especially clear on the cognitive claims of the 'mystics' and the mystical strands of all the religions, but is true of the strictly cognitive element in all religious types; not only the mystics).[28]

I have argued elsewhere that William James' threefold (not single!) set of criteria of assessment for truth in religion could be reformulated into contemporary philosophical and theological terms. In brief, three points must be noted: first, James's criterion of 'immediate luminousness' is translatable into contemporary hermeneutical criteria of truth as manifestation-disclosure. Second, James's criterion of 'reasonableness' is clearly translatable into either transcendental-metaphysical criteria or, alternatively, the criteria of 'critical rationality' and 'existential trust', producing the kind of 'philosophical reasonableness' which Küng's own earlier work argued for so persuasively. Third, James' ethical-political pragmatic criteria could be reformulated, as again by Hans Küng, into criteria of truthfulness, i.e. ethical humaneness, demanded by religion on religion's own ground.

My suggestion is, I hope, clear. Surely, Hans Küng could unite his present persuasive work on criteria of ethical humaneness (truthfulness) with his own earlier work on critical rationality and existential trust. Surely, he could, in principle, expand these analyses by reflecting further on his own implicitly hermeneutical understanding of truth as disclosure-concealment as entailed in the cognitive claims of the religions. Indeed, unless one believes (as Küng clearly does not) that finally truth is equivalent to truthfulness, then some more expanded set of criteria for assessing truth in theology and in inter-religious dialogue are needed. As far as I can see, there is nothing in Küng's amazing work to date that would disallow his acceptance of the suggestions for a development of his criteria noted above. But whether Hans Küng does accept my suggestions or not, one fact remains crystal clear: like every theologian who honours both truth and truthfulness, I will always be deeply grateful to the most truthful theologian of our too often dishonest century and our pluralistic, deeply ambiguous and beloved tradition – the incomparable and truthful Hans Küng.

Notes

1. In Küng's own work, see especially *Truthfulness, The Future of the Church*, and *Freedom Today*.
2. There is little doubt, for example, that in the English-speaking world, Catholic and Protestant, Küng is the best-known theologian not only to theologians but to a wide reading public.
3. Most recently, see his magisterial and daring study of *Judaism*.
4. From the North American perspective, the empirical and democratic Swiss cultural style of Küng's work has always been a major factor in his widespread influence.
5. This is best seen, of course, in Küng's remarkable and influential ecclesiological works, especially *Structures of the Church, The Church, Infallible?, Was ist Kirche?* and *What Must Remain in the Church*.
6. See, especially, the argument throughout *Truthfulness* for splendid illustrations of this Küngian dialectic of trust and honest critique.

7. For the transition from the more general studies of truthfulness in the church to the shifts in paradigms and the emergence of attention to such pervasive systemic distortions as sexism etc., see also the remarkable studies produced by the Institute for Ecumenical Research.

8. This seems to me implied in Küng's earlier work but explicit in such clear and systematic essays as those collected in *Theology for the Third Millennium*.

9. Ibid., 195–9.

10. Küng's care in calling the Christian message 'the Gospel of Jesus Christ' the 'norm' and 'experience' the 'horizon' is revelatory of his care to maintain the Christian theological character of the dialectic in his correlation. This is similar to Paul Tillich's famous hesitation to name 'experience' a 'source' of theology in his method of correlation.

11. A comparison of the methods especially in literature and in historical-critical method in these two Swiss Catholic theologians would prove fruitful for clarifying the two main contemporary Catholic theological options rendered substantive in the differences between the journal *Concilium*, where Hans Küng has proved a major voice, and *Communio*, where Hans Urs von Balthasar was so crucial. As always in theology, the methodological and substantive issues are mutually reinforcing.

12. Van A. Harvey, *The Historian and the Believer: The Morality of Historical Knowledge and Christian Belief*, New York 1966 and London 1967.

13. This is, of course, my own interpretation of the implications of Küng's careful distinction between the 'Jewish-Christian tradition', 'the Christian message' and the 'Gospel of Jesus Christ'. This fine insistence on the plurality within the tradition can be found in Küng's work as early as his famous exchange with Ernst Käsemann. See *Theology for the Third Millennium*, 64–84.

14. For one example, see the theological use of 'historical-Jesus' research in, for example, 'Theology on the Way is a New Paradigm', in *Theology for the Third Millennium*, 182–206, and the arguments on the theological role(s) of historical Jesus research in the magisterial *On Being a Christian*.

15. Clearly Küng is open to those other methods as well, as not only his collaborative work in his ecumenical institute at Tübingen shows but also his own work, as indicated in his essays in Hans Küng and David Tracy (ed.), *Paradigm Change in Theology*, Edinburgh 1989, 3–33, 212–19.

16. See, especially, David Tracy, *The Analogical Imagination: Christian Theology and the Culture of Pluralism*, New York and London 1981; and *A Short History of the Interpretation of the Bible*, with Robert M. Grant, Philadelphia and London 1984. I expressed fundamentally the same points in relationship to Küng's *On Being a Christian* in 'Particular Questions within General Consensus (reply to H. Küng and E. Schillebeeckx', *Journal of Ecumenical Studies* 17 (Winter 1980), 33–9 (also published in *Consensus in Theology? A Dialogue with Hans Küng and Edward Schillebeeckx*, ed. L. Swidler, Philadelphia 1980).

17. The importance of prepositions for Hans Küng's work in both christology (*in* Jesus Christ) and ecclesiology (*with* the apostles) is crucial. Indeed, it would be difficult to name another theologian who is so clear on what it means to confess *in* Jesus Christ ('the norm') *with* the apostles (the church and tradition) – *never* the reverse.

18. See especially his splendid studies in Walter Jens and Hans Küng, *Dichtung und Religion*.
19. See his 'Christian responses' to Islam, Hinduism and Buddhism in Hans Küng, Josef van Ess, Heinrich von Stietencron, Heinz Beckert, *Christianity and the World Religions*.
20. *Does God Exist?*, 115–26.
21. *Theology for the Third Millennium*, 227–56.
22. In the English-speaking world, the main proponents of the 'pluralistic' position are John Hick and Paul Knitter. I stand with Küng (and for the theological reasons he gives) in resisting the Hick-Knitter versions of a pluralistic option. For Hick, see *Problems of Religious Pluralism*, New York and London 1985; for Knitter, see *No Other Name? A Critical Survey of Christian Attitudes Toward the World Religions*, Maryknoll and London 1985.
23. See also Küng's recent and important development of his ethical argument here in *Global Responsibility*.
24. For a helpful philosophical study of the hermeneutical tradition on truth as manifestation, see James J. Di Censo, *Hermeneutics and the Disclosure of Truth: A Study in the Work of Heidegger, Gadamer, and Ricoeur*, Charlottesville, VA 1990. For the theological use, see my arguments in *The Analogical Imagination* (n.16) and *Plurality and Ambiguity*, San Francisco and London 1987, and, more explicitly in relationship to Catholic theology, in 'The Uneasy Alliance Reconceived: Catholic Theological Method, Modernity and Postmodernity', *Theological Studies* 50, 1989, 548–70.
25. *Theology for the Third Millennium*, 229–30.
26. For a helpful analysis of the implications of that debate in pragmatism, see Richard J. Bernstein, *Beyond Objectivism and Relativism*, Philadelphia 1983.
27. William James, *The Varieties of Religious Experience*, Cambridge, Mass. 1985, 11–30, 409–15.
28. Ibid., 301–61.

Kurt Koch

Catholicity and Ecumenicity: A Brief Plea for the Rehabilitation of a Theologian

Anyone who once again carefully studies from a distance of more than ten years[1] the long prehistory of the clashes between the *magisterium* of the Roman Catholic church and the theologian Hans Küng, which finally led to the withdrawal of the church's licence to teach on 15 December 1979 with the 'Statement by the Congregation of the Doctrine of Faith on some key points in the theological teaching of Hans Küng' could quickly come to the conclusion that the Roman withdrawal of its licence to teach was not so much grounded in theology as motivated by the strategy of the church's *magisterium* and by theological politics. This verdict is already reinforced by the simple observation – which unfortunately must remain historically hypothetical – that had the President of the German Conference of Bishops continued to be the great Cardinal Julius Döpfner, who died in 1976, Hans Küng's theological work would certainly never have been discredited by Rome. Similarly, one can speculate in the opposite direction for the future (and hope!) that were Cardinal Carlo M. Martini, Bishop of Milan and at present President of the Council of European Episcopal Conferences (CCEE), to become the successor of Pope John II (this dream for the church is also permissible), the official rehabilitation of Hans Küng by the church could be expected in the not too distant future.

On the basis of these speculations and hopes, does the Roman condemnation of Hans Küng consequently belong only in the history of the church's *magisterium* and thus to the human, indeed all-too-human side of the church, so that nothing remains to be done but to wait until promising changes have taken place in the personal politics of the world church? That would be to make things far too easy: behind both the wearisome controversies and the Roman decision lie elementary theological questions which need to be recalled and worked on. And as the Roman Congregation of Faith makes its condemnation of those doctrinal views 'which are of especial significance: the dogma of infallibility in the church and the task of interpreting authentically the one, holy faith of the word of God which is entrusted only to the living church *magisterium*, and finally those views which relate to the valid celebration of the eucharist' issue in the judgment that Küng cannot 'either be regarded as a Catholic theologian or teach as one', the first theological question to arise is that of the catholicity of Küng's theological thought, or more precisely what deserves to be given the predicate 'Catholic' in deed and truth.

1. Roman or evangelical Catholicity?

At the beginning of this century and right up to the middle of it, the word 'Catholic' was without doubt an honourable designation which both expressed delight in what was Catholic and could prompt enthusiasm for the Catholic Church. Not only could 'Hymns to the Church' be composed – with the spiritual vitality of Gertrud von Le Fort, who grew up a liberal Protestant and in the year 1925 was converted in Rome to the Catholic church, but it also expressed hope for the awakening of the church in human souls. Today, however, in wide circles the word 'Catholic' is no longer a token of honour even within the Roman Catholic church, but rather an indication of that weariness or even frustration with the church which is widespread in today's Roman Catholic church and is no longer articulated in the aggressively militant slogan of the 1960s, 'Jesus yes – Church no', but rather in the resigned and disappointed expression 'Jesus yes, Church no go'.[2]

A token of honour or a banner indicating a sense of having had enough of the church? There can be no doubt that neither of these two associations to be found in church praxis applies to Hans Küng, and that for his part he refuses to be taken over by either side. But in that case what does the word 'Catholic' imply for him – beyond the Scylla and Charybdis of optimism and pessimism about the church? In his latest remarks on this topic, in his explanation of the Apostles' Creed for our contemporaries, he writes: 'Only those are basically Catholic in attitude who are particularly concerned with the Catholic = whole, universal, world-wide church. To be specific, Catholics are those who are concerned with the continuity of faith and the community of faith in time (the two-thousand-year-old tradition), which has been maintained through all the breaks, and secondly with the universality of faith and the community of faith in space, which embraces all groups, nations, races and classes. The opposite of such catholicity would be "Protestant" particularism and radicalism, from which authentic evangelicalism and relatedness to the community are clearly distinct.'[3]

With this resolute insistence on the temporal and historical continuity and the local universality of the Catholic, Küng takes up what is not only the historically original but also the fundamental systematic meaning of 'Catholic' as it can already be found among the church fathers. For among them the Greek word 'Catholic', which is first found as a term used to describe the church with Ignatius of Antioch (died 117), denotes the qualitative universality of the Christian church, in the sense that on the basis of the finally valid saving will of God revealed in the Christ event, which is aimed at God's whole creation, it is in principle open to all human beings and therefore may not be limited to particular cultural circles or to individual races.

It follows automatically from that that Küng – with full justification – feels obliged to make a distinction between this Catholic church as confessed by Christian faith and the Roman Catholic confessional church which has grown up through history, and thus the plurality of different Christian churches which are there and can be experienced empirically, a plurality which has become a reality in history as the tragic result of numerous splits in the church and which goes back almost to the beginning of the church itself. For this fatal history of schisms in the church begins, as Küng has shown in his *magnum opus* on Judaism, with that division between Jews and Christians, or rather between synagogue and church, which the Catholic theologian Erich Przywara described as the 'primal rift' and from which he ventured to derive the subsequent progressive loss of totality in, not to say the complete failure of, the 'Catholica': 'The rift between Eastern church and Western church, the rift between Roman church and the pluriverse of the Reformation (the countless churches and sects) belong in the primal rift between Judaism (the non-Christian Jews) and Christianity (the "Gentiles" in the language of the letters of Paul).'[4]

In the baneful process of these numerous splits the word 'catholic', which originally articulated the Christian confession of the universal totality of the church, has increasingly become the specific property of individual confessional churches. That could raise the question whether in today's ecumenical age it would not be appropriate to dispense with the word 'catholic' altogether. Not a few Reformation churches have taken this course by deleting the word 'catholic' from their confessional vocabulary, even changing the Apostles' Creed radically so that it speaks of the universal rather than the catholic church. Probably without being aware of it or intending it, in this way they have made it even easier for the word 'catholic' to become the sole possession of a single confession, so that Roman Catholic Christians in particular no longer notice how extraordinarily paradoxical their own designation of themselves really is. If Reformed Christians also had the courage to confess the 'catholic church', it would inevitably dawn on every Roman Catholic Christian that 'Catholic' and 'Roman' are not simply synonymous, but that there is a tremendous tension between them. For as Cardinal Joseph Ratzinger once aptly observed earlier, in this self-designation a 'linguistic paradox' emerges which for its part unmistakeably manifests 'the scandal of the split within the Catholica itself' and spells out for Christian awareness the scandal of the split in the church.

To this degree the attribute 'Roman Catholic' is an absolutely honest self-designation for this confessional church. For it expresses the fact that this church, too, is no longer or not yet completely catholic. In this direction the Second Vatican Council's Decree on Ecumenism has self-critically conceded that in a state of division it is more difficult for the Roman Catholic church 'to express the fullness of Catholicity under every aspect in the reality of life'.[5] Here again it is Küng who has given the clearest expression to this intention of the Council: 'The *ecclesia catholica* of the Creed does not denote any confessional church, and despite its size even the Roman Catholic church becomes a particular confessional church by the addition "Roman", which has become customary only in recent times. "Catholic church" really means the whole, universal, comprehensive church. Like "Anglo Catholic", "Roman Catholic" is strictly speaking a contradiction in terms: particular-universal = wooden iron.'[6]

So it is no coincidence, but quite consistent, that Küng should not outline Catholicity from a Roman perspective or even identify the two, but that he should orientate the Roman on the Catholic and criticize this decisively in the light of the gospel in terms of a self-critical reference back to the gospel. In this thrust not only is Küng's theological thought to be described and evaluated as 'catholic', but in his own words it can be most adequately described as the paradigm of a 'critical ecumenical theology',[7] more specifically in four directions:

– First it seeks to be catholic, orientated on the universal and whole church, and at the same time evangelical, orientated on the gospel and directed by it.
– Secondly, it understands itself to be traditional because it is responsible for the great and splendid tradition of the Christian church, and at the same time 'contemporary', as it is prompted and moved by the questions of present-day people, the present-day church and the society of the moment.
– Thirdly, it proves to be 'christocentric', in that it concentrates on what is decisively and distinctively Christian, and at the same time ecumenical, in that it reaches out to the whole 'inhabited earth', i.e. to all Christian churches, all religions and regions of the world.
– Fourthly, it proves to be 'theoretical and scientific', by being concerned with the truth of Christian doctrine, and at the same time 'practical and pastoral' because it is inspired by human life and is concerned for renewal and reform.

2. The ecumene of the Christian churches

If we reflect on these four contours of the paradigm of Küng's theological thought, we will be fully justified in saying of it that it attempts to take the ecumenical emergency of the present moment of Christianity with radical seriousness. Indeed that must be our verdict. As the basic issue is that the ecumenical movement is concerned to regain the catholicity of the Christian church which is grounded in the Apostles' Creed, for Küng, 'ecumenical' proves to be the new name for 'catholic', and the important thing for him is to preserve this new name in those different forms in which the dialogical ecumenicity of the Christian church has now to fulfil itself.

Even if 'ecumene' is to be understood in its fundamental and original meaning as the whole inhabited earth, in the traditional sense this term is usually taken to refer only to that earth which is inhabited by Christians. This very limited understanding is documented most clearly in the classical and traditional conception of the ecumenical movement, according to which the ecumene presents itself in the form of the ecumene of Christian confessions and is understood as an attempt by the different Christian confessional churches to come together in a common faith and in the quest for a viable form of church unity.

At this first level of ecumenical dialogue Hans Küng has made definitive and pioneering contributions, as early as in his very first work, his theological dissertation on the doctrine of justification of the Swiss Reformed theologian Karl Barth from a Catholic perspective. With this book *Justification*, which appeared in 1957 and not only set many stones in the theological structure rolling but already at that point proved a stumbling-block for the *magisterium* and provoked the first entry in the Roman Congregation of Faith's 'heresy file' with the ominous protocol number 399/57/i, Küng produced the (over)due evidence that the Reformed doctrine of justification in the position of Karl Barth corresponds at all points with the doctrine of the Roman Catholic church – provided that that doctrine is rightly understood. In view of the consequences of this result one can understand why not only Karl Barth himself took Küng's book as a 'clear omen that the flood tide of those days when Catholic and Protestant theologians would talk only against one another polemically or with one another in a spirit of noncommittal pacifism, but preferably not at all – that flood tide is, if not entirely abated, at least definitely receding'.[8] But even the then dogmatic theologian Joseph Ratzinger praised Küng's work as a 'new starting point for an ongoing theological dialogue'.[9]

3. Ecumene of the religions

Since this first work, the development of a Christian ecumenical culture of questions and problems within the church has remained a decisive concern of Küng's, which is why even today he diagnoses the differences between 'Catholic' and 'Protestant' in 'different basic attitudes which have developed since the Reformation, though today their one-sidedness can be overcome and they can be integrated in a true ecumenicity.'[10] Nevertheless Küng's theological interest has increasingly shifted from the level of the ecumene of the Christian confessions to the level of the ecumene of the religions, in the

justified conviction that the special character of the Christian faith in the sense
of its universal truth can be expressed credibly by the church only when it
exposes itself to dialogue with other world religions, not only as *ecclesia docens*
but also and primarily as *ecclesia audiens*.

Be this as it may, it is to Küng's particular credit that he attempts to portray
Christian theology against the horizon of the world religions, more precisely
by resolutely taking up his previous ecumenical theology '*ad intra*', turned
inwards and concentrated on the Christian church, and now turning it '*ad
extra*', as it were outwards towards the world religions. Because it is Küng's
all too justified conviction that there cannot be and will not be world peace
without peace among the religions nor religious peace without dialogue
among the religions, he is concentrating his whole theological might on an
encounter of Christian faith with the great world religions, an encounter in
which the parties are ready for dialogue, understanding and mutually challenging.[11]

Behind Küng's concern for religious dialogue stands his legitimate basic
ecumenical conviction that the word 'ecumene' today can be used credibly
today only in a broad sense, which at the same time goes back to the original
meaning of the word. 'Thus "ecumene" today can less than ever be understood in a narrow, constricted, ecclesiocentric way; ecumene may not be
limited to the community of the Christian churches but must include the
community of the great religions, if ecumene – understood in accordance with
the original sense of the word – means the whole "inhabited earth".' So if
humanity today, 'despite all manifest hindrances and difficulties', at present
confronts the slow 'awakening of a global ecumenical consciousness' which is
proving to be one of the most important phenomena of the twentieth century,
even if it will come to full effect only in the twenty-first century, the response
to this development must be a serious ecumenical dialogue between the world
religions[12] of the kind which has been initiated by Küng in an exemplary way
and which has in fact been transformed.

Just as there can be no world peace without peace between the religions, so
too there can be no human survival without a common world ethic, of the kind
that Hans Küng once again posits clearly in the conviction 'that the one world
in which we live has a chance of survival only if there is no longer room in it for
different contradictory and even conflicting ethics. This one world needs one
basic ethic.'[13] As against this broad horizon the binding character of Christian
faith for human action can be credibly advocated only if this ethic accepts as
rivals other ethics with different orientations and foundations, the ecumene of
world views and ethics propagated by Küng proves to be urgent and indeed
overdue.

In the theme of the one humankind and its one basic ethic, the first stone
which Küng threw into the ecumenical waters has been able to make what has
so far been its widest wave. Of course this has also modified the centre of

Christian faith; on the other hand, it has never been betrayed. Rather, looking back on Küng's great work one may judge that in the all-embracing sense of a dialogical ecumenicity as briefly sketched out above his theology may be regarded as 'catholic' through and through.

4. A revision of papal judgments?

If the catholicity of Küng's theology is thus established, the question whether the condemnation of Hans Küng by the *magisterium* can and indeed must be revised becomes all the more urgent. Of course this is a fundamental theological question and cannot be discussed at depth in the present context. All that can be done is to give an example. This is provided by a papal revision of the position of the *magisterium* which has become famous, namely the theological controversy which was carried on in the fourteenth century over the question of the relationship between the ongoing life of the immortal human soul after death and its resurrection at the end of time. This controversy has gone down in history as the *visio* dispute; the Catholic dogmatic theologian from Paderborn, Dieter Hattrup, has described it as 'perhaps the most important dispute in the history of eschatology'.[14]

The occasion for this eschatological dispute was provided by the sermon of Pope John XXII at the Feast of All Saints in Avignon in the year 1331. At that time the pope did not just express the conviction, widespread since the early church, that those who were not fully justified had to go through a place of purification before they could achieve eternal bliss. He also taught that even the souls of the just and the martyrs would not immediately and directly after death attain to the vision of God, but only after the general resurrection of the dead and the judgment of the world. In the interim, while they would not suffer punishment, they would be kept, as the pope said with a biblical image, 'under the altar', i.e. under the protection and comfort of Christ's humanity. In taking up the doctrine of the waiting heaven, which had been put forward from the time of the church fathers to Bernard of Clairvaux, the pope stressed that human beings as individuals must wait for history to run its course as far as the judgment of God on all humankind before being able to attain personal consummation.

Because this doctrine of the waiting heaven clearly amounts to only a half-truth of the personal eschatology of Christian faith, this sermon by the pope[15] did not just provoke a long theological dispute about the point at which the vision of God would be experienced; there were also vigorous protests against the pope's doctrinal statements. Above all William of Ockham launched an energetic attack on the pope from Munich. And Philip VI, the king of France, commissioned a judgment from the Magister of the theological faculty of Paris, which moreover rejected the pope's new doctrine. Finally, the pope himself summoned a consistory and called on the cardinals, bishops and theologians to examine the question conscientiously and to make an unconditional statement, even if their judgment did not correspond with his. And he gave the theological commission under the direction of Cardinal Jacob K. Fournier the assurance that he would change his opinion if the counter-arguments should prove stronger than his own.

Cardinal Fournier used as his main support the theological examination of the doctrinal views of the pope on the equally traditional doctrine of a heaven open since the Ascension of Christ, and with the Second Council of Lyons (1274) stressed that the purified souls were taken up into heaven 'immediately'. When the commission had completed its work, the pope issued a revocation on his death-bed in which he acknowledged that the vision of God and punishment began immediately after the death of the righteous. And when after the death of Pope John XXII Cardinal Fournier was elected as his successor, under the name of Benedict XII he issued a revocation of his predecessor and in the constitution *Benedictus Deus* in 1336 taught the immediacy of the vision of God after human death.[16]

What does the recollection of this episode from the history of dogma mean for the problem of the revision of papal decisions? Contrary to those trends in present-day theology which in the context of the dispute over the doctrine of the infallibility of the First Vatican Council cite Pope John XXII as a fallible pope, it must first of all be emphasized that the pope at that time certainly did not want to describe his teaching as an official decision. Nevertheless, the fact remains that the pope was ready to revise his doctrinal proclamation on the basis of theological insights. Now if such a revision is possible in the case of theological questions of faith, how much more could an analogous revision seem necessary in the case of church disciplinary measures such as, indeed particularly in, the case of Hans Küng!

This question needs to be asked, especially since in his critical discussion of the First Vatican Council's doctrine of infallibility Hans Küng did not so much attack this doctrine as the extensive politics of the infallibility of the Roman *magisterium* which flow from it and are derived from it. However, this means, conversely, that it goes without saying that an official retraction of the verdict on Hans Küng would also necessarily imply a self-critical examination of the praxis of infallibility of the papal *magisterium*.

5. Open theological questions

But Hans Küng, too, would probably have to declare himself ready for some retractions, also and in particular in respect of his position in the dispute over infallibility. The decisive defect, or at least the one-sidedness, of his approach here lies not so much on the theological and doctrinal level as on the level of historical interpretation. For Küng tends to interpret the doctrinal statements of the First Vatican Council on the pope's primacy of jurisdiction and infallibility in a maximalist way and as it were to identify them with what was then the extreme ultramontanist position, in order to declare them untenable and finally to call for a 're-reception' of Vatican dogmas, and especially the dogma of papal infallibility.[17] At all events, that such a distinguished expert on the subject as the Bochum fundamental theologian and ecclesiologist Hermann J. Pottmeyer should come to the following conclusion provides food for thought: 'The proposal of H. Küng to reduce the infallibility of the *magisterium* of the pastors to the indefectibility of the church remains theologically superficial and found no support worth mentioning. The polemic which these authors introduced into the discussion hardened the fronts. They added to the obstacles which still stand in the way of a real re-reception of the two dogmas in the spirit of *communio* ecclesiology. The ultramontists tended, rather, to see this as confirmation of their position on this issue.'[18]

Closely connected with this over-interpretation of church history is a larger problem which relates to the hermeneutical approach of Hans Küng's theological thought. What is doubtless his great merit is that he orientates and constructs theology consistently on the New Testament testimony to the gospel and also, and in particular, attempts to express the Christian doctrine of the divine Sonship of Jesus Christ and the Triunity of God in such a way that it does not need to contradict either Jewish or Islamic monotheism. However, despite this extremely sharp eye for the biblically original and fundamental understanding of the reality of Jesus Christ and the Triune God on the one hand and the problems of the history of religions and the ecumene on the other, Küng has a certain blindness to the historical need that there was to translate the biblical message into the Hellenistic-ontological thought of the first centuries, a need which was also dictated by its content. Küng also tends to regard this process of the 'Hellenization of Christianity' as a dangerous shift in church history which distorts the biblical testimony.

This hermeneutic of suspicion runs though all Küng's publications, and of course has consequences above all for christology and the doctrine of the Trinity, the development and theological permeation of which he has neither rejected nor really appropriated personally – in contrast to those normative trends in present Catholic and Protestant theology which give the doctrine of the Trinity a dominant position at the centre of theological attention. From this it follows automatically that Küng cannot really assess the historical need for the translation of the biblical message into Greek Hellenistic thought generally and the development of the doctrine of the Trinity in particular.

That in this respect Küng in no way joins in the consensus of present-day theology is not only shown by the early interjection by the distinguished historian of dogma Alois Grillmeier,[19] but also documented by the contrary judgment of the Protestant theologian Wolfhart Pannenberg. The latter sees the combination of the Christian message with Hellenistic culture not only as 'the first example of an inculturation of the gospel' but also as something that 'remained basic to all subsequent procedures of this kind'.[20] Accordingly, he regards the development of the doctrine of the Trinity in Hellenistic thought as even providential. In his eyes it was required by intrinsic logic, or more precisely because Christian belief in the presence of God can be expressed in Jewish thought-forms only by extremely paradoxical phrases; and only Hellenistic thought – of course 'after relevant purification and transformation – could so express the reality of the God manifest in Jesus Christ that it could make the claim that only the trinitarian understanding of God describes the true reality of the one eternal God'.[21]

The revitalizing of this view of the history of theology proves indispensable for the present theological situation, not only for reasons of church history but also in the perspective of fundamental theology. If the Hellenization of Christianity were illegitimate at that time, and were open to the charge of being a falsification of Christian faith, which is the charge brought against it by the liberal Protestant theologian Adolf von Harnack, then the present-day modernization and renewal of Christian faith and theology in a postmodern paradigm, normatively initiated and developed by Hans Küng, would be equally unjustified.

6. Necessary rehabilitation

Although they have been sketched out only briefly, in my view these two indications of problems should make Hans Küng reflect self-critically once again and adopt a new position in his discussion with other theological approaches. Of course these are questions relating to theology, or more precisely to church history and hermeneutics, which do not touch on the Catholic substance of faith in Hans Küng's theological thought and therefore must – and can be – carried on among theologians themselves. Therefore they are also in no way capable of providing legitimation after the event for the condemnation of Hans Küng by the church's *magisterium*. Rather, they amount to pressure towards a revision of the church's disciplinary measures against him, so that the Catholic rehabilitation of the Christian Hans Küng and his theological work take place during his lifetime. What happened to Pierre Teilhard de Chardin, who was only reinstated after his death – albeit hesitantly and not without further posthumous accusations against his person – should not and must not happen to Hans Küng.

In heaven – Christians may rightly be bold enough to hope – Hans Küng will be rehabilitated anyway, along with that chuckling laugh which Karl Barth was convinced was the characteristic of the angels. It is also to be hoped, however, that even during his lifetime Hans Küng may again be granted official recognition by the church as a Catholic theologian, and – as a presupposition – again be rehabilitated by Rome. In his case it should be particularly easy for Rome to go back on its decision and as it were reverse the biblical promise of Jesus to Peter: 'Whatever you bind on earth will also be bound in heaven, and what you loose on earth will also be loosed in heaven' (Matt. 16.1), and with the rehabilitation of Küng anticipate on earth his heavenly justification. For anyone who really knows Hans Küng and has really studied his work cannot doubt, for all the disputatiousness which neither his tongue nor his pen avoid, the basic Catholic conviction by which with full justification he attempts to live on the basis of the gospel in the Roman Catholic church.

Notes

1. Here W. Jens (ed.), *Um nichts als die Wahrheit. Deutsche Bischofskonferenz contra Hans Küng. Eine Dokumentation*, Munich 1978, and N. Greinacher and H. Haag, *Der Fall Küng. Eine Dokumentation*, are still useful.
2. Cf. also W. Beinert, 'Angst und Kirche', *Stimmen der Zeit* 114, 1989, 219–35.
3. H. Küng, *Credo*, 136f.
4. E. Przywara, 'Römische Katholizität – All-Christliche Ökumenizität', in J.B. Metz et al. (ed.), *Gott im Welt. Festgabe für K. Rahner*, Vol. II, Freiburg im Breisgau 1964, 524–8: 526.
5. Vatican II, *Unitatis redintegratio*, no. 4.
6. Küng, *Credo*, 137.
7. H. Küng, 'Theologie auf dem Weg zu einem neuen Paradigma', in J.H. Bauer (ed.), *Entwürfe der Theologie*, Graz 1985, 181–207: 206.
8. K. Barth, 'A Letter to Hans Küng', in H. Küng, *Justification*, xli.
9. J. Ratzinger, review of Hans Küng, *Justification*, *Theologische Revue* 54, 1958, 30–5.
10. Küng, *Credo*, 137.
11. The first fruit of this truly ecumenical concern is tangible in his 1984 work *Christianity and the World Religions*, produced in collaboration with other scholars. This was later supplemented by *Christianity and Chinese Religion* (1988), in which he carries on an illuminating dialogue with Julia Ching, an expert in Chinese religion; he regards Chinese religion as the third religious river system.
12. H. Küng et al., *Christianity and the World Religions*, 440f.
13. H. Küng, *Global Responsibility*, 14.
14. D. Hattrup, *Eschatologie*, Paderborn 1992, 269.
15. For the wider background to his eschatological views cf. M. Dykmans, *Les sermons de Jean XXII sur las vision béatifique*, Rome 1973.
16. For his eschatological convictions cf. F. Wetter, *Die Lehre Benedikts XII. vom intensiven Wachstum der Gottesschau*, Rome 1958.
17. H. Küng, 'Zum Geleit. Der neue Stand der Unfehlbarkeitsdebatte', in A.B. Hasler, *Wie der Papst unfehlbar wurde. Macht und Ohnmacht eines Dogmas*, Munich 1979, XIII-XXXVII: XXXV.

18. H.J. Pottmyer, 'Ultramontanismus und Ekklesiologie', *Stimmen der Zeit* 177, 1992, 449–64: 451.
19. A. Grillmeier, 'Jesus von Nazareth – "Im Schatten des Gottessohnes"? Zum Gottes- und Christusbild', in H.U. von Balthasar et al., *Diskussion über Hans Küng's* Christ Sein, Mainz 1976, 60–82.
20. W. Pannenberg, 'Notwendigkeit und Grenze der Inkulturation', in G. Müller-Fahrenholz et al, *Christentum in Lateinamerika. 500 Jahre seit der Entdeckung Amerikas*, Regensburg 1992, 140–54: 149.
21. Ibid., 146.

Werner G. Jeanrond

The Rationality of Faith: On Theological Methodology*

Hans Küng is a unique phenomenon in twentieth-century theology: no other theologian has been published, translated and read so widely in this century; no other theologian has been the focus of such a major controversy; no other contemporary theologian has covered such a broad spectrum of theological themes. Virtually all important theological topics discussed in our time have been addressed by Küng at some stage in his career. His bibliography includes major works on God, Jesus Christ, the church, eternal life, theological method, the world religions, global responsibility, and the contribution of the arts to religion. Yet it was Küng's challenge of post-Vatican II ecclesiology and church management which brought him into lasting conflict with the authorities of his church. One effect of this controversy has been that Küng's contribution to modern theology has sometimes been perceived to be of a mainly ecclesiological nature and that his other achievements in theology have not been adequately appreciated. Moreover, the conflict between the Roman Catholic priest Küng and some of the members of the Roman Catholic episcopate has occasionally concealed Küng's important contribution to his own church before, during and after the Second Vatican Council.

This survey of Küng's theological development will therefore emphasize particularly those areas which are often treated too sparingly. However, it will not be possible to discuss all aspects of Küng's rich contribution to contemporary theology; instead I shall concentrate on his major works, and above all discuss the development of his theological methodology more closely.

Küng's theological development to date may be roughly divided into four periods:
1. his concentration on ecclesiological questions until 1970;
2. his treatment of major articles of Christian faith (God, Jesus Christ and eternal life) during the 1970s;
3. his reflection on theological method and the dialogue between Christianity and world religions and Christianity and culture since 1983;
4. his project *Global Responsibility* which is connected with all the previous questions, from 1990 on.

However, all of these periods are inspired by a strong commitment both to dialogue with all current religious, political and cultural forces in the world in general and to Christian ecumenism in particular. Küng's commitment to

Christian and then even global ecumenism must not be confused with a new kind of essentialism according to which all Christian traditions or even religious traditions are essentially the same. Rather, Küng wishes to bring Christians of all backgrounds and the different religious traditions of human-kind into a mutually critical conversation.

1. Beginnings in ecclesiology

Already in his first book, *Justification: The Doctrine of Karl Barth and a Catholic Reflection* (1957), Küng investigated the foundations for such an inner-Christian conversation. He examined the common ground of Protestant and Roman Catholic doctrine on this central aspect of Christian faith which has divided both traditions for centuries. But he remained critical of Barth's 'dangerous inclinations', such as his denigration of the ontic-creaturely aspect and his overemphasis of human sinfulness, and the resulting anti-Catholic polemics. Küng's study concluded that on the whole there exists a fundamental theological conformity between what Barth and the Roman Catholic church teach on justification. This insight shaped Küng's further questioning of how all Christian churches will have to change in order to promote the process of Christian unity and of what especially the Roman Catholic church ought to be doing in order to respond more adequately to the gospel in a new ecumenical age.

In the 1960s, the Vatican Council inspired all leading Roman Catholic theologians to reflect very thoroughly on the nature and structure of the Christian church. Thus, it need not surprise us that fifteen out of Küng's first twenty books deal with ecclesiological questions, among these publications most prominently *Structures of the Church* (1962), *The Church* (1967), and *Infallible?* (1970). *Structures of the Church* was written in response to Pope John XXIII's call for a renewed theological concentration on this topic with reference to the Council; *The Church* offered a systematic study of the nature of the Christian church on the basis of modern biblical exegetical knowledge; and *Infallible?* represented a first critical study of the Roman Catholic church in view of the increasing disenchantment among Catholics with the slow process of structural renewal in their church after the Council.

Perhaps Küng's approach to ecclesiology may be best characterized by his insistence on the need for a critical biblical foundation of all ecclesiology and the resulting insight into the essential difference between the church and the Kingdom of God. The church's mission is to serve the gospel of Jesus Christ, to respond to God's call in Jesus Christ, but not to produce God's reign.[1] Moreover, God's reign is proclaimed to sinners as good news. Thus, the church, itself a community of sinners, is called to preach the good news to the world, but not to rule the world. Like the Reformers in the sixteenth century,

Küng retrieved the biblical image of the priesthood of all believers. Christ's community no longer needs a mediation between the people of God and God, it no longer requires a priestly sacrifice of expiation. *All* Christians are called to proclaim God's word. Accordingly, Küng demands that any consideration of offices in the church must be spirited by this New Testament heritage.[2] This heritage rules out the establishment of a clergy–laity divide in the Christian movement. Therefore, Küng criticizes the formalism which has emerged in the post-biblical church, and he calls for a redefinition of ministry in the church as a service of love. This is not to rule out the special services of priests and bishops, rather it is to describe the proper theological basis of such a service.[3]

The question of authority in the church was to receive yet further prominence in Küng's theological work when Pope Paul VI issued his encyclical *Humanae vitae* in 1968 against all forms of artificial birth control. Together with a great many Christians within and beyond the Roman Catholic church, Küng protested against this encyclical. But he went further and criticized the entire Roman Church system which he saw 'still characterized by a spiritual absolutism, a formal and often inhuman juridicism and a traditionalism fatal to genuine renewal that are truly shocking to modern man'.[4] On the basis of his ecclesiological principles, Küng questioned the infallibility of both the pope and the Roman teaching office, pointed out past errors of both institutions, and described the peculiar context of the First Vatican Council (1869–70) which had formulated the doctrine of papal infallibility. Finally, Küng proposed a reappraisal of the traditional belief that the church as a whole is maintained in the truth in spite of the possibility of errors.[5] He also emphasized that there is no formal guarantee that even a council is infallible. 'Councils do not have authority over the truth of Christ. They can strive to attain it. It is for this that the Spirit of Christ is promised to the bishops and all participants, as it is also to every Christian.'[6]

As we shall see below, the controversy about Küng's ecclesiology continues to divide Roman Catholics, and although Küng's primary theological attention shifted now to the central theological questions of God and Jesus Christ, he never lowered his commitment to the renewal of the Roman Catholic church in particular, and the Christian church in general.

2. Major articles of Christian faith

Küng's turn to christology did not begin with his famous work *On Being a Christian* (1974) as is generally assumed; rather, this turn was prepared already in his less known work *The Incarnation of God* (1970, translated into English only in 1987). In this work Küng had already pursued the most crucial theological question, namely how God could be encountered in history and how God is related to the process of history. In this book Küng also offered a comprehensive introduction into Hegel's philosophy and theology. His main interest in Hegel derived, however, from this thinker's critique of the traditionally static concept of God. Using this critique, Küng wished to explore the foundations for a future christology.

Over against the classical concept of God influenced by Greek metaphysics, Küng – following Hegel – demands a new theological perspective. 'Hegel's philosophy begins by teaching us not to separate God from man and ends by teaching us not to confound them'.[7] Küng, however, does not follow Hegel's lead all the way. Rather, he reinterprets Hegel's speculative identity between the process of history and God as, in fact, not a totally closed system by pointing out that 'at the level of religion – not of philosophy – Hegel himself, for all his unmistakable emphasis on unity, stoutly maintained that there is an ultimate difference'.[8] On this basis of both identity and difference between God and the world, Küng sets out his prolegomena for a future christology. He calls for a christology 'from below' which is 'interested in the Jesus who meets us today, within the horizon of the world, humankind and God, as the challenge to faith which he personally embodies'.[9] This renewed concentration on historical Jesus research is, however, not seen by Küng as a means to present Jesus as he really was, rather it is understood as a critical tool which enables the theologian to scrutinize and verify the faith which has been handed down to us.[10]

Thus methodologically prepared, Küng constructed his christology in *On Being a Christian*. As the title of this book indicates already, Küng's primary concern in christology is not a theoretical one; rather he wishes to establish what it means to respond to Jesus Christ *today*. Therefore, he places his christology in the carefully analysed context of the contemporary challenges presented by both modern humanism and the world religions. In answering the question of what is special to Christianity in this context, Küng states that Christianity must not be equated with everything true, good, beautiful, and humane in this world. 'Christianity does not exist wherever inhumanity is opposed and humanity realized ... Christianity exists only where the meaning of Jesus Christ is activated in theory and practice.'[11]

In the main part of this work, Küng examines the dimensions of the Christian programme. He discusses Jesus' life and death in the context of religion and culture at the time, Jesus' proclamation of God's cause and Jesus' own identification with man's cause, the conflict which led to the death of Jesus, and the reactions to his life and death by the emerging Christian communities. The book concludes with reflections upon contemporary Christian praxis in the light of the christological dimensions presented earlier. We shall return to Küng's christology in the next section.

As indicated by Küng in *The Incarnation of God*, any adequate theological approach to God will need to examine the relationship between God and human history. Thus, it was only appropriate that Küng should treat of christology before presenting his thoughts on the concept of God in *Does God Exist?* (1978). The title of this book is somewhat misleading. Küng does not wish to follow the particular tradition of proving whether or not God actually exists. Küng's answer to that question is yes. Rather, in this book he examines the rationality of the Christian belief in God today.

The book takes the reader through the history of the contemporary understanding of God. It analyses the contribution to this understanding by the atheistic critique while it demonstrates at the same time that none of the leading atheists (Feuerbach, Marx, Freud, and Nietzsche) would have been able to disprove God's existence, as indeed none of the leading theists would ever be able to prove it. Instead Küng begins with the question of how the modern person relates to reality as such.

Since there is no one and absolute standpoint, our perceptions of the world can never be purely objective. Nor is any perception the exclusive product of a lonely subjectivity. Rather when we speak of 'reality', we always mean 'something that combines and embraces subject and object, consciousness and being, self and world'.[12] The decision which every human being faces, then, is a decision between two basic attitudes to reality: fundamental mistrust or fundamental trust. Moreover, this decision is a lifelong task and it concerns all aspects of our living, researching and activity in this world. Although Küng calls for a clear distinction between this 'fundamental trust' on the one hand, and 'faith in God' on the other,[13] he concludes 'that the fundamental trust in the identity, meaningfulness and value of reality, which is the presupposition of human science and autonomous ethics, is justified in the last resort only if reality itself – of which man is also a part – is not groundless, unsupported and aimless'.[14]

On the basis of these insights, Küng examines the traditional Christian approaches to God. He also notes the increasing interest in the question of God in our time. He forcefully rejects any attempt to divide reality into two spheres, a divine and a human. Rather he insists that God can be assumed 'only in a confidence rooted in reality itself'.[15] This in turn means: 'If someone affirms God, he knows why he can trust reality.'[16] Accordingly, there cannot be any outward rationality able to produce an assured security. 'There is not first a rational knowledge and then confident acknowledgment of God.' But there is an 'inward rationality, which can offer a fundamental certainty'.[17] Moreover, Küng stresses that belief in God must be considered 'a matter not only of human reason but of the whole concrete, living man, with mind and body, reason and instinct, in his quite particular historical situation, in his dependence on traditions, authorities, habits of thought, scales of values, with his interests and in his social involvement'.[18]

This need to consider the historical and social context of any belief in God brings Küng back to the specific Christian faith in God. After assessing the history of the Jewish and Christian traditions of believing in God, Küng concludes that the biblical faith in God 'is in itself coherent, is also rationally justifiable and has proved itself historically over many thousands of years'.[19] Finally, the God of the Bible has also a cosmic dimension, that is to say that the history of the entire universe is the area of this God's presence, not only the history of the individual believer. God operates 'in the world process: in, with and among beings and things. He is himself source, centre and goal of the world process.'[20] It is this God which Jesus of Nazareth proclaimed in his life, death, and resurrection. Here, Küng's theological and christological reflections merge again.

Although Küng had begun his christology and his examination of the rationality of faith in the Jewish-Christian God by analysing the horizon of the modern person who is searching for meaning, in 1982 he paid particular attention to this search for meaning in every individual life: his book *Eternal Life?* addressed the whole complex of questions related to the human hope for an eternal future. Küng interprets the various Christian eschatological symbols such as heaven, hell, eternity, and judgment, in the light of the Christian belief in the resurrection of Jesus of Nazareth. 'Jesus did not die into nothingness. In death and from death he dies into that incomprehensible and comprehensive absolutely final and absolutely first reality, was accepted by that reality, which we designate by the name of God.'[21] Thus, to believe in eternal life does not mean to hope to continue living for ever. But it does mean 'to rely on the fact that I shall one day be fully understood, freed from guilt and definitely accepted and can be myself without fear; that my impenetrable and ambivalent existence, like the profoundly discordant history of humanity as a whole, will one day become finally transparent and the question of the meaning of history one day finally answered'.[22]

This book concludes Küng's second period of theological work. In this period he attempted to address the major aspects of Christian faith and to correlate them critically with his interpretation of the contemporary cultural and intellectual horizon of theology.

3. Methodology and dialogue

The third period of Küng's theological work shows two distinct, though related moves: (i) Küng's reflection on theological method, and (ii) his studies of the relationship between Christianity and other world religions and of the relationship between religion and the arts. Both of these moves are in response to a changed awareness among many contemporary theologians: namely that the world with its plurality of religious and cultural traditions and movements, with its wealth of human insight and scientific knowledge, and with its ambiguous history, demands a new paradigm for theology.

Accordingly, in his book *Christianity and the World Religions* (1984), Küng calls for a global understanding of ecumenism. Ecumenism must no longer be limited to the inner-Christian conversation, but it ought to include the conversation between all great religions if ecumene is understood in its original sense as the whole inhabited earth.[23] For Christian theology that implies that the traditional Christian self-understanding marked by exclusivity and superiority must be overcome by an admission that none of us possesses the full truth, and that we are all on the way to the always greater truth. Such an understanding of truth demands, of course, that Christians broaden their knowledge and understanding of the other great religious traditions of humankind. Therefore Küng presents in this book introductions to Islam, Hinduism, and Buddhism in cooperation with leading historians of religion. Each of these introductions is followed by Küng's response from a Christian perspective. A dialogue with a Jewish scholar was already published in 1976;[24] and Küng's dialogue with the major Chinese religious traditions appeared in 1988.[25]

The search for a new paradigm of theology demands the close cooperation of scholars of different background and expertise. Thus, it is characteristic of this third period of Küng's work that many of his publications are produced in cooperation with other scholars: his dialogues with other world religions, his dialogues with literature,[26] and the results of an international conference on the subject-matter of the paradigm change in theology.[27] In addition, Küng presented a collection of his own reflections about the debate on theological method in his book *Theology for the Third Millennium* (1987), to which we shall turn later.

4. Global Responsibility

Methodological reflection on the demands of a postmodern paradigm for theology and experiences in dialogue with the various spheres of human creativity led Küng to direct his theological attention to the global context of present-day human existence. Here he is concerned to bring together reflections on religious, cultural, social, political, economic and ecological experience in a large-scale project, the programme for which was outlined in his manifesto *Global Responsibility* (1990, German title *Projekt Weltethos*). The German title clearly indicates the ethical concentration in Küng's thought. Whatever idealistic remnants may have been preserved in the course of Küng's thinking now give way to a programme with a rather pragmatic orientation which links the Christian approach to the world with a multi-dimensional interpretation of the present.

Küng's political interest, which previously was expressed only indirectly, now becomes explicit.[28] Human action needs ethical criteria in a global dimension. However, over against this need stand forms of religion which tend to be more provincial. So Küng's reform programme makes self-criticism within each religion a presupposition of world-wide inter-religious dialogue. However, in his view such self-criticism should also be applied by all non-religious trends of thought which seek to take part in the global quest for a new ethic. The criticism of every ideology becomes the starting point for Küng's ethical manifesto. His various analyses aim at 'a holistic view of the world and human beings in their different dimensions. For along with the economic, social and political dimensions there is also the aesthetic, ethical and religious dimension of human beings and humanity.'[29] However, 'holistic' is not to be confused with 'uniform'. Rather, the postmodern paradigm calls for an affirmation of the overall pluralistic constellation.

The goal and criterion of the new world ethic is the *humanum*: 'human beings must become more than they are: they must become more human!'[30] However, the *humanum* only comes really into view when all the dimensions of existence, i.e. the most humane society possible and an intact environment, are also included.[31] Küng rightly stresses that an analysis of the time which brackets out the religious dimension is deficient.[32] In addition he points out that the categorical nature of the ethical claim, the unconditional nature of the 'ought', cannot be grounded in human beings, who are conditioned in so many ways, but only in an unconditional: 'an Absolute which can provide an over-arching meaning and which embraces and permeates individual, human nature and indeed the whole of human society. That can only be the ultimate, supreme reality, which while it cannot be proved rationally, can be accepted in a rational trust – regardless of how it is named, understood and interpreted in the different religions.'[33] In this sense religion within the context of post-modernity receives new opportunities which ought to be exploited.

Küng cannot conceive either a survival without a global ethic or a stable world peace without religious peace. However, this presupposes an honest, critical dialogue between the religions, above all one which is based on self-criticism. The criterion of this dialogue remains the truly human, the *humanum*.[34] Such readiness for dialogue, though it must also be coupled with self-critical steadfastness, already furthers the capacity of religion for peace.

This is the point at which Küng's most recent research programme begins. His prime concern is to study the religious situation of our time, in order to locate basic insights into the possibility of inter-religious dialogue. Here his aim is, 'as far as possible to obtain the view of the whole of a religion ... However, the whole of a religion shows not only developments, historical sequences and dates but also structures, patterns of believing, thinking, feeling and acting. A religion is a living system of religious convictions, liturgical rites, spiritual practices and institutions of very different kinds, which develop further and which are highly complex.'[35] So this research programme envisages a multi-disciplinary study of religion, in order 'to do as much justice as possible to religions like Judaism, Christianity and Islam in their wealth, their complexity and their many dimensions'.[36] Above all Küng wants to cover the epoch-making shifts in these (and perhaps later yet other) religions, so that in each case he can identify their various periods and their structures, and offer prognoses.[37]

In the meantime, in his comprehensive study of *Judaism* (1991), Küng has succeeded in achieving a substantial part of this project on the religious situation of our time which I have just discussed. Studies on Christianity and Islam with a similar structure will follow soon. Although we cannot go into the precise content of this monumental study on Judaism here, a brief evaluation should be made of this unique work. For this is the first major study of Judaism by a Christian theologian to take Judaism seriously as a living religion and seek to grasp its own development as a whole.[38] The various paradigm shifts in the history of Judaism are clarified without reference being made to the Christian understanding of salvation, as had been customary in the two thousand years of hostile Christian studies. Of course Küng also investigates the tradition of this ideological approach and the annihilation of countless Jews which is at least connected with it, coming to a horrific culmination in the Holocaust and unfortunately still not at an end. Küng's attempt to inform, to develop an understanding of the other religion as other, and thus to perform a service for religious and world peace, sets standards for future dealings with other forms of religion.

5. Constants in theological thought

Our extensive survey of Küng's work has been necessary in order to draw appropriate attention to the wide range of his theological interests, developments and contributions and to offer an initial discussion of his major works. There are at least four unifying constants in Küng's theological work in the four periods described above: (i) his ecumenical interest (from originally an inner-Christian ecumenism towards a global ecumenism); (ii) his continuing ecclesiological reflection; (iii) his concern with the christological and theological foundations of Christian faith and with the rationality of that faith; and (iv) his search for an adequate theological method for today. Let us consider these in reverse order.

(i) Theological methodology

Küng's theological method can be studied both by distilling the implicit methodology operative in his major works and by discussing his more recent explicit discussion of theological method, especially in *Theology for the Third Millennium*. Both his implicit and explicit methodology reveal the same strong commitment to the Bible as the source and ultimate norm of Christian theology, a commitment which has been characteristic of most contemporary Roman Catholic theologians. For Küng, the second source of Christian theology is the wealth of human experiences in our modern or postmodern world.[39] Both sources, Bible and modern world, need to be interpreted, and both interpretations need to be critically correlated.[40] A similar model of critical correlation can also be found in E. Schillebeeckx and D. Tracy's approach to theology. While promoting this model in principle, Küng does, however, point out that this correlation between both sources may at times lead to confrontation, namely when biblical and contemporary experiences contradict one another. In such a situation of conflict, Küng attributes ultimate normative significance 'to the particular Christian experiences, or, rather, to the Christian message, the gospel, Jesus Christ himself'.[41]

In *On Being a Christian*, Küng had shown how he understands this ultimate norm to work. There he reminds us that 'narrative presentation and critical reflection ... must be united in Christian theology and proclamation'[42] and offers his own critical narrative and interpretation of Jesus' life, death, and resurrection. Here in *Theology for the Third Millennium* Küng emphasizes that his own interpretation of the principal norm of Christian theology, Jesus Christ, is informed by historical-critical scholarship which he considers to be essential for any appropriate theology today. He warns us, however, not to confuse historical-critical exegesis with a responsibly constructed historical-critical dogmatics.[43] The latter ought to include a systematic reflection on the (occasionally conflicting) results of modern biblical exegesis.[44]

The dimensions of the systematic task in theology are clearly outlined by Küng: as already indicated in our survey of Küng's work, for him good theology must be (i) ecumenical (in the global sense indicated above), (ii) truthful (that means not opportunistic), (iii) free (that means not authoritarian), and (iv) critical (not traditionalist).[45] Any candidate for an adequate paradigm for contemporary theology must respect these four essential dimensions.

(ii) Fundamental issues in christology and theology

In this context, however, Küng does not make totally explicit all of the dimensions which are operative in his systematic theology. Against the mediaeval-neoscholastic paradigm he insists that faith is not simply above reason; against the dichotomies of dialectical theology he emphasizes that faith is not against reason; and against the modern Enlightenment dichotomy he stresses that reason is not against faith.[46] For Küng, all our thinking and doubting, our intuitions and deductions are grounded on an 'a priori act of trust' of which we might not always be aware, but which, once we are, we may consciously affirm or reject.[47]

As we have seen, Küng's approach to God in *Does God Exist?* is based on this fundamental insight. Although Küng is critical of Rahner's theology because it was still part of the neoscholastic paradigm,[48] Küng's a priori act of trust does bear some resemblance to Rahner's transcendental experience.[49] However, there is also a fundamental difference between both approaches to God: while for Rahner the transcendental experience of any human being is always related (though not always thematically) to God, the God of Jesus Christ, Küng's a priori of trust is not simply identified with belief in God. But there exists an essential connection between trust in reality and belief in God. 'If someone denies God, he does not know why he ultimately trusts in reality.' And respectively: 'If someone affirms God, he knows why he can trust reality.'[50] The precise nature of this connection would need to be clarified further by Küng.

Like Rahner, Küng owes a lot to the Cartesian starting point, namely the individually thinking subject. While it is, of course, correct that any decision to believe in the Christian God is ultimately a decision made by an individual, it does not, however, automatically follow from this that the concept of God operative in the Christian movement must be exclusively grounded on individual trust. Rather it seems, and here Küng agrees, that there is a rich, but naturally ambiguous heritage of philosophical attempts which relate on-tologically God, Christ, the human being, and the universe. Many of these philosophical models are certainly inappropriate, as Küng himself has documented in *The Incarnation of God* with reference to the static concept of God in Greek metaphysics. Yet Küng does not sufficiently discuss his own use of ontological language which may lead to misunderstandings, particularly in christological thinking which has to wrestle with adequate expressions of the relationship between Jesus and God. When Küng writes 'For me, Jesus of Nazareth is the Son of God,'[51] he makes (if not only a value judgment) some kind of an ontological claim though existentially qualified. But even a qualified ontology is still an ontology. Similarly, his reference to 'reality' as the object of human trust has ontological implications.

Reality is always encountered through particular perspectives. These perspectives are always conditioned by all the dimensions of human experience, including the religious dimensions. Therefore the hermeneutical implications of the method of critical correlation between biblical message and human world would need to be discussed in more detail along the following lines: the contemporary human world is already present, of course, in perspectives which guide our reading of the Bible, as indeed the history of effects of the biblical texts is always present in our Western interpretations of the world. Therefore Küng's 'fundamental trust in reality' is already socially and religiously conditioned, a fact which Küng has not yet explicitly treated.[52]

For Küng, the norm of Christian theology is Jesus Christ. He is the centre of Scripture. Yet, he can only be reached through our interpretations of the different early Christian interpretations of his life, death, and resurrection. This hermeneutical situation causes a double pluralism: the contemporary pluralism of readings and the pluralism of early Christian 'readings' of Jesus as Christ. Coping with this double pluralism and the heritage of Christian interpretations in a responsible manner must include the risk of saying who Jesus Christ is in relation to God to the best of our knowledge. We have to make tentative ontological statements. Here Küng does implicitly agree. 'Jesus of Nazareth in fact has, in the last resort, no decisive meaning for me unless he is proclaimed as the Christ of God. Nor, anyway, does the divine Christ mean much to me unless he is identical with the man Jesus.'[53]

Therefore, tentative ontological statements must have a place in the new paradigm of theology in order to help us to express our particular faith in God both in terms of our own inner-Christian understanding of truth, and in terms of contributing meaningfully to the much wider search for truth in the conversation among different religious traditions.

(iii) The need for church reform

Küng has constantly kept to his demand for a thoroughgoing reform of the Roman Catholic church despite all the hostility and criticism from the church authorities which need to be reformed. His collaboration in the conciliar process of reform has permanently shaped his ecclesiology. His criteria for an appropriate ecclesiology, developed at that time, have remained a norm for him. For Küng, the Christian church is and remains a community of free men and women, who respond to God's call as disciples of Christ.[54] He himself sees his ecclesiological thought as shaped by three characteristics: Christian radicalism, constancy and coherence.[55] In the face of all despondency and depression which affect many committed Christians because of the present climate in the Catholic church, Küng constantly calls on them to maintain hope and to reflect on the authentic calling of the church as the trustee of Jesus Christ: 'I'm staying in the church because I have been convinced by Jesus Christ and all that he stands for and because the Church-community, despite all its failures, pleads the cause of Jesus Christ and must continue to do so.'[56]

In keeping with his ecumenical disposition, he constantly calls for re-cognition of existing church pluralism.[57] Such a recognition of course pre-supposes that a clerical minority no longer claims to direct church people as it were 'from above'. All Christians are called to apostolic discipleship.[58] All church members therefore have reciprocal obligations. 'The pastor has the obligation and the task of constantly preaching the Christian message to the community anew, even if it is uncomfortable for the community. Conversely, the community has the obligation and the task of constantly testing anew whether the pastor is remaining faithful to the task, whether he is acting in accordance with the gospel. There are not only false prophets, but also faithless pastors.'[59] Küng's ecclesiology of reform naturally also includes the call for a fundamental revision of the role of women in the church: 'So that the Catholic church, whose structure of ministry and power is completely dominated by males, may become a church for all people, women should be represented in every decision-making body: at parish, diocesan, national and world levels.'[60]

In contrast to many of his colleagues, Küng has not allowed himself to be driven into either resignation or cynicism by the conservative church policy at present being put forward by the Vatican. Rather, he is working with unbroken energy on his vision of a better church. This is all the more amazing when we reflect how attempts have been made to reduce Hans Küng's vision of the church to the 'Küng case'. This 'case' reached its sorry 'climax' with the withdrawal of his licence by the church in 1979. Here above all, three ecclesiological concepts were a matter of dispute between the self-appointed guardians of Catholic 'orthodoxy' and the Tübingen theologian: the question of the freedom of the theologian in the church, the concept of papal unfallibility and the clash of two different paradigms of theological thought.

However, Küng has never absolutized the freedom of theology. Rather, he constantly stresses that theology has its creative ground and its life in the Word of God, to which human beings bear witness.[61] Küng's theological approach and above all his criterion for judging forms of church authority and organization, which is grounded in the gospel, make it *a priori* impossible for him to accept a dogma of papal infallibility. In this connection Küng also points to the great difference between the paradigm of theology still defended by Rome and the paradigm of a critical and self-critical theology come of age which is represented by critical Christians and theologians today. While some Catholics still cling to a neo-scholastic paradigm, numerous others have long already been living in a new paradigm. One of the tasks of critical theology must therefore be to encourage communication between the defenders of both paradigms without simply claiming that the more recent paradigm is better because it is later. Its appropriateness may not just be asserted, but must be constantly tested afresh in public discourse.[62]

(iv) Global theological strategies

With his *Global Responsibility*, Küng has once again emphasized his global understanding of theological work. At the same time, with this project he has also brought out the impossibility of separating practical theological work from systematic theological work. Whereas contemporary theology often makes a tripartite division of theological work into fundamental, systematic and practical theology,[63] Küng implicitly emphasizes a twofold division, namely a distinction between fundamental and systematic-practical theological thought. The aim of fundamental theology is to reflect methodologically on theology in the inter-disciplinary context of present-day thought. Küng's paradigm theory belongs in this sphere. By contrast, the aim of systematic-practical thought in theology is to demonstrate a vision of Christian existence in the context of the present pluralism of religion and to develop strategies for Christian existence in the present global context. For Küng, the development of such strategies is always already ethical work. This concept of theology allows him always to understand Christian ecumenical theory and practice dialectically, and thus avoid the tiresome discussion of burdensome theory on the one hand or the dominance of theology by praxis on the other.

The one criticism that must be made in this connection is of Küng's hesitation to enter into the discussion of the concept of the human self in the framework of this global discussion. For most of those taking part in the discussion over the postmodern paradigm, the traditional self-understanding of human beings has become questionable. The Cartesian approach to the assessment of the self is no longer any use, since it largely ignores the interdependence on the one hand between human beings and on the other between the individual and the environment. Moreover it is necessarily still uncritical of all the strategies of suspicion which meanwhile have been advanced against the simple assertion of an independent human will or a trustworthy human reason.[64] But as Küng attributes central importance in his theological approach to both trust and reason, it seems appropriate that he should explicitly enter into this discussion today. It would also give his ethical and political perspective a much stronger foundation.

6. Hans Küng's theological achievement

Hans Küng has not only discussed all essential areas of Christian theology, reflected on necessary changes in theological method today, and opened many doors toward a Christian understanding of the world religions, but has also expressed his thoughts in such a way that every intelligent reader can follow them and thus receive the necessary information for entering into the discussion. Küng cannot be praised enough for the attention he has given to the presentation of theological thoughts. Countless people around the world have thus been allowed to nurture their theological interest and to transform their lives.

Perhaps Küng's two most important contributions to theological method so far have been (i) his proposal for a global theology which is aware of the many facets of human life in this world and of the different and often conflicting religious and cultural interpretations of reality; and (ii) his reconsideration of the nature of truth-claims in the context of such a global theology.

Küng's call on all human beings to enter into the discussion about the meaning and truth in our lives and to respect the open-endedness of such a discussion is inspired by his understanding of God's revelation in Jesus Christ. The resulting self-understanding of theology must therefore conflict with any theological paradigm which advocates a privileged access to truth for some people. Genuine conversation about truth cannot tolerate such privileged participants. This applics not only to the Roman Catholic *magisterium*, but to all human bodies in and outside of Christianity which claim such a special status and access to God and truth. Küng's vision of the global conversation about truth is based on his understanding of God's call in Christ that all people are called to relate to God without intermediary institutions.[65]

Küng's most significant contribution to the discussion of the central articles of Christian faith lies in his effort to demonstrate the rationality of this faith and to reflect upon the implications of this faith for human praxis today. Küng does not only wish to interpret the world, he wishes to help in transforming it by critically retrieving the radical humanism of the Christian faith. Even though Küng has not yet clarified all the philosophical presuppositions of his work, he has already contributed a lot to the radical transformation of the nature of theology in the twentieth century.

But he would be the first to admit that much more still has to be done. His work on the *Global Responsibility* programme and the survey of the religious situation of our time which is connected with this has only just begun, but it has already, as we saw above, produced very considerable results. At a time in which German-language theology in particular has become amazingly quiet, Küng is continuing to work with undiminished power and new ideas. His work has already stimulated many to critical thought and action and has thus contributed in its way to changing our world and our Christian self-understanding. What more could one ask of a theologian today?

Notes

* This is a revised and enlarged version of an article which originally appeared in David Ford (ed.), *The Modern Theologians* I, published by Blackwell, Oxford in 1989, pp.164–80. I am grateful to the publishers for allowing me to use the material here.

1. Küng, *The Church*, 96ff.
2. Ibid., 388ff.
3. Ibid., 363–480.
4. Küng, *Infallible?* 22 (I have corrected the English translation).
5. Ibid., 152f.
6. Ibid., 170.
7. Küng, *The Incarnation of God*, 462.
8. Ibid., 428.
9. Ibid., 491.
10. Cf. ibid., 492.
11. Küng, *On Being a Christian*, 125f.

12. Küng, *Does God Exist?*, 421.
13. Ibid., 473.
14. Ibid., 476.
15. Ibid., 570.
16. Ibid., 572.
17. Ibid., 574.
18. Ibid.
19. Ibid., 626.
20. Ibid., 649.
21. Küng, *Eternal Life?*, 145.
22. Ibid., 287.
23. Küng, *Christianity and the World Religions*, xiv.
24. H. Küng and P. Lapide, *Jesus im Widerstreit: Ein jüdisch-christlicher Dialog*, Stuttgart and Munich 1976.
25. H. Küng and J. Ching, *Christianity and Chinese Religion*.
26. See e.g. W. Jens and H. Küng, *Dichtung und Religion*; W. Jens, H. Küng and K.-J. Kuschel (eds.), *Theologie und Literatur. Zum Stand des Dialogs*, Munich 1986; W. Jens and H. Küng, *Anwälte der Humanität: Thomas Mann, Hermann Hesse, Heinrich Böll*, Munich 1989.
27. H. Küng and D. Tracy (eds.) *The New Paradigm in Theology*, Edinburgh 1989.
28. In this connection see also Küng's much-noted book *Die Schweiz ohne Orientierung? Europäische Perspektiven*.
29. Küng, *Global Responsibility*, 21.
30. Ibid., 31.
31. Ibid., 31f.
32. Ibid., 44.
33. Ibid., 53.
34. Ibid., 91. Hans Küng had already claimed in *On Being a Christian*, 554ff., that Christianity should rightly be understood as radical humanism.
35. Küng, *Global Responsibility*, 110f.
36. Ibid., 120.
37. Ibid., 125.
38. The excellent book by Franz Mussner, *Tractate on the Jews*, Philadelphia 1983, of course also takes the ongoing life of Jewish religion seriously, but is primarily interested in a Christian theological approach to Judaism. By contrast, Küng is attempting to understand the religious situation of our time.
39. For Küng's understanding of the term 'postmodern' see *Global Responsibility*, 19–24; *Judaism*, 443–7.
40. Küng, *Theology for the Third Millennium*, 108ff.
41. Ibid., 108 (my translation), cf. also 195–200.
42. Küng, *On Being a Christian*, 418.
43. Küng, *Theology for the Third Millennium*, 112f.
44. Ibid., 113f.
45. Cf. ibid., 101f., 203f.
46. Ibid., 202ff. and esp. 244f.
47. Ibid., 243.

48. For Rahner's concept of transcendental experience see K. Rahner, *Foundations of Christian Faith*, London and New York 1978, 75–81.

49. Küng, *Does God Exist?*, 571ff.

50. Ibid., 688.

51. For the dimensions of present-day theological hermeneutics, see Werner G. Jeanrond, *Theological Hermeneutics: Development and Significance*, London and New York 1991.

52. Küng, *Does God Exist?*, 687.

53. Cf. Küng, *Reforming the Church Today*, 54.

54. Ibid., 3.

55. Ibid., 10.

56. Ibid., 41.

57. Ibid., 79f.

58. Ibid., 86 (translation emended).

59. Ibid., 103.

60. Cf. Küng, *Freiheit des Christen*, 143.

61. Cf. Küng, *Theology for the Third Millennium*, 203–7.

62. See e.g D. Tracy, *The Analogical Imagination. Christian Theology and the Culture of Pluralism*, New York and London 1981, 54–82.

63. For these problems see D. Tracy, *Plurality and Ambiguity*, San Francisco and London 1987.

64. Küng, *On Being a Christian*, 481ff.

65. Ibid., 31.

III   The Ecumenical World

Lukas Vischer

Theology in the Service of the Ecumene: Protestant Perspectives

As one of Hans Küng's earlier writings programmatically puts it, the important thing is 'that the communion which already exists should grow. What we need is that both sides should create more and more common ground between us, until finally what separates us becomes insignificant and full unity is a reality'.[1] What has Hans Küng contributed to this goal which he himself has formulated? What is the significance of his theological work and his public activity in the eyes of Protestant Christians?

Without doubt he was one of the great active forces of the more recent ecumenical movement. More than one of his books was pioneering in every sense of the word, and though since his condemnation by Pope John Paul II his name no longer seems to exist in official circles of the Roman Catholic church, and even the Protestant side keeps silent about him in ecumenical dialogue for diplomatic reasons, this does not alter the fact that Hans Küng has made an essential contribution to the restoration of communion among the churches. Protestant churches owe him a special debt of thanks. For them he was a symbol of hope; as a Roman Catholic theologian he expressed their hopes for the ecumenical movement. They saw their concerns taken up in everything that he said and wrote. All at once the question 'Is Küng perhaps a Protestant at heart?' took on another emphasis. What in former, more confessional times would have been at least a secret wish now became a fear: that the Roman Catholic church could declare his theses 'Protestant' and put an end to further coming together. For many people, and especially for Protestant Christians, the withdrawal of his licence by Pope John Paul II, shortly after the latter's accession to office, involuntarily made Hans Küng a symbol of disappointed hopes. The supreme authority in the Roman Catholic church had made it unmistakably clear that Küng's theses were incompatible with the official doctrine of the church.

1. Renewal by councils and conciliar processes

Already in the 1950s Küng had made it his task to put in question the presuppositions of the confessional age. The ecumenical movement had been given considerable impetus after the Second World War, above all as a result of the foundation of the World Council of Churches. But there were still hardly any signs of a new awakening in the Roman Catholic church. Pope Pius XII rejected and forbade any official participation in inter-confessional encounters. However, already at that time Hans Küng began from the firm conviction that behind the established fronts was concealed far more common ground than was generally assumed. He sought to demonstrate this in an account of Karl Barth's doctrine of justification which led to what at that time was the completely surprising result that there were no unbridgeable conflicts between Karl Barth and the statements of the Council of Trent. At least in this respect, Hans Küng proclaimed with characteristic verve, Karl Barth's polemic against the Roman Catholic church had no foundation. Karl Barth had not understood the real meaning of the statements of Trent. In an accompanying letter Karl Barth confirmed that he felt that Küng understood him and that the statements of the Council of Trent as Küng interpreted them were indeed compatible with the Protestant understanding of justification. Nevertheless he raised the question whether the perspectives demonstrated by Küng did not rest on a new interpretation of the council. 'How,' he asked, 'do you explain the fact that all this could remain hidden so long and from so many both outside and inside the church?'[2] And today it sounds like a foreboding of things to come when he adds in conclusion: 'It will certainly take quite an effort, once (as we hope) the central area has been cleared, to make somewhat plausible to us matters like Transubstantiation, the Sacrifice of the Mass, Mary and the infallible papacy and the other things with which we are confronted ... in the Tridentine profession of faith.'[3]

The Second Vatican Council was the beginning of a new stage. Hitherto Küng had attempted to stress what was held in common above all by a refined interpretation of tradition. 'A truth of faith can always be articulated in formulas which are more complete, more adequate, and more perfect. Truth then is not restricted to some particular (time-bound) manifestation and can be embodied in a more comprehensive (though again finite) historical perspective. This embodiment of revealed truth takes place ... through the Holy Spirit of Jesus Christ working in the Church.'[4] Küng accused Barth of not seeing this vitality of the tradition adequately.

The announcement of the Council once again created a new situation. Right from the beginning Küng understood the Council as the occasion for a comprehensive reform of the Roman Catholic church – in both its thought and its life. The idea of reform was in the air. The World Council of Churches had developed the view that the unity of the churches could be achieved only by way of renewal. The keyword *aggiornamento* used by Pope John XXIII seemed to point in the same direction. In those fruitful years between the announcement and opening of the Council, Hans Küng made a vital contribution to giving content and form to this idea. The two writings which appeared at that time, *The Council and Reunion*, and *Structures of the Church*, made Protestant Christians listen. Would the Council in fact make so deep a contribution? Could it be possible that the Roman Catholic church would take a new direction instead of continuing the existing one?

The breakthrough achieved by the Council went far beyond most people's expectations. New perspectives opened up in almost all the areas with which the Council was concerned. A new framework was created for both theology and action, the worship and the spirituality of the churches. Was the Council over with the promulgation of the texts? Or could the stimuli contained in the texts be taken up and developed? Were the new elements corrections which had to be interpreted in such a way as not to contradict the tradition which had been valid hitherto? Or on the contrary, was it a matter of examining what had hitherto been valid on the basis of the new, and in any case providing a new formulation? Strong forces at the Council had concentrated all their intellectual and tactical capabilities on the task of making tangibly sure that the texts corresponded with the statements of earlier centuries. They *a priori* rejected any possible interpretations which took things further. I recall a conversation which I had with Hans Küng towards the end of the Council. What would finally be valid, I asked, the previous tradition which was expressly confirmed in the conciliar text or the new element, which made the real difference? The answer came immediately, 'Don't worry, we'll see to it that things don't slip back!'

Already during the last sessions Küng had reflected on the period after the Council. He emphatically pleaded for an open church in which the debate could be taken beyond the immediate questions. 'Theology has to perceive the negative-critical function which at the same time is a positive, constructive, critical function: time and again with every means and everywhere to point to the main concern, to the centre, and at the same time to allow the whole message to be expressed in its fullness. Need one spend long here in explaining that this task of criticism and correction cannot be settled once and for all, but must constantly be achieved anew in a laborious way?'[5] Küng was clear that further development cannot be brought about by theology alone but needs church structures to match. In an article 'Council – End or Beginning?' he suggested that something like a continuing conciliar process should be set up.[6] At the same time similar thoughts were also being developed by the World Council of Churches: could it not be possible to understand the ecumenical movement as a permanent conciliar process which allowed the separated churches to grow together step by step into union?[7]

The continuation of the conciliar discussions was particularly significant for ecumenical dialogue. The Second Vatican Council stated emphatically that it would enter into dialogue with the other Christian traditions. But must not this dialogue inevitably throw up new questions which the Council had not yet seen and discussed? And in that case, how were they to be treated? Taking up a proposal from the World Council of Churches, the Council had inserted the following statement in the 'Decree on Ecumenism': 'This sacred Council firmly hopes that the initiatives of the sons of the Catholic Church, joined with those of the separated brethren, will go forward, without obstructing the ways of divine Providence, and without prejudging the future inspirations of the Holy Spirit' (no. 24). How could this openness to dialogue be continued in practice, if not by a readiness for constantly new departures?

Küng kept his word. Along with many others, and also with Protestant theologians, he sought to put the new into practice. In breathtaking succession, theses and demands were presented which while suggested in the texts of the Council at the same time went far beyond them. Not only the texts of the Council but also the experiences which had been had in the course of the reception of the Council served as the starting point for new reflections. Within the ecumenical movement there was open talk of the reciprocal recognition of ministries and the joint celebration of the eucharist, and for a while it seemed as if it was only a matter of time before such demands were met. However, on closer inspection it was already clear at that time that sooner or later this movement must come up against limits.

First of all the question of the papacy, and especially of infallibility, had been bracketted out from ecumenical dialogues. Protestant Christians, too, were aware that the question of the authority of Vatican I had been one of the most disputed issues at the Council and that *a priori*, narrow limits had been set to an ecumenical dialogue on infallibility. Decisive and unavoidable as this question was for the future, initially by tacit agreement it was left untouched. It is to the credit of Hans Küng that he broke this tabu: he put the statements of Vatican I in doubt not only for ecumenical reasons but also on Roman Catholic premises. True as it is that the church is preserved in the truth of Jesus Christ over the centuries, there can be no doubt that it has erred, can err and will err. It is indestructible not because it does not err but because despite errors it is ultimately preserved in the truth by the Holy Spirit. Küng challenged the possibility of infallible statements. 'Thus not only has the plane of institutions and authorities been penetrated but also that of propositional truths in order to point to one and the same reality which lies behind the individual statements and alone gives them their truth – if necessary through very different statements.'[8] The contradiction from Rome came immediately. But it still took almost ten years for these theses to be condemned. Time and again it seemed as if Küng's position in the Roman Catholic church could at least be tolerated, even if it could not be approved. But at Christmas 1979 his licence was withdrawn.

Why did the *magisterium* intervene in this particular case? Why did it not perceive its 'weighty office'[9] of furthering and protecting the church's doctrine of faith and morals? We do not need to look very far for an answer. Küng's theses touched on the self-understanding of the *magisterium* itself. The *magisterium* seemed to have been put in question. The decision against Küng had both a theological and a church-political character. It gave a double signal.

It made it clear that everything that the Second Vatican Council had taught, everything that was being taught in the name of the Second Vatican Council, was in accord and had to be in accord with the statements of the First Vatican Council, and at the same time recalled that the task of interpreting the faith of the Word of God authentically was entrusted only to the living church *magisterium*. This was a clear option: the movement which sought to lead beyond the texts of the Council must not burst the banks: above all it could not remove itself from the control of the authentic *magisterium*.

2. Consequences for the ecumenical movement

The consequences were immense. One need only imagine what could have happened had the insights gained in the debate prompted by Küng become established, or even had they simply been tolerated in the Roman Catholic church. The little book which Hans Küng wrote shortly before his condemnation, *The Church Maintained in Truth*, shows the turn that the ecumenical movement could have taken on this basis. The vision developed here creates a new situation for Protestant Christians, not because they are 'Protestant' but because this understanding of the continuity of the one church of Jesus Christ in the truth could have made a common move forward by the separated churches possible. First of all it is important that Küng sees the origin of the indestructibility of the church only in Christ. 'So then the church is maintained in truth, in the truth of the gospel, in the truth of Jesus Christ. The Church does not maintain itself in the truth. It is maintained: by God, through Jesus Christ, in the Spirit.'[10] The continuity of the church down the centuries does not therefore rest in an intrinsic quality; it is given, in our keeping to the promise of Jesus Christ. But it is no less important that Küng could quite bluntly stand by the errors of the church. His understanding of the indestructibility of the church is free from the notable pressure to demonstrate that at all times the church has not only taught the truth but has taught the same truth. There is no need to take on the humiliating role of the magician who to the amazement of all draws the statements needed today out of the top hat of tradition. Küng does not feel it necessary to demonstrate the continuity in statements and structures. Error can be called error without the certainty of faith in the indestructibility of the church being damaged. 'Error on the part of the church's *magisterium* in serious definitions of faith and morals is in any single case a fact – and we are still alive.'[11] The church remains in the truth by Christ being made present in it. It is 'maintained in the truth not only where the right words are produced but wherever discipleship is fully realized in practice'.[12]

This view is so liberating for Protestant Christians because it makes possible an authentic dialogue between the separated churches. For now the issue is no longer that of making the truth taught infallibly in the Roman Catholic church at all times so clear that it can also be accepted and shared by Protestant Christians. The important thing is, rather, together to understand the apostolic tradition as it is present in all the churches broken in different ways, in such a form that it can be proclaimed and lived out credibly together today. The Protestant churches are no longer called on to deny their own past in favour of the Roman Catholic church because that is the only church in which the true tradition is infallibly handed down. Rather, with all the other churches it has a share in the working of the Spirit and with them can put itself under the guidance of the Spirit which will lead it into all truth. 'The Spirit of God cannot be restricted in effectiveness by the Church. The Spirit works not only from above but very decisively from below. He works not only in church ministries but where he wills: in the whole people of God. He works not only in the "Holy City" but where he wills: in all churches of the one Church. He works not only in the Catholic Church but where he wills: in the whole of Christendom. And finally, he works not only in Christendom but again where he wills: in the whole world.'[13]

The way in which Küng spoke about infallibility was also so liberating because with it the Reformation was given a firm place in the history of the one church. The Reformation no longer had to be interpreted primarily in terms of a loss. It could be seen as an event through which the true continuity of the church was guaranteed. 'But when popes and bishops pursued power, money, and pleasure, and theologians kept silent, slept, produced apologias, or even collaborated, there still remained those innumerable, mostly unknown Christians (among them at all times even some bishops, theologians, and particularly parish priests) who tried even at the worst times of the Church to live according to the gospel.'[14]

And at the same time the way was also opened up for a joint discussion about the indestructibility of the church. For Protestant Christians, too, are convinced that the church is maintained indestructibly in the truth. They, too, trust that God's word will not be completely absent at any time. However, the polemic against the dogma of infallibility has clouded their view of the questions which arise from this conviction. What has this church to do to remain in the truth? How does it give room to God's word in such a way that community is built up? In this respect Protestant Christians face a task that they have not tackled. Küng's proposal that the theme of infallibility should be worked on by an ecumenical commission would therefore not only have met with a ready response on the Protestant side but could also have produced new insights.

The decision of the *magisterium* against Küng put an end to all these hopes. By condemning his thesis, the *magisterium* made it clear that the continuity of the church had been maintained only in the Roman Catholic church. Whatever truth the churches separated from Rome proclaim and bear witness to is essentially the truth which is handed down in the Roman Catholic church. Since then the ecumenical movement has been burdened with a deep contradiction. The enterprise of dialogues, encounters and collaboration goes on. Who could have stopped the dialogue after all the experiences that the Second Vatican Council had made possible! The pope, too, is subjectively most deeply convinced that the ecumenical movement must go on and if possible lead to tangible results. The issues of the *Acta Apostolicae Sedis* are full of speeches which conjure up the aims of the ecumenical movement. And yet *a priori* such narrow limits are set to the dialogues that a real breakthrough is ruled out. A step into communion is possible for the Protestant churches only at the price of denying their own tradition. In particular the decision against Küng makes all discussions about the papal office and infallibility mere castles in the air. One dialogue commission after another comes to the conclusion that a papacy as described by Küng could in some circumstances be recognized by all the churches. But what is the use of such joint declarations if the *magisterium* in the church develops in precisely the opposite direction?

How seriously the supreme authority in the Roman Catholic church is concerned with the claim to truth is shown by a document of the Congregation of Faith, recently published with papal approval, on 'Some Aspects of the Church as Communion'. There is not a word in it to indicate that the continuity of the church of Jesus Christ is preserved in all the churches. Not a word to indicate that they can all contribute to the unity of the church, each with its gifts. Not a word, above all, that the Roman Catholic church falls behind other churches in even one respect. Its only wounds are the wounds of the other churches, in so far as they prevent it from developing its calling fully and simply. Listen to the argument: 'Since, however, communion with the universal church, represented by Peter's successor, is not an external complement to the particular Church, but one of its internal constituents, the situation of these venerable Christian communities also means that their existence as particular Churches is wounded. The wound is even deeper in those ecclesial communities which have not retained the apostolic succession and a valid eucharist. This in turn also injures the Catholic Church, called by the Lord to become for all "one flock" with "one shepherd", in that it hinders the complete fulfilment of her universality in history.'[15]

So that is the way the argument has to go after the condemnation of Küng! But how much sense does it make to carry on the dialogue between the churches in the face of so much sectarian spirit?

3. Questions to the Protestant churches

Küng's concern has always been primarily for the renewal of the Roman Catholic church. The thrust of his theological work from the beginning is towards self-examination. Each church is to create from within the presuppositions for the community to be able to grow. This concern for the renewal of his own church, however, obviously and unavoidably also contains the hope or the expectation that similar movements can also come about in other churches. Only when the same Spirit is heard on both sides can the hoped-for convergence come about. Indeed, perhaps even more can be said: if both sides really consistently listen to the Spirit, the churches *must* come closer together. And might not this comparable movement also be expected from the Reformed church, which from of old has inscribed the principle *semper reformanda* on its banner and in addition has at least in principle committed itself to a programme of self-examination and renewal? Did not Protestant Christians continually complain that by its reference to itself the Roman Catholic church prevented the development of the ecumenical community and as a result gave the impression that at any rate as soon as the situation changed they were ready for a new start?

In 1978 Hans Küng was invited to articulate his expectations to the Protestant churches in a speeech within the framework of the jubilee of the Bern Reformation.[16] He performed this task with the courtesy required by the occasion but at the same time with the clarity and firmness required by common commitment in the ecumenical movement. He recalled the progress which had been achieved in a short time. Differences which seemed to separate the churches at all times were being overcome in joint dialogues. A new period in the relationship between the churches could begin. Why did this not happen? Küng vehemently criticized the immobility of all the churches, but put to the Protestant churches above all the question why they were so little involved in the spiritual rivalry for unity. Why had they not taken steps which could have make it easier for the Roman Catholic church to draw wider-ranging conclusions on its side? There was impatience and disappointment in these questions. Why had the Protestant churches changed so little since the Second Vatican Council? Why in many respects were they even more unmovable than the Roman Catholic church? Concerns which had formerly been regarded as those of the Reformation had not only been taken up by the Roman Catholic church, but were often being implemented much more credibly than in the Protestant churches themselves – one need only think of the great importance attached to scripture, to the renewal of the liturgy, the revaluation of the laity, the deep awareness of the universality of the church and the reform of popular piety. In an unexpected way, in all these spheres the Roman Catholic church had raised questions about the encrusted praxis of the Protestant churches. And on the whole there had been no answer. People had played to the Protestant churches, but they had not danced.

Granted there was no lack of theological production on the Protestant side. There had been noteworthy achievements both in the ecumenical movement generally and in the response to the Second Vatican Council in particular. There was hardly a Protestant theologian who had not made his or her own contributions to this new dialogue. The theological questions to which the Council had led were readily being taken up and developed. Just as the observers during the Second Vatican Council had already done, numerous Protestant theologians were making it their task to influence the debates in the direction of more comprehensive openness. In many cases Protestant theologians were the driving force in the bilateral dialogues which the Roman Catholic church was undertaking with other churches. At the same time, however, the Protestant churches were marked by a remarkable lack of interest in the questions posed to them on the basis of their own presuppositions. Intensive as participation in the ecumenical dialogue was, the critical discussion with their own tradition remained unsatisfactory. What does the Reformation mean today in circumstances which have been changed by the ecumenical movement? How have the Protestant churches to perceive their task? What *aggiornamento* have they to achieve in doctrine and life? The Protestant churches could not give a common answer to these questions as churches. For all their theological vision they therefore remained remarkably unchanged because so much remained unresolved; in many respects their internal tensions and conflicts were even sharper. As churches, the Protestant churches were becoming immobile.

How could this happen? The most important reason is probably that the Protestant churches find it extremely difficult to act as churches. And to cope even to some degree with the questions raised by the Second Vatican Council and their own historical experience would take something like a 'Protestant Council'. But how could that come about? On what common basis could the Protestant churches embark on dialogue? And do they understand themselves sufficiently as one church to be motivated for such an enterprise? Küng began in his speech from the assumption that in response to the opening of the Roman Catholic church towards the Protestant churches, precisely the same movement could take place in reverse, namely that Protestant Christians could begin to take their membership of the church more seriously. He spoke of the reductions of the biblical message which lead to individualism, and pleaded for a deeper understanding of the eucharist. He argued for the significance of authority and church office, even the Petrine office. Do not the churches of the Reformation 'still hypostasize the authority of Jesus Christ as the only authority in the church? And in this way is not any church authority easily suspect as un-Christian authoritarianism, so that the problem of authority which now exists in the church, and which is different from that of a political democracy, is in fact overlooked? So in conflicts within the Protestant churches is there not often an evident weakness on the part of those holding office in the church, which in contrast to Roman over-direction tends towards under-direction? Who in fact speaks authoritatively for the churches of the Reformation? Who makes binding statements for the Reformed church of Switzerland? Does it help us to be told that scripture alone rules in the

Protestant church and that there is really no ministry, when this does not correspond to reality?'[17] The questions are all justified, but at the same time it is clear how infinitely difficult it is to realize these demands for greater ecclesial awareness. The spirit of a new start which prevailed in the time after the Second Vatican Council points, rather, in the opposite direction. In this atmosphere how could a new approach to the significance of *communio* be found? In order to be equipped to cope with the great questions together, the Protestant churches would have to learn in more than one respect to leap over their own shadows.

Nevertheless the task remains an unavoidable one. If the Protestant churches want to play a constructive part in the ecumenical movement, in the long run they cannot avoid the task of together achieving greater clarity about their role. They must meet together for common counselling. There must be something like a Protestant council, in whatever form, so that the Reformation heritage can be related to the present. The questions raised by the tradition which is grounded in the Reformation have not been superseded by the ecumenical movement. They remain relevant to all churches. But they have to be interpreted and brought up to date if they are to be heard. Real renewal will only be possible as a result of a new beginning by the churches.

The need for this task has become even more evident as a result of Küng's condemnation. Before this there could still be the hope that the unity of the church could be regained step by step, that the separated churches would gradually come closer together, and, after a time in which they had shared more and more with each other, would finally be able to recognize one another as that one church which leaves the confessions behind them and transcends them. Küng's condemnation finally showed that this expectation was an illusion. It showed that the differences in the understanding of the church, its authority and its witness are too deep to be combined in the same communion. The controversy has to be carried further for the sake of truth and communion, and the Protestant churches have to make their contribution to that.

For countless Protestants, Küng's condemnation was a welcome signal of a return to the old familiar confessional positions. 'Haven't we always said that the Catholic church will never change?' But remarkably, the number of those who did not allow themselves to be affected by the condemnation, but continued in their official ecumenical activities as though nothing had happened, was also great. Instead of seeing the condemnation as a 'Rome case', they also spoke of a 'Küng case'. Even today they guard against any criticism, in order not to disturb the 'good climate' which has been achieved so far. They add dialogue to dialogue as though that could change something in praxis. They pay courtesy visits to the pope and afterwards praise in well-drafted communiqués the constructive atmosphere which prevailed at them. Who can wonder if the supreme authority of the Roman Catholic church comes to the conclusion that the view of the church put forward by the Reformers has now in fact become groundless? Who can wonder if even Protestant Christians are so unclear about the voice of their own church that because of a decision of the pope which they cannot accept they leave – the Protestant church?

Neither the sterile confessionalism nor the uncritical ecumenism of the diehards will do justice to the situation which has arisen today. Only the wearisome and in many respects almost impassable way of reunion by conciliar process will really take the ecumenical movement further.

4. How long?

How are we to judge the prospects for the future? Will the hardening of fronts be only transitory, or have barriers become visible which can no longer be shifted? Has the ecumenical movement only been shown into a waiting-room, or has it come up against a firm rock which has to be reckoned with at all times?

Both alternatives are conceivable. There are good reasons for supposing that Rome's 'no' is no more than a cloud which must finally give way to the sun of stronger arguments. It is evident that Küng's view is now increasingly shared by thinking members of the Roman Catholic church, and it is hard to imagine that this growing theological consensus will allow itself to be suppressed permanently. The hour must come in which the 'no' has lost too much of its plausibility to be capable of being sustained. On the other hand, the weight of the tradition must not be underestimated. As we have seen, these theses of Küng's make deep inroads into the self-understanding of the Roman Catholic church. Precisely for that reason they open up such far-reaching new perspectives for the ecumenical movement, because they put in question the closed nature of the existing system. Will not this shake-up go too far? Is it not more probable that the question of the possibility of infallible statements will continue to be treated as a tabu?

Who knows which of these two scenarios is to be reckoned with? Küng himself seems to be convinced that the page will turn again. He writes: 'The achievement of a primacy of service calls for patience and undeterred commitment. There is no doubt that it will be realized in one form or another. The only question is whether once again it will be too late and thus with great losses.'[18]

This last remark is important. The time after the Second Vatican Council was something like a *kairos* for the churches. It has not really been exhausted. Presumably it will not occur again in precisely the same way. There will be further new experiences. The churches will have to cope with questions which they have not faced before. A new image of the church will be imposed on them. The changes that they have to tackle will be so far-reaching that the attempt to demonstrate the unbroken continuity of the church over the centuries will become a complete illusion. Rather, each, from its own tradition, will have to trust the Spirit which leads them into a future that was not foreseen in any of the divided traditions. What image, for example, will emerge from the insights of feminist theology? It can now already be said that the traditional views of authority in the church have been deeply put in question by criticism of the patriarchal order. What is the meaning of being the church in the multiplicity of cultures? Even now, it can be said that in a church of the future a much greater multiplicity in doctrine, theology and praxis must be reckoned with than the individual confessions are ready to accept today. What does a church look like which enters unconditionally into dialogue with the religions? It can already be said that it must renounce any attempt to lay down the limits of the world with a clarity which has already been decided. What does it mean to be the church in a world in which the victims of injustice and violence are on the increase? Even now it can be said that its credibility will be measured by its readiness for real solidarity, by the fact that in its midst it 'does not allow love to grow cold'. And above all, what does it mean to be the church in view of the fact that the survival of humankind and countless animals on this planet has become uncertain and that we cannot rule out an end which we have brought down upon ourselves?

None of the confessional traditions has ready answers to these questions. They must all insist that the future is in some respects open. 'We may not allow ourselves already to lay down a fixed form for the church. Whether the church of the future is large or small, institutionally stronger or charismatically more varied, whether it is a church of pastoral ministries or the decisive church community, whether the possibilities mentioned are alternatives at all, is something which lies in our hand only conditionally, as long as we do not know the form of future humanity.'[19]

The ecumenical movement came into being because here and there people listened to the one word of God. Things will be no different in this open future.

Notes

1. H. Küng, *The Council and Reunion*, 279.
2. H. Küng, *Justification*, xlf.
3. Ibid., xlii.
4. Ibid., 102f.
5. H. Küng, *Freiheit des Christen*, 113.
6. H. Küng, 'Konzil – Ende oder Anfang?', *Civitas* 20, 1964–5, 188–200.
7. *Councils and the Ecumenical Movement*, Studies of the World Council of Churches V, Geneva 1968.
8. H. Küng, *The Church Maintained in Truth*, 13.

9. N. Greinacher and H. Haag (eds.,), *Der Fall Küng. Eine Dokumentation*, Munich 1980, 88.

10. Küng, *The Church Maintained in Truth*, 21.

11. Ibid., 33.

12. Ibid., 20.

13. Ibid., 23.

14. Ibid., 31. Among other things, the Dialogue Commission between the Reformed World Alliance and the Roman Catholic Church took up the question of the significance of the event of the Reformation in the history of individual churches. The discussion proved difficult in every respect. Formulations which at first took things forward soon had to be given up. What was left was the statement that 'God's Word played a part in the event of the Reformation'. Another was immediately added: 'Not everything that happened can be attributed to the Word, because human sin also played its part in the separation.' From this the meaningless conclusion was drawn: 'As Roman Catholic and Reformed Christians we must not attempt to justify ourselves. We must all take responsibility for our own pasts and the element of the sin that we have committed.' The real question remains unanswered. Cf. H. Meyer et al. (eds.), *Dokumente wachsender Übereinstimmung* II, *1982–1990*, Paderborn and Frankfurt 1992, 656ff.

15. Congregation for the Doctrine of Faith, *Letter to the Bishops of the Catholic Church on Some Aspects of the Church as Communio*, 28 May 1992, 18.

16. H. Küng, 'Anfragen an die Reformation heute', *Reformatio* 27, 1978, 374–93.

17. Ibid., 383.

18. Quoted in W. von Loewenich, 'Ist Küng noch katholisch?', in H. Küng (ed.), *Fehlbar? Eine Bilanz*, 17.

19. Küng, 'Anfragen an die Reformation heute', 391.

Johannes Brosseder

Consensus in Justification Faith without Consensus in the Understanding of the Church? The Significance of the Dispute over Justification Today

Those who are concerned with the doctrine of justification, or more precisely with belief in justification, are not concerned only with one significant theological topic among others, but rather with the centre of Christian faith. They are concerned with the gospel of the mercy of God on the sinner; they are concerned with the fact that God bestows his righteousness on human beings, and in the cross of Jesus Christ has 'drowned' human sin; human beings do not achieve salvation by praising themselves for their works and merits before God, an activity in which they worship themselves; human beings achieve salvation only by acknowledging in faith the salvation bestowed on them in Christ by God. Such faith makes human works the place of the glorification of God and not a place of self-worship. The acknowledgment of God's divinity by human beings everywhere and in all places, also in the church and through themselves, is what God 'requires' of them. Jesus Christ has fulfilled this demand; in faith we shall have a share in this fulfilled demand; in faith, at any rate, human beings confess that they are not God and therefore cannot surround themselves with a divine aura: everyone's place is among their fellow human beings and not on God's throne.

1. The Reformation belief in justification and its Catholic fate

That also applies in the church. Here it is possible to see how the doctrine of justification is the cornerstone of Christian faith and works itself out in all spheres of human and interpersonal life. That also explains why everything else in theology and church depends on it. Anyone who is concerned with it is concerned with the heart of Christian faith and at the same time with the theme which in the sixteenth century brought about the collapse of church community within Western Christianity that has lasted to the present day. The break in church community was completed by Pope Leo X on 3 January 1521 by the bull *Decet Romanum Pontificem*, in which Martin Luther and his followers were excommunicated.

So there can be no dispute over whose is the historical responsibility for the announcement of the breakdown of church community; to foist it on the

Reformers was a tendency which dominated Catholic church history writing and Catholic dogmatics until deep into this century.[1] In the more harmless versions of this the Reformers were portrayed as heresiarchs, heretics, innovators and deliberate destroyers of church community. In the worse versions the penally relevant circumstances of the defamation were filled out. But in both versions the subsequent history of Protestantism was understood and evaluated only as the history of an ever-increasing apostasy from faith. Here the Reformers' doctrine of justification was made responsible for all the ecclesiastical and secular evils of modern times.

Of course this Roman Catholic cliché could not be sustained in the long run, since it manifestly did not correspond to the historical facts. It was Joseph Lortz[2] who in his work *The Reformation in Germany* (1939/40) introduced a shift in the presentation of the Reformation in Catholic church history writings; though this was unmistakably indebted to the traditional Roman Catholic church system and did not put it in question, it was capable of a fairer assessment of the events of the Reformation and did not spare its criticism of the state of the church in the sixteenth century. Initially, this shift in church history was not yet reflected in the systematic presentation of dogma as a whole. Granted, already in the 1920s, 1930s and 1940s some French- and German-speaking Catholic systematic theologians had entered into a critical discussion of Reformation theology, but this was almost exclusively concerned with the theology of Karl Barth and 'dialectical theology'. Moreover, here and there some theological interest could be found in the ecumenical movement, in 'Life and Work' and 'Faith and Order'. And there was the 'Una Sancta' movement, condescendingly mocked by some clergy and theologians because it was mainly supported by laity. But these were still peripheral to Catholic theology and the church as a whole. The church of those years was too much under the spell of anti-Protestant and anti-modernist theology and felt obligated to the Roman, centralistic and papalistic ecclesiology of the era of the Pius popes. Some theologians had combined this with romantic ideas about popular thought and an exaggerated incarnational christology in which the church as it was liked to present itself as an unassailable divine and human bulwark in the midst of a godless and hostile world.

And yet this era saw the beginning of theological studies and church practices which were to lead to a decisive turning point for the Catholic church in dealing with the churches of the Reformation and evaluating them theologically. Louis Malevez, Yves Congar, Jerôme Hamer, Karl Adam, Erich Przywara, Robert Grosche, Gottlieb Söhngen,[3] Hans Urs von Balthasar, Heinrich Fries and Hans Küng deserve special mention here. In particular, Gottlieb Söhngen's reflections on the *analogia fidei* and *analogia entis* from the 1930s, which caused Karl Barth great astonishment as early as 1940, prepared the ground for Hans Urs von Balthasar's 1951 work on Karl Barth[4] and Heinrich Fries's book on Bultmann, Barth and Catholic theology in 1955.[5]

However, it was Hans Küng[6] who, in his theological dissertation prepared in Rome and presented in Paris, turned to the central theme of the Protestant-Catholic controversy and made the doctrine of justification the topic of his first work. *Justification. The Doctrine of Karl Barth and a Catholic Reflection. With an introductory letter by Karl Barth* appeared for the first time in 1957, then in a fourth edition – with excursus – in 1964, and finally in a new impression in paperback in 1986 with a long new preface on the theme 'Justification today' and the address given by Hans Küng on the death of Karl Barth at the memorial service in Basel Cathedral in 1968.

2. Justification and its effect

Küng's book was the starting signal for a whole series of ecumenical studies on the doctrine of justification (or, more precisely, on justification faith) which, like Hans Küng, investigated the question whether because of this doctrine, which in the sixteenth century led to the breaking off of church communion by the church of Rome, the churches had to continue as they did before their division, or whether a theological consensus is not possible here. In his book, Küng made an attempt to investigate the Catholic tradition, and especially the Tridentine decree on justification, in the light of Karl Barth's doctrine of justification, to see whether it could stand up to Barth's questions, and to compare Barth's doctrine of justification with the traditional Catholic accents in order to see whether it took account of them. The conclusion Küng comes to is in both instances positive: 'there is a fundamental agreement ... between Karl Barth's position and that of the Catholic church in regard to the theology of justification seen in its totality'.[7]

The perplexity at this result was universally great: Karl Barth openly conceded it in the letter to Hans Küng which served as a preface to the book,[8] but at the same time confirmed: 'If what you have presented in Part Two of this book is actually the teaching of the Roman Catholic Church, then I must certainly admit that my view of justification corresponds with the Roman Catholic view; if only for the reason that the Roman Catholic teaching would then be most strikingly in accord with mine.'[9] Despite some detailed criticism, Hans Küng nevertheless found very broad assent among Catholic theologians to his account of the Roman Catholic doctrine, which has at least been seen as one alongside others which are possible. Hans Küng could not have achieved this result by his study had he not subjected all the confessional traditions and profiles in the understanding of justification to the verdict of Holy Scripture.

In 1957, Hans Küng compared the doctrine of the Council of Trent in the sixteenth century with the doctrine of the most significant Reformed theologian of the twentieth century, i.e. with that of Karl Barth. Stimulated by his study, ten years later Otto Hermann Pesch[10] investigated the theology of justification of the one who was the occasion for the Council of Trent, namely Martin Luther, and compared it with the doctrine of grace in Thomas Aquinas, who is regarded as the the embodiment of typically scholastic (Roman-) Catholic theological thought. The result of Pesch's investigation of the theology of justification in Martin Luther and Thomas Aquinas runs: 'As for the circle of questions discussed, a reciprocal anathema between Luther and Thomas is neither necessary nor responsible. On the proviso that in all the questions presented Thomas gives the teaching of the church and is rightly interpreted here, it must be judged that while Luther's doctrine of the justification of the sinner leaves the ground of the theology of his time and the previous period, it does not enter any new ground which would be prohibited to the Catholic theologian.'[11] Pesch sees the difference between Luther and Thomas in the different structures of the thought of the two theologians, namely the 'existential theology' of the Reformer and the 'sapiential theology' of Thomas. Each theologian has his Christian credentials. 'A reciprocal anathema with respect to theological structures as such would not be concentration here, but impoverishment.'[12]

With Pesch's investigation, high-scholastic Catholic theology, too, entered into a basic discussion of the original form of Lutheran Reformation theology. The studies of Hans Küng and Otto Hermann Pesch arrive at similar results. The result is understood as 'consensus on the doctrine of justification' and is a challenge to the churches. This consensus can no longer be banished from officious and official ecumenical conversations. It governs – to mention only three documents here – the 1972 'Malta Report' of the Evangelical Lutheran/ Roman Catholic Study Commission 'The Gospel and the Church'.[13] This states: 'Starting from the question of the centre of the gospel the question arises of the mutual understanding of justification. The traditional controversial theological disputes were given a particularly sharp profile at this point. Today there is a wide-ranging consensus over the interpretation of justification. Catholic theologians, too, stress in the question of justification that no conditions are attached to the saving gift of God for believers. The Lutheran theologians emphasize that the event of justification is not limited to the individual forgiveness of sins, and do not see in it a purely external declaration of the sinner as righteous. Rather, through the message of justification the righteousness of God realized in the Christ event is transferred to sinners as a reality which embraces them and as a result is the foundation of the new life of believers. In this sense justification can be understood as the overall expression of the saving event.'[14]

The Malta Report also rightly stresses that the confession of justification subjects all church traditions and institutions to the criterion of making possible the right proclamation of the gospel and not obscuring the unconditional character of the reception of salvation. 'It follows from this that church ordinances and rites may not be imposed as conditions of salvation, but can only be valid as a free development of the obedience of faith.'[15] We shall return in due course to the questions of the theological status of the consensus over the doctrine of justification and of whether the consequences for the life and doctrine of the churches are assessed equally on both sides – the Malta Report raises both questions explicitly.

The consensus in the confession of justification also dominates the 1986 study document 'Do Doctrinal Condemnations Divide the Churches?'[16] of the Joint Ecumenical Commission of the Council of the Evangelical Church in Germany and the German Conference of Bishops, in which the reciprocal condemnations of the sixteenth century on the topics of justification, sacraments and ministry were investigated to see whether these really did justice to the specific 'opponents' of the time and whether they must still be maintained today. The document says no to both questions. It states: 'As for the understanding of the justification of the sinner, the reciprocal ... statements of repudiation in the sixteenth century no longer apply to today's partner in such a way as to divide the church. This conclusion has all the more weight since historical insight into the dispute of the time shows that in many respects it did not relate to what the contemporary opponent really meant. Today, at any rate, both partners have learnt to listen to each other in a self-critical way. So each understands better what the other means, no longer engages in shadow-boxing and is careful to express itself in such a way that his partner does not misunderstand him but can recognize his special "concern", even though he himself cannot fall in with the other's mode of thought and expression. The doctrine of justification always has a specific function: to remind Christians that we sinners live only from the forgiving love of God. And this is a love which we only allow ourselves to be given; we in no way "deserve" it, in however qualified a way, nor can we attach prior or subsequent conditions to it. The "doctrine of justification" thus becomes the critical criterion by which all must ask themselves whether they can claim the name Christian for a specific interpretation of our relationship to God. At the same time it becomes the critical criterion for the church, by which it has to allow itself to be assessed at all times, to see whether its proclamation and praxis correspond to what is presented to it by our Lord.'[17]

Finally, consensus over the doctrine of justification is a mark of the 1986 Agreed Statement by the Second Anglican-Roman Catholic International Commission (ARCIC II): *Salvation and the Church*.[18] This states: 'The balance and coherence of the constituent elements of the Christian doctrine of salvation had become partially obscured in the course of history and controversy. In our work we have tried to rediscover that balance and coherence and to express it together. We are agreed that this is not an area where any remaining differences of theological interpretation or ecclesiological emphasis, either within or between our Communions, can justify our continuing separation. We believe that our two Communions are agreed on the essential aspects of the doctrine of salvation and on the Church's role within it. We have also realized the central meaning and profound significance which the message of justification and sanctification, within the whole doctrine of salvation, continues to have for us today.'[19]

Anyone who reads the texts will first be aware of the major changes and the tremendous effect in depth and breadth of the influence which Hans Küng began to exercise in 1957 with his first writing. This would not have been possible without the biblical foundation which marks out Hans Küng's theological reflection. Even now, this biblical profile has remained an outstanding characteristic of his theological reflection.

3. The situation in church and theology in the late 1950s

After this survey of the history of its influence, let us return once again to Hans Küng's book *Justification*. The theological and ecumenical significance of this book for its time can be assessed only if we duly take into account the situation of the Roman Catholic church in the 1950s. This was the late phase of the era of Pius XII. At that time everyone took it for granted that this era would be continued under a successor. In the era of the Pius popes, no one conceived of a church which would open the window and let in fresh air, a church which did not condemn but listened, a church which wrote conversion, penitence, renewal and reform on its banners, a church of brotherhood and sisterhood and collegiality, a church of ecumenical openness, a church which prescribed dialogue for itself, a church which took the side of the oppressed, the persecuted, the exploited, and lent its voice to those who had no voice, the sort of church which John XXIII and the Second Vatican Council and Hans Küng had a leading share in shaping, which set about giving itself a tangible form. It lay completely outside the perspective of the time.

It is only against this background that Hans Küng's extraordinary theological achievement in his first work is to be seen. At a distance of around thirty-five years after its first publication, of course we can now see even more clearly – and we need no special gifts for that art – how much of the Roman, i.e. the particular and therefore non-Catholic, eggshells of the time this book still has about it. Hans Küng was only later to be able to free himself from these. However, the reason for the effect that he had in this work of 1957 already lies in the absolute bond of theology and church to the word of God in Holy Scripture. This already made it speak in a variety of tones depending on the topic: the doctrinal tradition of the church and its normative character, the church's *magisterium* and the way in which it binds theologians, the primacy of the pope, the position of Mary in the history of salvation, the efficacy of the sacraments, the natural knowledge of God and so on (the specific topics are still discussed in a markedly apologetic way[20] – though not with facile apologetic).[21]

Some criticism of Reformation, especially Lutheran, positions still has no less apologetic a colouring. And in 1986, as already in 1957, Hans Küng still finds it difficult to get into writings of Luther's like *De servo arbitrio* and the *Sermon on Good Works*.[22]. We also find one confessional cliché or another, like the cliché of the isolated Protestant theologian who is left to rely only on himself, and who painfully lacks an ultimate bond in obedience and faith as compared with the Catholic theologian who, often in very sensitive subordination to the *magisterium* of the church, gives concrete expression to what it means 'to rely faithfully, in obedience and free commitment, on grace, on the Word of Jesus Christ which rules in and through the Church'.[23] And in 1957 Hans Küng still had not brought out clearly enough the explosiveness of the inner connection between the doctrine of justification and the understanding of the church. So with apparent unconcern he can still write: 'Through the church, in faith the individual shares in universal justification. So justification as it has taken place in Christ's death and resurrection has an essentially ecclesiological character.'[24]

Does the doctrine of justification really determine ecclesiology here, or does not ecclesiology rather determine the doctrine of justification? Küng also wonders why Karl Barth can draw such 'false' conclusions in his understanding of the church from his 'correct' doctrine of justification. He makes three factors responsible for that: the bias inherent in any theology, the polemically one-sided Catholic accounts of the understanding of the church and the discrepancy between Catholic doctrine and the Catholic life which disavows it.[25] If the explosiveness of the ecclesiological consequences of the consensus over the doctrine of justification had already been clear to him at that time, the result of the book on justification must inevitably have been that Catholic theology and Karl Barth are in fundamental agreement on the doctrine of justification and therefore they are also agreed that the church is pure instrumentality.[26] But in 1957 it cannot yet be said that Hans Küng has any understanding of the church as pure instrumentality, despite many pointers in this direction; though he can still say that 'one ought not to make demands from the Protestant side which do not seriously see the incarnation and the church as a divine-*human* configuration'.[27]

The 'human' in 'divine-human' has rightly been put in italics by Hans Küng because of its context: however, there is no doubt that at that time Küng could still speak of the church as a divine-human structure, especially as he speaks explicitly of incarnation in an ecclesiological and not a christological context. 'Church as a divine-human configuration' and 'church as pure instrumentality' are not mutually exclusive. The sacraments pose no objection to such a view, as these are not of the church, but in the common conviction of all Western churches of Jesus Christ himself. He is their Lord, not the church.

The church has to dispense them on his conditions, not its own. How far the Roman Catholic church is still removed from this insight, which also applies to it, is still the ecumenical crux in the theme of eucharistic communion, though this crux was caused by human beings, is perpetuated by human beings, and really has nothing to do with the cross of Jesus Christ. But the official church is fond of making such a connection. In the sacraments, too, the church as pure instrumentality makes its appearance and puts a large question-mark against all talk of the sacramentality of the church, which means more than pure instrumentality.

The critical perspectives mentioned so far have not been cited to show 'the weaknesses' in Hans Küng's *Justification*; they have been mentioned to show what difficult areas had to be covered. Hans Küng has had the courage to discuss the centre of the controversy between Protestants and Catholics pertinently, systematically and dogmatically: bringing together what had gone before, he has entered new theological territory and thus has taken a powerful ecumenical step forward. As was indicated above, since then the theme of justification has been *the* ecumenical theme, whether discussed openly or tacitly underlying all else. And here the Catholic church has not yet really discovered what it has to return to.

4. The consequence – the church as pure instrumentality

Hans Küng took a step forward that many still had to follow. Because he took this step, a first beginning could be made on reflecting above all on its ecclesiological consequences. Many people today think (still or already) in the way in which Hans Küng thought in 1957. Others have not yet even reached his state of knowledge in 1957 or have again fallen behind it. Hans Küng himself – evidently following the intrinsic tug of justification faith – was also quite specifically concerned with the theological questions of the church in the further course of his theological work: *The Council and Reunion. Renewal as a Call to Unity* (1960), *Structures of the Church* (1962), *The Living Church* (1963), *The Church* (1967), *Truthfulness. The Future of the Church* (1968), *Infallible? An Enquiry* (1970), *Why Priests? A Proposal for a New Church Ministry* (1971), *On Being a Christian* (1974), *Signposts for the Future* (1980).

Five perspectives are particularly important for the question of justification discussed in these books which are concerned with the church:
1. Ecclesiological statements are given a biblical foundation.
2. (Roman) Catholic doctrine is in accord with, or can be brought into accord with, the testimony of holy Scripture.
3. The praxis of the (Roman) Catholic church at the level of episcopal and papal ministry (John XXIII excepted) is often in flagrant contradiction to the biblical testimony and the church's own teaching. For example, in these books

Hans Küng leaves no doubt about the need for a 'Petrine service,' a papal primacy, as a service to the unity of the church as a whole. However, equally he makes it unmistakably clear that such a service can be provided only by a papacy which is renewed in the light of the gospel, and therefore cannot and may not present itself as the 'power of Peter'.

4. The ecclesiological questions are not explicitly subordinated to the criterion of the article on justification.

5. The concepts of the church as a 'divine-human' essence or a 'divine-human' reality, the church as an 'ongoing Christ' or as an 'extension of the incarnation' are explicitly rejected because they are open to misunderstanding – in contrast to Küng's book on justification.[28]

Anyone who is concerned with the theology of justification in general and that of Martin Luther in particular is immediately confronted with its ecclesiological consequences. So those who note the consensus in the doctrine of justification must also be able to note a consensus in the understanding of the church; if that proves impossible, then they are still far from sharing a consensus in the doctrine of justification.[29] At present the ecumenical dialogue of the churches is still hooked into this theme; because of that the ecumenical movement is stagnant, and even the smallest concrete steps towards church reconciliation are officially rejected by the Roman Catholic side.[30] In other words, the present Roman Catholic church does not find it particularly difficult by and large to speak of a consensus in the doctrine of justification, but it still continues to differ over *its understanding of the church*. This attitude has to do with a fatal distinction which arises out of more recent Roman Catholic church history. In 1970 Hubert Jedin could still write: 'In the past twenty years I have often said and written that in my view the gulf which divided Catholics and Protestants from one another did not lie in the doctrine of justification but in the sphere of the concept of the church.'[31] And as late as 1982 Erwin Iserloh wrote: 'It is not the "Reformation element", i.e. justification by faith, which divides the churches, nor even Luther's criticism of the church of his time, which necessarily derives from it, but his views of the church, the papacy, councils and priesthood – positions which he took up on the basis of the controversies of 1518/19. They put him outside the church of the time and even today still divide the churches ... Who will deny that ... in the question of the *magisterium* down to the present day that is a decisive – if not *the* decisive – question between Protestant and Catholic theology?'[32]

Evidently Catholic church history could only put things in this way because it did not see the significance of the criterion of justification faith as it had been unmistakably formulated by the Reformers for theological doctrine, for the traditions, orders and institutions of church and worship, and for the whole of church life. For the Catholic church, the article of justification is one article of faith among many others, which evidently has nothing to do with church orders, traditions and institutions; distinctive biblical origins are sought and found to legitimate these, even if they are presented in a somewhat forced way. However, the confession of justification means that for example all the church traditions, institutions, ordinances and rites are to be tested by the criterion whether they enable the true proclamation of the gospel and do not obscure the unconditional character of the reception of salvation. They may not be imposed as conditions of salvation. This is put well in the Malta report mentioned above, or can be read in almost every work of Martin Luther's.

There is no question that the true proclamation of the gospel can also come about through the present Roman Catholic church with its episcopal and papal ministry, and that the unconditional nature of the reception of salvation need not necessarily be obscured in it. Therefore it is completely legitimate for Hans Küng and Otto Hermann Pesch to call on the validity of Holy Scripture (Küng and Pesch) and the article of justification (Pesch) for the praxis of the church, since both theologians are convinced that its doctrine can in principle withstand this. But it is theologically unacceptable for this church officially to put forward the view that the church can achieve what the church is there for only through its tradition, the institution and order of the offices of bishop and pope, and not through other traditions, institutions and ordinances. This is the point at which the decision is taken as to whether the church really understands itself as pure instrumentality, or in a different way. If it under-stands itself as pure instrumentality, there is also consensus over the doctrine of justification; and in that case the church would have no problem in understanding other forms of church ministry, synodical structures of decision, etc. as another way of expressing itself as pure instrumentality.

In principle this means that, for example, the office of bishop does not constitute the apostolicity of the church but seeks to express it; it means that the apostolicity of the church can also be expressed in another way than through this office. The decisive thing is for the church to persist in the faith of the apostles. The 'guarantee' for that is the Holy Spirit and not some eternal form of an episcopal office, which cannot really be understood as the divine preliminary gift of a church structure which is therefore indispensable. Specifically, to understand the church as pure instrumentality also means that there must be completely new reflection on what Hans Küng describes as the 'Petrine service'. In his ecclesiological studies Hans Küng has argued vehe-mently for a Petrine service as service to the unity of the 'church as a whole'. This primacy is more than a mere 'primacy of honour' and it is also more than a 'primacy of jurisdiction'; it is a primacy of service, and not a primacy of power in the unity of the whole church.

It seems to me that this 'primacy of service', too, as merely a particular tradition of the Roman church, must be given a rest: it should not be forced on either the Orthodox or the Protestants; it can no longer even be forced on the Roman Catholic church and its members in this way. Throughout the whole of the second Christian millennium – apart from many other historical services to which Hans Küng also refers explicitly[33] – it has merely been the cause of the collapse of church communion and so far has constantly 'served' this. Whether an institution which for a thousand years has done the precise opposite to what by its own self-understanding it was 'really' provided to do can still serve the communion of Christian churches today seems to me to be more than questionable.[34] For too long the proof of its unsuitability for the task to which it lays claim has seemed to me to be obvious.

Nor is such a 'service' urgently required in the light either of the New Testament or of the life of the early church. Since personalities like John XXIII who might have succeeded in performing such a 'service' cannot be institutionalized, the institution itself must be put in question. How and in what way the Christian churches are to give expression to their future communion, the communion which exists between them, must be left for them to clarify. Here the notion of 'conciliarity' still perhaps has a promising future, since the papacy as an institution has proved incapable of solving this task. The Christian churches which have moved towards a restoration of communion between them do not need guarantees against schism.

One last example might be mentioned of the understanding of the church as pure instrumentality, namely the admission of women to all the ministries of the church. The criterion of the article of justification cannot accept any reason for excluding women from access to the ministries of the church. How much church traditions and ordinances seem to have the status of a condition of salvation here emerges indirectly from a letter from Pope John Paul II to the Archbishop of Canterbury, the ecumenical warmth of which can hardly be exceeded. 'Of course' it was sent on 8 December (1988), the feast of the Immaculate Conception. In it the pope, who is responsible for the present breaking off of Orthodox/Roman Catholic relations, writes that, like the Orthodox church and the ancient churches of the East, the Catholic church is firmly against the ordination of women and their consecration to the episcopate; it sees this as a break with tradition – such a break that the Catholic church cannot assent to it. The ordination of women to the priesthood in some provinces of the Anglican Communion and the recognition of the right of some provinces to proceed to the ordination of women to the episcopate really blocks the way to a mutual recognition of ministries. That such a text has become an integral part of the 1990 Agreed Statement by ARCIC II, 'Church as Communion', in which it is said of the eucharist that it unites men and women of every race, culture and social status in every generation, is the expression of an irresponsible unwillingness to listen and an insult to ordained women. That a similar passage also occurs in the 'Joint Declaration' of John Paul II and Archbishop Robert Runcie (2 October 1989) bears witness to the stubbornness with which the exclusion of women from the ministries of the church is regarded as a condition of salvation. Here it is said that the admission of women to the priesthood hinders reconciliation between the

Anglican Communion and the Roman Catholic church even where there is agreement on the eucharist and ministry. If the article on justification were really in force, there would be a sharper insight into how to distinguish appropriately between what can and what cannot appropriately be dispensed with in the church and how the church should understand itself as pure instrumentality.

The three specific themes mentioned above and the way in which they are dealt with makes it clear how fundamentally they disavow ecclesiological consensus in the doctrine of justification and virtually scorn it. Anyone who allows ecclesiology to be the criterion of the reconciliation or non-reconciliation of churches and refuses this role to justification faith has not even begun to take part in the human work of the restoration of the communion of the Christian churches by removing obstacles which have been put, and are still put, in the way of this communion. If the ecclesiological questions in the last resort are to be excluded from the consensus in the confession of justification, then at any rate there can no longer be serious talk of a consensus in the confession of justification. What was begun so impressively by Hans Küng in a difficult time would then prove to be ineffective. The *perennis reformatio* of the church would finally degenerate into a pious, meaningless phrase, and the ecumene could hardly be dismissed more emphatically – and that only a few years after a council which wanted to see the mobilization of all spiritual and intellectual forces for the restoration of the communion between the Christian churches. The spiritual criterion for the doctrine and action of a church on the way to the communion of churches is still faith in justification as the *articulus stantis et cadentis ecclesiae.*[35]

Notes

1. For Catholic dogmatics see A. Hasler, *Luther in der katholischen Dogmatik. Darstellung seiner Rechtfertigungslehre in den katholischen Dogmatikbüchern*, Beiträge zur Ökumenischen Theologie Vol. 2, Munich 1968.
2. J. Lortz, *Die Reformation in Deutschland*, reprinted with an Afterword by P. Manns, Freiburg, Basel and Vienna ⁶1982 (first edition in two vols., 1939/40).
3. For instances see H. Küng, *Justification*, above all 320–2.
4. H.U. von Balthasar, *The Theology of Karl Barth*, ET New York 1956.
5. H. Fries, *Bultmann – Barth und die katholische Theologie*, Stuttgart 1955.
6. See n.3.
7. Küng, *Justification*, 277f.
8. Ibid., xxxix–xlii.
9. Ibid., xi.
10. O.H. Pesch, *Die Theologie der Rechtfertigung bei Martin Luther und Thomas von Aquin. Versuch eines systematisch-theologischen Dialogs*, Mainz 1967.
11. Ibid., 950.

12. Ibid., 948.
13. Report of the Evangelical Lutheran/Roman Catholic study commission *Das Evangelium und die Kirche*, 1972, in *Dokumente wachsender Übereinstimmung. Sämtliche Berichte und Konsenstexte interkonfessioneller Gespräche auf Weltebene 1931–1982*, edited with an introduction by Harding Meyer, Hansjörg Urban and Lukas Vischer, Paderborn and Frankfurt am Main 1983, 248–71 (abbreviated as Malta Report in DWU I).
14. Malta Report in DWU I, 255.
15. Ibid.
16. Ecumenical Working Party of Protestant and Catholic Theologians, *Lehrverurteilungen – Kirchentrennend?*, Vol. I, *Rechtfertigung, Sakramente und Amt im Zeitalter der Reformation und heute*, ed. K. Lehmann and W. Pannenberg, Freiburg im Breisgau and Göttingen 1989.
17. *Lehrverurteilungen – kirchentrennend?*, I, 35.
18. *Salvation and the Church. An Agreed Statement by the Second Anglican-Roman Catholic International Commission* (ARCIC II), London 1987.
19. Ibid., 26f.
20. Küng, *Justification*, 121.
21. Cf. Küng, *Justification*, 99–122, above all 12ff., 278–82, etc.
22. Ibid., xiif.
23. Ibid., 121; cf. 120f.
24. Ibid., 225 (the English translation crucially omits 'through the church'!).
25. Ibid., 278–82.
26. I have taken over this apt term from Otto Hermann Pesch; see O.H. Pesch, *Gerechtfertigt aus Glauben. Luthers Frage an die Kirche*, Quaestiones Disputatae 97, Freiburg, Basel and Vienna 1982, 83; see also *Lumen Gentium* 1, second sentence.
27. Küng, *Justification*, 121.
28. H. Küng, *The Church*, 237, 239; cf. 203–60. Two further contributions by Hans Küng on the theme of justification are still worth reading: 'Rechtfertigung und Heiligung nach dem Neuen Testament', in *Begegnung der Christen. Studien evangelischer und katholischer Theologen. Festschrift Otto Karrer*, ed. M. Roesle and O. Cullmann, Stuttgart and Frankfurt am Main 1959, 249–70; 'Katholische Besinnung auf Luthers Rechtfertigungslehre heute', in *Theologie im Wandel. Festschrift zum 150jährigen Bestehen der Katholisch-Theologischen Fakultät an der Universität Tübingen*, ed. Katholisch-Theologischen Fakultät an der Universität Tübingen, Munich and Freiburg im Breisgau 1967, 449–68.
29. See in detail Pesch, *Gerechtfertigt aus Glauben* (n.26 above); also J. Brosseder, 'Martin Luther', in *Klassiker der Theologie I: Von Irenaeus bis Martin Luther*, ed. Heinrich Fries and Georg Kretschmar, Munich 1981, 283–313, 416–18, 432–34, above all 309–13; id., 'Verhinderte und verhindernde Ökumene', in *Gesellschaft und Religion*, ed. Jörg Albertz, Berlin 1991, 119–38, esp. 127–30. The otherwise extremely well documented work by S. Pemsel-Maier, *Rechtfertigung durch Kirche? Das Verhältnis von Kirche und Rechtfertigung in Entwürfen der neueren katholischen und evangelischen Theologie*, Würzburg 1991, answers the question with a resolute 'Yes/No' – her remarks cannot be understood in any other way. Unfortunately the value of this thorough study is further diminished by the fact that not a single

ecumenically explosive ecclesiological theme is discussed and subjected to the criterion of the article of justification.

30. Brosseder, 'Verhinderte und verhindernde Ökumene' (n.29).
31. H. Jedin, 'Reformation und Kirchenverständnis', in *Probleme der Kirchenspaltung im 16. Jahrhundert*, ed. Raymund Kottje and Joseph Staber, Regensburg 1970, 59–82: 67.
32. E. Iserloh, 'Luther und die Kirchenspaltung. Ist das Reformatorische kirchentrennend?', in *Weder Ketzer noch Heiliger. Luthers Bedeutung für den ökumenischen Dialog*, by Hans Friedrich Geisser, Gerhard Heintze, Erwin Iserloh, Hans L. Martensen, Gerhard Müller, Johannes Panagopoulos, Otto Hermann Pesch, Regensburg 1982, 73–92: 78, 80.
33. Cf. Küng, *The Church*, 447f., etc.; H. Küng, *On Being a Christian*, 497ff.
34. See my attempt, 'Ökumenische Katholizität', *Ökumenische Rundschau* 41, 1992, 24–39.
35. There are further important contributions on the topic in G. Maron, *Kirche und Rechtfertigung. Eine kontroverstheologische Untersuchung, ausgehend von den Texten des Zweiten Vatikanischen Konzils*, Göttingen 1969; J. Baur, *Einig in Sachen Rechtfertigung? Zur Prüfung des Rechtsfertigungskapitel der Studie des Ökumenischen Arbeitskreis evangelischer und katholischer Theologen: 'Lehrverurteilungen – kirchentrennend?'*, Tübingen 1989; U. Kühn and O.H. Pesch, *Rechtfertigung im Disput. Eine freundliche Antwort an Jörg Baur*, Tübingen 1991 (with bibliography).

Leonardo Boff

Christianity with an Authentic Face: Reflections on the Future of the Church in Latin America

There are two works by Hans Küng which have quite certainly helped Latin American, and particularly Brazilian, praxis and reflection: *The Church* and *On Being a Christian*. *The Church* served, and still serves, as an academic text in courses run by our institutes and faculties of theology and is constantly referred to at our theological and pastoral meetings for pastoral workers and in continuation courses for priests and bishops. The main contribution which the book makes in our context is that it has freed us from a fossilized picture of the church and opened us up to a process in which the mystery of the church is constantly inculturated anew. For us that means that the church must accept the challenge posed by the culture of the people and by the Latin American cultures, a challenge which is not taken seriously in the framework of mission. In this sense this book by Hans Küng has been a constant stimulus to a twofold loyalty which the church always has to preserve: to its New Testament source and to the appeals of the culture around it.

On Being a Christian has a particularly liberating dimension. It preserves the original intuitions of the Christian faith, frees them from their historical and cultural burden, and presents them as a source which provides meaning and life and advances humanization for the present. Partly devoted to the historical Jesus, it is valuable as an anthology. There are pages in it which I would not hesitate to count as being among the best that have ever been written from a perspective of liberation. Time and again these pages are read with enthusiasm, re-read and quoted by theologians and pastoral workers in ecclesial base communities and by social pastors working among the native population, marginalized mothers, the poor, blacks and Indios.

My reflections on the future of Christianity in Latin America seek to take further ideas which are present in the work of Hans Küng by putting them in the context of the realities which surround us.

The commemoration of the quincentenary of the conquest of Latin America celebrated in 1992 led not only to an assessment of what this time meant for the presence of Christianity on our continent but also to reflection on its future. What sort of a future can be foreseen for Christianity here if we also take into account the present process of crisis in the nation states and the accelerated tempo of the interweaving of economics, politics and the human drama which is taking place world-wide?

This topic is more appropriate for visionaries than for analysts. For one has to judge the future tendencies of an extremely complex phenomeon. It includes not only Latin America but really the whole world, to the degree that Christianity is a world-wide religious corporation. For this reason, the reflections offered here are decidedly fragmentary and hypothetical. They develop their vision from a particular perspective which is conditioned by a social (Latin American and academic) and ecclesial (Roman Catholic, liberation-theological) context which is incapable of achieving reasonable coverage of the whole range of topics involved here. However, that is no reason for despair, since this limitation is inherent in any thought.

A superficial analysis of the Christian reality in Latin America can distinguish seven main types of Christianity: Western Roman Christianity, the Christianity of the people, Western Reformation Christianity, popular Pentecostal Christianity, Christianity assimilated to other confessions, religions and mystical forms, historical and cultural Christianity, and world-wide Christianity.

Of course I do not have room here to analyse each of these expressions of Christianity and to prognosticate their possible futures. That would immediately lead to irresponsible superficiality. So I have made a choice, which might seem unfair. I shall be dealing with just three forms of expression, since they are the predominant ones and in my view *de facto* represent a theological and religious challenge. What is the future of Western Roman (hierarchical) Christianity? What is the future of popular Christianity and its best form of expression, namely the ecclesial base communities? And finally, what perspectives are offered by a Christianity which has become world-wide?

1. Hierarchical Christianity

The Christianity which came to Latin America was inculturated by European, Graeco-Roman-Germanic criteria. A religious institution was transplanted here as an element in the immense colonial project of military conquest and economic exploitation of the world that it was to dominate. There was no evangelization in the strict sense of the word. Evangelization in its totality presupposes that the groups which act in society encounter one another with their cultures, that otherness is accepted and that something new can develop out of the dialogue between the partners that has to take place. Under the conditions of the conquest, no real evangelization in the objective sense of the word could come about. Those who evangelized the indigenous population were of the same race, the same countries and the same groups as those who invaded the Amerindian territories and exterminated a large part of the population. The evangelizers of the slaves were the slave-owners who brought people by force from Africa and subjected them here to the terrors of slavery. The oppressed in the country and in the city were evangelized by their oppressors, those who took away their lands and paid them starvation wages. But what gospel can the fox preach to the chickens? So the issue is one of justice for the victims and honesty in recognizing the way in which we were evangelized, of recognizing that a distorted Christianity was introduced into Latin America. Therefore we have not celebrated 500 years of evangelization so much as the quincentenary of a certain type of colonizing church. Here the religious system of Roman, Westernized and hierarchical Catholicism spread, as it did in the Caribbean and in other places in Latin America which Protestantism reached with similar means.

What is Roman Catholicism? It is the result of a long process of encounter between religious power and political power. Within these wider limits most of the focal points of the Christian utopia came into being. First of all early Christianity was founded with communities of brothers and sisters. With the Constantinian shift in the fourth century Christianity began its political development. It turned into an institutional church with a hierarchical form which, as we know, in the end divides the body of the faithful into two parts: the clergy, who govern, and the laity, who obey. Up to the tenth century a Christianity predominated which had been assimilated to Byzantine culture in the East, while in the West a Christianity incorporated into Roman culture was gaining strength. In the course of the formation of the Western European states from the eleventh century on, a parallel structure was created in Roman Catholicism which has lasted down to the present day.

The dispute between the popes and the emperors, the internal struggles in the religious sphere and the confrontation with Western scientific and technical culture forged a type of Roman Christianity which – from a distance – was at all events a Western product. As such it is a complex entity which is made up of many elements and has Jewish-Christian roots. Its current form, as presented in the distribution of power, dogmatic fixity, legalistic structures and liturgical codification, derives from specific historical influences.

Official Roman Catholicism has been structured in terms of religious power. It articulates this religious power in the same way as the other dominant powers of society. This combination gave rise to Christianity as reality, myth and ideology. It shaped the material basis for the realization of the ecclesiastical project by developing its power structure, establishing its hegemonical discourse and securing lines of communication through the whole of society. This type of Roman Catholicism was reproduced in America.

A Latin church? In Europe it is autonomous; here it is dependent. There it is central; here it is peripheral and colonial. There it is the source; here it is the mirror. How was it reproduced in Latin America? In the first place by means of 'missionary catechesis'. The catechesis does not share in the least in the real lives of the Indios or the blacks, in their suffering or their hopes. It is a catechesis which conceals the deep difference between the conqueror and the conquered, between the master and the slave, between those with power and the powerless. It presupposes an equality which does not exist, as if the spirit and world of the indigenous population were the expression of a universal humanity or the homogeneous culture of the West. It begins from a clean sheet: the indigenous and the black have no religious culture to be assimilated. Their religion is demonized, their representatives are persecuted. Mission is an immense process which involves driving out the world of demons which dominates autochthonous culture. Despite his peaceful methods, not even Bartolomé de las Casas could avoid this process of the destruction of religion. Therefore catechesis does not in reality overcome the indoctrination of religious content worked out against the background of a Greek metaphysic (which was remote from biblical thought). As the hearers are not Western, assimilation is extremely small, as is also reported by the numerous testimonies of the missionaries.

Next came the 'settlements'. Here the natives were separated from their tribes, their earth and their traditions. They underwent the tailoring of Iberian culture. This was a tailoring of language and morals, of ways of working and organizing leisure time. The result was that the one who was settled was no longer an Indio, but not a Spaniard or a Portuguese either. This gentle force killed just as many as the harsh violence of the direct genocide which took place in the first battles in the sixteenth century.

Third came the strategy of 'pedagogical discipline and fear'. As Eduard Hoonaert puts it: 'With the settlement the idea gradually arose that the newly arrived natives were like wolves, beasts of the forest, wild beasts which had to be tamed with chastisements and penances until they finally became lambs, gentle and Christian Indios.'[1] After long doubts and heart-searchings, in his *Diálogo da conversão do gentio* (1556–1557) Nobrega came to the resigned conclusion that 'Fear seems to be the best and most certain way'; we must see that the Indios 'come to grasp faith through fear' and even become Christians 'by force'.[2] But is evangelization still meaningful if it is achieved only by force and compulsion? According to the criteria of official missiology the answer is, no. Nevertheless, we still speak without too much hesitation of 500 years of the evangelization of Latin America. This evangelization cannot escape critical assessment.

Finally, throughout the whole process there were 'popular missions' in which Roman Catholicism consolidated itself. Their purpose was to strengthen the link between popular Catholicism, which was autonomous and uncontrolled, and the hierarchical institution which had at its disposal the word, the sacrament and the criteria of church membership.

Under the domination of patronage, in this way the existence of hierarchical Catholicism was safeguarded throughout Latin America. With the advent of political independence and the secularization of the nation states, however, the Vatican administration adopted a strategy which is generally called 'Romanization'. It is based on a prior judgment which is quite clearly expressed in Pope Gregory XVI's letter of 12 June 1840 (*Beneficentissimo*): Latin America is an area in which 'the most wretched of people' lived, 'caught in the mists of the most serious errors' and unhappily living in darkness and the shadow of death. The institutional church had to be strengthened to reach – and convert – these people.

In 1899 the Latin American plenary council was summoned by Leo XIII in Rome. The perspectives of the Council of Trent (the clericalization of Christian life) and the First Vatican Council (the fight against modernity and affirmation of the papal primacy of jurisdiction) were codified here in the interest of a formidable strengthening of hierarchical Christianity. As far as pastoral strategy was concerned, this was brought into line with the central countries. So any manifestation of popular belief (as in the brotherhoods, the veneration of patrons and popular piety) was to be subordinated to the church authorities. In a word, this strategy was directed against indigenous Catholicism.

After the 1950s this process of Romanization came to something of a standstill with the rise of the laity and the social pastoral workers throughout Latin America. And it was stemmed even more effectively after the 1960s with the spirit of the Second Vatican Council. But under Pope John Paul II Romanization took on new force, and this strategy for the preservation of a hierarchical Christianity was now supported by a transnational perspective, implemented by transnational lay movements like Opus Dei, Communione e Liberazione, Focolari, Cursillos de cristandad, Catechumenate and others.

At present the implementation of a comprehensive reclericalization of church life is in full swing. The aim is to limit the new forms of ecclesiality canonically within an understanding of the church which is fundamentally hierarchical, dependent on the Vatican and subordinate to the centralist strategies of the Roman Curia. This includes mistrust of the conferences of bishops, control over the flourishing life of the orders through direct intervention in the Latin American Association of Religious (CLAR), a call for the incorporation of the ecclesial base communities (CEBS) into parishes, harsh criticism of the church of the poor, supervision of liberation theology and a curb on the theological activity of various theologians.

The instigators of this global strategy of the Roman Catholic universal church want to revive the myth of Christendom in a new form. This, they believe, must be the response to the present cultural crisis of the West and a proposal for the reunion of Europe after the collapse of so-called socialism. In the changed circumstances it can claim to be a moral Christianity, the heir to

Western values which are held to be Christian, and which in a new way could make Europe a community. From this perspective a model is being offered to the whole Roman Catholic sphere on the different continents. There is no point in analysing such a project in detail. I am convinced that it is not solid enough to serve as a principle of unity and practical inspiration.

2. The future of hierarchical Christianity?

What is the future of this type of Christianity in Latin America? The answer is complex. For really it does not depend on Latin America. Latin America is only a mirror; Europe is the source. The answer depends on the future of European Christianity, which has been shaped in Western culture.

First, this type of Christianity has a considerable intrinsic capacity for reproducing itself. In time it created a coherent self-understanding for itself. It succeeded in connecting this with God and the will of Jesus as its founder. So this understanding gained rights to untouchability and independence from history. It produced poweful images which – at this level – turned into archetypes of the Western soul. Prophetic figures and critics of the hierarchical system in particular are commandeered by the institution and now function as guarantors of the legitimacy of the institution, which represents itself as the true fulfilment of ancient promises.

Secondly, the social basis of hierarchical Christianity is grounded in the dominant forces of Western culture. Although this culture is experiencing a deep crisis of meaning and creativity, it has good stamina. Granted, we are talking more of dry bones than of a living organism, but dry bones in particular can last a long time. Here and there they are brought together in attempts at a resurrection, as in the various modern conservative movements of Europe. But this always results in a new strenghtening of the hierarchical church. By contrast, the capacity of hierarchical Christianity for inculturation is very limited and poor. The method of complete inculturation (*accomodatio*) attempted by Francis Xavier in Goa (1542), by Ricci in China (1598), by Nobili in India (1606) and by Rhodos in Vietnam (1662) was rejected in 1774 in the 'Rites Dispute' – all in the course of the strengthening of the Roman and Western paradigm. As a result the whole missionary process has been traumatized down to the present day.

Thirdly, this type of Christianity struck deep roots in Latin America. It was internalized in the soil of the people and is one of the elements of the established order. Time and again it manages to come to an arrangement with the dominant powers and so to secure for itself a sphere of relative autonomy in which to realize its religious project.

What future will this Christianity have? A very long one. It will endure over time, like its allies, but no longer through the inner force of self-reproduction. Generally speaking, institutional powers which succeed in rooting themselves in the world of a culture succeed in perpetuating themselves. That has happened with the colonial churches, baroque art, church music, the religious names of geography and the pantheon of popularized Catholic saints. Without question, we shall have to live for centuries with this type of Christianity, which is rich in history and institutional power.

On the other hand, if we think of history in the long term, we see that even the most venerable institutions collapse. After the Arab avalanche, there is almost nothing left of the Christianity of St Paul in Asia Minor, of St Augustine and St Cyprian in North Africa. But it is now important in a theological perspective to ask whether such a form of hierarchical Christianity corresponds to the gospel. Does it reproduce Jesus' dream of the immediacy of each individual to the Father, the dream that we are all brothers and sisters, that power is strict service, the dream of the pre-eminent worth of all human beings, since in the Son Jesus Christ we are sons and daughters of God? Or the dream that the poor stand at the centre if we want to understand the nature of the Father and the liberating content of the kingdom of God? These are questions which are hard to formulate and even harder to answer.

The alliance of the hierarchical church with the political powers of this world has in fact brought it about that the weight of historical contradictions falls on the official Christian tradition. One might think of the power of the Inquisition, the religious wars, complicity in the genocide of the Latin American population, complicity in slavery, systematic resistance to the ideas of modern freedom, the marginalization of women and the exclusiveness of the claim to revelation and religous truth. Although hierarchical Christianity exists – despite some prophetic manifestations at the heart of the episcopate – it bears within itself neither a greater hope nor a new discourse (what is said is always already known in advance), nor does it advance upwards and forwards the great dreams which are distinctive features of the rhetorical and liberating practice of Jesus. Hierarchical Christianity stands guilty here before human-kind and confessing Christians.

3. The Christianity of the people: a defenceless flower

This situation is not tragic, for there is another form in which Christianity is expressed. This obeys another logic and takes further the spiritual heritage of the Christian 'myth'. It is the Christianity of the people. Whereas the former is hierarchical, this is communitarian; whereas the former is clerical, this is lay; whereas the former is liturgical, this is devotional; whereas the former expressed itself in the dominant culture, this seeks its expression in popular culture. It represents a form of religion of resistance. It is thus a liberating Christianity because it forged its own synthesis of Christian faith in the paradigms of popular culture. Nevertheless it has an identity which is hard to understand. In a situation in which it is dominated, popular Christianity takes up elements of domination for the purpose of resistance and so has within it elements which are directed against the people. In other words, popular Christianity preserves a fundamental relationship to hierarchical Christianity.

Generally speaking, we can say with the support of some historians that in Brazil (as quite generally in Latin America) Christianity imposed itself in two ways: by mission and by devotion. The subject of mission is the official church (missionaries and hierarchy); its first audience is the Indios and its horizon the Council of Trent. By contrast, devotion has as its subject the family and the brotherhoods; its audience is the people generally and its horizon mediaeval piety. Devotion overcame the division into clergy and laity in the states of perfection (members of orders) and penitence (laity), and an attempt was made to live out the Christian experience in everyday life. Clergy and laity had to some degree to seek perfection in confronting life with faith.

The colonizers came steeped in the popular piety of the *devotio moderna*, a movement which had inspired European spirituality from the fourteenth to the sixteenth centuries. Important features of this trend, which had been shaped by the laity, were the spirit of community and the veneration of the saints. The spirit of community had always been strongly stamped on the indigenous and black traditions and on popular tradition. The veneration of the saints allowed direct contact with the saints. It was practised in the family and in the community, i.e. without priestly mediation. This gave rise to the strong saints, the novenas, the festivals, the sanctuaries, the processions, and especially the brotherhoods and the associations, which kept piety alive in an organized form. Afro-Latin American culture could grow together in this type of devotional Catholicism: it was 'syncretized'.

I do not want to analyse popular Christianity in detail, but merely to stress what the historians of the Latin American church emphasize: this Christianity of the people represents one of the most original cultural creations of Latin America. Barely controlled by hierarchical Christianity and official orthodoxy, it could develop quite freely by assimilating different elements of religious experience (the native, the black, the Romanizing, the sacramental and the liturgical tradition). As Eduardo Hoonaert aptly wrote: 'The brotherhoods gave the Christian world of ideas in Brazil its native colouring.'[3] They vastly enjoyed the popular religious festivals, even treating them as carnivals.

This Christianity helped to shape the Brazilian people as a mystical people, 'a people which trusts deeply in another world', a people which believes in the possibility 'of saving the whole world and finding something good and valuable everywhere'. This Christianity stamped a 'language which allows a people without possessions and without any possibility of communicating with its legal representatives to speak, to be heard and to receive the gods in its own body'.⁴ This popular Christianity came into being of its own accord, although it was exposed to the mistrust and even the scorn of clerical Christianity.

In the history of Brazil perhaps only three times have attempts been made to combine hierarchical Christianity with popular Christianity: in the plan for a patriotic church put forward by Pater Antonio Feijo, Imperial Regent after Independence (1822); by Pater Julio Maria after the proclamation of the Republic in 1889; and (from the 1960s) by the base communities. Pater Julio Maria was a real forerunner of liberation theology. He aimed for an alliance between the church and the people which would have encouraged a shift in the axis of discussion from the political and religious sphere to social questions. To put it in his own words: it was necessary 'to show the little ones, the poor, the proletarians that they were the first to be called by the divine Master, whose church, right from the beginning, was the church of the people. The great and powerful, the rich, could certainly enter, but above all it was to show mercy on the poverty of the people, to be a church of the poor'.⁵ The wide network of ecclesial base communities gave the church of the poor support and showed that a new, more communitarian and participative way of being the church can be taken.

As this theme is basic to the future of Christianity in Latin America, which is our concern here, I want to go into it in more detail.

4. Ecclesial base communities: the convergence of three historical forces

An analytic approach shows that the phenomenon of the ecclesial base communities brings together three historical forces: the utopia of the first missionaries, the rise of the laity and the first political movements among the poor.

The first force was the utopia of the first missionaries. I have already analysed the goal of an inculturated evangelization elsewhere. Missionaries of the mendicant orders did not dream of the expansion of the European church system into the Americas, but of the creation of an Indian church with Indian clergy, of an autonomous episcopal order directly subordinated to the pope. Not a mirror church but a source church was to emerge from the missionary effort. The basic feature of such a church was to be community. The spirit of community and simplicity, the characteristic of the indigenous populations and always praised in contemporary evidence (they did not even have the concept of private property), was the cultural value that the autochthonous culture already knew. This spirit of community already characterized popular culture, especially as a way of surviving in the face of marginalization at all levels by the rulers.

But this model could not establish itself. In close conjunction with the colonial project, the other, hierarchical Christianity won the day. But now it can emerge again in the ecclesial base communities. The dream of a church of the Indios – incarnated in the local culture – is again taking shape. Without arrogance we can say that the ecclesial base communities are the best fruit of the new evangelization. This already began in the 1960s, when the popular level penetrated the heart of the hierarchical church with communal celebrations, Bible groups and finally the ecclesial base communities. This communal movement associated itself with the communal spirit which was always present in the popular Catholicism of the brotherhoods, the pilgrimages, the veneration of the patrons with their work for the community and also the world of chapels and sanctuaries. The power of the ecclesial base communities can be understood in the light of these deep popular roots.

The second force which underlies the base communities is the significance of the lay movement in today's church. The crisis for ministries (the chronic lack of priests) put the hierarchical model of Christianity in a hopeless position. It had difficulties in reproducing itself. At the same time this crisis created spaces through which other Christian confessions and sects could penetrate. In this critical situation – in the interest of self-preservation as an institution – the church became open downwards in the direction of the laity.

After the 1950s there was great enthusiasm for various forms of social pastoral work. At that time the laity took on the role of critical and political mobilization. Perhaps the most important result was that through the laity (who on the whole came from the lower middle class) the social themes were put on the agenda of the bishops from the perspective of the oppressed and their liberation, and the whole church was wholly open downwards, in the direction of the oppressed and marginalized masses.

So the laity were called and took on responsibility for the church. The ecclesial base communities came into being on the initiative of the hierarchical church. But they were dominated by the spirit of community, the reading of the Bible in a way which set it against everyday problems, celebration co-ordinated by lay people in place of masses and sacraments (performed by the priest). Slowly they achieved a relative autonomy. Another way of being the church developed without having originally been intended, in other words *de facto*. It was communal and participatory, with popular forms of expression and deeply evangelical in spirit.

The ecclesial base communities made remarkable contributions to the four fundamental characteristics of the church: to the *word* (the laity took over the interpretation of scripture and the capacity for a spiritual approach); to *celebration* (the creation of new rites and new interpretations of the traditional rites); to *ministry* (the rise of a wide range of ministries, lay offices and charisms); and finally to *mission* (the creation of other communities which were embedded locally in the social situation in quite a different way). There is no denying that this new way of being the church represents a different distribution of religious power. It produces good symbols and creates a church consensus which differs from that of the hierarchical church. It finds its basis in the community, in a pedagogy which extends from below upwards, in a constant interchange of functions, in the central position given to the poor and their liberation, and the supreme significance of the gospel (the praxis of Jesus, the Spirit and charisms) in Christian life.

Despite certain contradictions and some ways in which it depends on the old model, the ecclesiologically new element in this communal model of being a Christian cannot be denied. It succeeded in attracting important elements of hierarchical Christianity. In particular, it turned the scales when the whole Latin American church formulated its option for the poor, against their poverty and for their liberation – the trademark of the new Latin American Christianity. The theology of liberation would be incomprehensible had it not been preceded by a church at the base, among the impoverished and marginalized, with its liberating praxis.

The third force which led to the establishment of a church at the base was the social movement of the people. From the 1960s on, all over Latin America organized movements of the poor and the oppressed came into being. They no longer accepted peacefully the standards of misery to which they had been condemned. They began to take account of the perverse character of the development which was going ahead at the expense of their impoverishment. They sought a way of liberation leading to another society in which the marginalized – having achieved self-awareness and having got themselves organized – would become the dominant agents in the change that was needed. The link with these movements was formed by the many Christians who were involved in the political project of the people, the project of a democratic, participatory, egalitarian society which was open to religious values.

These committed Christians began to ask in what way the kingdom of God and redemption by Christ were articulated in their struggles for liberation. They came to the conclusion that all-embracing liberation must also come about through social liberation, because Christ redeemed all of reality and not just its spiritual sphere. These convictions were deepened in the Bible groups and communities, and conversely they gave religious expression to the struggles of the trade unions, the country people and the popular parties.

The new feature of this encounter between political commitment and Christian experience is that the Christians of the ecclesial base communities are gradually extending their popular political project. The ecclesial base communities were of course very much at home in the base church – and thus among the poor. But they were also very much at home as an expression of the people's way of liberation. So the ecclesial base communities represent a concrete alliance between communal Christian faith and the people's concern. The active Christians in the ecclesial base communities thought that a popular, democratic society must also have a participatory, popular church. In other words, the social basis of the base church consists of the poor who are fighting for their lives and for a new society. The base church wants to collaborate in building up this new society – successfully.

So whereas hierarchical Christianity articulates itself as a project of the ruling forces (which is what it was in the colonial period and afterwards, up to the independence of the various Latin American countries), popular Christianity allies itself with popular concerns. The strength of the ecclesial base communities for the most part lies here. To opt for the poor over and above their evangelical and humanitarian value means (for hierarchical Christianity too) to give the political project of the oppressed political strength. And that has obvious consequences, since the hierarchical church is led by the option for the poor to support the popular struggle for land, housing and human rights, and to support the liberation movements of the natives, the blacks, the women, the young and the girls on the streets, and the other struggles which arise at the base of society.

5. The future of communitarian Christianity

What is the future of this kind of Christianity? It is the future that the oppressed themselves have. It is supported by dreams and the will to survive. Internally, communitarian Christianity is well rooted in the base communities. Undeniably it is permeated by the great inspirations of the gospel. That gives it the distinctive legitimation of the gospel. It takes up the great Latin American tradition of community among the natives, the blacks and the poor generally, and gives it ecclesial expression. It puts down roots in a devotional Christianity which is stamped by the laity and with its rich symbolism matches the people. The cultures to which Latin America bears witness (Aztec, Maya, Inca, Quechua, Tupi-guarani, Yanomomami and others), which had previously virtually never been evangelized, are now as a result adopting Christianity in their own way and within the framework of their understanding. The dominant methodology among the base communities – the way in which faith is set over against life, beginning from the demands of reality – makes the inculturation of the gospel easier for the indigenous Christians to achieve. So here the process begins all over again; here a challenge for the future of Christianity assumes a new form. It will no longer be exclusively Western and Roman but Mestizo, Afro-American and Amerindian.

By its inner power, communitarian Christianity successfully won over important sectors of hierarchical Christianity to its cause. That has given it inner solidity and protection against the attacks of highly conservative and clerical groups. Outwardly the power and future of this Christianity are thus guaranteed by its articulation of itself as a movement of social emancipation.

Popular social Christianity was able to take up the great political, emancipatory and religious goals of the people and give them a form compatible with
traditional faith and in accord with mass culture.

At the moment hierarchical Christianity is attempting to control this type of
Christianity. It is attempting to absorb the innovative power of communitarian
Christianity into the framework of the hierarchical church by transforming the
base communities into pastorates and reintroducing the clerical hegemony
instead of delegating religious power to the laity. Despite its strength,
however, I am convinced that hierarchical Christianity has not yet succeeded
in reshaping something which is so deeply rooted and so strongly supported by
its alliance with the great majority of survivors in our asymmetrical and unjust
society. This truly is a Christianity of hope. And hope always has the future on
its side and will keep it there.

6. The future of a world-wide Christianity

Today we are living in a unique era of history. An immense process of
worldwide globalization of human experience is under way. Cultures are
encountering one another and religions are discovering one another. The
internationalization of a particular model – whether of the economy, trade, or
religion – is experienced as violence and the survival of an imperialistic
mentality.

In a correct hermeneutical understanding, pluralism does not in fact mean
the collapse of a monolithic unity but the manifestation of the wealth of a
reality which is so all-embracing that no single symbol, no single discourse and
no single institution will ever be able to exhaust it. In the Christian dialect we
would say that the kingdom is so comprehensive and omnipresent that no one
by themselves could translate its whole historical scope. It is anticipated by all
and all give it merely a historical configuration.

Christianity gives the kingdom of God its unique form of expression, which
is permeated by the event of Jesus – who died and is risen – and by the
conviction that the spirit works within history, within humanity, and is given
life in religious manifestations and by those who continue to remember Jesus.
However, this unique character does not rule out other forms of expression of
the kingdom and of the revelation of God in history, as the Letter to the
Hebrews also recognizes: 'At many times and in many ways, God has spoken
to our fathers through the prophets' (1.1). And God continues to do so.

So in the light of the phenomenon of world-wide globalization the valid
paradigms of Christianity – the two which I have analysed here from a
Catholic position, but also others with a Western style – have to be relativized.
The time has come for Christianity to become really Catholic, i.e. to open
itself to the universality of human experience and to be capable of assimilating
itself

to any culture. Any centralistic claim or attempt at hegemony is to be rejected as sectarian, culturalistic or imperialistic.

We must understand the sayings of Jesus in the Gospel of John as a message for our time: 'The Spirit blows where it wills, and we do not know where it comes from or whither it goes' (cf. John 3.8): 'The time is coming when you will worship the Father neither on this Mount Gerizim nor in Jerusalem, but will worship him in Spirit and in truth ... Such are the worshippers whom the Father wants' (cf. John 4.21–24). Many people are ready to accept Christianity, but they do not accept its Western and quite accidental version. The greatest challenge for Christianity today is really to allow itself to be inculturated by the different cultures of humankind (and not just in church rhetoric). Either it takes its Western cultural roots seriously (with all the dogmatics and morality, its interpretation of the revelation event and monopolistic claims), or it will deviate more and more into sectarian behaviour and be regarded as a by-product of a culture of domination.

The worldwide globalization of Christianity will certainly be a highly dynamic process, especially from a Latin American perspective. It will focus on four poles: community, culture, symbolic identification and communion.

First, Christian life and not the institutions will stand in the centre. Christian life and Christian experience will be expressed in terms of communion: the mystery of God as human communion, the nearness of God in his incarnate Son, the enthusiasm of the Spirit who pervades history, the knowledge of the universal sacrifice for the redemption of all, the conviction of the good purpose of creation with the resurrection of all that is to the kingdom of the Trinity. The community will be the place at which faith and life meet and an exchange takes place not only of faith but also of our own lives.

Secondly, the communal form of expression of Christian experience will be achieved in symbolic images, in the values and terms of reference of the different cultures. Culture functions as a kind of Old Testament that allows dialogue with the Christian message. From this dialogue the New Testament emerges in every culture. Each time a different Testament is accepted as a communication from God. So if the Christian message is not involved in any process of cultural assimilation, it cannot make any history; it becomes irrelevant for human destiny and ultimately remains a scourge of Western inculturation. At this point the contribution of the feminine dimension, which today permeates all societies and also the churches, will be decisive. The whole experience of faith must be filtered and articulated through women's experience. In the end this will be able to make a contribution to the knowledge of the mysteries of God which was constantly denied to it over the past ten centuries. So by way of inculturation the different types of Christianity come into being as an expression of the unfathomable riches of the Christian 'myth'.

Thirdly, there is need for reflection on the need for a Christian identity. Here the different historical sensibilities of being a Christian come into play.

There is a Roman Catholic experience, then a Protestant experience, and also an Orthodox experience, quite apart from popular Catholicism, and so on. Such new experiences of the Christian message do not come into being in a religious vacuum. Rather, they grow out of particular basic figures which have already been consolidated historically. The new measures itself up against the traditional. It makes itself a synthesis and develops its identity from that. This represents a kind of family and genealogy (the Catholic community in Brazil, in China, in Ireland, and so on) within the spectrum of a particular type of 'historical experience'. Any actualization of the Christian 'myth' will be unique (a concrete universal), neither just the specific feature of a universal nor simply the concretization of a horizon which has been established beforehand, but specifically the unique phenomenon of the gospel energy which was initiated by Jesus and which continually brings about in history both new actualizations and the renewal of exemplary actualizations.

Fourthly, the culture of communion becomes an imperative, and does so within the various manifestations of Christianity itself. All must give up the claim to be the sole representatives of Jesus' dream; no church can represent the wealth of the Jesus event appropriately in history. Each Christian community will realize facets of it, and all achieve validity to the degree that they keep the heritage of Jesus alive in their own way and constantly take up its utopia afresh: as a source for the fulfilment of meaning and as a power which can intervene in history. It will be just as it is with the Gospels: each work, whether by Mark or John, will report Jesus and his message, but it will give this report with its own gestures and specific accents. There will be different forms of expression of the one living gospel which is the person of Jesus himself.

Fifthly, this communion must be open to all human religious manifestations. They too are the answer to the offer that the God of communion constantly presents to all persons and cultures. In them on each occasion God makes himself present, visits his people, and prepares it for life together in eternity. So a communion is necessary that is open to all sources which create meaning, i.e. to all that is nobly and deeply at home in the human mystery. In an ecologically threatened world the last question cannot be about the future of Christianity but must be about the degree to which it helps to preserve creation and to guarantee life in its various forms and in its mystery.

If Christianity represents a concrete service to life it will always have a future. Nevertheless, its most important concern will not be its own future but the future of human beings and the quality of life in the global ecological process. Authoritarian and sectarian forms have been able to maintain themselves in history. But they will not be able to create a new world of religious conceptions, so that human beings can dream of the kingdom of life and freedom, the kingdom of God.

We dream of the future of a Christianity which is bold enough to keep dreaming the dream of Jesus and which consistently attempts to translate this dream into institutions which are always provisional, concerned for the cry of the oppressed. This dream embraces the resurrection of all flesh, eternal life, and the enthronement of all creation with the rocks, animals, human beings, stars, the microcosm and the macrocosm in the realm of the Trinity. With its mystical, syncretistic and tolerant aura of freedom which is so close to the people, Latin American Christianity will have a unique and fruitful collaboration to offer to a Christianity which has become ecumenical and world-wide.

Notes

1. E. Hoornaert, *O Cristianismo moreno*, Vozes 1991, 58.
2. *Cartas Jesuiticas* I, Editora da Universidade de S. Paulo, Iatiaia, 1988, 229–45.
3. Hoornaert, *Cristianismo moreno* (n.1), 96. Boff often uses the Portuguese word 'moreno', taking up the title of Hoornaert's book. The term is usually translated 'dark brown' or 'dark'. In order to avoid fixing it to a skin-colour, with all the misunderstandings to which that could give rise ('redskin', 'brown', 'black'?), in the English text this has been rendered 'authentic' (see title) or 'native' [ed.].
4. Cf. R. da Matta, *O que faiz o brasil ser Brasil*, Rocco, Rio 1986, 117.
5. *A Igreja e a República*, Universidad de Brasilia 1981, 120–1.

IV   Christology and the Doctrine of God

Karl-Josef Kuschel

'Jesus Christ is the Decisive Criterion': Beyond Barth and Hegel in a Christology 'From Below'

'The change in the content of his christology can generally be described as
follows. In *Justification*, Küng sees Christ pre-eminently as eternal, pre-
existent Son of God. The incarnation taking place in history is merely the
revelation of the mystery of the God-man Christ which always remains the
same in God's eyes. The focal point of christology is thus shifted back to
that sphere of time which precedes concrete history and the incarnation
which realizes itself in time. Christology is determined by the eternal being
of the pre-existent Christ. In *On Being a Christian* the focus on the historical
existence of Christ has shifted to the subsequent period, to the value
experienced by the believing subject living after Christ ... The general
direction in the change of Küng's christology can be described with many
different pairs of terms expressing the abruptness and even the contradic-
toriness of the change. The focal point of christology has shifted from pre-
existence to the significance of Jesus which can be experienced in the
present, from the divinity of Christ to the humanity, from object to subject,
from truth to truthfulness, from ontology to functionality, from essence to
significance, from revelation to experience and "from above" "below".'

Thus the Finnish Protestant theologian Eero Huovinen in what is so far the
most extensive study of the christology of Hans Küng.[1] And that is the way in
which others among his critics (A. Grillmeier, W. Kasper, P. Hünermann,
H.G. Pöhlmann)[2] see him too: Hans Küng, the destroyer of dogmas or the
reductionist, who in the course of his theological career has undergone a
radical change above all in his christological thought, which can be summed
up as: all that is ontological and metaphysical in christology has been dissolved
in historicity and subjectivity. And indeed, did not a high orthodox christology
stand at the beginning of Küng's theological career (*Justification*, 1957), which
later seems to have been completely abandoned in his book *On Being a
Christian* (1974), with *The Incarnation of God* (1970) forming an 'intermezzo'[3]
which can almost be ignored? Has not the concern of classical christology
'from above', which found its last great advocate in Karl Barth, and which is
also presupposed as a matter of course in *Justification*, been completely
abandoned? The aim of this contribution is to demonstrate that the most
dominant systems adopted by Küng's critics for dividing up his christology
completely pass over the texts themselves. I shall demonstrate that for all the

discontinuity there is a great continuity in Hans Küng's christology, and that the concern of a christology 'from above' (Barth, Hegel) is 'sublated' – in the threefold sense of Hegel's term: taken up, done away with and transcended – even in Küng's later christology 'from below'.

1. *The interest in Karl Barth: christocentricity*

It primarily seemed to be a Catholic inheritance of Barthian christology when in 1957 the twenty-nine-year-old Hans Küng had his book on *The Understanding of Justification in Karl Barth* published. Moreover Küng's argument with Barth belongs in the history of the Catholic reception of Barth which had begun in Germany in the 1920s and 1930s (K. Adam, E. Peterson, E. Przywara, G. Söhngen) and was taken further in France during the 1940s (L. Malévez, H. Bouillard, J. Hamer).[4] This reception was not as obvious as all that, if we remember that Barth had uttered more passionate polemic than others against Roman Catholic theology and the Roman Catholic church. At that time every Catholic theologian could recall the statement with which in 1932 Barth had attacked the Catholic 'natural theology' (*analogia entis*) sanctioned dogmatically at the First Vatican Council: 'I regard the *analogia entis* as the invention of Antichrist, and I believe that because of it it is impossible ever to become a Roman Catholic, all other reasons for not doing so being to my mind short-sighted and trivial.'[5] As is well known, for Barth what lay behind this was the charge that the Catholic tradition was ready to accept a knowledge of God on the part of 'natural' human beings even independently of the revelation of God in Jesus Christ. Barth saw this as *the* basic error of Catholicism, which had led it to split the one true God, contrary to scripture, into a God known 'naturally' and 'supernaturally'. In this way the infinite difference between God and human beings, only to be overcome by God's action in grace, seemed to have been fatally levelled out.

Barth had proclaimed resolute resistance to this splitting of reality into nature and supernature, and had done so on the basis of his own christology, which he regarded as being given once and for all in the light of the biblical testimony and the tradition of the early church. So for Barth there is no knowledge 'before' or 'outside' God's revelation. There is strict equivocity between God and human beings which is transcended and overcome only by Jesus Christ the Son of God. For there is an analogy only between Christ's being and God's being, and only in so far as the world and human beings are part of the Christ event can there also be talk of a correspondence between God and human beings: an *analogia Christi* which is recognized in faith. Therefore for Barth the (Catholic) analogy of being (*analogia entis*) had to be replaced by a (truly biblical) analogy of faith (*analogia fidei*): 'If there is a real analogy between God and man – an analogy which is a true analogy of being on both sides, an analogy in and with which the knowledge of God will in fact be given – what other analogy can it be than the analogy of being which is posited and created by the work and action of God himself, the analogy which has its actuality from God and from God alone, and therefore in faith and faith alone?'[6] Unless one does this, the result is – as Küng was later to sum up Barth's concern – a 'fateful Catholic levelling down of God and human beings by means of a levelling concept of being; Barth thought that he had to protest against this in the name of a quite different god, in the name of the divinity of God'.[7]

But above all as a result of the pioneering monograph by Hans Urs von Balthasar, which appeared in 1951, Barth was now drawn constructively into an ecumenical dialogue with Catholic theology. Moreover, in Küng's estimation Balthasar's book meant 'a breakthrough for Catholic theology to an inner understanding of Barthian theology'.[8] This understanding proved all the easier since Balthasar in particular, with subtle analyses of the concept of nature, extracted the question of 'natural theology' which Barth felt to be so particularly divisive from the distorted contrasts which Barth had constructed and created the possibility of a consensus between Barth and Catholic theology.[9] And in fact Barth did not return to this problem later, but in his late theology made a constructive new evaluation of the concern of 'natural theology'.[10] We can start from Hans Küng's account: 'When as a young man in the mid-1950s – like many Catholic theologians disturbed by these problems – I approached Barth over this controversy – a man who had not only holy wrath but winning humour, he remarked, "In theology one never knows: does he have me or do I have him?" And in connection with the much-disputed *analogia entis*, which alone prevents one from becoming a Catholic, he merely said, "I've buried that now".'[11]

By contrast, in matters of christology, which Barth had restored to the centre of Christian theology to a far greater degree than any other twentieth-century theologian, Balthasar had already demonstrated a far-reaching consensus between Barth and the living Catholic tradition. In the light of the person of Jesus Christ Barth thought through once again the whole doctrine of God (Trinity), creation (Christ as the ground of creation) and redemption and changed it considerably in comparison with tradition. One would be fully justified in calling this 'christocentricity' in theology.[13] Granted, in his book the same von Balthasar had already drawn attention to the dangers of this Barthian christocentricity. Here already he had accused Barth of christological 'constraint';[14] other Catholic theologians like Hermann Volk[15] and Arno Quadt[16] followed him here and partly broadened this charge. In Barth's doctrine of creation in particular Balthasar felt that 'the whole work of creation must be stuffed into a christological mould'.[17] He said that to do this was to 'overstep the legitimate limits and competence of theology',[18] in a way which 'closes the doors on possibilities that are really open to God'.[19] Here he wanted 'persistently to lure', where Barth had 'pressed, cut and closed', but without 'dropping the supporting conception'.[20]

But what was the 'supporting conception'? From Barth, Balthasar had seen the opportunity also to give christocentricity new accents within Catholicism, to get out of the awkward scheme of nature and supernature which, the more time went on, had proved philosophically unsatisfactory and biblically un-founded. Balthasar did this with reference to numerous Catholic theologians of the past and present[21] and thus also introduced a 'christological renaissance' into Catholic theology which Barth for his part noted with satisfaction.[22]

In this attempt to ground christocentricity as decisively as Barth but without falling victim to his 'narrowness', Balthasar was followed above all by the young Hans Küng. Küng's dissertation on Barth's understanding of justifica-tion, written in Paris, appeared in 1957. This work was soon to attract considerable attention, since it had demonstrated that there was predomi-nantly substantial agreement between the doctrine of Karl Barth and the Catholic understanding of justification (for which the foundations were laid at the Council of Trent) if that were properly understood. This meant no more and no less than that division between the churches could no longer be justified in terms of this article of faith – for Protestants the *articulus stantis et cadentis ecclesiae*.

But in this book Küng too was not just concerned with the doctrine of grace and justification in the narrower sense; like Barth and Balthasar, he too put the problem of justification in a wider framework of christology and trinitarian theology. For Küng, too, it was clear that: 'Justification is not the central dogma of Christianity. This has always been Catholic teaching and Barth continues it against Luther in the best Catholic tradition. The central *dogma* of *Christ*ianity is the mystery of *Christ*, the mystery in which is revealed the mystery of the triune God as well as the mystery of the total creation which was created good, fell, was redeemed, and is to be consummated.'[23] Here – in the doctrine of the Trinity and the christology of pre-existence and incarnation which follow it – Küng, like Balthasar, saw a fundamental agreement between Catholic theology and Barth. Indeed as a theologian who was not yet thirty Küng was ambitious enough to present his own account of a speculative christology of pre-existence, the conceptual acuteness and speculative force of which is still unparalleled. His excursus 'The Redeemer in God's Eternity' set out to be no more and no less than a precise conceptual definition of 'how the pre-existence of the redeemer should be given theological clarification'.[24]

But why were young Catholic theologians at that time so fascinated by Barth's speculative christology, or better by the christocentricity which had its foundation here? We do not find the answer to this question along the lines of Eero Huovinen, whom I quoted at the beginning; he regards the 'main intention of the content' of *Justification* as being 'to interpret Christ in the light of his pre-existence',[25] and then – as we heard – reads the development of Küng's thought in matters of christology with a kind of decadence hermeneutic and plays off the different christologies in *Justification* and *On Being a Christian* against each other. Such an assessment completely fails to understand the significance of christology in *Justification* for Küng's life and work. For in this book the originality or even the main interest does not lie in a christology of pre-existence and incarnation; on this point in particular it was far too strongly dependent on Barth and traditional Catholic christology. No, the originality and thrust lay elsewhere, and here christology had a function which was ecumenically important. For the connection between justification and a high christology was on the one hand important for Küng for defusing Barth's polemic against the Catholic doctrine of *analogia entis* and on the other hand useful for overcoming the aporias within Catholicism in the understanding of nature and supernature. How are we to understand that?

2. The dispute over grace

In fact, under the influence of mediaeval and baroque scholasticism the Catholic tradition had developed an understanding of reality which can best be illustrated by the picture of a two-storey building. For it had a twofold order of knowledge and being: a natural basis and a supernatural superstructure. To be more specific, it had two forms of knowledge (natural reason and faith given by grace), two levels of knowledge (natural truth and truth of revelation given by grace), and two sciences (philosophy and theology). So in principle there were two storeys, clearly distinct and yet in no way in opposition: the lower one was constructed in the direction of the upper, higher one. And although this had often been caught up in crisis in the course of modern times (as a result of modern philosophy, science, historical criticism), in the politics of church and theology, it had once again been repristinated, externally modernized by more rational analysis and even less biblical theology, in particular in the nineteenth century with textbooks and editions, encyclicals and measures by the Inquisition, and finally given dogmatic sanction by Vatican I.[26]

But did that not result in a fateful split between nature and supernature, human beings and grace, philosophy and theology, or a purely external addition of the two levels ('the extrinsicism of grace')? Was not an autonomy of the human and the creaturely postulated here to which the grace of God was added to some degree only at a second stage, so that God's grace ceased to be the real centre or innermost goal of human existence? That at any rate had been the criticism of Karl Barth, who in addition had also directed his polemics against those divisions of grace which had been made in the traditional Catholic theology of grace (*gratia increata-creata, externa-interna, praeveniens-concomitans, supernaturalis-naturalis*).[27] Indeed Barth had put to

Catholic theology the decisive question whether it really took justification seriously as a free sovereign act of God, whether it really took grace seriously as grace, and whether its assertion of a unity of grace was more than an assertion.

Hans Küng had taken up this 'old fundamental question' of Barth's, 'addressed to Catholics', and stressed it clearly once again: 'Do you not covertly, though in all good faith, assert a ruinously un-Christian autonomy of the human, the creaturely, the natural, so that ultimately you make a hollow shell of *God's incarnation*?'[28]

Or, put even more sharply: 'Is God in *Jesus Christ* taken seriously in Catholic doctrine? ... Is Christ for all places and all times the *principium et finis*, Alpha and Omega, the beginning and end of all the ways of God? Does Jesus Christ have a role to play in the "Christian" teaching on creation in Catholic dogma? ... Do we not find too, in the Catholic theology of justification, an exclusive stress on an *analogia entis* which is not subordinate to the *analogia fidei*? And a simple juxtaposition of God and man, set beside each other on the same level, rather than an absolute subordinating of man as something beneath God and his grace? Is this not *the* crucial reason why the Reformers wanted to have nothing more to do with the Catholic Church? Is this not *the* reason why even today one cannot become Catholic?'[29]

Now of course after the Second World War attempts had been made, even within Catholicism, to break out of the awkward nature-supernature scheme. In 1946 the French Jesuit theologian Henri de Lubac had brought out a book with the title *Le Surnaturel*. On the basis of historical studies he had attempted to demonstrate that the notion of a 'pure' nature (natural order) of human beings with a purely natural aim had in any case arisen in the history of theology only in the sixteenth and seventeenth centuries, in the controversy over the theology of grace put forward by Bajus and Jansenius. In this way he in particular had made it clear that theologically one could give up the idea of a 'pure nature' of man – in fact the presupposition of the scheme of nature and supernature. For any created Spirit was *a priori* endowed by the Creator with a natural striving towards the infinite, towards the eternal bliss of the vision of God (*desiderium naturale beatitudinis*) which, while applying unconditionally, was ineffective in itself, without God coming to meet it. Consequently there was no *natura pura* of human beings which was directed only towards a purely natural final goal. Every human being strove, on the basis of the Creator's will, for eternal bliss, which was a gift (grace) of the Creator and was ultimately fulfilled only through God's grace. But the church *magisterium* had condemned this conception of de Lubac's. In his encyclical *Humani generis* of 1950 Pius XII saw 'the concept of an unmerited supernatural order of grace' undermined by the view that 'God cannot create any being endowed with reason without determining it and calling it to the view of bliss'.[30] Was there a theological way out here?

Young Catholic theologians at the time saw this way out in a stress on christocentricity. Moreover, in his book on *Justification*, in order to safeguard the unity of grace or, better, the unity of the reality of God and the world, Küng, too, resorted to christocentric and universalistic passages, above all from the Gospel of John and from Colossians and Hebrews, passages above all about the mediation of Christ at creation, which had also been key passages for Barth in his christology.[31] And the christo-logic? If all that exists, if the whole of reality had been created in Christ from the beginning, then the traditional theological distinction between a 'natural' order of being (i.e. one existing even independently of Christ) and a 'supernatural' order of salvation collapses. For 'in Christ' there is nothing 'natural', but only 'created', and so always determined by the grace of God. Consequently there was no such thing as a 'pure nature' (*natura pura*) of human beings, directed towards a purely natural final goal (without the vision of God).[32]

In other words, the reception of christology following Karl Barth made it possible for the young Catholic theologians of the time to overcome the traditional theological distinctions and the splitting up of reality into levels and to think of the relationship between creation and salvation, world and grace ('nature and supernature') in universal, unitary terms. 'All creation, being Christoform, has a hidden Trinitarian structure'[33] – thus Küng, and with this statement he more than clearly brought out his interest in this kind of christology. For him this christology was the basis for a unitary, undivided understanding of reality: 'Everything is in Christ, through Him and unto Him. Everything continues to exist in him.'[34]

Thus for Küng the reference to cosmic universalistic christology in Barth's sense represeted the possibility of bidding farewell to the awkward nature-supernature terminology with which even Balthasar had still largely operated in his book on Barth. As Küng wrote: 'Our point here, which according to revelation can in no way be compromised, is that in the present dispensation, man is man only through *Jesus Christ* but even in Jesus Christ man is *man*. Whether one should designate this man as "supernatural" or "natural" appears to be more of a semantic and therefore a secondary question.'[35] So in fact Küng – seven years after *Humani generis* – had written about the problem of grace in his book *Justification* without resorting even once to the current terminology of 'natural-supernatural' and the neo-scholastic-Thomistic 'theory of levels' which was associated with it.

It was the young Joseph Ratzinger who in his criticism of Küng's book on Barth agreed at precisely this point. He remarked that it was a 'contribution to the discussion particularly to be welcomed' that Küng had pointed to the 'concrete centre of a discussion which has been carried on all too much in abstract concepts (natural-supernatural, *analogia entis-fidei*)':[36] 'Jesus Christ; from here the conversation could and should indeed receive new life.'[37] Ratzinger saw one of the strengths of Küng's book as being precisely at this point: it brought out the close connection between creation and saving event which was also so important for Catholic theology. 'Creation,' Ratzinger remarked approvingly at that time, 'must also be understood as saving event in the Catholic view. Christ is in fact the ground of being of creation and the root of the structures of being. The reason why everything is created in Christ is the divine foreknowledge of human sin which is as it were caught up from the beginning in the prior determination of Christ. So creation and saving event are most inwardly interwoven from the roots: there are certainly stages of being in Christ on which our distinction between nature and supernatural rests, but everything is in Christ; the being of beings as such has a christological structure.'[38]

For the Catholic reception of Barth, this means that both Balthasar and Küng carried on their dialogue with Barth not least in the cause of renewal within Catholicism. In the process of what von Balthasar referred to as 'storming the bastions' of neo-scholasticism, Barth was a welcome conversation-partner within Catholicism who healthily 'forced' Catholic dogmatics, in the face of many aporias, to seek new christological dimensions in its own tradition and make them ecumenically fruitful. Precisely because both tried to legitimate christocentricity within Catholicism, they made a contribution to an ecumenical trend in Catholic dogmatics. Moreover, Küng never hesitated to speak of Karl Barth as one of the 'spiritual Fathers' also 'of Catholic renewal in connection with the Second Vatican Council', who as a 'fundamentally evangelical theologian' had challenged Catholic theology.[39] For Küng this was also the significance of Hans Urs von Balthasar's book on Barth: 'I will readily concede that without Balthasar's book on Barth my own work on Barth would have been impossible. I learned from von Balthasar that the Catholic and the Protestant could be reconciled precisely at the point where they are both most consistent with themselves. From him I learned above all that Karl Barth, precisely because he embodied the most consistent implementation of Protestant theology, also comes closest to Catholic theology: evangelically utterly orientated on Christ as centre, and precisely thus reaching out universally in a Catholic way: the possibility of an ecumenical theology.'[40]

3. From Barth the theologian to Hegel the philosopher of speculative christology

There is no doubt that to begin with the young theologian Hans Küng had 'exclusively advocated a christology "from above"'.[41] However, as I have indicated, this was by no means out of overbold speculation. With the reception of Barth's christocentricity, in his book *Justification* Küng first of all wanted to overcome the traditional terminology and structure of the doctrine of grace (nature and supernature) within Catholicism. But indirectly and cautiously at that time a second element was already evident. Referring to a key article by Karl Rahner on christology dating from 1954 ('Current Problems of Christology'),[42] Küng for the first time considered the problem of the immutability or the historicity of God. Moreover the excursus 'The Redeemer in God's Eternity' at the end of *Justification* ends with a significant quotation from Rahner: 'It follows from this statement [about the hypostatic union of Jesus Christ] that the assertion of God's "immutability", of the lack of any real relation between God and the world, is in a true sense a dialectical statement. One may and indeed must say this, without for that reason being a Hegelian.'[43]

Now one thing is certain: Hans Küng, too, did not mean to become a Hegelian when – with a view to a possible Habilitation – he turned to Hegel's christology. Rather, he was fascinated with the prospect of being able to think of God and Christ not only, like Karl Barth, increasingly along the lines of theological tradition, but now in dialogue with modern philosophy. The book is therefore anything but an 'intermezzo' or even a first slide down a slippery slope. It has its continuity with *Justification* in the matter of christocentricity, but this was now to be thought of less in theological than in philosophical terms. So Küng turned to Hegel: 'My view then was that it was precisely with Hegel's help that this christology from above, as it had been elaborated once more in Karl Barth's magnificent multi-volume synthesis, but also as it had been hinted at by Karl Rahner in a handful of articles – that this christology could be renewed for the present day with the help of Hegelian speculation. How this had to happen is expressed in the book, especially with relation to a possible becoming on the part of God and the dialectic that is thereby posited within God himself, as it is actualized in a dialectical conception of the divine attributes.'[44]

The reference is to *The Incarnation of God. An Introduction to Hegel's Philosophical Thought as Prolegomena to a Future Christology*, which appeared in 1970. This date seems remote from the beginnings, but the manuscript has already largely been written between 1956 and 1960. As early as 1957, after the end of Küng's student days in Paris, there was the first version of an account and critique of Hegel in manuscript, and in 1960, at the end of his time as Assistent in Munich, there was a second. However, the work then had to be broken off because of Küng's call to the chair of fundamental theology in the University of Tübingen. First questions of ecclesiology had priority: the Second Vatican Council, which had been surprisingly convened in the first half of the 1960s, had brought them to the fore. Books like *The Council and Reunion, Structures of the Church, The Church, Truthfulness* and finally *Infallible?* began to appear in the course of the 1960s.

When Küng then continued work on the Hegel manuscript, the intellectual landscape in Germany had suddenly changed. But as a result the subject-matter of the Hegel book took on a topicality which would have been thought impossible in the 1950s. For at that time no one could guess how basically philosophical the critical discussion with Christianity, the church and religion would once again become. After an intellectual shift brought about by the Third Reich, the war and the post-war period, in the 1960s there had been a revitalization of modern criticism of religion. The Frankfurt School (T.W. Adorno and M. Horkheimer) and critical rationalism (K. Popper and H. Albert) had come to play a leading role. Their attacks on religion blew like an icy wind through the lukewarm post-war air of self-assurance in theology and the church, and it was only of limited benefit to the Catholic church that at the Second Vatican Council it had just carried out some long overdue necessary reforms which had been in the wings since the Reformation and the En-lightenment. At the end of the 1960s countless intellectuals in Germany followed Nietzsche in taking the 'death of God' for granted, and indeed even theologians began to practise a 'theology after the death of God'.

In the face of this situation Hans Küng saw a new opportunity to react theologically to the changed intellectual landscape with his Hegel manuscript. The question of God had suddenly come into the centre to a degree which had not been the case since the crisis of the First World War. Here reference back to a great philosophical tradition was to help to overcome the spiritual crisis of the present. So for Küng, 'Whether the question of God is faced more with western secularism or with eastern Marxism, theology today is picking up the threads at the very point where, before the advent of dialectical theology, this issue last stood at the centre of interest, namely in German Idealism, and particularly in Hegel, the thinker who has so much to say both to secular bourgeois society and to Marxist socialism.' And there was another element: 'Whether the object of discussion is more the dead or the living, the present or the future God, theology today, like German Idealism, is concerned not so much with the "wholly other", unworldly God, as was early dialectical theology (the theology of diastasis), but rather with the God of the here-and-now. Precisely in this concern contemporary theology is forging fresh links between theology and christology.'[45]

So the transition from Barth to Hegel was also consistent on the grounds of the formation of christological theory and was in no way a complete departure from Barth. For it was Barth in particular who in an impressive essay on Hegel had called on theologians to 'learn' from Hegel.[46] According to Barth, Hegel also had 'something of decisive and lasting importance to say, or recall, to theology, and not only to the theology of his own time'.[47] And in fact: what was 'at the beginning', the meaning of 'God', 'being' and 'truth', had again been put at the beginning of philosophical thought, and by Hegel in particular. For Hegel had wanted once again from the start to put God at the focal point of philosophy.[48] Here Barth saw Hegel in particular as an ally against what he called 'modern cultural awareness', which for him was none other than the revaluation of human beings (anthropology) to the detriment of God (theology). With Hegel, Barth wanted to remind theology again of its most distinctive task, 'the possibility that truth might be history, event; that it might always be recognized and discovered in actuality and not otherwise. Theology might and should have known, not less well but better than Hegel, that its knowledge, its knowledge in particular, was only possible in the form of a strict obedience to the self-movement of truth, and therefore as a knowledge which was itself moved. It could let itself be reminded by Hegel that the source of knowledge of Reformation theology, at all events, had been the Word, the Word of God, the word of truth. But this also means, the event of God, the event of truth.'[49]

4. The interest in Hegel: thinking of the living God

So Hegel was concerned to think in philosophical terms of God's priority, indeed to take the living quality of God quite seriously. For him, to think of the living God meant to think of God in creation and history as living reality, as a God who himself undergoes a history and reveals himself in this history: in becoming the one who he is. Hegel wanted to trace God's 'career', the way of the 'absolute Spirit', as he emptied himself in the world and raised this world through all stages to himself and his infinity and divinity. For Hegel, the living God is the one who moves, changes, undergoes a history; a God who does not remain what he is but becomes what he is, a God who does not persist in himself exalted above the world but comes out of himself and empties himself: already through the coming into being of the world which has its climax in God's becoming man. Only such a God is for Hegel the true, and also the Christian, God: 'In brief, according to Hegel, the true God is the one who is both finite and infinite, both God and man in unity.'[50]

It is therefore evident that Hegel could also draw statements about christology in particular into his philosophical thought. Without exaggeration we may say that if Barth was the modern theologian of speculative christology, Hegel was its modern philosopher. For no philosopher of modern times has taken more seriously the subject-matter covered by christology (the infinite in the finite) than Hegel. For him the Christ event was not an event of mere private piety, but a world event of the Spirit, the significance of which for humanity as a whole he wanted to bring to light. The Christ event, the incarnation of the eternal Son of God, was for him the most visible expression of the sublation of the finite in the infinite. He saw the death and resurrection of the Son of God as the expression of the idea that even the 'death of God' could be abolished and transcended in God himself. Therefore according to Hegel the death of Christ in particular could not just be regarded morally as a 'sacrifice of empirical being'[51] but had to be understood in a truly philosophical way as the emptying of the divine Absolute itself. This was to be not just as a 'historical' Good Friday (that particular event) but rather as a truly 'speculative' (historical-eternal) 'Good Friday', which Hegel wanted to restore 'in the whole truth and harshness of its godlessness'.[52]

Could there still be any doubt that a Christian theology had to have considerable interest in this thought in particular? Was it not obvious that a good 150 years after Hegel's death, Christian theology for its part wanted to 'sublate', i.e. inherit, a thought which evidently put human beings in a position to consider the fleeting notions of God himself before the creation of the world with the dialectic of pure concepts of reason and thus understand the being of God itself – against all traditional, static metaphysics of being – as flowing, historical, dynamic? Was it not obvious that the Christian theologian wanted to make fruitful a way of thought in which 'the specifically theological crosses the christological'; that he attempted to grasp the possibility of himself thinking out 'the dynamic unity in the living Godhead'?[53] Indeed, Küng's interest in the Hegelian understanding of God consisted specifically in showing that Hegel made it possible to think of the classical concept of being and God in a dynamic and historical way and thus had laid 'the foundation for the comprehensive reconciliation of all antitheses'.[54]

Thus the contribution of *The Incarnation of God* lay above all in the vision of a 'God of the future', or better in the outline of a future understanding of God which was to be found at a point in time moulded by the criticism of religion and the philosophy of the Enlightenment. Küng derives from Hegelian philosophy key data for a future understanding of God which was to stamp his theology once and for all. 'Hegel's God is not a Spirit beyond the stars, who operates on the world from the outside, but rather the Spirit who is at work in the spirits, in the depths of human subjectivity. His doctrine of the Trinity is not a brand of conceptual mathematics remote from reality, but a trinitarian "*oikonomia*" brought into relationship with history. The creation of the world is not treated as an abstract *ex improviso* decision of the divine will, but is explained in terms of the essence of God ... Divine providence is not asserted in terms of an arbitrary God, nor is it proved along abstractly historical lines; instead, it is glimpsed in the concrete course of history. World history is not channelled into a constricted sacral *Heilsgeschichte* surrounded by profane history; on the contrary, the entirety of world history is seen as a single universal *Heilsgeschichte*, which, when looked at in religious terms, is centred on the event of incarnation.'[55] So it is understandable that in his book *Does God Exist?*, Küng can programmatically call for a 'post-Hegelian concept of God' and does indeed develop it.[56]

5. Criticism of Hegel along the lines of Barth

But despite all the significance of Hegel for a dynamic-historical understanding of being and God there is one decisive point at which Küng distances himself from Hegel. He resolutely opposes the almost compulsive Hegelian primal dialectic of being and nothingness in order to defend the freedom of God with a reference to the living God of scripture. Küng saw in Hegel the danger that 'God himself is so predetermined by this dialectic of being'[57] that God is no longer taken seriously as *the* principle of being and knowing. He saw the danger that the key christological statements in scripture about the incarnation, death and resurrection of the Son of God would ultimately serve only to illustrate the dialectic of being that had been postulated beforehand. And in that way the 'historical Good Friday' in Hegel had become completely 'speculative', a mere illustration of the primal dialectic of death and life, being and nothingness! Does not this philosophy really also need the historical Jesus, the concrete person of the man from Nazareth, in whose name this whole christology had been developed? Was there not here – in the 'sublation' of the concrete figure of Jesus Christ in a philosophy of the absolute Spirit – the 'eternal doubt'[58] which Hegel leaves: 'Is metaphysics Christianized here or is Christianity rendered metaphysical?'[59]

Thus Küng had resolutely taken his stand in the tradition of theological criticism of Hegel which extended from Kierkegaard to Barth and which had complained that in Hegel's speculative dialectic of God and the world there was already a levelling down of that difference between God and the world which for scripture could not be given up. So Küng did not want in any way to end up in a 'renewal of Hegel's system or of his speculative method'.[60] Here his criticism of Hegel was essentially in line with Karl Barth, who had similarly already written against Hegel: 'Hegel did not dispute the positive and historical nature of revelation, the uniqueness of Christ; rather he emphatically affirmed it. But with Hegel God and man can never confront one another in a relationship which is actual and indissoluble; a word, a new word revelatory in the strict sense, cannot pass between them; it cannot be uttered and cannot be heeded.'[61]

Hans Küng also insisted on this 'relationship which is actual and indissoluble' between God and man, and in this way showed how much *The Incarnation of God* had preserved Barth's great intentions – as far as the understanding of God was concerned. As he wrote: 'It is, theologically speaking, quite impossible to minimize the irrevocable difference between God and man ... We have been able to trace how internal philosophical criticism of his thought has itself upheld this principle against Hegel's speculative identity. Moreover ... this principle must be theologically radicalized ... in the *ontic* perspective we should see all God-world occurrence as based on God's free grace instead of on speculative necessity; and in the *noetic-ethical* perspective we should see all God-world mystery as based on trusting faith instead of on absolute knowledge.'[62] And in this criticism Küng referred explicitly to the 'biblical message' of the freedom and grace of God attested in the Old and New Testaments, just as Karl Barth had done. Barth had written in his essay on Hegel: 'Hegel, in making the dialectical method of logic the essential nature of God, made impossible the knowledge of the actual dialectic of grace, which has its foundation in the freedom of God. Upon the basis of this dialectic the attempt to speak of a necessity to which God himself is supposed to be subject would be radically impossible. But at all events the dialectic in which we ourselves exist, a method which we are ourselves at all times capable of using – this is not the actual dialectic of grace. Hegel did not open the gateway of this knowledge to theology, and it seems that it remained closed to his own perception too. That is probably the weightiest and most significant of the doubts about him which might be raised from the theological point of view.'[63]

6. The possibility of reconciling biblical and philosophical thought: the historicity of God

Once one has thus established critically the priority of biblical thought to philosophical thought, one can go on to interrogate the fossilized theological traditions anew in the light of philosophical thought, above all traditional church christology (the doctrine of two natures). For the remarkable thing about classical christology is that it has to conceive of the notion of a combination of the infinite and the finite, the notion that the infinite God enters into a history, becomes man, suffers, rises – but against the background of a static metaphysics of being with a Greek-Hellenistic stamp which strictly ruled out all movement, all becoming, all historicity of God: 'Thus God's eternity was looked on too much as a Platonic timelessness and too little as a powerful, living contemporaneity with all time. His omnipresence was seen too much as a static extension throughout the universe and too little as almighty dominion over space. His goodness toward the world and man was regarded too much as a natural emanation of the Good and too little as the free self-giving in love and grace of the God who acts in history. His righteousness was viewed too much as a distributive and retributive justice based on a timeless concept of order and too little as the saving righteousness rooted in God's fidelity to his covenant and promises. His incomprehensibility was pictured too much as the abstract absence of attributes in an anonymous ground of the world and too little as the otherness of the free God demonstrated in his acts. Thus while it is true that God appeared as the ground of the world, he was depicted too little as the one who is alive in a personal sense.'[64]

But the task of early Christian proclamation and theology, namely that of justifying in the Hellenistic intellectual world the Jewish-Christian concept of God as it had been made concrete in belief in Christ, had become so immense that it lost the opportunity of a 'radical transformation' of Hellenistic philosophy in the biblical spirit. According to Küng, there remained 'an ultimate dissonance between elements of biblical and philosophical provenance, along with an unbalanced tension potentially affecting christology most of all'.[65] Compromises came into being like the doctrine of two natures in christology, disputes over too much or too little divinity in Jesus Christ, aporias of christology on the narrow scale of the timelessness and historicity of God.

This explains the theological strategy of Küng's thrust: 'classical christology itself compels us to think beyond it and to take it more seriously than it could take itself insofar as it was hampered by the Greek metaphysical concept of God. Consequently we should avail ourselves of this opportunity and take the trouble, while presupposing classical christology's doctrine of the two natures, to think this notion further and to think it through consistently, even if we are convinced that – as will be demonstrated – an alternative way in to christology is possible in principle and at the present time even requisite.'[66] This is a highly remarkable statement given the overall conception of the book. For first of all Küng develops christological arguments 'presupposing the doctrine of the two natures', although at one point he is in principle to argue for 'another approach to christology', 'from below'. Here for the first time in the book we have an indication of a departure from the original conception which must be mentioned later.

However, first of all the whole book on Hegel ends up with the sketch of an understanding of God with a christological stamp, in which 'Hegel's major intentions' are to be brought to bear in a new way, but 'under decisively modified presuppositions'.[67] But the whole book lives by the hope that today it will be possible to go further along 'Hegel's lines' than classical christology: 'While the trains of thought developed from classical christology clearly led away from the Greek metaphysical concept of God, which proved too static or transcendent, they led at the same time toward Hegel's concept of God. The dialectical dynamism of the latter is manifestly better suited to express what must be stated by a classical christology which has been thought through to the end.'[68]

And so *The Incarnation of God* first of all finds its theological climax in a dialectical conceptual *tour de force* in relation to what is probably the most difficult chapter in the Christian doctrine of God: the impassibility of God, the dialectic of the divine properties, the immutability and coming to be of God. With great eloquence, New Testament Christian sayings about the surrender and humility of God, the impotence and suffering of the Son of God, the Son in the form of God and the form of the servant become great theological themes. And specifically? The suffering of the Son of God can no longer make

God appear an uninvolved, impassible God; he must be a 'compassionate God'. In the incarnation of the Son the immutable itself changes. And all this is in turn sublated dialectically in a new synthesis in which the Godhead of God can be understood to be not involved in a deficit but as a prodigal fullness, not subject to compulsion but as outflowing grace, not delivered over to time and history, but as a power over history free of time. All in all, then, this is a bold attempt 'to combine serious consideration both of the modern developments in our understanding of God and of the decisive features of the biblical understanding of God in a new understanding of the historicity of God, which would show itself to the world and to men and women as primordial historicity and power over history. As the living God, by way of contrast with a God who exists in an unhistorical mode of being, God both has a history and himself creates history.'[69]

Now that means that the understanding of God in *The Incarnation of God*, with its christological stamp, attempts:

1. A sublation of Hegel's great intentions: Küng wanted 'theology to avoid either cheaply and superficially harmonizing the "God of the Fathers and of Jesus Christ" with the "God of the philosophers" (according to the wont of apologists and scholastics old and new) or else simply dissociating the two (according to the practice of Enlightenment philosophers and biblicistic theologians)' but rather 'to *sublate* the "God of the philosophers" in the "God of the Fathers and of Jesus Christ" in the best Hegelian sense of the word, that is negative, positive and supereminent sublation'.

2. A sublation of Barth's great intentions. Anyone who knows Barth's christology, above all the new conception in Part Four of the *Church Dogmatics* which appeared in 1953, will clearly see the degree to which Küng's remarks about God's passibility, the dialectic of God's properties, the immutability and coming to be of God, indeed all the statements about God's historicity also correspond with Barth's christological dialectics. One only has to compare Küng's chapter on 'The Historicity of God' in *The Incarnation of God* with Barth's section 'The Way of the Son of God into the Far Country' in *Church Dogmatics* IV §59.

7. Criticism of Barth and Hegel in the light of a christology 'from below'

Had that solved all the problems? Had not the theological plans indicated in *Justification* (christocentricity) which were to be worked out with the Hegel book turned out extremely well? Were not philosophy (Hegel) and theology (Barth) reconciled under the sign of christocentricity – for all the irremovable difference between theology and philosophy? Had not theology again related scripture to modern thought? And had not at the same time an answer been given here to the modern criticism of religion?

However, something remarkable now happens. Instead of ending with such speculative christological syntheses, the author now adds another counter-point. Instead of ending along the line of Barth and Hegel with high flights of dialectical conceptuality about a movement in God, he makes a surprising shift. Instead of contenting himself with a biblical-modern doctrine of God under the slogan 'no going back behind Hegel', all at once he remarks 'no going back behind David Friedrich Strauss'. The slogan is now 'the historicity of Jesus – in a historical-critical sense'.[70]

What did that mean, given that christology had just been developed concretely and had been steeped in speculation? Given that there had been constant talk of the incarnation of the Son of God, his suffering, dying and resurrection? Given that the New Testament had been constantly present in the form of Johannine and Pauline christology and that it had even been used *against* Hegel's system? What did it mean, given that the author had described the significance of christology for a modern understanding of God with great speculative force and rhetorical verve? The answer is that Küng had noted that while along the lines of Hegel and Barth he had spoken in high theological terms of *Christ* Jesus, *Jesus* Christ had hardly appeared. Who this Jesus, in whose name this whole high christology had been developed, had been in concrete terms seemed unimportant, indeed was evidently not at all decisive for the doctrine of God. It had been enough to refer to the incarnation of the Son of God, his lowly form, his suffering, death and resurrection, in order to be able to present a new doctrine of God with full dialectical refinement. And these highly speculative christological and theological operations had in principle already been no problem for the young Küng as early as 1957!

When Hans Küng took up the manuscript in Tübingen for the third time after the end of the Second Vatican Council (1962–1965), he saw that here he had as it were lost the historical ground from under his feet and that he could no longer get away without the historical counterpoint: 'The more in Tübingen I occupied myself intensively (and this was the first time I had done so despite numerous lectures on exegesis at the Pontifical Biblical Institute and also in Paris) with exegesis on historical and critical principles, as exemplified in a very lively fashion for me by my colleague in the Protestant faculty of theology, Ernst Käsemann, who was a pupil of Bultmann's, the more difficult it became for me to maintain this speculation in connection with the under-standing of God and with christology. This doesn't mean at all that I had abandoned the positive intentions of a christology from above. But what increasingly became my goal – and I remember a long conversation with my then colleague at Tübingen, Professor Ratzinger, who endorsed me in this – was that it was from below that people of today could more convincingly strive to attain and could reach the statements of a "high" christology. Thus I then devoted myself with growing intensity to research into the historical Jesus.'[71]

So it should be noted that to the term 'historicity of Jesus' Hans Küng adds 'in a historical-critical sense'. For it is precisely here that he differs decisively from Hegel and Barth. For all their interest in the human Jesus of Nazareth, neither was ultimately interested in the historical question: who this person really was in history, in whose name this whole highly speculative theology and christology was being done. Already in Hegel's time, Ferdinand Christian Baur and David Friedrich Strauss of Tübingen had founded a tradition which – similarly an heir of the Enlightenment – investigated Jesus of Nazareth with the strict criteria of historical criticism. This tradition might not simply be ignored, especially as the historical questioning had undeniably gained acuteness and plausibility through the history-of-religions school, liberal theology and also Rudolf Bultmann and his school.

But what was the theological consequence of this turn towards research into the historical Jesus? Here too the consequence was first of all a criticism of the classical doctrine of two natures in christology. Just as Küng had wanted, with Hegel, to open the formulas of this classical christology in the direction of the historicity of God, now too he wanted to open them in the direction of the historicity of Jesus. On historical and exegetical grounds there was no question for him of an 'unhistorical repristination of classical christology'.[72]

Granted, even now Küng did not declare that involvement in the doctrine of two natures was simply impossible. It was historically justified and had often been the only real possibility for earlier times. But, Küng asked, 'Is this significance still so self-evident, indeed was it even so self-evident as far as the New Testament and especially the synoptic witnesses were concerned, that contemporary theology can simply proceed dogmatically from an established doctrine of the Trinity and presuppose the divinity of Jesus, i.e. the pre-existence of the Son, as a matter of course, so that it only remains to ask how this Logos who was pre-existent in the Trinity was able to assume and join to himself a human nature, in which process cross and resurrection must largely appear as little more than footnotes to the incarnation?'[73] And if that is so – what would be the consequence? Answer: 'Would it not be much more in keeping with both the New Testament witnesses and the historical thought of modern man to proceed from the man Jesus, his historical message and appearance, his life and fate and his historical reality and historical effect, in order to enquire about this man Jesus' relationship to God, about his unity with the Father? In short, is it not appropriate to eschew a christology organized speculatively or dogmatically from above in favour of one worked out historically from below?'[74]

But to take history seriously with a hermeneutics of historical criticism had consequences for the whole layout of the Hegel book and also for Hans Küng's further thought. For much as Küng wanted to lay the foundation for a present-day understanding of God with Hegelian philosophy in order to make it possible to listen again to the living God of the Bible who acts in history; much as Küng wanted to bring about a critical reconciliation of the 'God of the philosophers' and the 'God of the Bible', he could not reach this now along the lines of Barthian and Hegelian speculation. For historical and exegetical reasons Küng could now no longer achieve his statements about the historicity of God – as in the first two versions of his Hegel manuscript – by a dialectic of being within the Godhead along the lines of Barth and Hegel. Moreover, in the last version of the Hegel manuscript the speculative problems about God's capacity for suffering, the dialectic of the divine properties and the mutability of God, chapters which originally were to have been the conceptional crown of the whole work, had been relegated to excursuses. In this way, while *The Incarnation of God* did not take on the character of an 'intermezzo', it did become a propaedeutic ('prolegomena') – paradoxically enough, when one considers its extent. This propaedeutic character was the result of a self-problematization of the christology 'from above' which previously had been so much taken for granted.

Nevertheless, what was originally to have been achieved by a dialectic of being within the Godhead (on the basis of a few key christological statements in the theology of John and the deutero-Pauline letters), Küng now wanted to achieve by means of history. He wanted to preserve the same depth and height of the statements about God's being and action and yet not to engage in speculations on conditions within the Godhead. And what could only be hinted at in *The Incarnation of God* was developed in breadth four years later in *On Being a Christian* (1974). It is impossible here to go into his treatment of countless individual problems of christology. I shall keep strictly to my theme, which is how the intentions of Barth and Hegel are now also sublated in *On Being a Christian*. For we cannot understand the basic conception of that book unless we see that, for all the change in his christology, here too Küng has throughout maintained the basic intention of Barth and Hegel. In the case of Hegel that means that one cannot understand the basic conception of *On Being a Christian* unless one sees that Küng can bring out a surprising correspondence between the modern understanding of God and Jesus' understanding of God. The structural analogies are in fact staggering.

8. The revolution in the understanding of God

Of course Küng's starting point is that Jesus' understanding of God rests on very different cultural presuppositions from those of modern times: on another understanding of the world and reality. And this difference cannot 'be reversed today merely by an appeal to what Jesus said'.[75] But at the same time Küng asks: 'Should it not be possible also to understand the God of Jesus against such a modern horizon? Should it not be possible to bring what is decisive from Jesus' standpoint within this horizon? And on the other hand should it not be possible to answer and to answer unequivocally – particularly from Jesus' standpoint – what necessarily had to remain – as we saw – equivocal, vague, open, in man's general or philosophical understanding of God?"[76]

In the end these were rhetorical questions, but *On Being a Christian*, too, lives by the conviction that today in particular it is possible to *illuminate the God of Jesus under modern conditions*. How? By seeing that the God of Jesus is none other than the God of Israel. And this God is indeed already a historical, living, 'personal' God who is in the world and yet transcends it: at the same time of this world and beyond it, far and near, above the world and within it, future and present. This is no God who does not suffer, nor an arbitrary God; this is neither a primal natural principle nor a metaphysical being, neither a dumb force nor an anonymous power, but the living Creator God. And no greater misunderstanding of Küng's doctrine is possible than the charge of pantheism or Platonism, direct or indirect.[77]

Something else is decisive. Without being directed as before to a dialectic within God and categories like the self-distinction of God from God, Küng can now once again think through the properties of God dialectically and thus open up the ontological foundations of his doctrine of God. To be specific:

– God's eternity must not be understood as Platonic timelessness, but as powerfully living simultaneity with all time;
– his ubiquity is not inactive extension in the universe, but sovereign dominion over all space;
– his spirituality is not exclusive opposition to matter which is regarded as evil, but power infinitely superior to all created things;
– his goodness toward the world and men is not a natural radiation of the good, but freely loving, gracious attention;
– his immutability is not a rigid, elemental, dead immobility, but essential fidelity to himself in all his abounding life;
– his justice is not a distribution of rewards and reprisals based on a timeless idea of order, but a merciful, salvation-creating justice, rooted in fidelity to the covenant with men;
– his incomprehensibility is not the abstract lack of qualities of a nameless "whence" of our uncertain existence, but the otherness, uncontrollability, unforeseeability which are demonstrated in his action.'[78]

So it is understandable that Küng did not need a speculative dialectic in God to be able to speak of a revolution in the understanding of God. The proclamation of Jesus himself was a quite adequate basis for being able to say unprecedented, unexpected, revolutionary things about this God. But conversely, that means that for Küng, from the start, person and cause, messenger and message cannot be separated. Why? Because Jesus himself stands for the proclamation of *this* God – he and no one else, no Sadducee, no Pharisee and no Qumran monk. Certainly, this God of Jesus is in fact no other God than the

God of Israel, but this is a God proclaimed by Jesus in quite a different way. To put it pointedly: 'a God not of the devout observers of the law but of the lawbreakers, in fact – we must speak hyperbolically in order to bring out the contradictions and the scandal – not a God of God-fearers, but a God of the godless.'[79] In other words, Küng attaches the utmost importance to the fact that the unprecedented character of the understanding of God is not first to be attained by statements with a christological focus, but is itself grounded in the proclamation of Jesus. Where the new understanding of God is concerned, Jesus' proclamation and the later New Testament christology have a unity and continuity of content. In this way Küng had moved from a dialectic of being within God to a historical dialectic of revelation.

9. The dispute over christology

But did that mean that the concerns of Karl Barth's christology 'from above' had been given up? Had all that was ontological and metaphysical now been removed from christology and pure subjectivity and functionality been established? Was only the 'value experience of the believing subject living after Christ' now in the forefront of Küng's approach? In *On Being a Christian* was the historical Jesus no more than 'one who clarifies and embodies the initial value-experience which human beings already find in their own reality'? To put it bluntly, these questions ask whether christology had not become essentially superfluous, because even without Christ human beings already have a particular self-understanding, a particular 'value-experience'. Such a criticism of Küng's christology completely misses the point.

Already in *The Incarnation of God* Küng had made it clear that a christology 'from above' and a christology 'from below' cannot simply be set against each other so that, 'as often happened in the last century, it is simply derived psychologically from the pious consciousness and historically direct from history'. So here a christology which would be no more than the 'value experience of the believing subject living after Christ' is rejected. And here Küng expressly also took Barth's side: 'Notwithstanding its radical involvement in history, a christology from below is never tantamount to that "reverence before history" which earned the reproach of Karl Barth. On the contrary, faced with the Jesus who both proclaims and is proclaimed, such a christology finds itself confronted by the appeal of God in history, before which man cannot remain neutral. While heed must be paid to man's situation and understanding of reality prior to his hearing the Gospel, and while account must be taken of his changing world picture, a christology from below will nevertheless never mean simply a christology of human self-consciousness or of human piety, but rather a christology of divine revelation which radically lays claim to man's faith. Faith will not be regarded as merely a human attitude, a numinous feeling or a pious state of mind, but rather as a response to the God who acts in history as he is revealed in Jesus.'[80]

Similarly, in *On Being a Christian*, for all his reception of historical-critical questioning and all his criticism of the dogmatic tradition, Küng holds to a fundamental unity of christology, a continuity between the New Testament and the great church tradition: 'That God and man are truly involved in the story of Jesus Christ is something to be steadfastly upheld by faith even today ... In the light of the New Testament therefore no interpretation of the story of Jesus Christ can be justified which makes him out to be "only God": a God moving about on the earth, relieved of human defects and weaknesses. But neither must he be seen as "only man": a preacher, prophet or sage, symbol or cipher for universally human basic experiences.' Here too Küng explicitly stresses 'the uniqueness, underivability and unsurpassibility of the call, offer and claim made known in and with Jesus, ultimately not of human but of divine origin and therefore absolutely reliable, requiring men's unconditional involvement'.[81]

This becomes particularly evident in *Does God Exist?* (1978). In this book in particular, in the face of much criticism also from the church *magisterium*, Küng was concerned once again to make his christological position precise. Here, quite consistently, he had to reject as an 'incomprehensible falsification' of his christology the assertion that for him Jesus Christ was 'only an exemplary human being' and merely 'God's spokesman and advocate'. Küng equally explicitly rejects the suggestion that he denied the christological statements of the Nicene creed. On the contrary, it had been his aim 'to make it intelligible to people today'.[82]

Furthermore, along the basic line of *The Incarnation of God* and *On Being a Christian* Küng attempts to avoid alternatives in christology (like functional-ontological) which are open to misunderstanding. As he explicitly states: 'Functional statements – which are undoubtedly to the fore – and ontological statements must not be torn apart'.[83] Nor does he leave any doubt that even on his approach it is possible to confess Jesus as Son of God: 'In this comprehensive – not speculative but historical – perspective it can be made understandable even today that Jesus before Paul and then also in the Pauline tradition is understood as the revelation of God's power and wisdom, as head and lord of creation, as image, true image of God, as the Yes of God. In this light, it can also be understood and accepted that Jesus is described by John not only as God's Word but also indirectly as equal to God, even as Lord and God. And in this perspective we can understand such difficult and sublime statements as that in Christ lives the fullness of divinity, that God's Word became flesh. This, at any rate, is what we mean when we speak of "God in Jesus Christ". And in this sense, we agree also with the Council of Nicaea, in 325, when it speaks of Jesus Christ as "God from God, Light from Light, true God from true God, begotten, not made, of one Being with the Father".'[84]

In this closing statement it emerges that Hans Küng had to reject the construed alternative of either Jesus as a 'mere man' in whom God was present in action or Jesus as the 'only-begotten eternal Son of God', as being a pseudo-alternative. He declares unmistakably that this was 'no alternative' for the New Testament.[85] Why not? Because the New Testament is not concerned to tear the man Jesus and a heavenly being 'Son of God' apart but to recognize and confess the Son of God precisely in the human Jesus. Therefore in the light of the New Testament Küng rejects the alternative of ontology or functionality in christology: 'If "ontological" is meant as the opposite of "psychological" and the purpose is to reject a separation of person and work, being and interpretation, content of faith and act of faith, then I can sustantially agree, even if I do not much like the word in this connection. But if "ontological" in fact calls for a Hellenistic ontology (which is then perhaps adapted to modern times) of the kind that underlies the traditional doctrine of two natures, the christology of being and essences, along with many others I cannot accept it.'[86]

In other words, Küng attaches supreme importance to establishing that the christological confessions are not just a function of the understanding of faith, but say something about God's very being and thus in fact have ontological consequences. So there is no basis to the charge that Küng has not clarified the ontological presuppositions of his christology. On the contrary, precisely because Küng put such emphasis on the presence of *God* in the historical form of Jesus, at the same time his starting point was that this as it were also 'changed' the nature of God. Precisely on the basis of his historical approach Küng can make short, ontological, statements about the ground of being, the reality of God himself: 'I know that where Jesus is, there is God; that he tells me what is God's will; that where Jesus acts and talks, God is at his side; that where Jesus suffers and dies, there is God's hidden presence.'[87]

So for Küng Jesus is anything but an exchangeable religious factor, one which, changing historically, at one time puts one accent on God's cause and another time another accent – as hundreds of prophets, saints and founders of religion tend to do in turn. In the dialogue between religions in particular, Küng has consistently held to this position which some people find offensive or difficult to carry through – against all the tendencies towards relativization in a 'pluralistic theology of religion'.[88] Precisely because for Küng *God himself* has revealed himself in Jesus Christ and Jesus himself can be understood most deeply only in the light of God, Küng can show credibly why Jesus – as he himself says – 'should have this unique and authoritative signifiance for mankind and also for myself; why he in particular and no other of the great men – not Buddha, K'ung-fu-tse or Mohammed, nor even Marx or Freud – can call me with absolutely binding authority to discipleship'.[89]

So in this sense the christology of Hans Küng must be understood as an attempt to *sublate the major concerns of a christology 'from above' in a christology 'from below'*. His understanding of God proves to be moulded by Hegel, but is ultimately indebted to the biblical theology which he learned from Karl Barth. It was therefore no lip-service to this great Protestant theologian of the twentieth century when in 1987 Küng said that 'even today theology must keep resolutely to the great intentions of Karl Barth',[90] for all the criticism that needs to be made of Barth's approach. To keep to Barth's great intentions means specifically, for Küng: 'The biblical texts are not mere documents of philological-historical research but make possible an encounter with the "wholly other"; the utterly human testimonies of the Bible are concerned with God's Word which human beings need to recognize, know and confess. So more than neutral observation and interpretation is required of human beings: their repentance, conversion, faith is called for, a faith which remains a venture. Here human salvation and disaster are at stake. And the task of the church is to express uncompromisingly in society through the human words of its preaching this word of God on which human beings can constantly rely in trust. Both church proclamation and church dogmatics have to be utterly concentrated on *Jesus Christ*, on the one who for believers is not an exemplary "good man" but in whom God himself has spoken and acted: Jesus Christ is the decisive criteria for all talk of God and humanity.'[91] Here is the continuity of subject matter from *Justification* through *The Incarnation of God* and *On Being a Christian* to *Does God Exist?*. A 'hermeneutics of decadence' of the kind mentioned at the beginning of this article fails to note this continuity of substance. It is inappropriate for even beginning to understand Küng's christology.

Notes

1. E. Huovinen, *Idea Christi. Die idealistische Denkform und Christologie in der Theologie von Hans Küng*, Hanover 1985, 128f. Cf. the critical review by H. Häring in *Theologische Literaturzeitung* 112, 1987, cols. 377f.

2. W. Kasper, 'Christologie von unten? Kritik und Neuansatz gegenwärtigen Christologie', in *Grundfragen der Christologie heute*, ed. L. Scheffzyk, Freiburg im Breisgau 1975, 159–65; H. Küng, 'Anmerkungen zu W. Kasper, "Christologie von unten?"', ibid., 170–9; and again W. Kasper, 'Für eine Christologie in geschichtlicher Perspektive. Replik auf die Anmerkungen von H. Küng', ibid., 179–83; A. Grillmeier, 'Jesus von Nazareth – im Schatten des Gottessohnes?', in *Diskussion über Hans Küngs "Christ sein"*, Mainz 1976, 196–243; id., 'Wir glauben an den einen Herrn, Jesus Christus, Gottes eingeborenen Sohn. Unwandelbare Lehre im Wandel der Verkündigung', in *Zur Sache. Theologische Streitfragen im Fall Küng*, ed. L. Bertsch and M. Kehl, Würzburg 1980, 35–79; P. Hünermann, 'Information – Reflexion – Kritik. Zur Auseinandersetzung zwischen H. Küng und dem kirchlichen Lehramt', in *Zur Sache*, 154–71; H.G. Pöhlmann, 'Solidarität unter Vorbehalt. Evangelische Erwägungen zur Christologie von Hans

Küng', *Lutherische Monatschefte* 19, 1989, 525–7. The account of Küng's christology by D. McCready, *Jesus Christ for the Modern World. The Christology of the Catholic Tübingen School*, New York 1991, 261–96, is terrifyingly superficial. The author gives the impression that Küng's christology 'from below' is a kind of popular scientific christology for simple people without having understood the complex philosophical, theological and hermeneutical problems of the formation of a christological theory 'from below'.

3. Huovinen, *Idea Christi* (n.1), 75–92.
4. For the Catholic reception of Barth cf. H. Küng, *Justification*, 304f.
5. K. Barth, *Church Dogmatics* I.1 (1932), Edinburgh ²1975, xiii.
6. K. Barth, Church Dogmatics II. 1 (1940), Edinburgh 1957, 83; cf. Küng, *Justification*, 27–32.
7. H. Küng, 'Karl Barth und die katholische Theologie', *Theologische Literaturzeitung* 112, 1987, cols. 561–78: 565.
8. Ibid.
9. H.U. von Balthasar, *The Theology of Karl Barth*, New York 1972, esp. 191–227.
10. Cf. K. Barth, *Church Dogmatics* IV.3 (1959), Edinburgh ²1967, 103–65. What is meant here is Barth's 'doctrine of lights'. Küng has also drawn attention to it: *Does God Exist?*, 525–7.
11. Küng, 'Karl Barth und die katholische Theologie' (n.7), col. 566.
12. For Barth's christology cf. K.-J. Kuschel, *Born Before All Time? The Dispute over Christ's Origin*, London and New York 1992, 61–123 (with bibliography).
13. For the context of this theme in the history of theology cf. H. Küng, 'Christozentrik', *Lexikon für Theologie und Kirche*, II, Freiburg im Breisgau 1958, 1169–74.
14. von Balthasar, *The Theology of Karl Barth* (n.9), 184.
15. H. Volk, 'Die Christologie bei Karl Barth und Emil Brunner', in *Das Konzil von Chalkedon. Geschichte und Gegenwart* III, Würzburg 1954, 613–73.
16. A. Quadt, *Gott und Mensch. Zur Theologie Barths in ökumenischer Sicht*, Munich, Paderborn and Vienna 1976, 225–32.
17. von Balthasar, *The Theology of Karl Barth* (n.9), 184.
18. Ibid., 185.
19. Ibid.
20. Ibid., 256.
21. Ibid., 227.
22. K. Barth, *Church Dogmatics* IV.1 (1953), Edinburgh 1956, 768.
23. Küng, *Justification*, 123.
24. Ibid., 285–302.
25. Huovinen, *Idea Christi* (n.1).
26. Cf. H. Küng, *Theology for the Third Millennium*, 184–6.
27. Barth, *Church Dogmatics* IV.1 (n.22), 84–88.
28. Küng, *Justification*, 30f.
29. Ibid., 94f.
30. Pius XII, Encyclical *Humani generis* (12 August 1950), in *Heilslehre der Kirche*, ed. A. Rohrbasser, Fribourg CH 1953, 266 (no. 450 according to the numbering of the encyclical).

31. Cf. my study of Barth in *Born Before All Time?* (n.12).
32. Cf. also H. Küng, *Does God Exist?*, 518–22.
33. Küng, *Justification*, 136.
34. Ibid., 143.
35. Ibid., 145.
36. J. Ratzinger, review of Küng, *Justification*, in *Theologische Revue* 54, 1958, 30–5: 33.
37. Ibid.
38. Ibid., 32.
39. Küng, *Ansprache zum Tode von Karl Barth*. 1968.
40. Küng, 'Karl Barth und die katholische Theologie' (n.7), 566.
41. H. Häring and K.-J. Kuschel, *Hans Küng. His Work and His Way*, London and New York 1979, 153.
42. K. Rahner, 'Current Problems of Christology', in id., *Theological Investigations* I, London and New York 1961, 149–200.
43. Küng, *Justification*, 301.
44. *Hans Küng. His Work and His Way* (n.41), 154f.
45. Both quotations in H. Küng, *The Incarnation of God*, xiii.
46. K. Barth, 'Hegel', in *Protestant Theology in the Nineteenth Century* (1952), London 1972, 384–421: 417.
47. Ibid., 415.
48. Hegel's basic concern is summed up once again in Küng, *Does God Exist?*, 162–88.
49. Barth, 'Hegel' (n.46), 415f.
50. Küng, *The Incarnation of God*, 434.
51. Quoted from H. Küng, *Does God Exist?*, 140.
52. Ibid., 141.
53. Küng, *The Incarnation of God*, 433.
54. Ibid., 256.
55. Ibid., 468f.
56. Küng, *Does God Exist?*, 384.
57. Küng, *The Incarnation of God*, 264.
58. Ibid., 408.
59. Ibid.
60. Ibid., 422.
61. Barth, 'Hegel' (n.46), 419.
62. Küng, *The Incarnation of God*, 425.
63. Barth, 'Hegel' (n.46), 420.
64. Küng, *The Incarnation of God*, 440.
65. Ibid., 442.
66. Ibid., 445.
67. Ibid.
68. Ibid., 456f.
69. Ibid., 460.
70. Ibid., 465.
71. *Hans Küng. His Work and His Way* (n.41), 154.
72. Küng, *The Incarnation of God*, 466.
73. Ibid., 469.

74. Ibid.
75. H. Küng, *On Being a Christian*, 295.
76. Ibid.
77. Thus Grillmeier and Kasper (n.2).
78. Küng, *On Being a Christian*, 307.
79. Ibid., 313.
80. Küng, *The Incarnation of God*, 484.
81. Küng, *On Being a Christian*, 449.
82. Küng, *Does God Exist?*, 792 n.11.
83. Ibid., 685.
84. Ibid. There is more on this complex of problems in Kuschel, *Born Before All Time?* (n.12).
85. Küng, 'Anmerkungen zu W. Kasper' (n.2), 174.
86. Ibid., 176.
87. Küng, *Does God Exist?*, 686.
88. Cf. Küng's critical discussion of this theology in *Concilium* 183, 1986, 119–25, and K.J. Kuschel, 'Christology and Interfaith Dialogue. The Problem of Uniqueness', in *Christology in Dialogue*, ed. R.F. Berkey and S.A. Edwards, Cleveland 1993.
89. Küng, *Does God Exist?*, 686f.
90. Küng, 'Karl Barth und die katholische Theologie' (n.7), 571.
91. Ibid.

Kenneth W. Brewer

The Uniqueness of Christ and the Challenge of the Pluralistic Theology of Religions

Hans Küng's theology elicits antithetical responses that are never dispassionate. This is true specifically of Küng's understanding of the uniqueness of Christ. On the one hand, the German Bishops' Conference (particularly Cardinal Höffner) objected to Küng's christology because they felt that his method 'from below' and his emphasis upon functional categories reduced Jesus' uniqueness to that of a St Francis or Muhammad.[1] Küng received sharp criticism also from many German Roman Catholic colleagues. They agreed unanimously that Küng's understanding of Jesus Christ did not take classical christology seriously enough.[2] On the other hand, members of the 'pluralistic theology of religions' group criticize that Küng's view of the uniqueness of Christ presents an insurmountable obstacle for the Christian dialogue with other religions. Küng was not invited to their conference at Claremont, California (1986), but instead, he was subjected to critique. Küng was invited, however, to join the opposition group to the pluralistic theology of religions, but he declined. Subsequently, there is confusion about Küng's theology of religions. Has Hans Küng crossed the 'theological Rubicon', or is he still at the river's edge? This essay will attempt to set in relief Küng's understanding of the uniqueness of Christ and his relationship to the pluralistic theology of religions, which is represented largely (but not exclusively) by North Americans. Our first task is to profile the challenge of the pluralistic theology of religions.

1. The Challenge of the Pluralistic Theology of Religions

The pluralistic theology of religions group has challenged Christian theologians to rethink the uniqueness of Christ in the light of other religions in a recent book with the provocative title *The Myth of Christian Uniqueness* (1987).[3] The roots of the pluralistic theology of religions may be traced back to the early Christian attempt to deal with the phenomena of other religions by Ernst Troeltsch and Arnold Toynbee, who viewed all religions as radically relative and as essentially the same. The more recent history of the pluralistic theology of religions is grounded in the heightened awareness of the religiously plural world in which we live and finds its expression in the writings of two celebrated scholars, John Hick and Wilfred Cantwell Smith. Furthermore, the debate over Christian uniqueness is to be seen as the logical extension of the earlier debate over christology in the book *The Myth of God Incarnate* (1977).[4] Dennis Nineham summarized the intention of the first 'myth' volume as being 'to ensure as far as possible that those who continue to make such a claim for the uniqueness of Jesus ... are fully aware of the problems involved in making and justifying any such claims', and he added that 'it is impossible to justify any such claim on purely historical grounds, however wide the net for evidence is cast'.[5] The uniqueness of Christ, then, is the central problematic uniting both 'myth' volumes. This becomes clear above all in the essays that were delivered at the first gathering of the pluralistic theology of religions group in Claremont, California, which was organized to challenge programmatically any notion of Christian uniqueness.

The challenge of the pluralistic theology of religions is expressed by the metaphor 'crossing the theological Rubicon'. They mean by this rather cryptic metaphor the 'move away from insistence on the superiority or finality of Christ and Christianity toward a recognition of the independent validity of other ways'.[6] With explicit reference to Hans Küng, Paul Knitter has defined 'crossing the theological Rubicon' as follows: 'To cross it means to recognize clearly, unambiguously, the possibility that other religions exercise a role in salvation history that is not only valuable and salvific but perhaps equal to that of Christianity; it is to affirm that there may be other saviours and revealers besides Jesus Christ and equal to Jesus Christ. It is to admit that if other religions must be fulfilled in Christianity, Christianity must, just as well, find fulfilment in them.'[7] This appeal for Christians to view Christianity and Jesus Christ as 'equal' to other revealers and other saviours is an echo of Troeltsch's position that all religions are relative and of Toynbee's stance that all religions are basically the same. Emphasis is placed on the commonality of religious experience, and the distinctiveness of religious belief is rendered secondary in importance.

John Hick's conception of the 'Copernican Revolution' in theology clarifies the pluralist programme further. Hick advocates a paradigm shift in theology similar to that which took place in the natural sciences from the Ptolemaic to the Copernican world-view. In the Ptolemaic world-view, the earth was understood to be the centre of the universe with the other planets circling around it. In the Copernican world-view, however, the sun stands in the middle of the universe. The Copernican revolution, then, was from a geocentric to a heliocentric world-view. Applied to theology, Hick maintains that in the centre stands not Christianity, nor the church, nor even Jesus Christ, but God himself – the 'Eternal' or the 'Real'. A paradigm shift is encouraged away from traditional exclusive and inclusive Christian positions, which place Christianity, the church or Jesus Christ in the centre, to that of the pluralistic theology of religions, which is reality-centric or soteriocentric. 'The

Real' may be experienced universally and is described in various ways from the historically contingent language of diverse cultures. The 'Eternal' or the 'Real' is, consequently, not the special possession of the Christian faith.[8]

A fundamental presupposition of many pluralists is Wilfred Cantwell Smith's contention that religious faith is to be separated sharply from religious belief. Smith views 'faith' as the core religious experience and 'belief' or the 'cumulative tradition' as the complex of symbols used to express the meaning of this core religious experience. The former is always personal and existential, while the latter is not necessarily so. The underlying faith experience is said to be the most important, universal and generic human quality. Smith regards the history of religions as a 'single' tapestry. It is from the assumption that all religions share a common religious history that he desires to construct a 'world theology'. The great variety of religious symbols, beliefs and doctrines is always derived from the underlying faith experience, so that what is primary in the religions is this core experience and not the diverse symbols used to articulate prereflective faith. This interpretation of the relationship between faith and belief makes it possible to view religious language as largely mythological in character.[9]

It is important to specify the sense in which uniqueness is labelled a 'myth' by the pluralists. The pluralistic theology of religions group insists that Christian uniqueness is not simply erroneous and must be discarded. Rather, they claim that Christian uniqueness must be re-evaluated. They concede that Christianity 'is unique in the precise and literal sense in which every religious tradition is unique – namely that there is only one of it and that there is therefore nothing else exactly like it'.[10] Contributors to the volume organized against the pluralistic theology of religions have pointed out correctly that uniqueness in the sense denoted by the pluralists is 'unproblematic and indisputable'. They specify further that it is 'at the theological level when claims are made ... about the definitiveness and normativeness of the revelation of God in Christ that difficulties occur'.[11] More precisely, then, pluralists maintain that the literal understanding of Christian uniqueness to 'signify the unique definitiveness, absoluteness, normativeness, superiority of Christianity in comparison with other religions of the world' is a myth (= false).[12]

The option for religious faith over belief and the view of religious language as mythological in character are fundamental assumptions which persuade the pluralists to interpret the uniqueness of Christ as a myth. They contend that the christological language of the New Testament is restricted to the poetic, mysterious, confessional and wholly metaphorical expression of the love, devotion and commitment of the early Christian community towards the man Jesus of Nazareth. The language in the New Testament is not to be taken literally or non-metaphorically. Rather, it is to be understood in a purely symbolic sense, although a cognitive component to faith language is acknowledged. To make too much of the cognitive content of the language of the New Testament, however, would be in the pluralists' view an abuse of religious language, for it would transform the faith symbols derived from religious experience into dogmatic ontological statements about the nature of reality as such. The classic expression of this view is John Hick's often quoted statement: 'that Jesus is my Lord and Saviour is language like that of the lover for whom his Helen is the sweetest girl in the world'.[13]

The arguments set forth by the pluralistic theology of religions to support their claim of the myth of Christian uniqueness are threefold. Tersely summarized, the pluralists contend that: 1. the awareness of historical-cultural relativity limits all knowledge and religious beliefs. Consequently, the assessment of other truth claims from one's own point of view is severely limited, if not rendered impossible altogether (Kaufman, Hick, Gilkey); 2. God is infinitely beyond our grasp and it is inconceivable for any one religion to possess the 'only' or 'final' word about this absolute Mystery (Cantwell Smith, Samartha, Panikkar, Yagi); and 3. any claim to absolute or final norms is intrinsically unethical and exploitative (Radford Ruether, Suchocki, Pieris, Knitter, Driver). The conclusion and consensus from these arguments, although the reasoning is admittedly varied, is that Christian uniqueness is a myth and that crossing the theological Rubicon is justified. Two of these arguments have been directed to Hans Küng.

2. The pluralist challenge to Hans Küng

In an early essay, John Hick regarded Küng's paper delivered at the Eucharistic Congress in Bombay, 'The World Religions in God's Plan of Salvation' (1964),[14] as the boldest attempt 'so far' in abandoning the ecclesiocentric view of 'No salvation outside the Church'. He applauded Küng's shift from an ecclesiocentric to a theocentric view of salvation and his distinction between the 'extraordinary' way (the church) and the 'ordinary' way (the world religions) of salvation. In the end, however, Hick contended that Küng's inclusive model was only an 'epicycle' of the old Ptolemaic theological world-view. He admitted that Küng pointed in the direction of his Copernican revolution, but charged that Küng fell short of carrying it out with his emphasis on the uniqueness of Jesus Christ.[15] Paul Knitter has commented further that Küng's shift from ecclesiocentrism to theocentrism is in reality simply a '*move to christocentrism*'.[16] Recently, the pluralist Alan Race has confirmed that Küng's inclusivism is not 'enough' for pluralist sensibilities since Küng affirms the uniqueness of Jesus, however qualified.[17] As a result, members of the pluralistic theology of religions group object to Küng's understanding of the uniqueness of Christ for two reasons.

A. The ethical-practical objection

The feminist theologian Rosemary Radford Ruether questions whether the Christian claim to be the one universal faith by which all persons are related authentically to God is still credible. She has come to the opinion that: 'The idea that Christianity, or even the biblical faiths, have a monopoly on religious truth is an outrageous and absurd religious chauvinism. It is astonishing that even Christian liberals and radicals fail to seriously question this assumption.'[18] Ruether makes visible here the pluralist goal of moving beyond not only conservative exclusivism, which posits that salvation is only in Christ, but also beyond liberal inclusivism, which grants that salvation is possible in non-Christian religions but does so only from within a specifically Christian framework. Her feminist perspective declares that it is just as exploitative to herald Christianity or Jesus Christ as the norm for all religions as it is to universalize male experience as the norm for all humanity. The Christian view of itself as a universal religion should be replaced by the awareness of its own finiteness and particularity. The emphasis on Christian uniqueness only breeds contempt for other religions.

That the emphasis on Christian uniqueness only leads to the degradation of other religions was the claim of Gregory Baum just after Küng gave his lecture on 'What is the Christian Message?'[19] at the World Congress of Theology (1970). Baum charged that Küng's stress on the centrality and uniqueness of Jesus Christ was in effect an ideological 'rhetoric of exclusion'. He argued that the church's language about Jesus Christ has introduced 'seeds of division and conflict' that were never meant by Jesus himself. Furthermore, he noted that: 'The division of the world into "Christians" and "non-Christians", as many similar divisions between "we" and "they", has created a language that led to the self-elevation of the we-group and the degradation of the others.'[20] Baum believes that this language affects the way the church thinks and treats 'outsiders'. It makes the church 'vulnerable to evil' and will eventually result in 'inhuman treatment'. He cites the persecution of the Jews as a classic example of this 'rhetoric of exclusion'. Baum, therefore, questions if it is possible to affirm with Küng the uniqueness of Christ without advancing a rhetoric of exclusivism with regard to other people.

Avery Dulles, although not a pluralist, resonated initially with Baum's critique of Küng's emphasis on the centrality of Scripture and the uniqueness of Jesus Christ. Dulles cautioned that this emphasis of Küng's could lead to 'unhealthy exaggerations' and that 'this formula is quite acceptable for many Catholics and Protestants, but it is not the most natural meeting place for other segments of mankind'.[21] He argued that what is unique to Christianity often detracts from what it has in common with other religions and weakens the basis for dialogue. Dulles, however, is at odds with himself, for not long after he made the above remarks he reviewed Küng's book *On Being a*

Christian and praised the central position given to the life and teaching of Jesus. In addition, Dulles criticized Küng's use of functional categories to describe Jesus' uniqueness as weak. He maintained that: 'If Jesus is in a singular way God's revelation in the flesh, there must be something special about Jesus that makes Him, rather than anyone else, such a revelation.'[22]

The pluralist Marjorie Hewitt Suchocki has also sought to illustrate that Küng's understanding of Christian uniqueness is unjust. Her thesis is that 'universalizing one religion such that it is taken as the norm whereby all other religions are judged and valued leads to oppression, and hence falls short of the norm that liberationists consider ultimate – the normative justice that creates well-being in the world community'.[23] She rejects, therefore, the absolutizing of one religion as the norm for all others. Like Ruether, Suchocki sees a correlation between absolutizing one religion over others and the patriarchal universalizing of male experience as normative. Suchocki regards Küng's book *On Being a Christian* as a chauvinist defence of Christian superiority over the other religions. She charges that Küng belittles the other religions by pointing out their negative characteristics and by comparing these unfairly to the most noble ideals within Christianity. Suchocki's claim is that the same destructive dynamics at work within sexism are likewise activated in Küng's understanding of Christian uniqueness:

> ... just as women are measured and judged by masculine experience, even so Küng measures and judges other religions by Christian experience. Further, the form of sexism that separates reprehensible qualities from men and projects them upon women is also operative in Küng's treatment. The qualities which he specifically names as negative in other religions have parallels within Christianity. These parallels are not acknowledged. Rather, they are rendered invisible in Christianity by projecting them as somehow appropriately descriptive of other religions. Here the exclusivist attitude toward women finds its echo in an exclusivist attitude toward other religions.[24]

B. The historical-relativity objection

Pluralists have embraced Ernst Troeltsch's position that radical consequences result for the universal claims of Christianity from the awareness of 'historical relativity'. Troeltsch's central problem was with 'the clash between historical reflection and the determination of standards of truth and value'.[25] Troeltsch and pluralists conclude from the awareness of historical relativity that all religions with their moral and truth claims are relative in the sense that they all are derived from and may be explained entirely by their particular social location. Any claim to absoluteness, superiority, definitiveness, normativeness, finality, or uniqueness, is thoroughly value-laden. As such, these

204 Christology and the Doctrine of God

claims reveal more about what is important to a particular group or religion than they do about reality. Awareness of historical relativity, therefore, forces one to admit the limitation of making universal judgments about one's own religion and of adjudicating conflicting moral and truth claims. Langdon Gilkey concurs with this view, but admits that the danger of historical relativity is historical relativism, whereby the foundation for prophetic critique of 'intolerable evils' is swept away. Despite this, all are agreed that religions should abandon their universal claims in order to promote inter-religious dialogue. John Hick concedes, however, that a claim to universal validity is possible if it is grounded in empirical/experiential data. Nevertheless, he finds such data lacking.

Paul Knitter has applied the argument that any claim to uniqueness and normativity must be tested by empirical evidence for Küng's view of the uniqueness of Christ. His thesis is that historical-critical methods of investigation do not permit any claim to the uniqueness or normativity of Christ. He argues that: 'the claim for Jesus' exclusive uniqueness does not form part of the central assertions of Christian texts ... and that although the New Testament does claim that a new 'mode-of-being-in-the-world' is revealed in Jesus, the claim that this took place only in Jesus is the result of 'the historically conditioned world view and thought-patterns of the time'.[26] Knitter sees no reason why there should be only one definitive revelation of God or only one saving figure from God. To deny the possibility of other revelations or saviours equal to Jesus Christ, Knitter charges, would be a form of 'exclusivism'. Knitter also contends that Küng spends 'too much time trying to establish the risk of faith on scientifically reliable knowledge of the historical Jesus'.[27] In doing so, Knitter thinks that Küng has not only violated the limits of historical relativity, but has missed the power of myth. Knitter holds that the traditions about Jesus are permeated with mythological language to such an extent that it is futile to attempt to verify the uniqueness of Jesus on the basis of historical analysis. In the end, the story about Jesus is regarded as more important than the history of Jesus. Knitter assesses that Küng's inclusivism is more dangerous than overt exclusivism, since it possesses a 'subtle, camouflaged narrowness'. Knitter, therefore, challenges Küng to abandon 'the scourge of inclusivism' and join those who have already crossed the theological Rubicon.[28]

The pluralist Tom Driver also chides that Küng's use of the historical-critical method to recover the 'historical Jesus' is nothing but 'naive historicism' and 'naive scripturalism'. Driver believes that the emphasis upon the 'scriptural Jesus' and the 'historical Jesus' as the centre, model and norm for what is Christian must be abandoned. This emphasis, he argues, has led to devastating moral and political abuses. He advocates a thoroughgoing historical relativism. Driver regards the pursuit for the historical Jesus such as Küng's as wrong-headed, since historical research cannot confirm or deny the historicality of events in the New Testament. He says: 'It is a fundamental error, and a costly one, for theology to seek the truth of God and the truth of Christianity exclusively in Christ past, to the neglect of the truth involved in Christians' encounter with their changing environments. This is a prevalent error, to be found even in so open-minded a theologian as Hans Küng.'[29] On the constructive side, Driver argues that God has more than one history and that this fact is the basis for positing other salvation histories outside Christianity. Driver's pluralist view affirms not only that God has different names, identities and modes of involvements in the world, but that the Godhead itself is plural in that it possesses different natures.[30]

To summarize, the pluralist challenge to Küng's understanding of the uniqueness of Christ is intended to prod Küng to go one step further in his shift from ecclesiocentrism to theocentricism to that of a reality-centrism or a soteriocentrism. Pluralists want Küng, as well as exclusivists and other inclusivists, to relax the Christian emphasis on the uniqueness of Christ. Pluralists hold that the unique and normative claim for Jesus is both impossible historically and inconceivable epistemologically. Pluralists claim that the Christian emphasis upon Jesus' uniqueness only leads to a chauvinistic, divisive, exploitative, exclusive, imperialistic, and 'crypto-colonialist' form of Christianity. Are the pluralists correct?

3. Critical evaluation of the pluralistic theology of religions

Some questions for clarification regarding the challenge of the pluralistic theology of religions to Christian uniqueness are in order. Although the focus is upon the pluralist critique of Küng's understanding of the uniqueness of Christ, our critical evaluation goes beyond this specific interest. With an open spirit, the pluralists have invited theologians and the Christian community to evaluate the content, coherence, adequacy, appropriateness and faithfulness of the pluralistic theology of religions to human experience and to the Christian tradition. While it is not possible to make an extensive evaluation here, several issues will be considered under the following questions.

A. Can Hans Küng be numbered among the pluralists?

This question might seem surprising given the sharp polemic against Küng by the pluralists cited above. Nevertheless, Scott Cowdell in a recent article entitled 'Hans Küng and World Religions: The Emergence of a Pluralist' (1989) has argued that Küng crossed the theological Rubicon initially in his book *Does God Exist?* more obviously in his Christian responses in *Christianity and the World Religions*, and completely in his essay 'What is True Religion?'.[31]

Cowdell notes correctly that a shift has taken place in Küng's theology of religions on the issue of the normativity of Jesus Christ. Formerly Küng viewed Jesus Christ as the *norma normans* for all religions. Now Küng asserts that Jesus Christ is the *norma normans* directly for Christians and only indirectly for non-Christians. The question is, however, does this modification constitute Küng's 'conversion' to the pluralist position?

Although it is true that Küng has gravitated increasingly toward a more open posture to the world religions, it is false to conclude from this that he has embraced the pluralistic theology of religions. With Paul Knitter in mind, Küng has referred to the pluralistic theology of religions as an 'old doctrine from the spirit of Protestant liberalism'.[32] Knitter reports that when he challenged Küng directly to cross the 'theological Rubicon', Küng refused for two reasons: 'it would alienate him from his faith community and it would tend to diminish the depth and firmness of Christians' personal commitment to Jesus Christ'.[33] Moreover, if the decisive criterion for being a pluralist is as Knitter has defined it, i.e., to concede that other religions and other religious figures are equal to the revelation and salvation of God manifested in Jesus of Nazareth, then Küng is definitely not to be numbered among the pluralists. The question of whether or not Küng is a pluralist must be answered in the final analysis in the negative for two basic reasons: 1. it goes contrary to Küng's own self-understanding, and 2. it contradicts the pluralists' continual appeal for Küng to cross the theological Rubicon. Alan Race locates correctly Küng's theology of religions 'mid-way between the full pluralist theology and the inclusivism of the post-Vatican II Catholic approach exemplified by Rahner'.[34]

B. Can the uniqueness of Jesus be demonstrated on historical grounds?

Against Tom Driver's historical scepticism, Küng points out correctly that the New Testament writings are the only source of authentic information concerning Jesus and Christian origins. To focus only on the human experience of Christ in the present is to take an ahistorical approach and to disrupt the critical correlation between the two principal sources for theology, i.e., Christian texts and human experience. Furthermore, Küng attempts to steer a middle course between a 'superficial credulity' and a 'radical scepticism' with regard to the New Testament witness. In spite of the difficulties of inquiring into the history of Jesus, Küng finds it necessary, meaningful and possible. Paul Knitter's view that the claim for Jesus' exclusive uniqueness does not form part of the central assertions of Christian texts is only partially correct. It is true that the word 'uniqueness' does not occur in the New Testament. But he dismisses artificially all the exclusive claims in the New Testament with regard to Jesus as being 'the result of the historically conditioned world view and thought-patterns of the time'. This is to resolve the problem of Jesus' uniqueness too facilely.

Knitter is correct to point out that the uniqueness of Jesus cannot be established strictly from a historical perspective. He is wrong, however, in thinking that this is what Küng attempts. When we turn to Küng's understanding of the uniqueness of Christ, we find that the historical and the theological often flow into one another. In many cases the historical is permeated thoroughly with the theological. This fact raises serious doubts about establishing Jesus' uniqueness from a strictly historical point of view. Küng does maintain, however, that the claim to the finality, normativeness and uniqueness of Jesus is theologically appropriate since 'to do otherwise would be to abandon the central statement of all the scriptures which are normative for them [Christian theologians], and which almost two thousand years ago came to form the New Testament, the foundation document of Christianity. Whether it is convenient or not, Jesus is normative and definitive for the whole of the New Testament: he alone is the Christ of God ...'[35] Küng, therefore, holds that the uniqueness of Jesus may be established responsibly from a historical-theological basis. Furthermore, Küng does not think it necessary to discard the specifically Christian criterion in the inter-religious dialogue, as do many of the pluralists.

C. Is there a necessary connection between uniqueness and arrogant superiority?

The pluralists are right to remind Christians of the past abuses which have transpired in the name of Jesus: antisemitism, sexism, burning of heretics and witches, Western imperialism, colonialism and domination, destruction of the environment, nuclear build-up, etc. But are they right to make a necessary connection between the uniqueness of Christ and the negative effects of an arrogant superiority? Is it true that universal norms always lead to oppression and injustice of 'outsiders'? While no one can dismiss the fact that such 'unhealthy exaggerations' have occurred, it is beyond the evidence to say that it occurs 'necessarily'.

Two things must be said against the pluralists' critique of Küng on this score. The first is that Küng has qualified his conception of the normativeness of Jesus with his conception of the *humanum* in the essay 'What is True Religion?'.[36] What Suchocki means by her norm of 'justice' can be reconciled quite easily with what Küng means by his general ethical criterion of the *humanum*. Küng understands the *humanum* to mean anything that protects and promotes that which is humane and advances human dignity and worth. Applied to the religions, whatever enhances the dignity of human beings is true and good, whatever diminishes the dignity of human beings is false and bad. The essay in which Küng developed his understanding of the *humanum* was available to Suchocki at the time of her writing against Küng. Had she consulted this essay instead of narrowly focussing on *On Being a Christian*, she would have had to revise her reading of Küng.

Secondly, the specific Christian criterion of the normativeness of Jesus Christ does not contradict the normativeness of the *humanum*. In fact, Jesus of Nazareth gives a concreteness to such abstract conceptions as 'justice' and '*humanum*'. The concrete historical person of Jesus of Nazareth, Küng maintains, possesses an impressiveness, audibility and realizability that is lacking in abstract principles, universal norms and systems of thought.[37] Moreover, if we consider the character of this concrete historical person, Jesus of Nazareth, then we find the personification of a new way of thinking and relating to God and to humanity. Jesus makes clear that what God wills is the total reorientation of human thought and action. Küng specifies that God's will is nothing less than the advantage, greatness, dignity and well-being of humanity. The concrete historical Jesus puts a human face on God and reveals God to be in solidarity with the weak, the sick, the neglected, the poor; with women, children, people ignorant of religion and moral failures. The Jesus of the New Testament is a servant-messiah who calls his followers to be servants as well. When Christianity behaves contrary to the God manifested in Jesus Christ, what is called for is not the abandonment of Christian norms, but the retrieval of the highest and best ideals within the Christian tradition.

D. Is unthematized 'faith' radically detached from thematized 'belief'?

A distinction must be made clearly between prereflective faith experience on the one hand and religious symbols, beliefs and doctrines on the other. But is it appropriate to separate sharply 'faith' experience from rational 'belief' and to give priority to religious experience over the cognitive component of religious beliefs, as many pluralists do? This move results in the unjustified preference for the 'mystical' and the rash depreciation of the 'prophetic' element in religions. It also allows one to emphasize too easily what is common to all religions at the expense of their contrasts and differences. Moveover, granting priority to a generic faith experience leads to the evasion of the difficult problem of adjudicating conflicting ethical and truth claims found among the religions. Furthermore, questions abound concerning the accuracy of the description of the relationship between religious experience and religious belief by the pluralists. Does not their bias for mystical religious experience promote a devaluation of religious language and an all too facile conception of religious language as 'mythological' in character?

Here we find that Hans Küng again departs appropriately from the pluralistic theology of religions. He not only argues that there should be no simple agreement among religions and that the differences should not be 'smoothed out', but he also notes that 'the utterly ambiguous inward religious experience must not be made absolute, as if all the religious statements that can be articulated, all revelations and creeds, authorities, churches, rites and manifestations were irrelevant by comparison with this inward religious experience'.[38] Thematized religious belief, therefore, and unsystematized religious experience may be distinguished, but Küng posits a more dialectical relationship between them so that these can never be radically separated from one another. In fact, religious experience and reflection belong together. Küng describes the relationship of outward reflection and inward experience in the following manner. On the one hand, 'Without religious experience, religious reflection is empty; reflection lives by experience,' and on the other hand, 'Without religious reflection, religious experience is blind; experience needs the critical illumination and assurance of reflection.'[39] Against the pluralist conception, then, Küng argues that all religions cannot be gathered under one umbrella of a common essence or core religious experience. This is due to the fact that 'there never is a religious experience in isolation, in itself, free of all interpretations. Religious experience from the beginning is interpreted experience, shaped by the religious tradition in question and its various forms of expression.'[40] This postulate is the epistemological basis for Küng's historical-theological understanding of the uniqueness of Christ, to which we now turn in conclusion.

4. Küng's argument for the uniqueness of Christ[41]

Christology is a central systematic organizing rubric of Küng's theological method. This is especially evident in his theological work dating from 1970. Here Jesus of Nazareth is heralded as the unique and distinctive feature of Christianity, beginning with his address on 'What is the Christian Message?' at the World Congress of Theology in Brussels (1970) and throughout his three most popular works, *On Being a Christian* (1974), *Does God Exist?* (1978) and *Eternal Life* (1982). Representative of his view is the statement: 'The special feature, the most fundamental characteristic of Christianity, is that it considers this Jesus as ultimately decisive, definitive, archetypal for man's relations with God, with his fellow man, with society: in the curtailed biblical formula, as "Jesus Christ".'[42] Hence, what is unique about Christianity is nothing other than Jesus of Nazareth. This emphasis continues in Küng's dialogues with the great religious figures (Moses, Muhammad, Krishna, Confucius and Buddha) in *Christianity and the World Religions* (1985) and *Christianity and Chinese Religions* (1988), as well as in numerous essays.

Küng objects to establishing the uniqueness of Christ through the hermeneutics of dogma characteristic of 'Denzinger theology'. Rather, he begins with the historical Jesus of Nazareth 'from below' and then works toward a christology 'from above'. The uniqueness of Christ is therefore grounded in historical analysis, but it is not restricted to it. Küng is confident, moreover, that 'we know incomparably more that is historically certain about Jesus of Nazareth than we do about the great founders of the Asian religions'.[43]

Because of the lack of historical certainty surrounding many founders of religions, Küng has called for quests for the historical Buddha, Confucius, and Muhammad. He cautions, however, against superficially placing the great religious figures side by side for comparison. Nevertheless, Küng ventures a comparative, historical-theological analysis of the uniqueness of Christ in the light of other figures in the history of religions. The following features of Jesus' uniqueness become transparent in Küng's theology.

A. Jesus is unique with regard to his Jewish social context

Jesus eludes the 'cross of co-ordinates of options within Judaism'.[44] Jesus did not belong to any of the established ecclesiastical groups of his day. He was not a priest of the religio-political establishment (Sadducees), nor a political revolutionary (Zealots), nor an ascetic monk (Essenes, Qumran), nor even a devout moralist (Pharisees). Küng asserts that 'it shows considerable understanding of Jesus if we do not attempt to integrate him within the quadrilateral of establishment and revolution, emigration and compromise: He fits no formula. He is provocative, both on the right and on the left: apparently closer than the priests to God. At the same time freer than the ascetics in regard to the world. More moral than the moralists. And more revolutionary than the revolutionaries.'[45] Like her majesty's 'loyal opposition', Jesus was a 'critical catalyst' who avoided all attempts to domesticate him within the reigning 'cross of co-ordinates of options'.

B. Jesus is unique with regard to his message

Jesus' message is different from that of Moses' law, from that of Buddha's monastic rules, from that of Muhammad's revolutionary world conquest and establishment of theocratic states, and from that of Confucius' traditional morality and aristocratic ethics. The manner of Jesus's speaking is also without parallel in the Jewish world. He spoke not like the prophets, saying 'Thus says the Lord', but rather said, 'I say to you'. Jesus' message was that of the kingdom of God. This message conflicted with the religio-political theocracy anticipated within Judaism. Küng concludes: 'The superiority of Jesus becomes apparent, not in the often completely comparable individual statements, but in the unmistakable orginality of the whole teaching.'[46]

C. Jesus is unique with regard to his person

Unlike other founders of religions, Jesus' words cannot be abstracted from his life. Rather, the historical Jesus is the sum and substance of the Christian message. He is the normative embodiment of the will of God. His message is inseparable from his person. God's forgiveness was offered personally in him.

Jesus exhibited love for enemies, unconditional forgiveness, and the renunciation of power and rights. Küng remarks: 'Jesus as the crucified and living Christ [is] the Christian message. He is this message not abstractly, but quite concretely; nor just theoretically, but practically; not on the periphery but in an explicitly central place, not only factually but deliberately programmatically. With this concrete programme this message is simply him: not Socrates and not Buddha, not Moses and not Muhammad, not Marx and not Freud.'[47]

D. Jesus is unique with regard to his humble existence in view of his world impact

Miracles and extraordinary events surrounding Jesus' life are not unique to him. What is miraculous, however, is that the life of such a humble figure could have vast world-historical significance. Jesus' profile appears quite meagre compared to other religious figures: he did not grow up in Pharaoh's court as did Moses, nor was he the son of a king as was Buddha; he was not a scholar and politician like Confucius, nor a rich merchant like Muhammad. Moreover, many of the places and dates of Jesus' life are obscure. In addition, Jesus had no support from his family; had no special education; had no money; held no office; received no honours; was not backed by any authorized party; and was not married. And while Buddha established a monastic community, Confucius founded a training school, Moses transferred his leadership to Joshua, and Muhammad organized an expansionist state, Jesus left behind no established church, creeds, cultic practices or ministries. From this evidence Küng concludes: 'Hence Jesus is *not* what is generally understood as the founder of a religion or of a Church.'[48]

E. Jesus is unique with regard to his relationship to God

Jesus' relation to God is often depicted by the concept of incarnation. Küng argues that the concept of incarnation is not an un-Jewish idea. It is compatible with the Jewish view of the transcendence and immanence of God expressed by the concept '*Shekinah*'. This indicates God's special dwelling in the sanctuary, the tent of meeting, and the Temple. Küng sees no reason why this concept cannot be applied to Jesus of Nazareth in order to understand his relation to God.[49] The New Testament title for Jesus also indicates his unique relation to God. This unique relationship, Küng maintains, may be expressed today by the notions of God's 'advocate', 'deputy', 'representative', 'delegate', 'trustee', 'plenipotentiary', or 'spokesman'. Jesus is the advocate of God in the sense that the real revelation and countenance of the one true God are made manifest in him. There is a unity of revelation and will between Jesus and God. Beyond the dispute over titles, Küng asserts that it cannot be contested that 'Jesus acted on the basis of an unusual **experience of God, bond with God,** and immediacy to God …'.[50] As a consequence, God comes to be understood quite differently and unambiguously in Jesus of Nazareth.

F. Jesus is unique with regard to his death

The question of what ultimately distinguishes Jesus from all others can be answered only by reference to the cross. Küng contends that a comparison of the deaths of the founders of religions highlights Jesus' uniqueness. With Jesus, we have 'a young man of thirty, after three years at most of activity, perhaps only a few months. Expelled from society, betrayed and denied by his disciples and supporters, mocked and ridiculed by his opponents, forsaken by men and even by God, he goes through a ritual of death that is one of the most atrocious and enigmatic ever invented by man's ingenious cruelty.'[51] What is particular about Jesus is that: 'Jesus died not merely forsaken by men, but absolutely forsaken by God. The unique fellowship with God, which he thought he enjoyed, made his foresakenness by God in death all the more unique …'[52] Jesus' unique death is intensified by the claim that he transcended death by resurrection. Küng observes that it is the resurrection from the dead that accounts for the 'enigma' of the emergence of Christianity after Jesus' shameful crucifixion. It also explains the shift of focus from Jesus the proclaimer to Jesus the proclaimed. With the resurrection we see the dawning of a new age; the beginning of the general resurrection from the dead. Küng remarks: 'In him and only in him has the new life out of death been revealed.'[53]

These six features constitute Küng's position on what is special, distinctive, and unique to Jesus in light of other religions. They are not exhaustive. It must be pointed out in conclusion, however, that the emphasis on the uniqueness of Christ has been tempered somewhat in Küng's most recent *Global Responsibility*. This new departure is not in contradiction to his earlier thinking. Rather, Küng distinguishes between the 'inside' perspective (the position from one's own faith tradition) and the 'outside' perspective (the view of another tradition, not one's own), so that he is able to hold firmly to his Christian identity but have a maximum of openness to others. In its entirety, Küng's theology of religions presents a real alternative for Christians who are searching for a new way to relate to other religions, but who do not want to get their feet wet in the Rubicon.[54]

Notes

1. The discussion of Küng's christology by the German bishops is found in *Küng in Conflict*, ed. Leonard Swidler, Garden City, NY 1981.

2. The most serious criticisms were: Karl Rahner, 'Zu Hans Küng's neuestem Buch: Erste Eindrücke und erste Fragen', *Theologie der Gegenwart* 18, 1975, 80–7; Walter Kasper, 'Christologie von unten? Kritik und Neuansatz gegenwärtiger Christologie', and 'Für eine Christologie in geschichtlicher Perspektive – Replik auf die Anmerkungen von Küng', in *Grundfragen der Christologie heute*, ed. by L. Scheffczyk, Freiburg, Basel and Vienna 1975, 141–70, 179–83; Joseph Ratzinger, 'Christ sein – plausibel gemacht', *Theologische Revue* 71, 1975, 354–64; Alois Grillmeier, 'Die Einzigartigkeit Jesu Christi und unser Christsein: Zu Hans Küng, Christ sein', *Theologie und Philosophie* 51, 1976, 198–243; Helmut Riedlinger, 'Radikale Rationalität: Zur Methode in Hans Küngs "Christ sein"', *Theologie und Philosophie* 51, 1976, 185–95; and Hans Urs von Balthasar et al., *Diskussion über Hans Küngs 'Christ sein'*, Mainz 1978.

3. *The Myth of Christian Uniqueness: Towards a Pluralistic Theology of Religions*, ed. John Hick and Paul F. Knitter, Maryknoll, NY and London 1987.

4. *The Myth of God Incarnate*, ed. John Hick, London and Philadelphia 1977.

5. Ibid., 194–5.

6. Paul Knitter, 'Preface', in *The Myth of Christian Uniqueness* (n. 3), viii.

7. Paul Knitter, 'Hans Küng's Theological Rubicon', in *Towards a Universal Theology of Religion*, ed. Leonard Swidler, Maryknoll, NY 1987, 225.

8. Hick's 'Copernican Revolution' is found in: *God and the Universe of Faiths*, London, 1977; *God Has Many Names*, London and Philadelphia 1982; and *An Interpretation of Religion: Human Responses to the Transcendent*, London and New Haven 1989.

9. Wilfred Cantwell Smith, *Faith and Belief*, Princeton 1979; *Towards a World Theology* Philadelphia and London 1981.

10. Paul Knitter, 'Preface', in *The Myth of Christian Uniqueness* (n. 3), vii.

11. Gavin D'Costa, 'Preface', in *Christian Uniqueness Reconsidered: The Myth of a Pluralistic Theology of Religions*, ed. Gavin D'Costa Maryknoll, NY 1990, x.

12. *The Myth of Christian Uniqueness* (n. 3), vii.

13. John Hick, *The Centre of Christianity*, London and New York 1978, 32.

14. Hans Küng, 'The World Religions in God's Plan of Salvation', in *Christian Revelation and World Religions*, ed. Joseph Neuner, London 1967, 25–66.

15. John Hick, *God and the Universe of Faiths* (n. 8), 128–9.

16. Paul Knitter, *No Other Name: A Critical Survey of Christian Attitudes Towards the World Religions*, Maryknoll, NY and London 1985, 134.

17. Alan Race, 'Christianity and Other Religions: Is Inclusivism Enough?', *Theology* 89, 1986, 178–86.

18. Rosemary Radford Ruether, 'Feminism and Jewish-Christian Dialogue: Particularism and Universalism in the Search for Religious Truth', in *The Myth of Christian Uniqueness*, 141.

19. Hans Küng, 'Was ist die christliche Botschaft', in *Das Unverzichtbare am Christentum*, ed. Volker Hochgrebe und Norbert Kutschki, Mainz 1971.

20. Gregory Baum, 'World Congress at Brussels: Liberation', *The Ecumenist* 8, 1970, 97.

21. Avery Dulles, 'The Theology of Hans Küng: A Comment', *Union Seminary Quarterly Review* 27, 1972, 141.

22. Avery Dulles, 'Dogmatic Theology and Hans Küng's *On Being A Christian*', *America* 135, 1976, 342.
23. Marjorie Hewitt Suchocki, 'In Search of Justice: Religious Pluralism from a Feminist Perspective', in *The Myth of Christian Uniqueness* (n. 3), 149.
24. Ibid., 153.
25. Ernst Troeltsch, 'The Place of Christianity Among the World Religions', in *Christian Thought: Its History and Application*, ed., with an introduction by Baron von Hügel, London 1923 reissued New York 1957, 36.
26. Paul Knitter, 'World Religions and the Finality of Christ: A Critique of Hans Küng's *On Being A Christian*', *Horizons* 5/2, 1978, 154.
27. Paul Knitter, *No Other Name* (n. 16), 71.
28. Paul F. Knitter, 'Hans Küng's Theological Rubicon', in *Toward a Universal Theology of Religion*, 224–30.
29. Tom F. Driver, *Christ in a Changing World: Toward an Ethical Christology*, New York and London 1981, 47.
30. Tom F. Driver, 'The Case for Pluralism', in *The Myth of Christian Uniqueness* (n. 3), 212.
31. Scott Cowdell, 'Hans Küng and World Religions: The Emergence of a Pluralist', *Theology* 92, 1989, 85–92.
32. Hans Küng, *Global Responsibility*, 98.
33. Paul F. Knitter, 'Toward A Liberation Theology of Religions', in *The Myth of Christian Uniqueness*, 194–5.
34. Alan Race, *Christians and Religious Pluralism: Patterns in the Christian Theology of Religions*, London and Maryknoll, NY 1982, 67.
35. *Global Responsibility*, 99.
36. Hans Küng, 'What is True Religion?', in *Toward a Universal Theology of Religion*, 231–50.
37. Hans Küng, *On Being a Christian*, 540–4.
38. Ibid., 102f.
39. Hans Küng, *Does God Exist?*, 611f.
40. Hans Küng, 'What is True Religion?', in *Toward A Universal Theology of Religion*, 235.
41. For an extensive treatment of Hans Küng's theology of religions see Kenneth W. Brewer, 'Hans Küng's Theology of Religions: A Historical and Thematic Analysis' (PhD diss., Drew University, forthcoming 1993).
42. *On Being a Christian*, 123.
43. Ibid., 147.
44. Hans Küng, *Judaism*, II B.II; *On Being a Christian*, C.I.
45. Hans Küng, 'On Being a Christian: Twenty Theses', in *Signposts for the Future*, Garden City, NY 1978, 13.
46. Hans Küng, *On Being a Christian*, 259.
47. Hans Küng, 'Was ist die christliche Botschaft', in *Das Unverzichtbare am Christentum*, 34.
48. Hans Küng, *On Being a Christian*, 286.
49. *Judaism*, 384f.
50. Ibid., 331.

51. *On Being a Christian*, 335.
52. Hans Küng, *Eternal Life?*, 95.
53. Ibid., 108.
54. I want to thank Joy McDougall, Steffen Lösel, and especially Karl-Josef Kuschel for making valuable suggestions regarding the style and content of this article.

Hermann Häring

Trust as Resistance against Nothingness
The Question of God as Raised in *Does God Exist?*

'Should God exist, then we would have found a fundamental solution to the
riddle of the questionableness of reality itself, a fundamental answer to the
perennial question of the origin and destiny of the world and of humankind.
That God exists can only be asserted in an act of trust grounded in reality
itself.
Thus there is no ground to speak of a stalemate between affirmation and
negation of God. Those who say yes to God know why they can put ultimate
trust in the reality surrounding them.
Belief in God can thus be justified before reason. Its rationale manifests
itself in the practice of a venturesome trust in reality itself: fundamental
trust and trust in God are bound up with each other.'[1]

While Hans Küng's book *Does God Exist?*, which appeared in 1978, is not
perhaps his best-known work, for me it is still his most interesting work and
the one which is theologically most important. Having previously dealt
intensively with issues relating to the Bible and the history of faith (one need
think only of *The Church* and *On Being a Christian*), the scholar who had at an
early stage worked on Sartre and later intensively on Hegel now returns to his
sources in philosophy and systematic theology to bring both starting points
together in connection with the question of God. The present article was
originally written as an answer to the question why Küng's arguments for the
existence of God convince me. It forced me to sound out the background and
the wider context of Küng's position. As a result I found myself caught in a
complex network of questions relating to the history of ideas, hermeneutics
and language. Above all I attempted to examine the significance and scope of
what Küng calls 'fundamental trust'. I leave it to my readers to judge whether I
have been successful. It will be clear to them that I do not have the linguistic
elegance and clarity of my teacher.[2] However, I would like to show that we his
pupils learned from him how to think – for the benefit of the church and
theology.

1. Hermeneutical demarcation

Hans Küng presented his arguments for the existence of God in 1978, in his book *Does God Exist?*. The crucial text covers thirty-six pages in the original.[3] In accord with many contemporary theologians, Küng begins from the assumption that the existence of God cannot be proved directly. He proposes to verify God as the all-determining reality indirectly, namely through the reality of human beings and the world as it can be experienced.[4] Now the thesis that God cannot be proved has long since become a virtual truism on all sides. Before I go into three crucial points of Küng's argument, I should like to make some hermeneutical observations.

The intrinsic connections between the question of God and the way in which we speak about God are complex in the extreme. First of all, the language which we use does not simply depict reality, but creates a new reality on the basis of its relation to reality.[5] This can be seen especially where language leaves the empirical sphere as its point of reference. That is quite certainly the case with the statement 'God exists'. Alongside its ontological references, the assertion 'God exists' also includes references to the speaker. Furthermore the argument leads to modally qualified results. Thus the statement 'God exists' is – like all statements – either meaningless or meaningful. But God's existence itself is recognized as impossible, as contingent or as necessary,[6] and according to Jüngel even as 'more than necessary'. These modal qualifications are themselves only the logical consequence of the question how 'necessary' God is for our own existence and self-understanding as human beings. Where the concept 'God' appears in a culture, questions of faith, the meaning of life, anxiety or hope do not prove to be groundless. Thus the objective level of the argument has a reciprocal effect on the concept of God in God's relation to us.

Finally, it is necessary to note the context of the argument.[7] We can legitimately talk of God's existence indirectly only by noting the disclosure situation of 'God exists'. Obviously statements about existence cannot be understood independently of that which has a particular existence. The formal equality of the statements 'the stone exists', 'good exists' and 'Gorbachev exists' must not be allowed to disguised the far-reaching differences in the meaning of particular statements about existence. Such statements break through the classic pattern of proof. We cannot fill the statement 'God exists' with content prior to concrete experiences. Lexically it is to some degree empty and has to be deciphered entirely from its communicative function.[8] This causes particular difficulties in a cultural context in which talk of God's existence can no longer be seen as self-evident.[9] Therefore the concept of God, understood in terms of statements about existence, presupposes a concrete, language-centred understanding of the problems of the question of God. So we can decide appropriately on the truth of a statement about existence only if we know its associations for speaker and listener. There can be no focussing on the context of legitimation before that.

2. Faith in the face of nihilism

For these reasons Küng's argument begins well into the 'foreground' of our question. In brief, it presupposes modern experiences of the question of God. I shall neither summarize nor analyse Küng's exemplary, highly informative and exciting 'report' of around 450 pages here. I shall begin at the point where, after centuries of assertion and criticism, for Küng the problem has been worked out which we have to confront today. This happens with Friedrich Nietzsche, who does not simply dispute the existence of God or criticize the way of life of believers but in his 'nihilism' – radicalization and consistent atheism all in one – tries to unmask all existing values, including the supreme value, 'God'. Nietzsche's plea is for a consistent atheism, the aim of which – to quote a well-known phrase – is the overcoming of man by man. That is the extreme counter-position to belief in God, since now even the certainty of reason has gone. Translated back into ontological language it means that the 'fundamental assurance of being itself' is affected. So for Küng this marks the only adequate counter-position in the dispute over God from which a dialogue can be carried on. Here the statement 'God exists' is no longer a statement which is limited to the level of 'true or false'; rather, nihilism is about the response to reality itself, and this alone can determine the context in which the statement has meaning and is discussed.

So is nihilism in principle as possible, irrefutable and unprovable as the existence of God,[10] so that there is a stalemate between faith and nihilism? Initially that is certainly the formal result. However, Nietzsche has clearly shown the full extent of this stalemate. He discloses in Küng's argument the nihilistic core of a consistent atheism which is not only asserted theoretically but experienced concretely. In so doing he uncovers the refusal of any trust as the consequence of atheism, which he understands as militant unbelief. Only on the basis of this position can Küng then, as I shall demonstrate later, relate an ultimate trust in reality to faith in God. First, belief in the existence of God had simply become implausible and incredible. There was hardly any more to be said. Now the true extent of the apparently plausible atheistic solution becomes evident; for Küng it becomes the decisive context for the discovery of the question of God. Nietzsche not only analyses atheism as a critique of the praxis of faith but also investigates its nature and its consequences. That is why he has become so important. He is as it were the anti-theologian *par excellence*.[11]

It is to Küng's credit that he has taken up this radicalization of the question of God and investigated the basis for it. This has three consequences for his further argument.

1. As is well known, the arguments for the existence of God are no longer compelling on the level of abstract proof. Küng sees this disadvantage as also being an advantage in their use. The question of God can no longer be discussed without consideration of human beings and reality. We can discuss it only at a more complex level by continually taking together three poles: the statement about existence itself, patterns of human and social action, and the convictions of those who believe in God. The truth of God's existence carries conviction only if it is related to plausible values (correctness) and embedded in convincing behaviour (credibility). As a result, the question of God moves from an ontological to a hermeneutical horizon. Küng develops his question of the existence of God as a hermeneutic of what he calls fundamental trust. His concern is to reject God or to understand God as the content of our trust.

2. The arguments for the existence of God are resolved as a question of the meaning or meaninglessness of the reality which we experience – as it were every day. So first of all we must learn to understand reality in such a way that the question of God emerges in it, and not just behind it.[12] Here attention to the limit conditions of our experience is decisive. In the dispute between belief and nihilism we can no longer objectify these conditions in terms of their own foundations or connections. Küng develops his question of the existence of God as a hermeneutic of what he calls the meaning, the ground, or the goal of reality. So it is a matter of saying that God is dead or 'thinking' of God as the centre of our own reality.

3. Against this background it becomes evident that the stalemate in the terms 'unproven – not refuted' can only be provisional. There is no more need to give lengthy explanations as to why we can no longer ourselves objectify the probative force of an argument than there is to explain at length that our reality is full of intrinsic contradictions. The only question is how long a practical rationality – however fragmentary – will assert itself, and whether we are not always already caught up in trust in reality. Moreover the grounding of the truth of God (like that of any truth) becomes clear only at the end.[13] Before any further analyses we can see that this process of understanding immediately leads to existentially binding insights – and in the end to a binding character which no longer knows any 'Yes, but'.

Küng's assertion that belief in God is the more meaningful (if not the only meaningful) solution lays claim to validity against the background of the modern dispute, in other words in the face of a prior negative decision. Nietzsche was not interested in arguing either about a provisional God or about a reality which would be regulated superficially (i.e. by technology or culture). So he was not concerned with a God whom we could still decipher functionally as humanity. Rather, he was concerned with a God the concept and experience of whom was developed in the monotheistic (and in this sense radical) intellectual culture of Christianity. The monotheistic concept of God in particular is not related to specific parts of reality, to central experiences, gaps or origins (say of a religious kind), but in the strict sense to reality as a whole and its all-embracing transcendence. In his survey of the intellectual history of modern times Küng has brought out the singificance of the statement 'God exists' in narrative form. Following this, he faces the task of bringing together the result systematically. The question is how he will tackle this hermeneutical task in such a way as to achieve a trustworthy, meaningful and binding result.

3. Yes to reality?

Nihilism has made it clear that the debate over the question of God is directly embedded in the debate about our reality. A God whom we think of independently of our reality as a purely transcendent being ultimately loses any significance for the inner understanding of reality.[14] But if God remains external as the ultimate cause or ultimate goal of his world and thus becomes a rival to human freedom, he has not merited the name 'God'. True, Küng paraphrases the concept of God with metaphors like 'supreme instance', 'ground', 'support', 'goal', and verbs like 'define'. But these metaphors are not to be deciphered as external causality, goal or ordering principle.[15] As Küng understands it, God's 'causality' appears as the working of the things themselves, God's 'final cause' as the dynamic of human beings and the world, and God's 'ordering principle' as the structure, the life-principle or cultural process of reality itself. 'Determining' denotes the experience of an ultimate comprehensive unity which is intrinsic to what is, which is beyond our disposal, but which encounters us in our reality itself. So God's relationship to the world surpasses reality as a whole, that is, reality both in its totality and in each of its parts. Anyone who wants to cope meaningfully with the question of God must therefore investigate the meaning or meaninglessness of this reality. Furthermore, since Nietzsche, not only the question of God but even before that the question of our reality is up for discussion. So it is the debate over this ontological and hermeneutical nihilism which leads Küng to distinguish the two levels – God and our reality – and at the same time to relate them to each other. Methodologically, therefore, Küng prefaces the question of the existence of God with the question of reality generally.

First of all, however, we need to consider the claim of this reality to be binding. No human being would deny his or her own being and life. Whether we like it or not, we have to affirm our own existence and identity. We can accept or reject ourselves, give or deny an orientation to our life, understand our future as meaningful or as ultimately chaotic. But it is virtually impossible to behave without any attitude (however unreflected or pre-scientific). So we can never begin to think without a prior decision, from a neutral point. That would itself in turn be unhistorical thought.[16]

Knowledge comes about in this process of individual and collective acceptance or rejection, coping with contrasts, with what is given and refused, with joy and sorrow. It grows out of what Edward Schillebeeckx calls 'contrast experiences'. In some constellations of experience we can then see irrefutably the degree to which knowledge is shaped by prior decisions. It is in particular those who have 'previously' accepted meaning who can find it in their often wretched lives (and perhaps can do so because they have accepted these lives).[17] Conversely, people who are unable to accept life as given cannot find any meaning in a rich and unproblematical life (and perhaps because they do not accept it). In other complexes it can emerge that sceptical restraint, the pathos of objectivity or more sublime criticism already betrays a basic position.

Küng speaks of a 'fundamental attitude' with many nuances which in the debate over nihilism can be classified as an alternative between a 'fundamental mistrust' and a 'fundamental trust'.[18] But if the model described holds – especially with its element of binding unity – fundamental trust and fundamental mistrust cannot be equal possibilities, for only those know this reality from within who accept it positively and in a binding way. No small child can grow up healthy without a fundamental trust, and no life worth living is possible without trust.[19] We have always already laid claim to trust when we stand for light against darkness, relations against relationlessness, life against death, being against nothing.

Now a decisive breakthrough in Küng's approach seems to me to lie in his distinction and correlation between 'reality' and 'God'. Here, as we saw, there is not only a distinction but also – and this is even more important – a reciprocal relationship. Because God shows himself to us as an element within our reality, we can learn the appropriate way of dealing with the question of God – or at any rate its basic structures – precisely in dealing with this reality. In the debate, in dealing with ourselves and our lives, we at least prefigure our attitude to the question of God; so – to put it cautiously – without reference to our reality, a hermeneutically responsible way of dealing with the question of God is unthinkable. Just as the material concept 'reality' becomes an empty shell for those who do not know how to deal with their reality, so the content-centred statement that God is the all-determining supreme instance becomes lexically empty if those who use the term cannot at the same time report what is being determined in what way by this supreme instance. That leads to a double structure in the question of God: it is about the truth of God, but the truth as embedded in its worldly meaning. What we arrive at perhaps with inductive logic has to be clarified and ordered hermeneutically. It is no use adopting an assertive position ('Yes, it is true., . . .') if nothing is also said about its meaning ('if you understand it like that'). This tension lies at the heart of the argument.[20]

What follows from this is important for understanding Küng's enterprise. His formal argument does not set out to draw conclusions but to open up possibilities. For Küng it serves as an incitement and invitation[21] to interpret the trustworthiness of the implications of meaning in one's own existence.

With this rather abstract reflection we have jumped ahead of Küng's argument. Now it is time to consider the core of Küng's text.[22] Küng seems to cause himself difficulties. On the one hand he speaks of an inner reasonableness which rules out any reifying approach from outside. On the other he appeals to this vulnerable and inwardly-directed reasonableness in a situation in which the statement 'God exists' has lost its plausibility. So in view of the nihilism which has been described we can no longer rely on any form of apparent clarity. Only an 'inner reasonableness' which is wholly in the matter itself can help us. But in this situation it can also become clear how appropriate this help is.

This is indeed the result of modern thought and modern criticism. Not only the answer 'God' but also the correct question about God threatens to disappear. The nihilism of Nietzsche is so valuable because all he leaves as the result of modern thought is the radical 'questionableness' of reality. Is this 'questionableness' simply the result of a highly philosophical view of the world, or do we also find it in our own experience, so to speak as fear of the reason of our own heart? For Küng it is clear that the world and human beings affirm themselves and can affirm themselves over wide areas. But despite all the self-affirmation, we cannot explain ourselves satisfactorily in our own terms. For centuries this discovery has found expression in amazement *that* the world is. According to Küng, it begins among those who are ready to accept and to understand their reality in trust. However, a remark of Weischedel applies to this attempt: 'Anyone who proposes to ask the question of God philosophically in our age must take account of the situation from which this question begins: he must put himself at the zero point from which alone truth can emerge in a new way, if it can emerge at all, in the absence of all security.'[23]

4. Yes to God?

This zero-point situation corresponds to the totalizing of a question which Küng consistently attempts to translate into the dimension of present identity, our origin and our future. He takes up the three classical questions of philosophy, 'Who are we? Where do we come from? Where are we going?'[24] He is thus concerned with the foundation, goal and meaning of reality. As ultimate reasonableness of these dimensions is to be expounded, Küng designates these dimensions 'primal ground, primal support, primal goal'. He talks of 'primal support' in connection with the worldly contingency of our existence, and (taking up the philosophical tradition) of 'being itself' when referring to the ground of existence.[25] To achieve a clear argument and clear identifications of existence, and thus comprehensibility, 'God' must be expressed conceptually. However, it is also *a priori* clear for a hermeneutical approach that no such conceptual precisions can be adequate, since the specific basic experience which opens up a perspective on God must be reconstructed in all experiences *together*.[26]

The argument is thus so complex that it cannot lead to any compelling proof. But in that case how is a reasonable account and confirmation possible?[27] The assertion that Küng too has not 'proved' the existence of God, which can often be read, says nothing against his plan. Küng's starting point is that the broad complexes of experience in human life can never be brought together to form a completely coherent theory of the existence of God. Therefore the assumption of God's existence always remains 'problematical' for him, and even later he does not retract this proviso in any way; for by way of indirect verification (which must be taken, and cannot be relativized as a provisional approach) experiences can also always be cited which tell against God's existence. As in the case of basic decisions in and about the life that we can experience, so too on the way to a positive claim about existence the pre-reflective and pre-scientific position of those engaged in the argument have an underivable role. We are already shaped by attitudes and decisions before we can formulate 'objective' arguments. So we are not compelled but invited; confronted not with an irrefutable proof but with a problematical situation. The process of verification on which Küng sets out is in fact indirect in two ways.

(i) The indirect goal of the verification is not the existence of God as such, but the legitimacy of accepting this existence. It is a long way from reasonable certainty to what John Hick has called 'eschatological verification'. So it is not 'God' but our decision about him which is the immediate object of reflection.
(ii) The goal of verification is not the irrefutable correctness of such a decision but its intrinsic (shall we say hermeneutical) reasonableness and grounds for belief. The issue is one of 'authentication', of 'confirming' and of 'credibility'.[28] Against this background Küng develops the structure of 'proof' in three steps.

Step 1. The urgency of the question

'Without authentic transcendence there can be no authentic transcending. Thus the question of religion, indeed the question of God, is raised.' It is not only the history of the question of God which has already been described, but a consideration of human beings and the grave questions which human beings and society face, which make the question of God inescapable. As has already been explained, the world remains confined in an ultimate radical questionableness. The world as a whole and human beings cannot ground themselves in themselves, cannot achieve a coherent understanding of human beings and the world or find an ultimate answer to questions about the origin, meaning and goal of human beings, history and the world. So the question whether God exists at all is to be answered in and from a situation of radical questionableness.

Küng not only points out that the question of the existence of God exists *de facto* (and inescapably). He also points to the field of experience of human beings and the world, where the question emerges with extreme urgency, demands and makes possible an answer. No one – and Küng is clear about this – can put the question of God to one side as irrelevant. At the same time he shows that and why the argument must be conducted with an eye to its consequences and that these cannot be ignored. The connection between theory and praxis must be kept in view from the start.

For this reason, no method can be shown by which we can find the way to God or gods independently of persons. If God really is the 'all-determining reality'[29] (that is also the reality which is the ground of everything, which keeps everything in being and gives it meaning), then God is connected with our concrete experiences.[30] For Küng, the assertion 'God exists' has meaning only in so far as it establishes meaning. So the issue is not the construction or proof of God, but the justification of what is always *de facto* talk of God's existence. Thus what stands at the beginning of the operation is not the question of the concept of 'God' but the meaning of God's existence for (the understanding of) human beings and the world as it is revealed in our history. This is a constituent element in Küng's argument.

Step 2: The hypothesis

Having hermeneutically clarified the definition of 'God as all-determining reality', as a second step Küng makes a conditional connection between God's existence on the one hand and an ultimate grounding of reality on the other. If God were to exist, then reality would not ultimately be without a ground, support or goal. The answer to the questions of our experience of reality, which for the moment is given hypothetically, has a twofold form.

(i) In respect of reality as a whole, Küng says: 'If God exists, then the grounding reality itself is not ultimately groundless. Why? Because God is then the primal ground of all reality ...' This conditional relationship is then transferred to the different aspects of the question (support, goal, being).[31]

(ii) In respect of our own personal reality and our own history, that means: 'If God exists, then despite all the menace of threat and death I can with good reason confidently affirm the unity and identity of my human existence. Why? Because God is the primal source also of my life.' This connection too is developed in terms of the meaning, hope and ground of being of life.[32]

This in no way robs the counter-arguments, which are discussed at length, of their force. Reality *remains* 'questionable' – although Küng denies that the counter arguments are the last word.[33] Nevertheless, the existence of God 'would' give the decisive condition of possibility.[34] Now on the presupposition of the definition given and the explicitation of its content, the indissoluble connection between condition (= God's existence) and the given consequence (= answer to the ultimate questions) is in fact irrefutable. But what are we to conclude from it? If it only follows that atheism can neither be proved nor refuted,[35] Küng would seem to have done himself a disservice. Nothing is left other than a *possibly* true assertion. So it is not a matter of proof, but of the question what we are to do with this result.

Step 3: Inner confirmation

This brings us to the core and the decisive points of the argument. As such, the connection noted above shows only what significance the question of God has for human beings and reality. Of itself it does not yet say anything about the truth of God's existence. Although the question is urgent, a sceptical restraint is fully justified. At this point Küng introduces the key thought in his argument. It is: 'That God is, can be assumed only in a confidence rooted in reality itself.'[36] In my view this statement has four epistemological implications.

(i) Küng rejects objectifying procedures designed to yield compelling proof. This exclusion of compelling procedures for legitimation gives the rest of the argument its decisive quality; for now all the attention must be paid to a process of grounding which dispenses with the compulsion of objectifying logic.

(ii) The renunciation of compelling proof makes room for a shift in perspective. Methodologically, as has already been said, this is a hermeneutical procedure in which concrete object- and subject-centred constellations of meaning are discovered. In this sense it is a question of the 'overall truth' of the real: 'God' is understood as the truth content of all-embracing reality and thus the almost tautological stringency of the connection described above, formulated in an unreal way ('IF God existed, then a fundamental solution WOULD BE GIVEN') is operationalized. It becomes the occasion for understanding our experiences of reality in terms of their ground, support and goal, in the light of the existence of God. In a way comparable to Pascal's wager,[37] 'God' is offered in the best sense of the word as a working hypothesis for thought and life. This proof therefore convinces only those who can follow it through in their own or in shared experiences.

(iii) Küng calls the readiness to rely on a recognized constellation of meaning 'trust'. In so doing he criticizes the neutrality of reason in the face of the question put to it as sham, seeing it as a lack of readiness to assent, as a disguising of refusal. The concept of trust should be examined closely in this context. Küng does not add a new, fundamentally irrational quality to knowledge from outside; rather, he pleads for 'trust' again to be recognized as a basic condition of understanding itself and for understanding again to be recognized as a genuine dimension of trust.[38] So '(fundamental) trust' simply means the (fundamental) readiness to rely on the matter despite its unpredictable binding character. So trust and a ground for it are thought of together, and are envisaged as disclosing themselves as a meaningful unity only to the one who trusts. Küng could also have spoken of inner commitment, of a will to recognition or a readiness to enter into binding commitments or to undertake a 'dangerous' enterprise; for to acknowledge God (and thus one's own God) is not without its dangers.

For this reason this trust at first extends only to reality as it can be experienced immediately. Only as a second step does it direct itself towards God and is it traditionally called 'faith'. But this faith, too, is not an expansion, but a basic condition and an inner dimension of knowledge. So faith, too, lives primarily by a passive element: I rely on what shows itself to me (in some circumstances unobtrusively); I would give this space if I allowed it to be expressed. Understood in this way, knowing begins as silence, as hearing, as perceiving. It would be attractive to draw lines from here to those theories for which religious knowledge comes about as emergence, as the appearance of the holy or – linguistically much simpler – as disclosure (I.T. Ramsey).

(iv) This interconnection makes clear why for Küng the yes and the no to the meaning of reality and the existence of God cannot stand side by side with equal rights. For only in affirmative thought (willing to perceive) about reality and its ultimate foundation can an assent be evident. Here it is *a priori* clear that this evident nature or transparency can never be completed. So anyone who rejects this affirmative thought in any case brings thought to an end too early – i.e. before it can arrive at assent. In that case the meaning of reality cannot be grappled with unconditionally.[39] Understood in this way, belief in God lies in the consistency of trust in reality, because every meaning brings out (and must bring out) its own foundation.[40]

But is there meaning in this trust in reality, meaning in this belief in God?

'As radical fundamental trust, belief in God can suggest the condition of the possibility of uncertain reality.'[41] Perhaps Küng should have expressed himself more cautiously at this point: 'Anyone who affirms God has formulated a reason why – in accordance with his experience and his way of knowledge – he can trust reality. But he must also wait for the definitive confirmation of his experience, the final goal of his way of knowledge.' Only if the proviso about the refusal of faith is set against the self-proviso of faith does the answer remain, as intended, in the air, with that status in which alone meaningful connections can come about.

Therefore we must not over-stylize this statement – a danger when reading Hans Küng – so that once again it becomes a convincing proof. Küng is in fact simply describing the experience of those who affirm trust and faith. He can only sound out inner connections of meaning and therefore speaks of an 'inner' reasonableness. Now as long as we want to explain and argue, we can describe an 'inner' reality only as the experience of those who experience it. So inner reasonableness is not a logical strategy but an anarchic experience.

Step 4: Rationality and trust

What is the nature of this reasonableness which cannot be proved, which discloses itself in this trust? How can it be given concrete epistemological form, as what Küng describes with the psychological category of 'trust'? Let us remember once again that this basic trust must really have its reasonableness in itself, because nothing else is left but un-reason. The fundamental act of trust cannot be preceded by a justification. So trust appears as a dimension which only confirms itself in knowledge, because knowledge comprises a basic attitude of openness which if need be can also be disappointed. So inner reasonableness cannot (and will not) completely overcome the possibility of disappointment. That is the price of the original symbiosis of recognition and knowledge.

Now this attitude of trust relates to experiences which, while we may call them exemplary in contexts of grounding, cannot be universalized and thus made available to discourse which is logically compelling.[42] This gives the question of God a two-fold tension. First there is a tension between universality and particularity. Experience is and on each occasion remains particular, although it contains a universal claim. Precisely for that reason, no successful winning strategies can be developed here which avoid the personal decision of individuals. Secondly, there is a tension between description and normative validity. On the one hand we can describe the meaningful connections that we discover only as experience, but on the other hand they are full of claims to validity. If these experiences in fact had no universal validity, they would be false.

Inner reality, grounded in concrete experience, is inevitably lost when conveyed in theoretical discourse, so it remains related to the report of concrete experiences. The religions therefore keep resorting to the linguistic form of the report (stories, narrative, myth), which is then recalled in abstract discourse as the 'IF-THEN' rule. Therefore even the symbiosis of recognition and knowledge mentioned above always remains both memory and hope at the same time. What was then must always be redeemed again. Only on this condition does ordinary rationality, which can be and is at our disposal, carry conviction.

These considerations make it clear that the concepts of 'trust' and 'fundamental trust' are not simply to be understood as a psychological construct.[43] In the context of the epistemological discussion, Küng is concerned with a readiness to take account of those concrete experiences – which often cannot be objectified or universalized because they are practical ones – experiences which are left out of rationalistic scientific discussion with its ideals of the possibility of direct empirical verification, of quantification and repetition at will.[44] In connection with the problem of nihilism the question is what comprehensive scheme of interpretation can assimilate the experience of reality in affirmation or negation. But in connection with the problem of God the question is whether we can combine in any binding way the affirmation of the existence of God and the binding affirmation of reality.

However, this last question shows that we have not yet gone completely through the critical zone. Who gives us the right to solve the radical 'questionableness of reality' – even if only hypothetically – in the direction of the existence of God? Does not the formal hypothesis already open up a way for all possible answers for people who cannot live in absolute scepticism and the negation of meaning, without the acceptance of ethical and other values? Is not Küng opening the door to all kinds of projections, functionalizations and ideological misuse? Protestant theologians in particular tend to leave the discussion of linguistic questions here, arguing that God's existence cannot be grounded.[45] It is this to which Küng, coming from the Catholic theological tradition, resolutely objects. In the language of Dalferth, but in diametrical opposition to Dalferth's conclusions, Küng claims that it is precisely the ontic, ontological and anthropological primal fact, the questions of goal and meaning, of norms of behaviour and the basis for them, which compel us to speak of God's existence *at least as a question*. This in no way changes, say, the underivability of the Christian confesssion of God, but through the category of questionableness gives it its place at which the question must be put – in an ultimately world-wide context. Anyone who speaks of God, of an ultimate salvation and an ultimate redemption, must be able to indicate before that what 'God' means, what they can be redeemed from and what can bring their salvation.

What is involved here is in fact the tension of a God whom on the one hand we already know (though, granted, this is in hope of ultimate groundings), but of whom on the other hand we still have to hear everything. Anticipatory construction ('If God is ...') and subsequent reconstruction ('... my life would be') interlock. Before anything at all can be said of God's existence, it is necessary to identify unmistakably what is to be proved.

The provisional construction of the concept of God thus sets a hermeneutical reconstruction in motion. First the reconstruction can see to it that the existence of God can be convincing on intrinsic grounds and that 'God' does not degenerate to become the product of some kind of fantasy of utopia, anxiety or power; is not projected on to the screen of another world. Only this course ensures that we can put critical questions to the historical conceptions of 'God' (including the biblical and specifically Christian conceptions) on the basis of the fundamental human experience. We must pay careful attention to this polarity of construction and reconstruction, because the shift from a convincing inner rationality to its ideological misuse is easy to make. In short, only in confrontation with the radical questionability of human beings and reality does God really remain God.

5. 'God exists'

Küng focusses his argument on the statement 'God exists'. But what does this statement mean – independently of Küng's immediate argument? Of course the existence of God which is claimed corresponds to the existence of finite things only by way of analogy. But what does 'analogy' mean here? Another approach may perhaps take us further. The claim that God exists puts talk about God explicitly in an ontological context. There is something in God which transcends the reference to me, which of itself is only as it is. It thus contradicts any functionalization of the concept.[46] Thus the assertion of existence resists any attempt to understand God only as an aspect or an ultimate legitimation of something else. So up to now is there no analogy, but identity of meaning, in the word 'exists'? However – and here the analogy may begin – the problem of nihilism in particular can make it clear that the assertion of the existence of God changes one's understanding of the existence of the world because God's existence embraces the existence of the world. Thus the relationship of original and derived meaning moves in opposite directions: according to the origin of our concepts, existing originally of course means what we experience as existing. God exists 'in himself' and primarily (if God exists), but himself, of himself, in the full meaning of the word. All other things in their existence need a reference to him.

Here Küng undertakes an enterprise which is sometimes criticized by theologians. What in fact is really said of 'God' if – alongside an extremely abstract 'questionableness' – we keep to this dry statement about existence? Certainly we have already made a distinction between anticipatory construction and hermeneutical reconstruction, and shown that for Küng the statement 'God exists' represents a framework which first has to be filled out by the history of the question of God or, conversely, which figures as an abstraction of the modern question of God. But the question remains whether this procedure is legitimate at all. It is said that anyone who limits the question of God to the abstract question of 'God's existence' (and restricts it to a general assertion of existence) does not take God's Godness seriously. This is to understand God as an objectifiable being who in principle does not transcend the world and human beings. Many theologians (especially Protestants) therefore will not have the question of God reduced to a reified 'there is'. They are fond of referring to Bonhoeffer's famous statement, 'A God who is there, is not God.' Küng agrees with this statement in so far as it reduces God to a something that is there 'like Lake Geneva, or the Matterhorn, or love between two human beings'. But at the same time he counters this objection with a remark by Brecht: 'I advise you to consider whether your conduct would change in the light of your particular answer to this question …'[47] Küng therefore also gives an extended answer to this question: what would be different if God existed?[48] In so doing he has made concrete precisely what I have said above on the question of existence. We may have questions about these concretizations, but the perspective in itself is not overlooked.

To answer the objection I shall now go more deeply into two questions discussed in the analysis of religious language. The first question runs: if we say 'God', how can we know what we are talking about? And from there we return once again to the question: what is the nature, connected with that, of the assertion of the existence of God?

Let us turn to the first question. In accordance with the basic structure of any proposition, the word 'God' can serve as subject or as predicate. In that case, as linguistic analysis puts it, it can serve as a 'designator' or a 'predicator'. That may be a grammatical triviality, but it leads to the question what the word 'God' originally is and how it is to be used – as designator, as predicator, or in both functions. First let us ask whether God functions as a 'designator' in this context. In this case 'God' appears as the subject of further statements, and here in turn there are two possibilities: 'God' functions as a proper name (as Israel, for example, speaks of 'Yahweh') or, less strictly, as an identifying description. If 'God' is a proper name, then I enter as it were directly into a personal relationship with God. But God is invisible, and we cannot in any way presuppose that others experience him. So I name God without having described God further. For those who unfortunately still know nothing of God, 'God' is a pure mode of reference. But since I do not just say 'You', I seem to know him (as I know Fritz or Barbara), so that I only need point to him.

Now this theory has many adherents among Christian theologians, since at first glance it corresponds to the biblical notion that there is only one God who has revealed himself with his name. But what are those to do to whom God has not revealed himself, though they too are perhaps in search of the true God? How are they to get to know God? And how can I convey my personal knowledge to my conversation partners simply by mentioning a name? But if 'God' (second possibility) is used generally as an identifying description, as a generic term, then I am certainly also communicating some basic descriptive elements which distinguish God sufficiently clearly from other beings. But from where do I get this prior knowledge of God, if 'God' serves exclusively as a 'designator', i.e. as the starting point and point of reference for all further statements (yet where I cannot experience him empirically). In any event, caution is called for. Anyone who wants to understand God only as a proper name or on the basis of certain specific experiences (say biblical or Christian) is in essence breaking off the dialogue with representatives of other religions, with philosophy, and, in a secularized society, with many contemporaries. The representatives of other religions then name their own God, and many people what they regard as God, on the basis of very particular experiences. If these monotheistic motives are all that there are, they lead to individual positions which are incapable of dialogue.

In the second case 'God' is introduced as a property, as predicator. Being God is predicated of a (another) subject. For example it can be said that 'Love is divine' or 'Yahweh is God'. There are weighty reasons for this usage, particularly at the point where God is really still unknown. Therefore arguments for the existence of God in particular are also aimed at conversation partners for whom 'God', if he can be introduced at all, can at first be introduced only as predicator. This also applies to the discussion within theology, because otherwise any further argument would have to be broken off even among those who shared one's convictions. Now this approach, too, has its representatives. They are fond of pointing out that the ancient Greek world started from a predicative usage. 'God' at the same time means 'divine'. Properties and values, experiences and hopes, are elevated to a divine status. Moreover, those with a sceptical standpoint or who are critical of religion are more likely to introduce 'God' as predicator (cf. Feuerbach). Furthermore, the predicative use has its specific function where false gods are being rejected. Not Baal or Mammon but Yahweh is the true God.[49] However, such an argument can (and must) end with the recognition that in the end 'God' can be defined only by 'God' himself. 'God' can be understood only as God. But we must first come to this insight by a general question and tentative awareness of God. The knowledge of God is essentially a transitory insight, even when it is a question of God's existence.

So the designative and predicative uses complement each other. A prior construction of the concept of God (predicative) is unavoidable because otherwise a process of identification (designative) cannot be put in motion. At the same time the (designating) name must be filled out by the constant reconstruction of those experiences which make 'God' verifiable at all.[50] That is a predicative process. Now for the assumption of God's existence everything depends on taking the step from the predicative to the designative usage. But that calls for a leap, a grasp forward, a decision, a resolute change of hermeneutical position, which can only be made by the knowing subject (and his or her credibility). Now this change of position presupposes the existence of God as God. That is what is meant in talk about God's existence.

Let us now turn to the second question. What kind of a statement is 'God exists?' It is a statement about existence, and thus belongs to a class of statement which is particularly unmanageable in logic, and which has led to complicated analysis. This is particularly the case with the existence of God. According to a widespread conviction, statements about existence make sense only if they relate to individual identifiable entities. All other statements presuppose that what is designated must exist. For example, 'The tree is green [if it exists].' But here the statement is that it exists (the tree, God), and so the basic condition of all (other) statements, becomes meaningless: 'This tree exists [?if it exists?].' Evidently such 'singular statements about existence' go far beyond linguistic questions. They explicitly include ontological presuppositions[51] which can be clarified only in the light of the basic framework of the assertion. However, such statements in general also have a second implication. They are always made by a speaker who validates the statement: '[I assert that] the tree is green [if it exists]', or '[I assert] that the tree exists (? if it exists?]'. If I assert that the tree exists, then I am evidently no longer relating my statement to the fact that I can depict or fictitiously create a reality in my statements (hence [if it exists]). So what am I referring to? Quite evidently, as Dalferth remarks, following Anglo-Saxon positions, myself as the speaker. There is a connection in reality between the tree and myself. As early as 1981 Dalferth concluded in connection with this question: 'So with the assertion "God exists" I am postulating a connection in reality between God and myself, in which each has a place and stands in a relationship which is capable of explanation.'[52] In 1984 he took this line of thinking further and attributed a trans-categorical and transcendental function to statements about existence. Such a statement does not add a further meaning to the object, but rather relates my thinking to reality. The 'existing' object confronts me as irreducible truth.[53] Speaker and spoken are 'both localized in the context of the existent'.[54] They are 'both in principle identifiable in the same way'.[55] In traditional terms, what we have here is the wonder that reality exists, that I am myself, that we can make a distinction between reality and fiction.

So statements of this kind about existence are not only constantly presupposed in our talk about reality,[56] but in fact transcend, explicitly or implicitly, the propositional dimension. Viewed as speech-acts, at the same time they presuppose a binding character which affects the speaker.[57] In statements about reality as a whole this binding character is implicit. In statements about God, as the concept is generally understood, they become an explicit theme. The ontological commitment which comes into play with general statements about existence is thus made propositionally explicit in statements about reality as a whole and in statements about God introduced into the tradition of a way of speaking which has been canonized over millennia. Küng describes this shift from description to the explicit acceptance of the binding character which has arisen as 'trust'; the radicalization of this binding dimension of trust is brought into play as 'faith'.

Closer analysis of Küng's argument could show that it is not just questions of knowledge which are to be solved by appeals to trust. The attitude of trust primarily means a readiness of binding knowledge. What is also involved is a readiness to affirm explicitly the presuppositions of knowledge which are made implicitly, so that they guide knowledge as well as formulate the grounds for propositions. So the reference to basic trust can be seen as a reference to the intrinsic consistency of a binding character which has come about.

It is therefore worth reading the non-real 'IF-then-WOULD BE' structure of the argument against this background. From a Kantian perspective, God or the trustworthiness of reality as a whole are a postulate. The important thing is to fulfil all needs for meaningful knowledge and acceptance of reality. From the perspective of a transcendental theology schooled in Heidegger, the intelligibility and goodness of the real (or the existence of a God who is the ground for these values) arise as the 'conditions of possibility' for truth and the value of the real generally. Küng's argument does not coincide with either of the two outlines sketched out,[58] since he takes note first of all of the distinction between thinking and an explicit process of grounding, and secondly of the element of freedom (and subject-relatedness) which is involved in binding processes of understanding. The thought process as such can be presented in the 'if-then' form. Its contents are to be introduced into the differentiation of their linguistic (and thus objectifying) formulation. The dialogue situation in which the hearer first has to be convinced with reasons cannot be ignored,[59] if the suspicion of an implicit moral reproach or authoritarian command of faith is to be avoided.[60] The thought process must thus remain related to a *possible* conclusion as something non-real. This non-reality does not arise out of an irrational chance factor in reality itself, but from the fact that human freedom is incalculable at the moment at which it is woven into the ground of its own existence.

The situation is so complicated because a dialogue situation in which the argument is carried on hermeneutically from a discovery context usually presupposes understanding, which is then to be woven into a context of legitimation. How is the context of discovery to be translated into a context of legitimation? Küng formulates a conditional relationship, the members of which stand in a differentiated relationship to the reader whom he is to convince. Certainly a reason must be given for the existence of God. Everyone expects that of a theological book with the title 'Does God exist?' But contrary to expectations, what is to be legitimated appears in this conditonal relationship not as the consequence of a premise but as the sufficient condition for a consequence which concerns reality as a whole. God's existence, says Küng, answers all the questionableness of the world and human beings. But the consequence of the condition (namely that a last word can be given) is not simply verifiable either. Rather, the opposite is empirically viable, namely the scandalous radical questionableness of the world and human beings.

So what has been proved? Is not Küng going to absurd extremes? According to both self-critical discourse and the preceding history of atheism and nihilism, what has been proved is God's non-existence rather than God's existence. In fact Küng turns the whole strategy of argument against himself and thus brings the cognitive impasse into focus. He himself has presented the questionableness of reality as the result of the history of thought which determines us and has demonstrated the helpless reaction of theology. So he forces himself into a situation in which – on the level of legitimating thought – no further argument is possible. And that is precisely what he is aiming at. Therefore no strategy of counter-arguments which could refute, mitigate or disarm the negative result is developed either.[61]

This what we might call self-imposed aporia in the argument thus forces a shift in its context. How is that to happen? Let us recall that statements about existence always also involve the situation of the speaker. Now while we can describe this context in general statements, we can no longer formulate it as a singular context of legitimation. Perhaps we can still achieve something in the hermeneutical context of a binding discovery. But this is only possible for those who voluntarily enter into this situation. Küng describes this condition with the category of trust, and has something to say about its different dimensions. 'That God exists can only be acepted in ... a trust.' Küng does not speak here of 'faith'. He does not mean to make the almost tautological assertion 'that God exists must be accepted in faith'. Trust in the sense used involves a hermeneutical dimension. So in this context of argument it relates to God only in so far as at the same time it relates to reality as a whole.

In this situation, then, the basis-consequence relationship is reversed. Nothing can be proved, because no one who – in the interpretation of believers – does not accept the situation explicitly puts themselves in the wrong. Now Küng asserts that the context can be disclosed and explained in a reasonable and positive way by anyone who follows him in translating the situation of binding disclosure into an attitude of trust. To such a person this trust discloses itself from a faith which becomes aware of its own reasonableness. So proofs of God cannot be more than invitations to accept the binding quality of comprehensive thought in the light of its grounding – no more, but also no less. Anyone who believes will see. That is a provocation presented in the non-real and with a claim to reasonableness.

6. Crossing the boundaries

As we saw, Küng develops the argument for the existence of God against the background of a long history of problems. This context is important not only because the basically narrative structure of the book, which conveys the experiences of others, corresponds to the appeal to an inner rationality, but also because Küng deliberately wants to go beyond the three classic boundaries of theological discussion so far, which are almost aporias. These are the boundaries between philosophy and theology, between (to put it in a sweeping way) Protestant and Catholic tradition, and between a scientific and a 'prescientific' order of thinking. These boundaries have grown up historically and are often strictly maintained, understandably defended by logic and strict conceptuality. Apparently compelling proofs or refutations then appear within their particular rules. But these rules, too, are always also the result of decisions which have been made in history, in which the complexity of our experience has been reduced.

1. Küng strives to cross a boundary between philosophy and theology. It was drawn at least from the Enlightenment by a philosophy which emancipated itself on the basis of the Cartesian ideal for the legitimation of theology. As we already saw, Küng understands trust to be a rationally responsible framework for our access to reality. A relationship of trust, interest and readiness for assent cannot be excluded either *de facto* or methodologically, as scientific theory has also recognized.[62] Along this line faith emerges, i.e. 'trust in God as qualified, radical fundamental trust',[63] and thus as an action with philosophical quality.

2. Küng strives to cross a boundary between Protestant and Catholic tradition. This is clear from his attitude to the question of natural theology.[64] Granted, at present we speak in our cultural sphere on the basis of Christian presuppositions about God, but faith and trust are also possible outside the Christian message. Here the content and form of faith are not reduced to a 'Christian philosophy', but theological reflection is opened up unconditionally to philosophical discourse. There is no regionalizable storm-free zone of a knowledge reserved for Christians.

3. Küng crosses the customary boundaries of a science which argues in a rationalistic way, which can no longer perceive trust and faith as legitimate modes or presuppositions of language. We may not avoid the demand for sober argumentation by the call to trust, but must take account of the

dimension of all truth which is abidingly pre-scientific because it belongs to practical life. This applies in the first place to a truth which can lead to binding consequences for the one who recognizes it.[65]

Thus Küng understands the statement 'God exists' as a summary statement of faith in God which need not be committed to any particular faith system, but which cannot exhaust itself in a detached intellectual attitude.[66] However, at the same time he understands the statement as the summary of a complex of problems by which the history of Christian culture is deeply moulded. So he cannot suppress the history of the criticism of religion which still determines the problem today. Against this background the argument is conceived as being a simultaneous challenge both to church language and to a theology which often enough still fails to take the problem seriously. Küng the theologian is ultimately concerned that the Christian churches should learn to proclaim their faith in God in a contemporary way, so as to enter into an open dialogue with all other religions and with them work for a world in peace and freedom. Küng's argument can be understood as an indication of the need to speak of God's existence within the religions in such a way that the world with its questions to God is not forgotten but taken seriously. So it is an indication, not a conclusive result.

If Küng's argument – with its course shaped by the history of ideas and its philosophical orientation – is to have any effect, it needs translations from the context of people with questions in the light of that context. The abstract concept of 'questionableness' has to be developed as the threat to human beings in the world. The attitude of basic trust has to be deciphered as steadfastness in and resistance to nothingness. How we live will then have to show whether and to what degree faith in God opens up meaning and makes meaninglessness tolerable. Like the abstract question 'Does God exist?', so too the abstract answer with a reference to radical trust and faith can be no more than a preparation for and a structural indication of that everyday trust and everyday faith which can be offered as Jewish, Christian or Muslim faith, as the faith of another religion, or even in the guise of concepts from world views in many places and in many garbs.

Notes

1. Theses 6–13 in H. Küng, *24 Thesen zur Gottesfrage*, 6f., which has not been translated into English. In this short work Küng sums up *Does God Exist?* in the form of theses. Reading the latter is of course an indispensable requisite for understanding him.
2. This article is an abbreviated and revised version of an article which originally

appeared in English: 'Does God exist? The Argumentation of Hans Küng', in T. Miethe and A. Flew (ed.), *Does God Exist? A Believer and Atheist Debate*, San Francisco 1991, 236–69 [however, the translation here has been made afresh from the German text printed in the *Arbeitsbuch*].

3. H. Küng, *Does God Exist?*; the part mentioned, F IV, has the title 'God Exists', 552–83.

4. Ibid., 548.

5. The linguistic theory of L. Wittgenstein's *Tractatus Logico-philosophicus* (1918), put forward polemically, was already out-of-date philosophically by the time of its publication. Wittgenstein's great contribution is, however, that he refuted his own misunderstanding in an enormously productive way. His *Philosophical Investigations* (1945–49) should be required reading for every theologian.

6. The significance of this investigation becomes clear, for example, in Kant's classic critique of the proof of God from Anselm of Canterbury's *Proslogion*. Anselm concludes the necessary existence of God directly from the *id quo maius cogitari nequit* (that greater than which cannot be conceived), and thus already anticipates the proof of God in the definition of the term 'God'. For Jüngel's position cf. E. Jüngel, *God as the Mystery of the World*, Edinburgh and Grand Rapids 1983, 3–55.

7. In its positivistically simplified version, the principle of verification recognized only directly empirical verification. This simplified focus is understandable in the modern understanding of proof since – apart from the problem of induction, which has long been recognized – it allows only means of proof or results which are compelling in an objectifying way. Here I.U. Dalferth (*Religiöse Rede von Gott*, Munich 1981, 505f.) uses the famous well-known parable of the gardener which A. Flew took over from J. Wisdom to show that the problem of verification had long represented a much wider problem. The question is not the verifiability and falsifiability of individual propositions but much more generally whether religious discourse can be rational at all, and justified in a rational way.

8. 'Before attempting to express existence propositions through existence quantifications, it is necessary to clarify what "exist" means in them and whether this meaning corresponds to what the existence quantor expresses or is explained in an acceptable way by this ... Thus it has not been demonstrated *a priori* that "exists" in "God exists" has to be understood in the sense of the existence quantor or indeed can only be understood in this way. Simply to translate this statement into the language of predicate logic is therefore not of itself a sufficient answer to the question of the meaning of the assertion made in this statement in Christian discourse' (I.U. Dalferth, *Existenz Gottes und christlicher Glaube*, Munich 1984, 94f.). According to Dalferth (*Religiöse Rede*, 631), 'expressions like "I", "you", "he", "here", "there", "now", "then" represent "orientational features of language which are relative to the time and place of utterance"' (J. Lyons, *Introduction to Theoretical Linguistics*, Cambridge 1968, 275ff.). They can only be understood correctly if one notes how they are centred on the speaker in each particular use, and their concrete meaning on any occasion can only be understood in terms of their pragmatic function of structuring a field of language and discourse in space and time in relation to the speaker. In a similar way, the meaning of transcendental expressions like "true", "good", "something", "being", "exist", and so on cannot

be fixed generally; they can only be explained in concrete terms with reference to a particular usage. To some degree they are lexically empty and are to be deciphered wholly from their usage in pragmatic communication, which consists, for example, in achieving shared certification of the object of a statement, in judging its characterization, evaluating it and what is said, and so on. In contrast to the deictic expressions, however, these terms are not orientated on the speaker but – one might say – on the object: their particular concrete meaning arises out of their function in respect of the subject-matter on which the debate is focussed.

9. For important problems within the triangle of text, context and experience which have hardly yet been considered, cf. H. Häring, 'Eerlijk voor God? Over de resultaten van een voortgaande discussie', *Tijdschrift voor Theologie* 31, 1991, 285–315.

10. Küng, *Does God Exist?*, 425ff. 'Proof' here is understood in the most general sense of the term: a process of providing grounds which includes the claim to validity and can defend itself against any (possible) objection. To the degree that the validity of a proof is not weakened by any counter-argument, according to a universal use of language the proof is regarded as 'compelling'. The current problem over 'proofs for God' lies in the fact that the element of the 'winning strategy' (i.e. the refutation of objections) no longer works, and by virtue of its hermeneutical structure cannot work in respect of the whole of reality.

11. In fact it has proved virtually impossible to arrive at any qualitatively new perspectives for the polarity of belief in God and nihilism since Nietzsche. Sartre formulated impressive anthropological connections. Furthermore conclusions are drawn, to the point of an absolute fragmentation of the question of meaning in post-structuralist thinkers, who formulated their approaches in intensive critical discussion of Nietzsche. This does not mean that post-structuralism owes itself to Nietzsche. What is new is the fact that post-structuralist philosophers resort to a *complete* fragmentation of the experience of meaning and formulate this in terms of structuralism and a psychoanalysis with a linguistic orientation. Cf. lectures 7–11 in J. Habermas, *Der philosophische Diskurs der Moderne. Zwölf Vorlesungen*, Frankfurt 1985, 191–389.

12. To make what he calls 'inner reasonableness' more precise, Küng could have referred to the discussion of 'experience' as a basic anthropological category, which has been carried on in European theology over the last decade. See E. Schillebeeckx, *Christ*, London and New York 1980, 27–64 (which appeared after the manuscript of *Does God Exist?* was completed). For a short summary of this issue see J. Splett, 'Über die Möglichkeit, Gott heute zu denken', in W. Kern et al. (eds.), *Traktat Religion, Handbuch der Fundamentaltheologie* I, Freiburg 1985, 136–55, esp. 140–4.

13. Augustine defines the relationship between faith and knowledge against the background of a way. Faith does not precede knowledge because the believer knows more, but because inner assent opens the way to knowledge. To this degree knowledge is and remains the goal of faith.

14. In this case God is imagined as a quasi-physical cause, as a quasi-physical or quasi-psychological goal, as a model that can be imitated, a quasi-pedagogical model, as the constructor of a world which can be of use to human beings. God

then intervenes directly in extraordinary situations. Thus God acts as human beings do, although God is not a rival to their freedom but the founder of it. The great theological and philosophical tradition of our history of thought has always associated God's transcendence dialectically with his immanence in this world. At this point it is not a matter of correcting or simply rejecting a metaphysical theology, but of taking its differentiated claim to truth seriously once again.

15. These concepts derive from Aristotle's theory of causes. In addition to the two 'external' causes (effect and goal) in the context of hylemorphism this knows material and formal causes as 'inner' causes.

16. This unhistorical thinking is one of the great temptations of modern times and has not been overcome even at their 'end', as postmodern trends in particular show. H. Peukert, *Wissenschaftstheorie – Handlungstheorie – Fundamentale Theologie. Analysen zur Ansatz und Status theologischer Theoriebildung*, Düsseldorf 1976, has shown that in both philosophy and theology even history itself can think unhistorically (and may not so think, in view of the unjustness and the victims of history). Unhistoricity has recently been propagated as an ideology by F. Fukuyama, *The End of History and the Last Man*, New York and London 1992.

17. I need not spend time here pointing out in detail that precisely such a result becomes the source of resistance. Cf. the still seminal book by D. Sölle, *Leiden*, 1973, 111-48.

18. Küng, *Does God Exist?*, 438.

19. Ibid., 444–64.

20. That, say, the notion of an endless chain of causes transcends and does away with itself is as obvious a logical conclusion to the argument as the comment that this formal argument can only be convincing as a generalization of concrete experience.

21. Küng locates his verification between an 'empiricistic' and a 'general hermeneutical criterion of verification'. The first would have to establish God empirically; the second would content itself with making the word 'God' and the statement 'God exist' understandable. By contrast, Küng is concerned with a 'knowledge of God related to experience'. Thus what is meant is not a compelling derivation from an allegedly evident experience but a 'clarifying illumination of the experience which is always problematical and which invites a positive decision' (ibid., 550f.).

22. Küng, *Does God Exist?*, 552–76.

23. W. Weischedel, *Der Gott der Philosophen* I, Darmstadt 1975, XIX: 'In this question, the questioner himself comes into play in a special way. He is himself part of the totality of beings, and is so in an exemplary sense, in that he has the possibility of putting this whole in question. When he asks about the whole he is at the same time asking about himself, the part of the whole which puts it in question. Therefore it is of decisive importance for his self-understanding whether and how this whole can be understood, i.e. whether it is possible to make statements about God as the ground of being as a whole, or whether this is impossible for human thought; and that means whether our human situation is unavoidably godforsakeness, so that we cannot do other than either praise this enthusiastically, bear it soberly or lament it painfully, or whether even today it is still possible to utter the *De profundis*' (ibid., XVIII).

24. See e.g. the beginning of the Foreword to E. Bloch, *The Principle of Hope*, Oxford

and Cambridge, MA 1986: 'Who are we? Where do we come from? Where are we going? What do we expect? Many feel themselves confused. The ground under their feet is swaying: they know neither why nor wherefrom. This condition is that of anxiety. When it is concretized, it becomes fear.'

25. Before rationalistic critics denounce this way of speaking as 'conceptual salad' (see H. Albert, *Das Elend der Theologie. Kritische Auseinandersetzung mit Hans Küng*, Hamburg 1979, 82) they should take these connections into account. Albert has by no means grasped, nor does he want to grasp, the hermeneutical complexity of a truly adequate definition of the term 'God'. He would unhesitatingly call such a neglect 'shoddiness' among others.

26. This totality in the qualified sense of the word (because it transcends immanence and transcendence, part and whole) remains as it were the abiding hermeneutical mystery of the kingdom of God. 'From below' we can at best achieve it in approximations: finally it must disclose itself as such in an underivable act. In this context Rahner has developed the theory of the *potentia oboedientialis*, but it too approaches the matter only from a limited and thus limiting perspective.

27. This starting point can also be accepted by philosophers who do not go on to conclude that all arguments for the existence of God are meaningless or impossible: 'The proofs of God's existence have not become superfluous because they have lost their strict demonstrative character. Instead they continue to serve as a certification of believing. They represent paths of thinking that, when originally thought out, seize the thinker with the self-conviction of the deepest event of living and that, when reflected upon with understanding, make a repetition of this certification experience possible' (K. Jaspers, *Philosophical Faith and Revelation*, New York 1967, 34f.).

28. Küng, *Does God Exist?*, 550.

29. 'All-determining' is likewise a metaphorical statement that can be given meaning depending on the concrete conditions of experience – how could it be otherwise? For it remains open how God can determine reality and how in fact God does determine it. It is indeed a central problem of modern faith that this 'determination' by God does not fit with the experience of human freedom, and so its metaphor cannot be developed further.

30. By concrete experience I mean for example the experience of a quite particular, definite event which can be distinguished in space and time. Otherwise it would not be possible at all, because no event can be experienced by all people or by all people in the same way. Here the starting point of the writer is that all human beings are confronted with experiences of such a class, e.g. pain, grief, disappointment, joy, etc.

31. Küng, *Does God Exist?*, 566.

32. Ibid., 567.

33. What remains open in Küng's argument is whether the arguments against are merely outnumbered by the arguments for (and are thus weakened by comparison), or whether they turn into positive arguments. This can be clarified by asking three questions: 1. Does Küng just mean to say that the questionableness of reality forces us to ask the question without giving the answer, or is he being led by the transcendental theological argument that implicitly the questionableness

implies an answer? 2. Do negative experiences (of death, evil, etc.) merely mean that the assertion of God's existence remains threatened by corresponding assertions to the contrary, or do these negative experiences ultimately require the assumption of God's existence if the problem is to be settled at all? 3. Finally, do the counter-experiences serve as (indirect) falsification or – from a changed hermeneutical perspective – along with the positive experiences do they similarly serve indirectly to verify God's existence?

34. Küng, *Does God Exist?*, 568.
35. Ibid., 569.
36. Ibid., 569f.
37. Ibid, 61–3.
38. Augustine describes believing as *cum assensione cogitare* (thinking with assent). For him, too, the dividing line does not run between faith and thought, but between false thought on the one hand and right thought and faith on the other. An analysis of his understanding of faith could make it clear that the modern model, according to which 'thought' and 'faith' are in competition, or externally supplement each other, is not the only possible model.
39. Presumably this no longer amounts to an unreserved perception of the questionableness of reality. If that is the case, then the one who trusts can be more painfully disappointed in a binding trust than the one who holds back his position in an intermediate field of indecision or scepticism. Here it cannot be ruled out that Nietzsche put more trust in reality than some of his opponents. However, we are no longer in a position to pass judgment on that. In theological terms, only God sees into human hearts. So, much as Küng also makes a plea for the connection in principle between the finding of meaning and trust, his concern is not to verify belief and unbelief empirically.
40. To this degree Küng does not exclude an implicit faith in God. For him, the question whether and how far this implicit faith is identical with trust in reality is an open one.
41. Küng, *Does God Exist?*, 574.
42. The best example of this kind of reality is provided by knowledge and conviction that someone loves me, means me well, or perhaps is even ready to share their life with me.
43. Küng is not concerned just with a 'concretion' (important though that is, 453–73). However, this distinction could have been expressed more sharply (W. Pannenberg, *Anthropology in Theological Perspective*, Philadelphia and Edinburgh 1985, 224–30).
44. Küng, *Does God Exist?*,' 460–77.
45. I.U. Dalferth then draws a very sweeping conclusion from his differentiated remarks: 'That something exists at all, that more than one thing exists, that this plurality exists as a multitude of objects in space and time, and that among these objects such exist as are in a position to know and are capable of knowing this, does not say anything about the existence of God or about the truth of the assertion "God exists". Rather, it speaks only for itself. The certainty of the existence of God which is expressed in the Christian assertion of God's existence does not have its origin in the provocation of the ontological, ontic or anthropological primal fact,

as though these compelled us to speak of God' (*Existenz Gottes*, 169). What is at issue is not the alternative 'origin or not' but the precise effect of the provocation of which Dalferth speaks and which can also represent a figure of origin.

46. Thus e.g. when 'God' is interpreted as a cipher for love, cohumanity, finality, incomparable power, unconditional moral demand, the experience of an extreme limit, contingency, etc.

47. Küng, *Does God Exist?*, 561f.

48. Ibid., 562ff.

49. The Dutch theologian H. Kuitert (*I have my Doubts*, London and Philadelphia 1993, 32) makes this clear by the story of Elijah and the priests of Baal. At the end of the dramatic event the people cry out, 'Yahweh is God, Yahweh is God' (I Kings 18.39). 'God' becomes a predicator where he is called on by name.

50. Dalferth, *Rede*, 565–95.

51. Dalferth, *Existenz*, 100–54.

52. Dalferth, *Rede*, 591.

53. Dalferth, *Existenz*, 114–18.

54. Ibid., 152.

55. Ibid., 154.

56. Ibid., 88f. Dalferth reports W.V.O. Quine's thesis of 'ontological commitment', according to which in all speaking the existence of some objects is assumed. 'Thus in all talk the speaker commits himself to the existence of precisely those objects which take the place of the logical variables for which they stand when the statement is translated into the formal logic of value corresponding to the judgment about the truth of the proposition. Thus anyone who asserts that God created the world is saying that there is God and that he has created the world, and thus binds himself to an ontology which reckons with the existence of God.' For the present context, two questions follow from this: 1. Can we describe reality in all its parts, analyse it and understand ourselves as part of it without the implicit assumption that as a whole it is intelligible, good, and worthy of our assent in its structure of space and time (i.e. limitedness, origin and goal)? 2. Can we speak of the good foundation, purpose and meaningfulness of reality as a whole without ontologically presupposing talk of the existence of God? In that case the question about the reconstruction of already existing statements about existence runs: is the statement that God exists irreducible?

57. In connection with the theory of speech-acts, we should presumably speak of the illocutionary dimension of statements about existence.

58. Whereas Kant must deny the 'postulate' the quality of a rationally conclusive argument on epistemological grounds, transcendental theology makes an over-hasty virtue of this necessity. Kant's question is misused as it were as an arsenal for conceptuality, which is all too hastily taken as a proof of God in that the problem – namely the transition from practical to theoretical reason – is obscured with a resultant category mistake (see C.F. Geyer, 'Marginalien zum Thema: "Transzendentalphilosophie und Theologie"', *Franziskanische Studien* 65, 1983, 334–50).

59. The parables of Jesus could serve as an example, as could fairy tales and poems. They cannot be understood without a prior acceptance because they construct

discovery contexts into which they seek to draw their audience and do not want to set up connections which can be detached from involvement and assent.

60. This is illustrated, for example, in the reception of K. Barth. His reference to God's only true Word may well be understandable and capable of being grounded in the light of the inner connections of his discourse, but he can no longer translate the grounding into the inter-subjective situation of a group in which believer and non-believer want to enter into a conversation about God. This attitude takes another authoritarian turn where the grounding of God's existence is taken back to the demand that God is to be 'thought'. The deliberate failure to note the difference between 'thinking' and 'grounding' does not take account of the unique situation of theology. Its theme, namely the existence of God, is not understood as plausible, but it is not seen as a negligible quantity either. So in our period there is probably no other assertion for which the need for a foundation has been claimed so extremely as that of God's existence. Here there can be no context of grounding which – once outside the zone of what is generally plausible – is as complex as this proof.

61. This apologetic procedure is still often used in theology. As a rule it is not noted that such arguments only prove their own weakness because they reduce the place for experiencing God or for God's disclosure to narrowly drawn sectors of reality. Here too God dies, as Wisdom's famous parable impressively shows, the death of a thousand qualifications.

62. Cf. E. Stöker, *Einführung in die Wissenschaftstheorie*. Darmstadt 1977, 13–38.

63. Küng, *Does God Exist?*, 572.

64. Küng takes up the discussion carried on in Europe since the 1950s which in the Protestant sphere was dominated above all by Karl Barth. For a long time this was contrasted polemically with what was called the 'Catholic' side but was in reality the rationalistically narrowed position of Vatican I.

65. So Küng's reference to his earlier *On Being a Christian*, in which he developed the argument for the first time (57–68), is important for the understanding and effect of the arguments. There the arguments are not put in the framework of the abstract question of the existence of God but as a preliminary to the question of the Christian God.

66. For the Christian theologian, the confession of the existence of God accordingly becomes the ultimate summary of belief in the God of Jesus Christ.

Nevill Mott

An Answer to the Question of God in Modern Times?
A Physicist Reads *Does God Exist?*

1. *A personal horizon*

I met Hans Küng for the first time in the autumn of 1977, when, with my wife, I was the representative of Cambridge University at the celebrations of Tübingen University's five hundredth anniversary. I heard his address in the Stiftskirche, and introduced myself to him at the subsequent lunch. The following day my wife and I continued our journey to Marburg, where I have many friends with common scientific interests. Here at a lunch in the restaurant, Die Sonne, I learned from a telephone call that I had been awarded the Nobel Prize for Physics, jointly with two Americans whose work was closely related to my own. A few days after my return to Cambridge, there arrived through the post the English edition of Küng's *On Being a Christian*, inscribed 'Für Sir Nevill Mott. Zur Erinnerung an Tübingen mit herzlichen Glückwünschen zum Nobelpreis'.

This book has become one of my most precious possessions. Often, when in trying to clarify my own beliefs I find some Christian doctrine puzzling, I look for it in the index of this or one of Hans Küng's other books. I have quoted his views in sermons in my local church and elsewhere, and have occasionally checked with him to make sure that I have stated them correctly.

The invitation to contribute to this *Festschrift* is, among other things, the result of a book that I edited, *Can Scientists Believe?* (1991),[1] containing essays by fifteen men and women who have had experience of research, on how their science and religion relate to each other. In my own contribution, Küng's views are of course quoted several times.

To show how they have influenced me, I must say something of my own intellectual and religious development. My parents both started adult life as physicists, and indeed met in the Cavendish Laboratory in Cambridge, though they did not remain in a scientific profession. However, from the earliest days that I can remember, I knew about the great physicists, and wanted to follow them. I started research in 1926, just at the moment when the new quantum mechanics of Heisenberg and Schrödinger was being formulated. I learned the German language so as to read their papers. After studying with Niels Bohr in Copenhagen and Max Born in Göttingen, the wave-particle duality and the uncertainty principle were as familiar to me as simple arithmetic; they seemed quite natural and as obviously correct as the proposition that two and two equals four. I have made my career by applying these principles to problems of everyday importance, such as semiconductors, the strength of metals, photographic processes and superconductors.

My parents, both coming from Church of England families, early in their married life found the teaching of that church unsatisfactory and abandoned church-going, so neither I nor my sister were baptized. Except for compulsory worship at boarding school, I rarely if ever attended a church service until the age of about fifty, when I was director of the Cavendish Laboratory in Cambridge. Then the priest in charge of the University Church, Mervyn Stockwood, an intimate friend at that time and later a bishop, asked me to give a talk in his church in a series about religion and science. To prepare for this, for the first time in my life I read a good deal of theology, and was deeply interested in this world of thought, so different from that with which I was familiar in my normal work. I asked myself what is the nature of religious truth and came to the conclusion that I must think of a doctrine as something worthy of respect because of its acceptance by our ancestors, which should be examined by any thinking man to see if it had relevance for him, and to see if it helped in his understanding of God. Religious truth was, I concluded, quite different from scientific truth, which according to Popper is susceptible to falsification but within that limit accepted from Washington to Moscow (this was in the period of the Cold War). I was very conscious of the role of Christianity in our history; I felt that the culture which gave us a countryside studded with Gothic churches of wonderful beauty could not be based on pure falsehood, nor could Bach's St Matthew Passion be based only on a superstitious myth. Attending a church service regularly each Sunday, as was my duty as Master of a Cambridge college, I wanted to give what meaning I could to that which I heard there – and to realize that doctrines like the Virgin Birth, unacceptable and indeed rather repellent to me, could nonetheless be respected as part of the culture of an earlier time. So later, when I met Hans Küng's teaching that doctrines could be acceptable if interpreted for the twentieth century, it fell upon ground which was well prepared.

2. Problems of faith

Some of the ways in which I have been influenced by Küng are set out in my contribution to the book *Can Scientists Believe?*, which I have already mentioned. For instance, in discussing Bultmann on demythologizing I say how much I owe to Hans Küng, who tells me (if I understand him correctly) that

Christian doctrines are true if they are interpreted adequately for people of the twentieth century. Thus he writes of the literal truth or otherwise of the story of the empty tomb: 'Anyone who perceives the real point of the resurrection message will regard some fiercely contested questions as peripheral.'[2] Although I have read that the historical evidence for the empty tomb is rather good, I feel that this does not really matter, and hope I am with Küng there.

I have read that in an interrogation of Küng by two representatives of the Vatican he was asked, 'Do you unreservedly believe that Jesus is the Son of God?' 'Of course,' he replied, 'but in the modern world the important thing is to interpret this statement, is it not?' This could not have pleased his interrogators.

The doctrine that the crucifixion was a sacrifice for sin has always been repellent to me, and I was eager to see what Küng had to say about it. In *On Being a Christian* I found that he writes that this interpretation of the crucifixion was introduced by Bishop Anselm and is not for our age, but derives from the legal system of the eleventh century. If you believe in free will – as I do – one cannot believe that the crucifixion was preordained: Pilate or the Roman or Jewish authorities had free will to choose otherwise. The event, showing that utter evil can prevail in the short term, is something we know only too well in our own century. That it has seized the Christian imagination, so that a suffering Christ confronts us in almost every east window in churches, is clear. But many men and women have faced death for what they believe. I would rather say that Jesus taught us to live than that he taught us to die.

The concept of God is at the heart of all religions. I believe that this concept is very difficult to define, and perhaps has a different meaning to each member of a congregation in any church. To me God is an entity, external to ourselves, neither omniscient nor omnipotent, but who gives meaning to our lives. That God gives meaning is also a recurrent theme in Küng's writings. In some ways I am attracted to process theology – the teaching of Whitehead, for example – but not entirely: God must be external to us, not something we create. I asked myself why I believe this. Not because it is proved, but by an act of will: because I want to believe it. To me we have this mystery of human consciousness existing somehow alongside natural law; and to give it meaning, a belief in a God who is outside us has become necessary to me. Without that belief in the unknowable that we call God, life can seem a tale told by an idiot.

Again I looked up what Küng has to say about the origin of faith. Does one will to believe? He writes in *On Being a Christian*:

> Is Christian faith a matter of understanding?
> To take faith simply as an act of understanding, as theoretical knowledge, as acceptance of the truth of biblical texts or ecclesiastical dogmas, even as an assent to more or less improbable assertions: this is the intellectualist misunderstanding of faith.

Is Christian faith an effort of will?
To understand faith simply as an act of will, as resolution of the will in face of inadequate evidence, as a blind venture, as a *Credo quia absurdum*, even as merely a duty of obedience; this is the voluntarist misunderstanding of faith ...
Christian faith is none of these things. In absolute trust and complete reliance, the whole man with all the powers of his mind commits himself to the Christian message and to him whom it announces. It is simultaneously an act of knowing, willing and feeling, a trust which includes an acceptance of message and person as true.[3]

Of course Küng does not make faith wholly an act of will – but to me the act of will comes first. Finding that I believe in God because I wish to do so, I have perhaps been less influenced by *Does God Exist?* than by some of Küng's earlier books. But some parts have impressed me deeply. To show this, I reproduce a sermon I gave recently in our local church.

3. The problem of Christ's cross as a sacrifice

Anyone coming into this or any other church sees in the east window the image of a suffering Jesus hanging from the cross. If we think about it, perhaps while waiting for the rector to come in, what thoughts does this bring to our mind? Is it his sacrifice for our sins? Or that God can suffer? Or that our own suffering – and for none of us is life always a bed of roses – is meaningful because of his? We all have faced suffering and ultimately we face death, and in suffering, the loss of a loved one perhaps, we must have asked, 'How can the loving Father of Jesus Christ have done this to me?' I want to ask whether that suffering figure in our east window gives us an answer.

So I turn to our Christian faith and its history. The Christian religion, evolved over three thousand years in the Old and New Testaments, seems to me to contain some doctrines that contradict one another, so that each one of us has to choose those that *we* find helpful to our understanding of God. The crucifixion as a sacrifice for our sins is a part of Christian doctrine. It is a doctrine expounded in detail by Anselm, Archbishop of Canterbury in the eleventh century. Anselm is a very interesting figure in church history. Most of his adult life, before he went to Canterbury some thirty-seven years after the Norman Conquest, he spent in the monastery of Bec in Northern France. The mediaevalist Richard Southern wrote that he was the first really constructive religious philosopher in Western Christendom for six hundred years – since St Augustine and the fathers of the first four centuries. Anselm was a man who asked the fundamental questions. For instance, how do we know that God exists? Did God become man in Jesus Christ? Was this necessary? What exactly did it achieve, and how? What is the relation between our reasoning on these subjects and our faith? And how should we interpret the sacrifice for sin?

Anselm also said, 'I want to *understand* something of the truth which my heart *believes* and *loves*. I do not seek thus to understand in order to believe, but I believe in order that I may understand.' This is important. Faith came first for him, and this is how he understood the sacrifice for sin.

The eleventh century was a period when the study of jurisprudence was flourishing: in Anselm's mind this was important for theology. Anselm claimed that through Adam's sin God's honour had been infinitely offended, and it could only be made good by the voluntary infinitely valuable death of a God-man. Although this theme, his sacrifice for sin, has inspired hauntingly beautiful hymns like 'When I survey the wondrous cross ...', do we really believe in a God who demands retribution and sacrifice? Do we believe in a God like Abraham's Jehovah in whom Abraham believed when he prepared to sacrifice his only son Isaac?

The approach to religion of an Anselm, asking questions about the nature and actions of God, seeking to resolve them and asking the faithful to accept the results, has led in our sister church in Rome to the conclusion that mankind needs an infallible guide, and in the last century to the doctrine of the infallibility of the Pope when pronouncing on dogma – a doctrine that we do not accept in our church. But we can find among mediaeval writers a rather different view on dogma. Think, for instance, of Meister Eckhart. Born in 1260 in central Germany, a man who preached, not in Latin to the monks but in German to the common people, he spoke not of the subtle points of theology but of the immediate presence of God in the individual soul. I quote from one of his sermons. 'I have often said that there is a power in the soul which neither time nor the world can touch. This power proceeds from the soul and belongs to the soul for ever. I have sometimes called this power of the soul a fortress, sometimes a light, sometimes a spark in the soul. But now I can say it is more than any of these things.'

I do not want to imply that Eckhardt and Anselm would disagree; they both had the same faith. But they come down to us with a different view. A modern writer who – it seems to me – starts from God in the soul and our struggle with him there is Harry Williams. His book *The True Wilderness* describes his battle with God in his own soul – with little interest in doctrine.

Turning then to sacrifice from a point of view like that of Eckhart, even seven hundred years before the birth of Jesus, the Hebrew prophet Micah, with that astonishing capacity of the Jewish prophets to foresee the God preached by Jesus, wrote:

> With what shall I come before the Lord,
> and bow down before the exalted God?
> Shall I come before him with burnt offerings,

with calves a year old?
Will the Lord be pleased with thousands of rams?
With ten thousand rivers of oil?
Shall I offer my firstborn for my transgression?
The fruit of my body for the sin of my soul?
He has showed you, O man, what is good,
and what does the Lord require of you?
To act justly and to love mercy
and to walk humbly before your God (Micah 6.6–8).

Can we see in the death of Jesus, whose teaching was so like Micah's, something which is not a sacrifice for sin, but which can give some meaning to our own suffering and death?

Suffering is not all due to human wickedness – as was the suffering of the Jews in the Holocaust and that of Jesus on the cross – and it cannot be *sent* to try us – it cannot be willed by God. I do not believe that God willed either that or the wickedness that we see in our own world today.

If I ask myself why I believe in God, and I was not brought up in any such belief, it is because I do not believe that the life of any human being is meaningless; it is not a random movement of atoms. Life is not a tale told by an idiot. Life must have meaning, and it is to God we look to give it meaning. And that man in our east window, dying – it must have seemed at the time – a pointless death, is the supreme example of *meaning* given by that which came after the event – which at first seemed to his followers to be the end of everything. Hans Küng writes in his book *Does God Exist?*: 'Only one thing – but it is decisive – can be said on the life and suffering of this one man to those who are apparently pointlessly living and dying. Even obviously pointless human life and suffering *can* have a *meaning*.'4

God, I think Küng is saying, has taken this cruel and wicked deed, and through the events that came after it, the resurrection and the teaching of countless Christian thinkers, has given it profound meaning through two thousand years of Christian history. God has given the death of Jesus the meaning that has inspired our church. We are told, and can believe, that God gives our lives a meaning too. Is that – perhaps – what we can see in our east window?

This sermon shows clearly that Küng's teaching on Jesus has affected me very deeply – though I find it difficult, knowing so little of what Jesus actually said, to be sure whether St Paul and the evangelists interpreted him correctly.

I add another bit from *Does God Exist?* on suffering, as I think that this is the heart of what I have learned from Küng and the basis of my belief in Jesus:

In the light of the suffering and death of this One, who senselessly suffered and died, only one thing can be said, but this is decisive: even manifold suffering and death can have a meaning, can acquire a meaning. A hidden meaning. Man cannot himself attach this meaning to suffering, but he can accept it in the light of the perfect suffering and dying of this One. A meaning is not given automatically: no wishful thinking is to be satisfied, no glorification of suffering proclaimed, no tranquillizers provided and no cheap consolation offered. But *a meaning is offered* which can be freely accepted. Man has to decide … He can accept it in believing trust in him who endowed the senseless suffering and death of Jesus with meaning. Despair is at an end.[5]

In the book *Eternal Life?*, Hans Küng writes that we must accept the hope of eternal life through trust in God, but that it is outside time, and to us totally unimaginable. I find this comforting; eternal life, in its popular form, is both horrifying and unimaginable: to sit up there for ever, watching the sun cool down and life on earth disappear, as in H.G. Wells' *The Time Machine*, is a prospect from which I shrink. But – it seems to me – Küng in his writings speaks of Jesus as living here and now, in real time.

A few years ago my wife and I attended a Nobel Prizewinners' meeting in Lindau, and Küng asked us to lunch; the Lindau organization kindly provided a car to drive us to Tübingen and back. It was further than we expected, and we did not have enough time to talk, but when I asked the question, 'Is it the same kind of eternal life for us and for him?', Küng said 'Yes'. But at that moment the other guests, Tübingen physicists whom he had invited to meet us, came in, and I still have not fully understood his answer to this question.

With Küng's ongoing battle with the Congregation for the Doctrine of Faith and with the present pope, I can only stand on the sidelines and cheer. In the Anglican church, in spite of its deep divisions, we do have almost complete freedom. I was admitted to the church, baptized and confirmed, on the simple statement that I believed in God and that I could find much of his nature in Jesus Christ. But I recognize the unique position of the Roman church in Christendom, as did John Henry Newman. I once told a Catholic friend that if Küng became pope, I would become a Catholic, but she said there was not much chance of that.

And in a review by a leading Anglican churchman of his latest book attacking Vatican policies (*Reforming the Church Today*), I read: 'If the Roman church goes Küng's way, there will not be much theological justification for *our* separate (Anglican) existence.' True enough – and a very devout Catholic friend of mine always describes Küng as a Protestant. This I think is not quite fair – though Küng certainly protests; but I feel that he believes that the Catholic church is the hope of mankind, if only we can *interpret* its teachings. The prayer for Christian unity that we repeat in our churches is something to which I shut my ears: as we both are now, we should stay separate; but if Küng's vision is realized, that would be a different matter.

4. Religion and science

The editors of this book have asked me to say something about Küng's discussion of modern science as it is to be found especially in *Does God Exist?*.[6] As is only to be expected, Küng demonstrates his very clear understanding of modern quantum mechanics, the theory of relativity, molecular biology and its influence on the theory of evolution, which he takes as proved. His description of the controversy between Einstein on the one hand – whose thought he understands fully and clearly – and Heisenberg, Born and Niels Bohr on the other is particularly interesting. He sees how the latter put forward a very different view, and as it were drop the principle of causality overboard. There is apparently no 'causal' explanation for the ultimate processes of nuclear physics, like the decay of the radio-active atom which may take place today or tomorrow. Küng sees this limited validity of causality as a relief which enables us to overcome the mechanistic picture of the world in Newtonian physics. But he does not want to go too far. He quotes Heisenberg: In the end we do succeed in understanding this world, by representing its organizational structures in mathematical forms; but when we want to talk about them, we must be content with metaphors and analogies, almost as in religious language.'[7] Küng mildly criticizes this statement when he writes: 'But an acosmic existentialism is not an answer to a cosmological scientism.'[8] Beyond question Heisenberg was writing under the clear impact of the surprise that his intellect had caused him. Today's scientists, who have grown up with quantum mechnics and its everyday application, by contrast find the strange behaviour of the electrons as normal and as matter-of-fact as anything else in physics – a meditation on the indeterminacy relationship no longer leads them to reflect on the magnitude of creation or the unfathomable ways of God. Rather, indeterminacy and so on is all part of every-day work.

Of course there are also eminent scientists in today's world who long for Einstein's certainties and are attempting to construct a new atomic theory which achieves as much as quantum mechanics but with a restoration of causality. I personally believe – and, I must confess, hope – that they are unsuccessful.

If I have understood him rightly, Hans Küng would hope the same thing. He seems completely at home in the physics and biology of 1978 and yet can write, 'I believe in God the Creator.' On the very next page, however, he asks whether there was just a moment in the development of life or of human beings at which a direct intervention of the Creator would have been necessary. He comes to the conclusion that it is impossible to see any necessity at this particular point for such a direct intervention by the Creator God. And yet again a few pages later the following quotation appears: 'For the natural scientist, it is a question of deciding in faith whether to assume an ultimate groundlessness, unsupportedness and meaninglessness or a primal ground, primal support and primal meaning of everything, a creator, ruler and finisher of the evolutionary process.[9]

When I read these paragraphs yet again and thought about them, I got the impression that had Küng concerned himself with modern science without his Christian faith, he would not have come to the conclusion that a Creator God existed. Faith tells him that this is so, and it seems to me that those who learn from Küng should not expect all his arguments to take the same course. Is it perhaps possible that in our complex and mysterious world conclusions can be both true and untrue at the same time?

Perhaps I should add something else. Did not a very famous Anglican clergyman once remark that any theologian who attempted to marry theology to science in a particular decade would risk finding it a widow in the next? After the publication of Küng's book, Stephen Hawking's extraordinary bestseller *A Brief History of Time* appeared. This puts forward a form of relativity theory in which the curvature of the dimension of time suggests that it has no beginning. But the publication in 1986 of Barrow and Tipler's book *The Anthropic Cosmological Principle* may be even more important. Since 1978 it has become increasingly clear that both the origin of the universe and that of living beings would not have been possible without an extraordinary series of apparent 'accidents', either in connection with a planet on which life could arise, or in relation to the development of thinking beings. The temptation is becoming increasingly great to see God's finger at work here, in the very sense which Küng disputes. I hope that Küng is nevertheless right and that his thoughts in this connection do not suffer a sorry widowhood. The picture of the finger of God, the mistake and the new attempt, which is so welcome to so many theologians, seems far removed from our understanding of God here and now, the loving Father of whom Jesus spoke. But the evolutionary processes of the cosmos and life are hard to understand and to reconcile with the picture of a God who is here and now and to whom – as Küng believes – we can turn.

Finally, since I have been asked to say how Küng's teaching has affected me as a scientist, I assert that for me science and religion are separate worlds; to comprehend them both one has to wear two hats; for a complete life one must perhaps wear many hats. But my science teaches me not to respect authority, not even Einstein's when he says 'God does not throw dice', and it teaches me that the solutions to the everyday problems in physics turn out to be simple and elegant, even if abstract. My instinctive belief is that the unseen world is like that too.

And finally, how can I describe God? Although when I try to define God, he disappears, I learn from Küng that God is the one who gives meaning to life and in whom we can trust. And although many of the doctrines of the church are hardly acceptable, and must be interpreted, it is better to stand within it than outside.

I received many letters about the book that I have already mentioned and some articles about it in the press. Whereas some of the writers wanted to continue to understand the old assured statements of the Bible literally and criticized me for my 'liberalism', there were others who expressed great relief that they could continue to be active in the Christian churches without having to accept all the statements of the creed in faith: 'born of the Virgin Mary', 'comes to judge' ... I write back to such people and advise them to read Hans Küng's books.

Notes

1. N. Mott (ed.), *Can Scientists Believe?*, London 1991.
2. H. Küng, *On Being a Christian*, 361.
3. Ibid., 162.
4. H. Küng, *Does God Exist?*, 694.
5. Ibid.
6. Ibid., 628–59.
7. Ibid., 630.
8. Ibid.
9. Ibid., 648.

V   Dialogue with Judaism

Editors' Preface

This section, 'Dialogue with Judaism', differs from the others by virtue of its documentary character. It documents some of the most important Jewish reactions so far to Hans Küng's book *Judaism* – above all from the German- and English-speaking world – and Küng's answers to his critics. Not least against the background of the most recent scandalous outbursts of anti-semitism in Germany, we have decided to underline the importance of the dialogue with Judaism. Furthermore, the role of Jewish-Christian dialogue in Hans Küng's theology (from *The Church* through *On Being a Christian* and the published dialogue with Pinchas Lapide to *Judaism*) is itself great enough to justify a separate section. A documentation has the further advantage that the reader can for once follow a 'dialogue in progress' through concrete examples. It was always Hans Küng's conviction that a dialogue consists not only in the exchange of courteous compliments but also in a struggle to arrive at the truth which each partner obviously sees in different ways. Anyone who reads the following documents will be able to see how there is an argument over central questions which are common to Jews and Christians and which still divide them. But it will also become clear that a dialogue is meaningful because it is only in conversation that misunderstandings can be removed, mutual corrections are possible, and agreement can be reached. This section opens with an autobiographical text by Hans Küng indicating the background to *Judaism* in which he depicts his encounters with living Judaism. This text shows particularly vividly what effects and challenges these encounters represented for his theology.

Hans Küng

My Encounters with Judaism

Yes, I have encountered living Judaism, repeatedly, as it were from my youth up, though constantly in different ways. In contrast to some German colleagues of my generation (I was born in 1928), from the start I went to a school where there were also Jewish pupils, in Switzerland during the Second World War. We all accepted them as a matter of course and the only striking thing about them was that they did not come to lessons on Saturdays. There was no animosity on either side, but there were no discussions of questions of faith or religious practice either. The Holocaust? We young people learned of the abominable atrocities committed by the Nazis against the Jews from the Swiss press during the last years of the war; however, we had no inkling of the dimensions that this genocide had assumed.

We left school together, Jews and Christians, in 1948, the year of the foundation of the State of Israel. I went to Rome, to study philosophy and theology there for seven years under the strictest Roman discipline. Apart from the usual Old Testament lectures I heard hardly anything at the Papal Gregorian University about the Jewish people: Judaism was not communicated to us rising Catholic priests in Rome as a relevant factor either politically or theologically. Indeed the people Israel had been completely superseded by the church of Christ, and Jerusalem had been replaced with Rome: that was the Catholic view which was presented quite naturally. It took the *Church Dogmatics* of the Protestant theologian Karl Barth to open my eyes, as a Catholic student, during my last years in Rome, at least to the theological explosiveness of the theme and the undeniable dialectic of synagogue and church. However, through all my seven years in Rome I did not hear a word about Christian complicity in the persecution of the Jews, even in the Nazi Holocaust. Pius XII – was he not *the* great pope of the century?

It was first in Paris, where I went to do my doctorate after being ordained priest, that it became clear to me that this pope who was so admired had kept silent in a decisive historical situation. Not only the Jews, but also Polish Christians, had expected clear words from him when the German army invaded Poland in 1939, and Pius XII in Castel Gandolfo at the outbreak of the Second World War had not wanted to take his place as the 'common Father of Christendom'; significant Catholic theologians were illegitimately disciplined by this pope, but the Catholic Adolf Hitler, despite his unprecedented crimes, was neither indicted nor excommunicated. At the same time, in Paris, through Jewish professors at the Sorbonne I came into contact with a Jewish spirituality which had remained alive.

Nevertheless, despite, or because of, many positive experiences I still had insufficient theological or political awareness of the problem which people refer to – in a very narrow way – as 'the Jewish question'. Moreover in my 1960 book *The Council and Reunion* (warmly welcomed ecumenically in the preparatory phase of the Council) there was no mention of a possible ecumene, an ecumenical coexistence with Jewish brothers and sisters. It was only when an American rabbi had attacked me vigorously for this silence and pointed out that the Fourth Lateran Synod in the high Middle Ages (which I had praised as a reforming council) had already initiated all those discriminatory actions which the Nazis were then to carry through in great industrialized style that the terrible history of relations between Christians and Jews began to dawn on me. I wanted to investigate this question, both historically and theologically, as soon as possible.

It was the time of the Second Vatican Council, in which I was able to take part as a council theologian. John XXIII, that unforgettable first ecumenical pope, had given the signal for a new attitude of the Catholic church to the Jews by changing the Good Friday prayer *pro perfidis Judaeis*. The significance of this question for my own church became increasingly clear to me, above all in work with American theologians and bishops. A declaration on the Jews and on freedom of religion was in preparation. When curial obstruction to this declaration increased and we theologians around Cardinal Bea were informed that Paul VI had yielded to political and church-political pressure and decided to drop the declarations on the Jews and on religious freedom, I felt compelled (and I resorted to this kind of well-organized indiscretion only in this one case) to inform the most important international newspapers about these scandalous goings-on. Through my then colleague Joseph Ratzinger, Cardinal Frings was alerted to the seriousness of the situation, and French friends mobilized French cardinals as agreed. Under the impact of the storm in the press and after preliminary personal discussions between a group of cardinals and the pope, both the declaration on religious freedom and that on the Jews were finally rescued. Granted, they had been toned down on individual points, but despite everything they represented an epoch-making shift in the relationship between the Catholic church and Judaism. However, to the present day the Vatican, which has made pacts with every possible authoritarian régime, has yet to grant the democratic State of Israel diplomatic recognition.

Meanwhile I had made thorough studies of the history of Jewry in Christianity for my book *The Church* and come to a conclusion which I found oppressive: 'an indescribably dismaying history of suffering and death, lasting over many centuries, which came to a monstrous culmination in the Nazi murder of millions of Jews: how was it all possible?' And in answering this question of motivation something became clear to me which I maintained explicitly in my summary of the Second Vatican Council: 'National Socialist antisemitism would have been impossible without the centuries of anti-semitism practised by the Christian churches.'

It was this statement which earned me my first serious rebuke, though still in the form of a personal letter, from the President of the German Conference of Bishops, at the time Cardinal Julius Döpfner. Since I had by then worked out the whole chapter on 'The Church and the Jews' for that book, I sent him the manuscript as a reply. I heard nothing more from him on the matter.

Two years after the end of the Council, in 1967, I travelled for the first time to Jerusalem. All the hubbub around the birthplace in Bethlehem and the tomb in Jerusalem did not prevent me from taking in deeply the people, countryside and places where the Jew Jesus of Nazareth, who for Christians is the Christ, lived, fought and suffered. In the meantime I had long become aware that it is impossible, as the Gospel of John does, to make 'the Jews', even the Jews of that time, responsible for that death of Jesus, for which in fact only the religious and political establishment of the period was to blame.

At the same time, however, I asked myself increasingly intensely who this Jesus really was and what his original purpose had been. This question was brought home to me with oppressive persistence by a young European Jewish woman in a hotel in Jerusalem: 'I have come to this city and everywhere I see and hear the name Jesus Christ,' she said, 'but I cannot understand why this Christ is important for Christians. You're a theologian, can you give me an answer?'

Yes, Judaism is alive and I have encountered it, time and again in the form of questioning Jewish men and women. At that time I had not yet concerned myself intensively with the Jesus of history. But I instinctively felt that the usual dogmatic answer, that he was the Son of God, the second person of the Trinity, the God who had come down from heaven for our redemption, would end the conversation as quickly as it had begun.

Now for the first time, as it were from the perspective of the Jewish disciples of Jesus themselves, I tried to explain (for today) what the disciples experienced from him and with him and in him (and what we experience today): that he did not just proclaim the word of God but embodied this word of God in a unique union of life and teaching, living and dying, and thus is God's word bodily. That was as it were the birth hour of my quite personal perspective of 'a christology from below', which I then presented seven years later at length in my 1974 book *On Being a Christian*.

Since then I have become convinced that Christians should allow themselves to be asked by living Jews whether they have really understood in the right way down the centuries this Jesus of Nazareth, who appears in the New Testament as at the same time a pious and a rebellious Jew. Did they not, in the circumstances, drop what was originally Jewish and Hellenize him far too early? Did they not, as Pinchas Lapide once remarked, thus put the Jews off him: namely, by all the compulsory measures with which Christians down the centuries have sought to impose the message of Jesus as Messiah on the Jews and compel them to accept it?

A 'christology from below' certainly does not mean that we overlook God or even cut him out. How would that be possible, where Jesus himself proclaimed the kingdom and the will of God: hallowed be *his* – God's – name? Anyone who encounters Jesus of course encounters 'his God'. But 'from below' means that we do not appropriate to ourselves the divine perspective, so as to look at everything simultaneously from heaven, in judgment or condemnation. It means that we dare to look at, and ask questions about, the story of Jesus from the earth and its conflicts and problems, from the perspective of the people of the time (and of today): what have people seen in Jesus, how did his Jewish disciples understand Jesus, and how can we understand him today? According to the Synoptic Gospels this man from Galilee did not simply come and say 'I am the Son of God', but he came and proclaimed God's kingdom and God's will. And this perspective 'from below' makes it possible for us Christians to share a long stretch of the way with our Jewish brothers and sisters because from it they too can ask, 'Who was this man?'

Now if the *Jew* Jesus of Nazareth continually becomes a critical question for us Christians, in a no less serious sense he can represent a challenge to believing Jews. Already in the earliest Gospel, that of Mark, right from the beginning there is a recognition of the fatal conflict between the Jew Jesus of Nazareth and certain Jewish circles of his time which is clearly dominated by the Law: sabbath observance, the regulations for cleanness, the marriage rules. Had Jesus only called, like the prophets – acknowledging the authority of Moses –, for the true observance of the Law; had he merely, like the rabbis, the scholars in the Law, issued a call to follow the Law better, the last fatal conflict ending in his execution would never have come about. To present it merely as a crime by the Romans, as a political intrigue in the interplay of Roman and Jewish authorities, overlooks the real religious problem. The ultimate issue is the question which still leads Judaism, at least Orthodox Judaism, and Christianity to go their separate ways: according to this Jew Jesus, the sabbath, the divine commandment, the divine law, is there for human beings; human beings are not there for the sake of the sabbath, the divine command, the divine law. Freedom from the law, a freedom which, after the execution of Jesus, Paul, the pupil of Jewish rabbis, thought through and lived out consistently, represents a critical question put by Jesus to Judaism, at least Orthodox Judaism, today.

Now all these questions could be discussed further, and since I became aware of them I have taken it for granted that I must be in constant dialogue with Judaism. This dialogue has also found published form in my conversation with Pinchas Lapide (1976). I am convinced that the loss of Jewish Christianity and a one-sided Hellenization was extraordinarily disastrous for Christianity. Granted it enabled Christianity to survive, culturally and spiritually, in a Europe moulded by Greece, but at the same time it removed Christians from their Jewish origins and made it uncommonly difficult to transfer Christianity to another spiritual and cultural sphere (for example Asia or Africa).

The consequences of this alienation are particularly evident even today, because to the dialogue with the Jews has now also been added the dialogue with Islam, which in the Qur'an seems to me to have preserved many concerns of Jewish Christianity with respect to the figure of Jesus. For me there is no doubt that the understanding of God must be seen in the light of the common Jewish-Christian-Muslim tradition, and that this common basis of the faith of all three Abrahamic religions has tremendous significance for today. Indeed, I am convinced that the dialogue between Christianity and Judaism can be carried on meaningfully only in the context of the triangular relationship of Christianity, Judaism and Islam and that the dialogue must lead to a trilateral conversation, a 'trialogue'. Judaism is alive, Christianity is alive, Islam is alive, and one can encounter the One God in all these three religions. If anything makes a brighter horizon shine in this dark time it is this: these three great religions, at enmity over the centuries, can today have a common future. Of course, this does not eliminate all the differences between them but it will lead to a mutual recognition, challenge and enrichment. No peace between the nations; no peace, especially in the Near East, without peace between the religions, and especially between the religions of semitic origin!

(Source: R. Walter [ed.], *Das Judentum lebt – ich bin ihm begegnet. Erfahrungen von Christen*, Freiburg im Breisgau 1985, 121–8)

Shalom Ben-Chorin

A Handbook of Instruction and Introduction

The Swiss Catholic theologian Hans Küng, who was born in 1928 and works as Professor of Ecumenical Theology and Director of the Institute for Ecumenical Research at the University of Tübingen, has just produced an extensive volume, *Judaism*, which indicates his deep intimate relationship with the mother religion of Christianity.

The volume has the subtitle 'The Religious Situation of Our Time', and has appeared shortly after a more than 500-page book by the author and his colleagues on Islam, Hinduism and Buddhism.

It was immediately preceded by the programmatic work *Global Responsibility*, which bears the dateline 'Tübingen, May 1990'.

What Küng has produced recently is almost beyond belief. The church may have withdrawn the *missio canonica* from him, as he has put papal infallibility seriously in question, but Küng is able to continue his teaching activity within the context of his university. Despite his attitude of opposition he still has the status and function of priest.

Küng begins from the basic recognition that there can be no peace among the nations without peace among the religions; no peace among the religions without dialogue between the religions; no dialogue between the religions without research into the foundations of the religions.

He terms the three monotheistic religions – Judaism, Christianity and Islam – 'Abrahamic religions'; chronologically Judaism stands in first place and is their root.

Küng displays an amazing knowledge of the substance of Judaism. He divides his work into three main parts: The Past which is Still Present, The Challenges of the Present, and Possibilities for the Future.

A radical biblical criticism prevails in his consideration of the early biblical period, so that for example the conquest described in the Bible is largely put in question.

Throughout Küng uses the concept of paradigms. By this he means groupings and modes of behaviour which can be demonstrated side by side in the long history of Judaism. He starts from the correct insight that Judaism is not a monolithic entity but always was and remains a pluralistic society, divided into these paradigms. He already relates this to the tribes in the ancient Israel of the period before the state.

There are broad descriptions of the central leading figures of Abraham and Moses, followed by the history of the kingdom under David and Solomon and finally the division of the kingdom into North and South, Israel and Judah, until their downfall. The theocracy of post-exilic Judaism leads through the Judaism of the rabbis and the synagogue to the Middle Ages, and the first part ends with assimilation and the beginning of modernity: Moses Mendelssohn is called the first modern Jew.

The second part leads from the Holocaust to the State of Israel. Then follows the controversy between Jews and Christians, and the question of dialogue is investigated. The figure of Jesus in recent Jewish literature is reported very carefully, and there is an objective account of why Judaism cannot see Jesus of Nazareth as Messiah or Son of God.

The old opposition of the author to his church becomes particularly evident in his clear reckoning with the pope who kept silent over the horror of the Holocaust, Pius XII, but on the other hand he rightly sees the significance of the pioneering figure of Pius's successor, John XXIII, who brought about a Copernican shift in Catholicism, not least in relation to Jews and Judaism. The Second Vatican Council which he called continued some of the approaches of this pope on a wide scale, but unfortunately the course was not maintained under John XXIII's successors, and above all positive statements by the Council on the revision of relations between the church and Judaism are again being forgotten.

Küng does not always see the nuances clearly in his discussion of the situation within Judaism in the modern period: in the figure of Samson Raphael Hirsch, the founder of neo-Orthodoxy in Frankfurt am Main, he sees only the radical reaction to the Reform movements; he describes Hirsch as an exegete who simply ignored the Bible and does not recognize that in observing a strict piety of the law Hirsch opens up the way to secular education.

Küng is too fascinated with American Judaism. He emphasizes two figures in present-day American Judaism: Abraham Joshua Heschel from the Conservatives as a representative of an anthropologically centred theology, and Joseph W. Soloveichik from Orthodoxy, who, beginning from halakhic man, developed a philosophy of subjection of reality to the yoke of the law.

There should have been greater emphasis on Israel, particularly in connection with the problem of unbelieving Jews, as here we have the type of the secular Israeli whose Jewishness is exhausted by living as a Hebrew-speaking Israeli citizen in the historic homeland of the Jewish people.

Küng's teaching at American Jewish colleges like the Jewish Theological Seminary in New York and the University of Judaism in Los Angeles has largely shaped his perspectives. It was here that his living encounter with Judaism took place.

Küng has succeeded in creating a compendium of Judaism which contains a wealth of material for both Christians and Jews, arranged by a skilful hand, and provides a survey and a view of the future. Küng ends his epilogue with an appeal for peace: 'In all synagogues, churches and mosques there should not only be prayers but also an active concern and work for peace.'

Extensive notes and indexes round the book off and thus make it a handbook of instruction and introduction for which the author is due boundless thanks.

(Source: *Israel Nachrichten*, 6 December 1991)

Pinchas Lapide

No Preconceived Christian Pattern of Thought

'Why should Christianity bother with Judaism, when for two thousand years it has done its best to deprive Judaism of any future?'

At the beginning of his new book, Hans Küng not only puts this blunt question but at the same time gives it impressive answers. He does not want to cram Judaism into any preconceived Christian pattern of thought or into a prescribed dogmatic. How welcome this approach in Küng's great venture is, when one reflects that:

– the self-appointed 'new Israel' has been contrasted with the 'disinherited, sinful, old Israel';

– 'late Judaism' has been attacked as a dusty relic from antiquity. From which the conclusion would have to be drawn that Jews today are really museum pieces who have long since forfeited their right to exist;

– in broad Christian circles it is taught that 'the Old Testament' is 'obsolete', indeed 'superseded and fulfilled' by the New Testament.

This 'concerted action' of hostility always sounded very suspicious and still does. Is it not perhaps the expression of a deep Christian insecurity in the face of the fact that Christianity is the only world religion whose saviour was once the adherent of another religion? All the more so as he was also crucified by pagans for his Jewish faith!

Or can so many Christians not take in the fact that the churches' essential vocabulary of salvation comes from the heart of Judaism – matters of faith by which Christianity stands and falls? For example: heaven on earth, redemption, repentance, the forgiveness of sins, grace and mercy. Indeed even the concepts and contents of Messiah and messiahship are and remain primally Jewish.

Of course the later church was quite free to develop its faith away from Judaism into the heart of paganism. The church owes to this Hellenism among other things the Trinity, the doctrine of the two natures, the Greek notion of divine sonship – and indeed celibacy and hostility to the body. However, the earliest community in Jerusalem, with Peter, James and the apostles and all the great Jewish women, remained to the end Jews faithful to the Bible, as their master had been.

How welcome Küng's words are – in comparison with those of his former Tübingen colleague Cardinal Joseph Ratzinger, who, even at the end of 1987 in Rome, could commend the convert Edith Stein as an example of how it is only when a Jew becomes a Catholic that he or she becomes a true, complete, Jew. Küng aptly comments here: 'The racist antisemitism which reached its climax of terror in the Holocaust would not have been possible without the previous almost two-thousand-year history of the religious anti-Judaism of the Christian churches.'

But for all the praise that it deserves, here and there in Küng's good book there are still glimmers of anti-Jewish prejudice. Thus for example the author claims that 'Jesus no longer wanted to take any notice of the natural opposition between those who were alien and those who were not, between Jews and Samaritans/Arabs.'

Here one may ask where Jesus ever mentioned Arabs or even Samaritans and Arabs in the same breath? Rather, one might point to the following sayings of Jesus which run diametrically counter to the insinuation above:
– 'Go nowhere among the Gentiles, and enter no town of the Samaritans' (Matthew 10.5).
– 'I was sent only to the lost sheep of the house of Israel' (Matthew 15.24).

Similarly, Küng states that Jesus seemed 'really too liberal'. How are we to understand that, in the face of the way in which the rabbi of Nazareth explicitly makes the Torah more pointed, as we can read in the so-called 'antitheses' of the Sermon on the Mount, which are not really antitheses at all? Even with a magnifying glass one can find no 'liberalizing' with Jesus of Nazareth. On the contrary, not only murder but slander is forbidden, as he emphasizes in the Sermon on the Mount. Five further radicalizations of the Torah then follow in this vein – and not a single antithesis.

A quite different topic which needs discussion is Küng's attitude to current politics in the Near East and his suggestions for peace. I share his opinion that Judaism today in the Diaspora and the State of Israel is in a severe post-Holocaust crisis. Conflicts and dilemmas over identity are seething under the surface, and they will only be resolved when there is peace in Israel. For lack of space I shall limit myself to asking Küng one political question: does he really believe that there is no focal point of conflict in the Arab world other than Israel/Palestine?

Even if the state of Israel were to go up in smoke, would not a variety of Arab states still continue to want an 'Arab atom bomb'? Or does Küng not believe that Gaddafi, Saddam Hussein and the rulers of Iran and Pakistan and elsewhere are making urgent efforts in this direction?

However, all in all I agree with Hans Küng in his diagnosis that the establishments of all three monotheisms are suffering from hardening of the theological arteries. I also agree fully with his thesis that there can be no stable world peace without peace among the religions.

(Source: *Die Welt*, 8 October 1991)

Charles Middleburgh

The Amazing Vitality of Judaism

With good fortune, one may, in a lifetime, read a few books that will make a deep impression and leave one feeling immeasurably richer. *Judaism* by Hans Küng is one of those books.

It is massive, superbly researched and intricately argued with 633 pages of text and 91 pages of instructive notes.

Judaism is the first of a trilogy on the world's three Abrahamic religions, a trio that I suspect will be rated one of the masterpieces of modern religious scholarship. Professor Hans Küng, the highly controversial but much respected Professor for Ecumenical Theology at Tübingen University, Germany, writes about Judaism as a devoted friend of the Jewish people. He portrays the stages of Jewish history as paradigms, defined as 'an entire constellation of beliefs, values, techniques and so on, shared by the members of a given community' which he first described in his earlier work *Global Responsibility*.

His description of the development of Judaism and the events of Jewish history is always fascinating, sometimes challenging and controversial and occasionally amusing, as when he describes *Chanukah* as having become 'a kind of Jewish Christmas'. Küng does everything he can to demonstrate, in a manner that some might find surprising in a Catholic theologian, how Judaism is 'an independent entity with amazing continuity, vitality and dynamism'.

His approach to certain subjects is quite critical on occasion, particularly in his description of Christian anti-Semitism and the attitude of the Vatican and the German churches to the Nazi regime and its programmatic persecution and destruction of the Jews. If this brings pleasure to some Jewish readers, his section on Israel, especially that entitled *The Tragic Conflict*, will upset a great many others. Although I am personally in broad agreement with all his points, particularly in the section concerning the *Intifada* and the *Palestinian State*, I cannot deny that Küng hits hard where he feels strongly in a fearless style that some may find unacceptable. It would be wise to remember though that throughout the book, Küng's deep commitment to both the survival and development of the Jewish people is evident and we ought to consider ourselves fortunate in having such a loving and honest friend.

He is well aware of the crisis of faith provoked by the Holocaust, which he considers both thoughtfully and sensitively and discusses its implications for Jews and Christians without fear. His conclusions may not suit everybody but they are worthy of thought: 'Because there is Auschwitz, say the godless, the idea of God is intolerable. And those who believe in God, whether Jews or Christians, may answer, "Only because there is a God is the thought of Auschwitz tolerable to me at all"'.

I found the section entitled *For the Sake of Human Beings* a little confusing, because I was not able to decide what Küng the 'honest broker' was attempting to achieve in his sustained emphasis on the common ground between Jews and Christians, especially through the person of Jesus the Jew. The hint that I felt was contained in the text, that things might be better if we became part of the community which sees 'doing of the will of God aimed at love which is above any law' as the best human endeavour, left me slightly uneasy.

The final section, *Epilogue: No New World Order without a New World Ethic*, is rather disappointing and facile and somehow unworthy of the high standard set by the rest. Nevertheless, I unreservedly recommend this book to anyone with an open mind who, like Küng, wants to see enhanced dialogue between those of different faiths, a reassertion of belief in God in a troubled world and a renewed commitment to the key ideals which dominate this text:

No survival of the world without a new world order.

No world peace without religious peace.

No religious peace without religious dialogue.

(Source: *Manna*, Autumn 1992)

Albert H. Friedlander

A Catholic on the Jews

Some of the best books on Judaism are written by Christian scholars. When these books are examples of meticulous scholarship, an outsider's view of the Jewish tradition presents few traps for the reader, even when one must be on guard against isolated Christian prejudices. The danger rests more on the other side; a philo-Semitism can sometimes be seen which can distort the overall picture.

In this magisterial study Hans Küng asks: 'How can a Christian theologian dare to involve himself in matters which are the internal concern of Jews?' And again: 'How can a Christian theologian dare to go so far to meet Judaism, for example, in connection with the origin of Christianity from Judaism?' These questions have to be asked so that they can be dismissed.

Küng's objective presentation of contemporary Jewish thought honours the authenticity of a religious pattern which derives its dynamism from the tension between its polarities; and Küng's questions about interfaith dialogue, Jesus, the Muslims and Israel are all asked with deep sensitivity and understanding. Almost all Jewish readers will welcome the text and rise to its profound challenges.

The Christian reactions may be anticipated from the responses of the past, where this stormy petrel of the Catholic faith has often been a harbinger of controversy.

The book's framework presents a challenge. *Judaism* is the first part of a mammoth undertaking – *The Religious Situation of Our Time* – with two more volumes to follow which will deal with Christianity and Islam. Küng therefore emphasizes Abraham's role here, the Semitic wanderer and alien, who is the ancestral father of the three faiths.

The true preface to this great enterprise is Küng's book of last year, *Global Responsibility: In Search of a New World Ethic*. That work can be summarized in the words Küng sets as the key words to *Judaism*:

No peace among the nations
without peace among the religions.
No peace among the religions
without dialogue between the religions.
No dialogue between the religions
without investigation of the foundations of the religions.

Hans Küng uses the new language of postmodern theology, which sees religions passing through changing 'paradigms'. The world religions, he states, are all '... living international and transcultural systems transcending the individual, which, in the course of their history ... have gone through a variety of epoch-making paradigms'.

He follows Judaism through this pattern of change in the course of history; and Christianity and Islam will be fitted into the same framework. Although I see the individual in Judaism at times transcending the system, Küng does capture the full sweep of Jewish history and thought.

And of course, there is the over-riding goal for the whole presentation: the need for peace, the need for a world ethic. In *Global Responsibility* Küng emphasized the role of religion in fomenting wars, and called for a coalition between believers and unbelievers which would find a working peace ethic. Here he presents the Judaism in which the ethics of peace have endured through its historical changes. In the modern world, he shows a devout orthodoxy adapting the earlier theocratic mode to challenge modernity; and he describes the progressives moving between assimilation and the attempt at co-existence with modernity. The schema does not always capture the reality of Jewish existence fully. But there is enough truth within it to make us confront ourselves.

Küng discusses Jewish postmodern faith after Auschwitz and the birth of Israel. For him, Christ dies in Auschwitz – not God – representing suffering humanity. Here, one must end with Wiesel's reminder that one cannot have a theology about (or after) Auschwitz; but one may still try. The fact that there was prayer in Auschwitz entitles us to pray now. And Küng's quest for a universal ethic begins with compassion for all of suffering humanity. His superb book travels a long way towards his distant goal.

(Source: *The Times*, 26 March 1992)

Tony Bayfield

Interpreting the Jews

Many years ago, I used to stand on the terraces at Upton Park and watch a winger by the name of Harry Redknapp. 'Arry Boy – as he was known to the Chicken Run – was the most brilliant and the most infuriating footballer I have ever seen. One minute he would be flying down the wing with a skill and flair that made George Best look pedestrian. The next minute he would be taking a corner worse than a Skoda. Hans Küng's enormous study of Judaism (well over 700 pages, including the notes) reminds me of 'Arry Boy. It is brilliant but infuriating; dazzling but outrageously over-elaborate; fearless and honest but about as tactful (note the breadth of your reviewer's sporting knowledge) as Geoffrey Boycott on Ian Botham's fitness.

Much of the book is devoted to a historical evaluation of Judaism, tracing its organizing ideas through the paradigm shifts of history. Küng is magnificent on the Hebrew Bible. Though at times one may quarrel with the minutiae of the scholarship, he acknowledges, as few Christians before him, the massive contribution that biblical Judaism has made to Western religion. He underlines its fundamental universalism, he acknowledges the enormity of the gift of monotheism, he identifies its central ethical commitment, its transforming, eschatological message. Biblical Judaism receives its full due from Hans Küng.

But Küng is simply awful on rabbinic Judaism. He becomes obsessed with the *halakhah*, the Jewish legal tradition, and his unremitting criticism is reminiscent of the worst of uncomprehending Christian condemnations of 'the Law'. He fails utterly to identify the true purpose of the enterprise, the enshrining of divine values in the prosaic acts of everyday life. He sees the halakhic tradition as self-segregating rather than protective, and dismisses its intellectual rigour as casuistry.

We emerge into the modern world with Küng's staggering knowledge of twentieth-century Jewish thought, where his sympathies appear to lie with Buber rather than Rosenzweig and with Borowitz rather than Soloveitchik. I share his enthusiasms.

Some way through the book, however, the story gets hijacked by the emergence of Christianity. Once again, Küng is superb in his grasp of the details of the period and his understanding of Jesus as a Jewish figure of his day. But he feels the need to lapse into long sections on Resurrection, Trinity and Incarnation, in what appears to be an attempt to convince Jews that none of these ideas falls outside the bounds of Judaism. Later on, if I understand correctly, he suggests that Judaism and Christianity do not need separate sabbath days.

Küng deals at considerable length with the Holocaust. His section acknowledging Christian responsibility, flaying the Vatican in the process, brought tears to my eyes. When he suggests that Jews today can misuse the Shoah for political purposes or for emotional blackmail, he is far from wrong. But in calling for us to draw a line under the Holocaust, his head appears to be shutting him off from the understanding of the heart. He sounds like a well-meaning but frustrated relative instructing the widow to come to terms with her grief and look sharp about it.

The book deals at length and in many places with the state of Israel. He is unequivocal about the importance of Israel to the Jewish people and about the right of Israel to exist. As he says, 'What is required ... is critical solidarity of Christians with the state of Israel.' He is rightly and unstintingly critical of some of the policies of Israeli governments since 1967. But at times he goes way over the top and is uncomprehending of the psychological trauma experienced by Israelis during the Gulf War in anticipation of gas attacks involving German technology. Brilliant insights sit cheek by jowl with flashes of blindness. He can say, for instance, that the 'dispute over the state of Israel is the main reason for the tensions between the Western world and the Arab world'. In fact, the reverberations of the Crusades will continue long after Israel has signed peace treaties with its Arab neighbours.

Küng goes on to consider the future of Judaism. He underestimates the extent to which Jewish demography will focus anxieties and influence policy. But he foreshadows Eugene Borowitz's brilliant new book, *Renewing the Covenant*, in suggesting that covenant rather than law will be the future paradigm. In so doing, he echoes the best of liberal Judaism, but underestimates the continuing vitality of orthodoxy and the *halakhah*. Few people have summed up the present state of Jewish thought better than Küng: 'Just as Jewish religion and post-modern theology continue to have a negative stamp as a result of the catastrophe, the Shoah, so too they have a positive stamp as a result of the rebirth of the Jewish state.'

All this is to give you some idea of the exhilaration and frustration that I felt in reading the book. But I have a more serious problem with Küng's enterprise.

As I understood *Global Responsibility*, Küng's thesis was that the future of the world depended upon the religions of the world making common cause on the basis of a shared commitment to the humanum. He would then, in a series of books, identify that which each religious tradition could contribute to the common purpose, what each needed to give up and where each needed to be self-critical for the sake of the shared goal. I could not be more enthusiastic about the enterprise. But, midway through this book, the conviction began to grow that Küng had taken his eye off the ball and lost sight of his objective. It was summed up for me by a characteristically erudite passage summarizing the writings of the great American Jewish theologian, Abraham Heschel. Küng omits to say that Heschel was one of the leading figures in the American civil-rights movement.

So the book becomes a monologue. It is weighed down by Küng's personal preoccupations – his intense dislike of religious law, and his determination to demonstrate the accessibility and even acceptability of Christian theology to Jews. This is surely quite unnecessary to the agenda of *Global Responsibility*, and renders the enterprise far less persuasive than it might otherwise be. It is also lacking in tact if he wishes to gain the support of the Jewish 'establishment' for his enterprise.

Finally, one wonders whether 700 pages is the best way of pursuing the objective. Although the book *appears* to be highly structured, it is in fact remarkably untidy, and has an unfortunate habit of causing the hackles to rise before allaying the annoyance 50 or 100 pages later. Küng is splendidly served by his translator, John Bowden, and not one of the pages ever sounds like heavy German theology. But if only Bowden had got his hands on the original German manuscript before its publication in Germany and had been able to prune, refine, and remind Küng of his purpose. Like Harry Redknapp, Hans Küng is brilliant, exhilarating, challenging. But if he had tried to do a little less in a more disciplined manner, the boy 'Ans would have been more likely to score.

(Source: *Church Times*, 27 March 1992)

Hans Küng

Response to Albert H. Friedlander and Tony Bayfield

Sir, A Christian theologian who ventures to write about Judaism is in a rather difficult situation, because he can easily be accused of 'interfering' in other people's affairs. And anyone who wants to advance conventional Jewish-Christian dialogue by a friendly but honest discussion of controversial issues at the centre of the debate can get into real difficulties and lose friends. However, if such a theologian also seeks to show his passionate concern with the future of Judaism as a living religion, he can count on honest sympathy from his Jewish conversation partners.

I felt this sympathy last week in London, when, on the occasion of the publication of my book *Judaism*, I was able to speak to a variety of Jewish and Jewish-Christian audiences. Whether it was to the large gatherings in St James's, Piccadilly, and with the Council of Christians and Jews, or on a smaller scale, at the reception given by Sir Sigmund Sternberg and at a private lunch given by my publisher, John Bowden, I had the same good experiences: deep attention everywhere, committed questions, a sense of shared struggling over the old questions common to Jews and Christians which still separate them, and always authentic sympathy. I think that people felt my conviction, particularly as a Christian theologian, that despite the way in which Judaism itself has been torn apart and invaded by secularity, it has a future as a religion, and is learning to overcome the challenges of the postmodern world for the benefit of future generations. As a Christian theologian, I am also concerned that faith in the God of Abraham, Isaac and Jacob should remain attractive to those to come. Since I believe in the same God, I am not an outsider to Jews but an insider, not a stranger but a friend. I regard my book as an ecumenical service to Judaism in the interest of a better understanding between Jews and Christians. So I would like to express my thanks to all those who helped to make these days in England such a success for me.

I am particularly grateful to Rabbi Albert H. Friedlander and Rabbi Tony Bayfield for studying the book and introducing it sympathetically to the public in such detail so soon after it appeared. Anyone who reads the critical review by Rabbi Bayfield in the *Church Times* of 27 March will feel the passion with which he discussed the questions raised in my book. He has much praise for the book, but also makes some critical points which give me a chance to clarify my concern once again.

He says I feel 'the need to lapse into long sections on Resurrection, Trinity and Incarnation, in what appears to be an attempt to convince Jews that none of these ideas falls outside the bounds of Judaism'. But had I kept silent above all on these dogmatic questions I would rightly have been accused of reprehensibly concealing central differences.

A Christian theologian's book on Judaism deserves to be noted not only where it praises Jews and censures Christians, but also, I feel, where it questions traditional Jewish positions. And surely I had to express all my deepest concerns in the dialogue with Judaism in this one book, since the next two volumes will be devoted to Christianity and Islam. Our dialogue has so often been polite, tactfully avoiding awkward questions. If one is gentle but at the same time frank, does one risk lapsing into a 'monologue'? Rabbi Bayfield proves the opposite in his review, and I am grateful to him for it. I am sure that the dialogue will go on.

(Source: *Church Times*, 3 April 1992)

Tony Bayfield – Hans Küng

An Exchange of Letters

The Sternberg Centre for Judaism   31 March 1992
The Manor House
80 East End Road
London

Dear Hans,

John Bowden has passed on to me your comments on my review of 'Judaism'
in the *Church Times*.

First may I say how honoured I am that you have taken the trouble to take
my remarks so seriously. I am extraordinarily flattered to be in correspondence with you and do hope that next time you are in London, we can meet
and continue our dialogue. I am not sure that we can go a great deal further
through exchange of letters but I would like to respond briefly to your
comments.

1. You are absolutely right in correcting my point about Heschel and the
Civil Rights Movement. I went back to the relevant section and cannot
understand how I missed the sentence that you cite. My apologies.

May I add the following? I still think that the agenda of *Global Responsibility*
could have been pursued much more explicitly. Part of the continuing
contribution that Judaism can make lies with its prophetic tradition. There is
no doubt that Heschel's participation in the Civil Rights Movement flowed
directly from his understanding of the prophetic imperative. The example of
Heschel should be used to encourage us to further efforts in the future.

Let me suggest, albeit tentatively, that the prophetic commitment to social
justice is subtly different from the Christian tradition that flows from Jesus'
involvement with people on the margins of society. This is not to make a value
judgment between the two. But one might well argue that the Jewish doctrine
of social justice flows from confrontation at the centre of society (prophets
chiding kings and governments), whilst the Christian 'bias to the poor' is
focussed on action at the periphery. A dialogue between the two positions
might prove very fruitful.

2. I re-read your chapter 'The Law as Liberation'. Please do not misunderstand me. I am overwhelmed and humbled by the scope of your reading
and the courtesy that you pay Judaism in taking so many of our thinkers
seriously. I, too, find David Hartman challenging and interesting. But in the

last analysis, you are critical of Hartman. Furthermore, the overall impression in the book is one of negativity towards *halakhah*.

If you ever have the time to read the essay that I sent you, you will see that I, too, feel the need to critique *halakhah* and argue for a post-*halakhic*, covenantal position. But I acknowledge the fact that *halakhah* did seek – I think successfully – to embody great values and principles. It made a heroic attempt to make them operative in the mundane acts of everyday life. It took the obligation to search out God's will seriously. One only has to look at the way in which the halakhah tried to concretize the prophetic concept of social justice – making provision for the poor and the needy, regulating the courts and access to justice, seeking a degree of income redistribution – to see what I am driving at.

Moreover, there are real questions about whether a minority could have survived within the Christian and Muslim world without the halakhic framework to sustain it. This is clearly still an issue and there is always the possibility that, in a few generations' time, the only Jews who will have survived will be those who have clung to a strictly halakhic and separatist mode. I do not take that view and could not adopt that stance but it does not mean that I am right!

Finally under this heading, you can see how you have engaged me and Jonathan Magonet and Albert Friedlander in dialogue. But we are liberal Jews. I wonder what Jonathan Sacks' response would be to your critique of the *halakhah*.

It is always worth remembering that rabbinic Judaism produced much more than the *halakhah*. You make relatively little in your book of the aggadic and midrashic traditions and seldom cite them.

3. I will, indeed, re-read the chapter dealing with resurrection, trinity and incarnation, etc. My problem here is, however, two-fold.

First, I had assumed that up to that point in the book, you were addressing me. You turned to address a Christian audience at this point without really signalling that.

Second, I was particularly taken by your explanation of resurrection. It was utterly comprehensible to me as a Jew and echoed a sentence from our modern funeral service: 'We do not die into the grave but into the love of God.' However, I am not just interested in the common ground between Christianity and Judaism. I am interested and excited by the points at which our ideas and insights differ. It is by struggling with difference that I expand my religious horizons and grow. But this is a dialogue point and, as I have said before, perhaps more marginal to the agenda set by *Global Responsibility* than the space allotted to it in your book.

4. I applaud the switch of language – from forgiveness to reconciliation. I am absolutely convinced that if you call upon Jews and Christians to further the work of reconciliation post-Shoah, you are more likely to get a positive Jewish response than if you speak of forgiveness which has ceased to be a

helpful starting point. We must never underestimate the propensity amongst many Christians for minimizing the Shoah or characterizing it as mere history. Equally, we must never underestimate the extent to which Jews and Judaism have been damaged by the Shoah. It is very important that people point out to us where we misuse the Shoah for political or other advantage. But it is equally important that people do understand the scope of the damage and the duration of the mourning process.

I think that you have set yourself a most extraordinarily difficult task. Perhaps the single most important requirement for the future is that religions move into a much more self-critical mode. However, self-criticism is never easy and Jews, at least, find it even harder to respond to a call for self-criticism from someone outside our faith than they do from one of our own co-religionists. My educational background tells me that criticism has to be balanced by genuine praise and it is vital that Jews see more clearly than we do at the moment how we can contribute to global responsibility and the *humanum* – what we can give positively as well as where we have to change. Like it or not, yours is not merely a theological but a diplomatic task – and diplomacy and complete honesty were never the best of bedfellows! – 'Human kind cannot stand too much reality'.

I hope that you are aware of my unbounded respect and admiration for you – and my preparedness to assist you in any way that I can.

Thank you once again for taking me so seriously.

Warm regards,

Yours sincerely,

Tony
Rabbi A.M. Bayfield

Professor Dr Hans Küng,
7400 Tübingen   31 March 1992

Dear Tony,

I've just got your reply. Many many thanks. I am so happy that you understand my intentions, and we shall go on in our dialogue!

Shalom,
Cordially,
Hans

VI World Religions

John B. Cobb, Jr

Inter-religious Dialogue, World Ethics and the Problem of the *Humanum*

I

No Christian has contributed more to inter-religious dialogue that Hans Küng. Whereas such strong statements are dangerous to make in many fields, in this one they are safer. Although interreligious dialogue has occurred in earlier generations, it has been primarily a phenomenon of the post-World War II period. Hence competitors with Küng for this honour are his contemporaries. Comparisons are, therefore, easier.

Contributions to such dialogue occur at many levels, of which I will distinguish five. 1. There is Christian theological reflection that shows that in principle a dialogical relation to other religious communities is appropriate. 2. There is actual participation in such dialogue and promotion of it. 3. There is reflection about what happens in dialogue and how it can be improved. 4. There is the interpretation of other religious communities that encourages dialogue and shares its fruits. 5. There is clarification of the role and importance of dialogue in the total human situation.

There are others who have given more concentrated attention and leadership at one or another of these levels. For example, some have written more extensively, and perhaps more rigorously, on the Christian reasons for engaging in dialogue. A few have devoted more time to actual participation in dialogue or to promoting dialogues. Certainly some have gone further in particular dialogues with Jews, Muslims, Hindus or Buddhists. Others would compete with Küng in terms of reflection on what actually happens and can happen in dialogue. There are historians of religion who have provided more information about other communities of faith. But there is no one who has done all of these as extensively, as effectively, and as influentially as Hans Küng. Hence, my original statement, far from being exaggerated, is not strong enough. Hans Küng has contributed *more* than any other Christian to inter-religious dialogue.

I have made this assertion without commenting on the fifth level of dialogue as identified above. It is here that his contribution is most distinctive. Most Christians who engage in dialogue do so to share and to learn and to express solidarity with representatives of other religious communities. These are laudable motives, and Küng supports them. The World Council of Churches promoted dialogue chiefly for practical purposes of co-operation on shared goals, tending to contrast these purposes with specifically religious ones. Küng agrees that dialogue has profoundly important social purposes.

But Küng understands the purpose of dialogue in a broader context than either of these. This context is nothing less than the total global situation of the present. He presents inter-religious dialogue as an indispensable element in dealing with this situation. But he shows that it can work in this way only if it engages in genuinely religious interaction of the sort of which the World Council has been suspicious. When this contribution to inter-religious dialogue is included, Küng's leadership is without peer.

This leadership is not merely an intellectual and scholarly one. Küng is recognized in the public and political world as a spokesman to whom it is wise to listen, one who can speak for the wider religious community rather than only for one tradition. Furthermore, as he identifies needs, he shows how they can be met and, indeed, does himself much of what is needed. No other Christian plays an analogous role.

What is distinctive in Küng's contribution comes to expression most clearly in *Global Responsibility: In Search of a New World Ethic* (1990). This builds on work that Küng had been doing since the mid-1960s (perhaps earlier), and announces programmatically a whole new project, one of daunting proportion! This essay will take this book as its focus for interpreting Küng's most distinctive contribution to dialogue among the religious communities.

In different books, and often within the same book, Küng writes from two perspectives. As a Christian theologian he describes these as 'external' and 'internal'. This book is written primarily from the external perspective, but with important sections in which the internal perspective is explicitly adopted.

The external perspective allows Küng to survey the global situation as objectively as he can. What is happening, and what role is being played by the religious traditions? He does not justify the focus of attention on these traditions by his own participation in one of them or by any special pleading. His arguments for their importance are quite objective. First, they are crucially involved in some of the most intractable international problems, problems recognized by statesmen everywhere. Second, instead of contributing as they do to the difficulties faced by political leaders, they are capable of making a fundamental and indispensable contribution to the solution.

The role of religion in causing problems is too obvious to require much of Küng's time or ours. More important is his analysis of the positive role that religious communities can play, and indeed must play, if there is to be a viable future for humanity. The dilemma is that societies cannot exist without a shared ethos, and yet most national societies are now religiously pluralistic. The democratic state is expected to remain neutral on those matters on which the religions disagree. The danger is that where there is no common ethos, the state must exert raw power. The alternative is that the religious communities work together to form the needed common ethos.

The problem is even more acute because so many of the decisions that must now be made are global rather than national. All peoples must agree on certain principles and directions if catastrophe is to be avoided. Hence the need is not only for a shared ethos within nations. It is for a world ethos.

The problem is still more complex. Although historically the religious traditions have shaped the ethos of their several communities, today tens of millions of secular people are little affected in their own values and commitments by the pronouncements of religious leaders. The world ethos that is required must commend itself on secular as well as religious grounds.

This might suggest that the task is to get from philosophy a neutral, rational system of beliefs and directives. But this will not do even if agreement were reached among philosophers. First, religious communities will not accept a secular ethos imposed upon them. Second, secular ethics does not have the depth and power needed to redirect human thought and life. That depth and power reflect the religious dimension of human experience.

Küng does not suppose that all the religious traditions overlap in their ethical teachings in such a way that all that is needed is to bring their historic agreements to the fore. He knows that differences run deep. He knows also that for the most part they have historically resisted some of the teachings that are now indispensable if they are jointly to aid humankind in its crisis. The required agreement among them must be forged out of the present situation, not merely discovered in their sources.

Simply to have identified this urgent need and to have called for dialogue that would help to respond to it would have been a distinctive and important contribution. But Küng did not stop there. On the contrary, at least since 1984 ('What is True Religion? Toward an Ecumenical Criteriology', a lecture delivered at a conference at Temple University and published in Leonard Swidler, ed., *Toward a Universal Theology of Religion*, Maryknoll 1987, 231–50), Küng has proposed that the needed ethos can be developed from the idea of the *humanum*. All religious traditions, he is convinced, as well as secular people, are committed to human well-being and fulfilment. Their ways of relating their ultimate commitments to this ethical one differ. But a shared ethos can nevertheless be developed. Küng had an opportunity to try out this important proposal at a UNESCO meeting in 1989, and he was encouraged by the response of representatives of many traditions.

Once again, this is a contribution of enormous importance. Küng could well have offered his proposed solution to the world and encouraged study by representatives of the several traditions to test their readiness to accept it. But once again, Küng has not stopped here. Instead, he has launched a whole new programme. He will survey the several great traditions himself to examine their present situation, especially as it relates to the possibility of joining in the support of the urgently needed world ethos.

Coming from some other scholar nearing his sixty-fifth birthday, such an announcement might have been greeted with scepticism. Surveying the present situation of any one tradition would be considered by most scholars as more than a lifetime's work! But Küng does not affirm the kind of academic sensibilities that call always for more detailed studies of particulars and draw attention away from the larger picture. He knows that it is the larger picture that shapes decisions about the future. And he is convinced that there are responsible ways of providing this larger picture. Furthermore, he has repeatedly demonstrated his gifts in this respect.

Should there have been any lingering doubt of Küng's serious intention or ability to carry out his project, this would have been dispelled by the publication, already in 1991, of the first volume of the new series, *Judaism*. In 900 pages, Küng uses paradigm analysis to characterize the several stages of the development of Israel and Judaism, to describe recent events in some detail, and to reflect on possibilities for the future.

II

This whole programme swims against the stream, not only of university scholarship in general, but also of trends in current Christian theology. Küng is fully aware that in both Catholic and Protestant contexts, the trend is conservative, where he is unabashedly progressive. But even among those who are seeking new responses to the changing context, most are moving in one of two directions, quite different from Küng's.

One group, sharing Küng's enthusiasm for inter-religious understanding and mutual respect, is superficially similar in its desire to identify what is common to the great traditions. But it differs in two respects. First, although Küng spends much of his time viewing matters from the external perspective, as in the analysis of the actual and possible roles of the religious communities in the global situation, he enters dialogue always as a believing Christian committed to Christian truth. Second, he eschews all a prioristic theories of what is common to the traditions, working instead with great care individually with each. Among his most impressive writings is *Christianity and the World Religions* (1986). Here he listens to scholarly accounts of Islam, Hinduism and Buddhism and then provides a detailed critical response to each as a Christian theologian. He followed this up with *Christianity and Chinese Religion*, a similar response to Julia Ching's scholarly accounts of the religion of Chinese antiquity, of Confucianism, of Taoism, and of Chinese Buddhism. These volumes contain the most extensive and wide-ranging Christian criticisms of the other religious traditions that exist anywhere. If Küng had written nothing else, these books would have established him as a major and distinctive contributor to dialogue.

More than any other theologian, Kuong has worked theologically with the whole range of religious traditions. He deals with each in its particularity. This means that when Küng indulges in generalizations about all these traditions, as he occasionally does, he has earned the right to do so! And in any case, the commonality he hopes to find is the capacity to support a shared ethos, not already existing support.

The other group more obviously diverges from Küng. Many thoughtful Christians, especially Protestants, finding themselves in a situation in which Christendom no longer exists as political establishment and is fading as a cultural one, claim this situation as an opportunity for a truer faithfulness to Christ. They see this faithfulness as a renewal of the distinctive Christian ethos, its language, beliefs, symbols and practices. They eschew negative statements about those who do not share this faith. But they want to renew the congregation and deepen its immersion in a pattern that was greatly weakened by the church's internalization of Enlightenment values. Precisely the way Küng affirms the *humanum* is, for many of them, the sort of influence of the Enlightenment from which the church should free itself.

From Küng's perspective this movement can only be seen as a retreat from public responsibility at a crucial time. But from the point of view of these theologians, Christians cannot make their proper contribution to society except out of the particularities of their distinctive heritage. The whole effort to find common ground either with the secular world or with other religious communities belongs to the Enlightenment or to the modernity that is now dying.

This is a profoundly different reading of postmodernity from Küng's. I mention it here, not to support it, but to indicate the obstacles to gaining support for Küng's project among Protestants. Instead of progressing in the direction in which Küng calls us, much of the best of Protestant energy is directed toward undercutting all such projects! A generation ago support would have been more readily forthcoming.

III

Although I do not participate in this current trend and hope that it will not go too far, I do see a related weakness in Küng's characteristic formulations of the inner and the outer perspectives. They seem almost disconnected and at times even in tension. When he writes from the outer perspective, he seems to claim perspectival neutrality in the manner of objective discourse. He pronounces on the strengths and weaknesses of the several traditions as a scholar and a humanist. Then he shifts somewhat abruptly to the profession of his own faith. In that context he makes rather startling statements to the effect that Christianity is *the* true religion.

Both voices are offensive to some who believe themselves to be truly reflective of the new, postmodern situation. The first is offensive since it seems to ignore the social location of the writer and the way that affects what he sees. The second is offensive since, despite all qualifications, it sounds arrogant.

Much can and should be said in defence of Küng against these criticisms. He knows, of course, who and what he is. But the emphasis on one's social location easily leads to the relativization of what one says and, indeed, to avoidance of bold analyses and overviews of the sort he offers. It may be better to get a clear proposal before persons in other social locations for their response than modestly to limit oneself to reflecting on one's own perspective. In particular, white male Europeans too easily abdicate the responsibilities that go with their social location by emphasizing what that social location is.

In response to the charge of arrogance, we can see that in the same paragraphs in which Küng affirms that for him Christianity is *the* true religion, he affirms that there is the truth in others as well. Throughout his account he emphasizes the importance of self-criticism in all traditions, and he engages in a great deal of criticism of Christianity. His affirmation that Christianity is *the* true religion does not lead to harsher criticisms of others or any lack of appreciation for their contributions either to Christianity or to the world situation as a whole. Küng is anything but a Christian chauvinist.

Further, many people will be able to deal with his book more easily, given the sharp distinction of the two perspectives as he presents them. For example, secular people will be interested in his overall analysis. Many of them will be able to take it more seriously because it presents itself as a secular view of the religious role in global affairs. They can discount the sections clearly labeled as 'internal' in perspective.

More important, many representatives of other traditions will be able to share the overall account. Then, when they come to the sections that are specifically Christian, they can substitute their own, specifically Muslim or Hindu perspectives, for example. This will enable the proposal to get a good hearing from those to whom it is especially directed.

IV

Despite my recognition of all of these arguments in Küng's favour, I share in the discomfort felt by some as a result of the sharp distinction of the inner and outer perspectives. Even though I recognize that there are practical advantages in writing in this way, I wonder whether, in the long run, it will not cause more problems than it solves. And from the point of view of full intellectual honesty, I believe it distorts somewhat the real situation.

I believe that ultimately Küng engages in the study of the global situation as he does because he is a Christian. That does not mean, as I see it, that his being a Christian introduces a bias that he could escape by putting on the hat of the objective scholar. On the contrary, I believe that his Christian passion causes him to see features of the global situation that persons lacking that perspective – however scholarly and objective they claim to be – consistently neglect.

Indeed, there is no scholarly, objective or 'external' perspective as such. There are academicians of many diverse interests and convictions with varied social locations who examine the same world situation. Each highlights particular features. Most underestimate the importance of religious traditions. Some underestimate the importance of the ethos in general. Others overestimate the capacity of secular rationality or some philosophical tradition to provide the needed ethos.

Küng makes none of these mistakes. In my view, that is, from my perspective, his depiction is more accurate precisely because he brings to bear what he knows and feels as a thoughtful and learned Christian. But one does not have to share his Christian perspective to recognize the truth of what he says. The fact that one's special perspective enables one to discern what others have not seen does not mean that they cannot see it when it is pointed out to them.

Hence, to acknowledge and emphasize one's perspective is not to relativize what one sees. Economists see some features of the situation more clearly than do those without that training. That does not, or should not, cause us to deny that what they see is there to be seen. The same is true of cultural anthropologists, political scientists and ecologists. The total situation is so complex that no one analysis begins to exhaust it. For particular purposes, some correct analyses are more useful and more important than others. Küng's is extremely important for all those who hope for a happy future for humanity. To say that it attends to some features of the situation rather than others, and that his selection is affected by his Christian faith, does not diminish that importance.

I doubt that I am saying anything here that Küng denies. My point is only that, perhaps for practical purposes, he does not make this Christian theological character of his whole analysis explicit. That may be a prudent decision, but it has a price. It gives the reader the impression that Küng remains very much the child of the Enlightenment in respects that post-modern thought has rightly criticized.

It also makes the transition to the internal perspective uncomfortably abrupt. In my opinion, just as what Küng thinks of as the external perspective is informed throughout by the internal one, so also, what he affirms in the internal perspective is informed throughout by the external one. Just as there are Christian reasons for his highlighting of particular features of the global situation, so there are external reasons that he finds truth in his Christian faith. It is better to think of two poles in one continuous mode of thinking rather than of two perspectives.

I picture my own situation, which is similar in many ways to his, more as follows. I can engage in study and reflection only where I now am. I am formed by my Christian history and my repeated decisions to affirm my Christian identity. Hence all my thinking is affected by my Christian perspective. But one of my reasons for reaffirming my Christian identity is that it motivates me to be as honest and open to evidence as possible, and especially to evidence that is critical of the Christian position I have adopted. If I found that being a Christian inhibited openness and honesty, I could not remain a Christian. This is not because I am more committed to openness and honesty than to Christ, but because I understand commitment to Christ to involve commitment to openness and honesty.

I also find that being a Christian enables me to discern aspects of the real situation that other perspectives do not clarify. Of course, I see that others discern aspects that I miss. But it has seemed to me that my Christian perspective does not inhibit my learning from them. As I learn from them, my Christian understanding expands and deepens. Whether any other perspective allows those who embody it to learn as freely from others as I think my Christian one does, I do not know. I am quite sure that some do not, including many that call themselves 'Christian'. But I can confess the liberating and illuminating power of Christ without making negative statements about others.

From this point of view, I am uncomfortable with the statement that Christianity is *the* true religion. I am quite comfortable in saying that Christian faith opens me, in principle, to all truth. Of course, that is not to claim that I am free from defensiveness, but it is to assert that I experience that defensiveness not as faith but precisely as idolatry and lack of trust in Christ.

None of this means that Küng should make no distinction between what he is saying when he talks about Christianity in much the way he talks about other religious traditions and what he says when he confesses or describes his reasons for repeatedly reaffirming his Christian identity. But the distinction seems to me overdrawn and misleading in some of Küng's formulations.

On the one hand, I hesitate to make this criticism. Küng is moving ahead on an extremely important project. We theologians have the habit of criticizing one another's projects in such a way as to inhibit any bold undertaking. It is easier to show some limitation in another's formulations than to launch one's own initiatives. And once one has criticized, one can excuse oneself from giving the support the project deserves! My criticism is not intended in that spirit. Even if I am correct, this does not invalidate Küng's project or reduce the reasons for supporting it.

On the other hand, my quarrel is not a trivial one. Indeed, from my perspective the long-term ability of theology to support the kind of project Küng advocates depends on undersanding that project as Christian and theological. Küng could be read as saying that the definition of his project is purely secular. This secular project is then brought to the attention of believers in the several traditions. At that point he will put on his theological hat and work on the Christian response.

If the book is read in this way, it is not an invitation to other theologians to share in this venture or to engage in similar ones. The theological task is limited to the internal thinking that appears at certain points in the book. The tendency is for theologians to limit themselves to the theological task; so the survey of the global situation and the identification of the role religious communities need to play will be left to others.

I believe, in contrast, that Christians, and especially those who are set aside as theologians, are called to identify the most important needs of God's creation, to clarify what they are, and to propose ways of responding. Küng is a model of this kind of theological work. But his distinction between the external and the internal perspectives obscures this fact. It is because I want much more of theology to follow in the direction Küng has pioneered that I am so critical on this point.

V

Perhaps related to this formal criticism, that at a deeper level is intended as support, are some material criticisms. I wonder whether the *humanum* is today an adequate basis for the ethos that is needed. I am not at this point raising the question of the relation of the *humanum* to ultimate reality, a topic deftly treated by Küng. My concern is with the relation of the *humanum* to the other creatures.

Küng is himself quite sensitive to environmental issues, and many of his statements indicate that he has transcended the anthropocentrism of the Enlightenment. Yet the choice of the *humanum* as the basis of the needed ethos does not transcend anthropocentrism, even when the relation of human beings to the other creatures is emphasized. Indeed, much of the discussion of the *humanum*, even in this book, accents its close relation with the Enlightenment.

Küng is surely correct that the gains of the Enlightenment, such as the emphasis on the dignity of every human being, should not be abandoned in postmodernity. But the need now, I think, is to affirm human dignity without the anthropocentrism of the Enlightenment. It is also to avoid the individualism so characteristic of the Enlightenment. Other religious traditions, such as Hinduism and Buddhism, and certainly the primal religions, can help us find ways to do that.

At this point my criticism *is* directed to Küng's specific proposal. *This* criticism *is* a reason for not supporting that proposal in its present formulation. But I do not want to be primarily negative. In my book with Herman Daly, entitled *For the Common Good*, we criticized the Enlightenment model that has dominated economic theory, and we proposed the model of person-in-community. We went on to clarify that the community in view is not only the human one but also includes other creatures.

This could be viewed as simply a proposal as to how to understand the *humanum*. I would argue that even if it is only that, there would be some gain in formulation. It would work against an individualistic understanding of the *humanum*. However, more is involved in including both human community and other creatures from the outset rather than only later in the process of unpacking what is meant by the *humanum*.

I make my proposal hoping that, should it be accepted, it would not slow down or inhibit the important work of involving the several traditions in moving toward a common ethos. It is my opinion that the weaknesses in the focus on the *humanum* stem from its connections with Enlightenment individualism and dualism, and that these have not had comparable effects in other traditions. The notion of persons-in-community-with-one-another-and-with-other-creatures is not alien to the other traditions or to our own. Today this communitarian character of personal life and its embeddedness in the natural context are gaining recognition both in religious communities and in secular ones. Many of the principles Küng advocates follow more directly from this model than from focus on the *humanum* alone.

VI

The issue of social location comes out more clearly on another point. Hans Küng writes, inescapably, as a citizen of the First World. There is nothing wrong with that. It is probably easier for affluent people to think in global terms than for those who struggle to survive; so First World people have a special responsibility to give leadership in this direction. Furthermore, what happens in the First World is of utmost importance for what happens throughout the planet. And Küng writes as a citizen of the First World who is deeply concerned not only with that world but with the Third and Fourth Worlds as well.

However, there *is* a problem with developing a *world* ethos that generalizes so clearly from the problems and situation of the First World and does not acknowledge this slant. Even when it refers also to the problems of the Third and Fourth Worlds, it discusses them from the perspective of the First World. This is where explicit acknowledgment of social location would help. We could then be assured that as the global problematic is developed other voices would be heard, so that other features of that problematic would find their place.

One way in which the First World orientation shows itself is in the minor attention given to economics. The writing sometimes implies that after the Second World is lifted to First World standards, something like this can happen in the Third and Fourth Worlds also.

But in fact this is impossible. Already our affluence is overtaxing the global biological and chemical systems. If the inhabitants of the Third and Fourth Worlds consumed at current European rates, the collapse of the biosphere would be rapid indeed!

In any case no serious proposal has been made that would even lead in this direction. The only proposal before the global community that deals with economic growth in the Third World is the Brundtland Commission report. That calls for a six-fold increase in production in the Third World. But it envisions achieving this goal by a six-fold increase in the size of the economies of the First World! The absurdity is patent.

When the only proposal before the global community for alleviating the suffering of the Third and Fourth Worlds is patently absurd and while that suffering deepens year by year because of the 'restructuring' of the economies of many Third World countries required by the International Monetary Fund, the suggestion that First World businessmen, by subscribing to a better ethics, can make a great difference, seems simplistic. We desperately need a new ethos. But unless that new ethos expresses itself in new economic theory and practice, it will do half of the world's people little good.

One reason for my great concern about the nature of the ethos that the religions will support is that the economic theory and practice that is destroying the Third and Fourth worlds stems from an individualistic and dualistic anthropology. As a result, for the sake of increasing Gross National Product, it has systematically assaulted traditional community and exploited the other creatures, animate and inanimate. Current policies and proposals are no different in these respects. I see little hope for Third and Fourth World peoples unless this changes. Nothing said about the *humanum* in Küng's book indicates that it would give significant support for the needed change. If we order economic development instead to the strengthening of human communities in their natural contexts, there is a chance for real improvement even though the GNP will not be much affected.

Küng's profound analysis and responses are ordered to making a real difference in the real world. That is why I take them so seriously. I am forced to confess that in the past my work in inter-religious dialogue has not been informed by a full understanding of what is at stake. I have been converted.

But just for that reason a critique of the details of the analysis and response is not a merely academic exercise. If Küng's proposals are taken seriously, and he is in a better position than anyone else to promote them, the results will be of world-historical importance. It would be tragic if they did not genuinely help the Third and Fourth Worlds as well as the First.

Elisabeth Moltmann-Wendel

Dialogue between Religions without Women?
Women's Perspectives in the Abrahamic Religions

Dialogue between religions has begun today on many levels. It remains unsatisfactory for those who 'bear half of heaven' – i.e. women – that so far their perspectives on a dialogue have been little discussed and hardly taken into account. For as Moritz Winternitz has aptly remarked, 'the woman has always been religion's best friend, but religion has by no means always been woman's friend'. That would mean today that the direct involvement of women in their religion should again be taken seriously and at the same time there should be a new look at the critical relationship between woman and religion. This could open up new insights for the dialogue of the religions: from a woman's perspective do they not have more in common than appears from a man's perspective? For example, the loss of female self-determination runs parallel in all three Abrahamic religions. Criticism of a male-conditioned understanding of sexuality unites many women who have very different notions of God. What appears to be a male consensus could here have become religious dissent. The community of women, which has always been regarded critically in the West, can become a new value.

For women too, many questions are still open or do not allow simple solutions. A dialogue between religions today should remain open to groups whose thought runs counter to it, and the religions should accept the criticism of women, without whose active participation there can be no peace among the religions. In this article I shall give an account of the significance of the three Abrahamic religions for women today.[1]

At first glance the situation of women in Judaism, Christianity and Islam is very different. In the area of Western Christianity women have introduced the two women's movements of the nineteenth and twentieth centuries, and on the left, Protestant wing they have achieved full religious equality with men as pastors and bishops, whereas in many Islamic areas women have to conceal themselves under their chadors and actually want to do so. But again there are the most varied nuances between these two extremes, undermining the Western prejudice that the West is highly developed and the East under-developed. There are Christian women in the powerful Western, Catholic, church to whom the priesthood and the diaconate are still barred. By contrast, for some time women have been able to become rabbis in Jewish Reformed communities, and the number of women professors on the teaching bodies of Islamic universities in Turkey and Egypt is said to exceed that of women professors in Western countries.[2]

Moreover, in addition to the religious factors which encourage or get in the way of women's liberation, we also have the most varied social systems, which extend from highly technocratized American society to the nomadic tribes. I want to take up the various themes relevant to women in the three religions which are still influential in adaptation to and confrontation with social developments.

1. Common features of the three religions

First of all we should note what is common to the three religions: they are Abrahamic religions, and thus all derive from Abraham as their ancestor: Old Testament traditions are their common source. Moreover they are monotheistic religions. Their revelation has been conveyed by men – Moses, Jesus, Muhammad – and they are religions of the book, which refer to their sacred scriptures: the Hebrew Bible, the Old and New Testaments and the Qur'an. A common feature of these holy scriptures is that they have an extremely ambivalent position on the question of women. They contain elements of equality between men and women (created equal: Gen. 1.27 – the same responsibility for conduct: Surah 3.195; 4.124; 9.71, etc. – equality in Christ: Gal. 3.28). On the other hand they emphasize the pre-eminence of the husband over the wife (Gen. 3.16; Surah 2.228; 4.34; Eph. 5.21–23; I Tim. 2.9–14, etc.). In all three religions over the course of the centuries these passages have been reinforced by interpretations which are hostile to women and have given women's life a negative stamp.

There are elements of hostility to women throughout the history of the three religions. At the beginning stand women, primal mothers in each tradition, who have contributed to the consolidation of the community: Jewish women like Miriam and Deborah, whose earliest battle songs and women's songs have been handed down. There are Christians like Mary Magdalene and the women who as disciples followed Jesus to the death and without whom the Christian message is unthinkable. In Islam there are Hadisha, Muhammad's wife, who set him up in his camel business and who influenced him and strengthened him in his religious self-understanding; Aisha, the wife who was later preferred and given rights in his subsequent harem; and Fatima, his fourth daughter, the prophetess, who became highly significant for the Shi'ites. But these traditions, too, were treated and handed down differently. The independence of women was played down on all sides. Miriam was made Moses' sister, Mary Magdalene the great sinner, and the inspirations of Hadisha were forgotten.

Alongside these common features, however, there are differences in religious education and socialization, in the understanding of marriage, in the significance of sexuality, which still have an effect today and can further liberation or get in its way. Not least, the women's movement has had very different concerns within the three religions. I shall sketch out these four themes briefly here.

2. Education and socialization

First, I shall select some features relating to the different socialization of boys and girls. Whereas in Judaism the boy is accepted into the covenant of God, the Jewish community, with circumcision on the eighth day, for the Jewish girl this acceptance takes place without ceremony – at birth. Any child who is subsequently born from this girl belongs to the Jewish community, is automatically a Jew. The Bar Mitzvah, the reception of the boy into the synagogue community, also lacked a female parallel for a long time. At the age of twelve the girl, too, belonged to that community, but again without any ceremony. In modern times parallel ceremonies have now been created: since 1930 Bat-Mitzvah ceremonies for daughters, and since 1970 also rituals on the birth of a daughter. But it is primarily biology which creates different religious presuppositions.

In Islam boys are similarly circumcised, and in Islamic tradition there are no female parallels. The excision of the clitoris which is customary in some Islamic countries (Sudan, Somalia, Egypt) is tolerated in Islam but has no religious legitimation there. The female embryo, which in other countries (China, India) is in some danger of being aborted, is in no danger in Islam. The killing of infant girls was forbidden as early as the time of Muhammad. However, as in other poor countries, it can be seen that small girls are looked after less well than their brothers. Female mortality is thus greater, but similarly there are no religious grounds for this.

In Christianity there is the same ceremony of reception for both sexes, baptism. Here boys and girls have the same religious start. Confirmation, too, is also administered for both sexes equally.

It is probably the case in all the countries of the world that the birth of a son fulfils other expectations than the birth of a daughter and that in cultural and religious life there are many subtle disadvantages, for example the question of ministrants in the Catholic church, the banishment of Islamic women to certain parts of the mosque, and of Jewish women to the gallery in Orthodox groups. Such experiences make it clear to girls at an early stage that they are the other sex.

The right of women to religious education and further education has also always been a matter of dispute in all religions. Women today refer to early evidence that they were given equal opportunities. Thus the Hebrew Bible still obliges women along with men to hear the Torah read out every seven years (Deut. 31.9–12; Neh.8.2–3). Women could also pray with men in the synagogue with equal rights and even become leaders of the synagogue. Women were also included in the calculation of the *minyan*, the ten people needed for worship. However, from the sixteenth-century Shulkhan Arukh, a law book of Orthodox Judaism, women were no longer counted among the persons needed to form a quorum for a service. The right of women to equal education was also lost. Nevertheless there were continually women teachers of the Law and women, above all rabbis' daughters, who taught the Talmud. In 1845, at the time of the first women's movement, Reform Judaism again required the same religious education for boys and girls. Since 1972 there have been women rabbis in Reform Judaism and there are now around 200 of them world-wide. With them interest is growing in tradition and its interpretation in favour of women.

Spiritual activities among women are also known from the early Islamic period. Muhammad is said to have allowed women even as imams: in public, specifically only for women, but at home also for a household consisting of men and women. However, the religious role of the woman has never been laid down legally. Women who have a command of the Qur'an and Hadith now teach in groups of women and girls. The purdah society (society with a strict division of the sexes) still limits the work of women in religious education. Nevertheless there have continually been specialists and individuals who are expert in questions of law, and holy women (like Mama Sliman) who have tackled religious questions in their books.

In Christianity the convents created islands for female theological thought within a patriarchal church which excluded women from the active practice of religion. On these women's islands an early women's theology grew up, the significance of which for male theology as well is now being discovered (mysticism). It was made possible by the celibate form of life encouraged in Christianity. The dissolution of the convents in the Reformation also meant an end to independent female education. Women's religious education was certainly required and encouraged by the Reformation; ultimately, however, over the following centuries it was again left to individual women.

3. Attitudes to marriage

In all three religions marriage has an almost sacred role, since it is the prerequisite for procreation and thus for the existence of the community, above all in the Jewish and Islamic views. 'He who is not married is not a full man,' we read in the Talmud. 'Marriage is the sole way of virtue,' says Muhammad.

But the accents are placed very differently. In Judaism the significance of marriage lies in procreation, intimacy and the fulfilment of erotic needs. Here human needs are seen and integrated which are also important for women.[3] The Song of Songs is explicit testimony to sexual mutuality. Sometimes it seems that it is the desire of women to marry which makes marriage necessary. However, the initiative always comes from the man. The woman goes from the protection of her father to the protection of her husband without a break (Deut. 22.16; Ex. 21.7). Polygamy – which is still permissible to the male in the Hebrew Bible – disappeared because of cultural circumstances. While still regularly practised in Islamic areas, in Christian countries under Christian influence it was prohibited in the twelfth century. Divorce was originally initiated by the husband. The woman could ask him for a letter of separation in cases of illness, failure to consummate the marriage and other basic needs. But under Christian influence, from the eleventh century onwards the consent of the wife was also necessary for divorce in Christian countries. Divorce could become the decision of a public rabbinical court, and could also be applied for by a woman. But in Orthodox circles to the present day women are at a considerable disadvantage over the right to divorce.

In Islam marriage is regarded as an order of creation. Polygamy, as reported of Muhammad, is also anchored in the Qur'an (Surah 4.3). It is possible to marry four wives and slave girls. However, in modern circumstances the wife can insist by contract on monogamy. The significance of marriage is stronger than in the Jewish understanding. Nothing is said about the fulfilment of erotic desire. The woman's sexual availability can even be compelled by physical force. 'Men stand above women because God has marked them out by nature' (Surah 3.34). 'Men stand a step above them' (Surah 2.228). Women can seek divorce in certain instances: sickness, no financial support, complete incompatibility. But the husband can dissolve the marriage with or without the wife's consent. However, in the case of divorce the wife's dowry gives her financial security.

The Christian household tables of the New Testament also show a hierarchical order of marriage. According to Ephesians (5.21ff.) the husband is to 'love' the wife and she is to 'honour' (or fear) him. What Troeltsch called a 'patriarchalism of love' seems continually to have undermined harsh patriarchal customs. But it is important for Christianity that since the Jesus movement there has been the idea and the formation of the *familia Dei*, which leaves behind all current patterns of marriage and even breaks through patriarchal structures. According to Mark 10.29f. those who follow Jesus have no fathers, only brothers, mothers and sisters. In this way the spiritualization of forms of life and at the same time ascetic celibate solutions were envisaged. 'It is good to marry and better not to marry' – this saying of Paul would not have been a real alternative in Judaism and Islam. In Christianity it became a momentous challenge which extended as far as the question of women. The ascetic ideal, which exists in Judaism and Islam only in the tiniest marginal groups, began to shape Western Christian culture, and this offered new models of life for women also outside marriage. In Islam it is the married man rather than the monk who is the ideal, so in early Islam the single woman was a 'complete failure',[4] and in Judaism too the unmarried woman has no tradition. By contrast, on Christian ground the possibility of an independent female way of life arose at an early period.

4. Evaluation of sexuality

This brings us to the most serious difference between the Abrahamic religions: their asssessment of sexuality. Sexuality relates to the deepest and most intimate human experiences, and the way in which it is experienced and evaluated sheds decisive light on human self-understanding. Whether one controls sexuality anxiously or experiences it positively as an experience of totality also always depends on the respect in which women are held. In a culture which is determined by males who have made their models of rule, organization of life and self-control social ideals, the suppressed areas of the emotions, intuition, nature, the corporeal, the irrational are always projected on to the woman, feared and despised.

A first common feature among the three Abrahamic religions is that sexuality is never given an exaggerated religious significance, as for example in Hinduism and in other, above all pre-patriarchal cultures. But sexuality, which is concerned with the mystery of life, is protected in various ways, and the rules, laws and customs associated with it stamp the lives of women.

In Judaism there are the levitical laws which regulate dealing with birth, pregnancy, menstruation and the emission of seed (Lev. 15). Menstruation and the flows of blood as a result of disease are regarded as uncleanness, and the regulations for the monthly period isolate women and interfere not only with their everyday life but also with their religious life. However, we can also learn to see what 'uncleanness' is in another way. Because the ovum which is expelled in menstruation, the process which causes bleeding, is unfertilized, the process can also be understood as a 'principle of death'.[5] Starting from the understanding of life, the menstruating woman is exposed to this process of death and thus is 'unclean'. The status of the menstruating woman – called *niddah* – is a status of separation but also of autonomy. On the other hand, as Monika Fander[6] points out, the term *niddah* in early Jewish literature, where it is also to be translated as 'cast out', 'abominate', comes dangerously close to being identified with moral transgression or with pollution and impurity (Qumran). Thus impurity and feminity are brought together. As the isolation of a woman lasts twice as long after the birth of a daughter as after the birth of a son (Lev. 12.18), the suspicion is intensified that what were originally laws of protection ultimately imply the inferiority and uncleanness of the woman. Thus female sexuality is characterized as a realm of particular danger.

Early Christianity now breaks with these traditions. It is reported of Jesus that he touched the woman with an issue of blood who had approached him and who according to the logic of the laws of cleanness must have been unclean (Mark 5.25–34 par.). Above all Matthew's version of this story literally takes up the Greek text of Lev. 15.33 (Matt. 9.20).[7] Instead of avoiding the woman, Jesus heals her. By transcending this and other levitical laws relating to the dead and to food, Jesus put 'the contrast between remoteness from God and nearness to God' solely 'in the human conscience'.[8] This practice remained possible in early Christianity until around 300, when the old laws of purity relating to sexuality again found their way into the church, and in the Western churches priesthood and celibacy were combined. The old thinking about cleanness was further sharpened by the Western Graeco-Roman dualism which thought of body and spirit, soul and body as opposites, whereas Hebrew thought did not know these oppositions. On the basis of this dualistic thought, female sexuality became a power to be feared. The Eve story in the Jewish tradition did not become the story of the Fall just in patristic tradition, but already in the New Testament (I Tim. 2.13f.), and then nourished the dogma of original sin. The persecutions of witches, which despite the usual contempt for women have no parallels in other religions, may be regarded as an expression of anxiety and opposition to dogmatized sin and sexuality. With the dogma of original sin and the persecution of witches, Christianity sadly took on contours which were to the detriment of women.

However, the possibilities of celibate asceticism which opened up on the other side could free women from biological pressures. In the pre-modern period virginity could free women from the domination of a father, a brother or an uncle. Here forms of life were created which later became productive in the women's movements of the Western world: 'chastity as autonomy'. From this perspective Chrsitian traditions take on a new status in contemporary feminist research. At all events it becomes clear that not only the married couple but also the individual woman became a model of Christian life. Not only marriage but also virginal celibacy could become a model of discipleship. But this was just one phenomenon in Christianity, important though it was. As already becomes clear in the household tables of the New Testament, marriage and partnership, and with them heterosexuality, ultimately become the main social model for Christian life.

The distinctive feature of Christianity as opposed to Judaism and Islam remained the breaking of the tabu with biological and social norms. In recollection of the Jesus movement and the praxis of the early church the Reformation churches again took up this practice, broke with celibacy, and with their doctrine of the equality of male and female before God made it possible over the next centuries for women to enter the pastorate. However, this theory of equality then made it difficult to develop a distinctive women's culture which corresponded to the rhythms of feminine life. In other words, the powerful effort of Christianity to overcome biology ultimately encouraged a monastic spirituality remote from the body and a modern culture of repression and domination which forgot the body, something of which we are only now becoming aware. Every now and then women could rediscover themselves in both these cultures. Both shaped the West and the emancipation movements, including the women's movement. But even today women ask critical questions about both, and their ambivalence must be recognized.

The Islamic attitude to sexuality is the most restrictive. Sexuality is understood as an energy which has to be regulated. Anyone who is sexually unsatisfied is regarded as potentially dangerous. An ascetic life-style is rejected. But feminine sexuality is the territory which men have to defend and protect. The honour and shame of a family are bound up with the notion of virginity. Shame must be avenged, often with blood. In order to preserve their virginity, the freedom of girls is throttled from puberty on. In some countries the chador, which really only goes back to the saying in the Qur'an (Surah 24.31), 'Enjoin believing women to draw their veils over their bosoms', has become the complete concealment of the female body except for a slit for the eyes. It is meant to make femininity invisible and not desirable. Freedom of movement returns for a woman only after the menopause. In modern conditions operations on the hymen have become possible which make it possible to hand the bride over to the husband intact after pre-marital intercourse. This 'virginity mania' ultimately rests on an ignorance of sexuality, and perhaps on the error that sexuality is to be defined only from the male perspective.

Fatima Mernissi sees the difference between the Western and the Islamic understanding of sexuality as being that the West fights against sexuality as such, and Islam fights not against sexuality but against the woman. In Islam woman is characterized by an active sexuality, and her sexual self-determination must be prevented out of fear of chaos (*fitna*).[9]

If the Western individual is split in the conflict between body and spirit, the male Muslim sees disorder, *fitna*, not in himself but in the woman. The drives are energies which can have both a destructive and a constructive effect. Satisfaction through sexuality is the basis of cultural work – but this is envisaged as being for a society consisiting of males.

This anxiety about the structure of human drives, which is also rampant in the West, could be demythologized by the recognition of the variety and colourfulness of human drives and could do away with the fixation on sexuality.

Here the insights and experiences of women from all cultures come together. Just as in Western countries women develop a very wide understanding of sexuality which is not limited to coitus, so the Egyptian Dr

Saadawi judges that 'sexuality does not occupy any disproportionately great space in the life of an emancipated, intelligent woman. Ignorance, oppression, fear and every possible limitation transcend the role of sexuality in the lives of women and girls.'[10] But women still live in a world dominated by male ideas and male anxieties, and have to survive in it.

The Western sexual revolution with its marketing of the female body is rejected by many Islamic women. The question arises for them whether they are not all too quickly being changed from 'oriental-style sexual objects' to 'Western-style sexual objects'. Could not even the chador serve to restore the dignity of women because it compels people to assess them by their gifts and personality and not just by their bodies?[11] *Tearing the veil from their bodies would also inevitably entail tearing it from the spirit of society. Only a transformation of the social, economic and not least religious presuppositions of the patriarchal societies and churches and a change in men could bring about a fundamental culture-change here.* In the last resort the women's question is a men's question, and the liberation of women is possible only when men too are liberated from clichés, prejudices and anxieties.

5. The women's movement in the religions

Religion is not a male invention, but its control and the regulation which emerges from it lay for centuries in the hands of men, and women have always led only a marginal existence in religion. Their rights and freedoms were given to them. They agreed, secretly objected, or – but only in the rarest cases – offered open resistance. In the first women's movement which arose out of the Euro-American context of the Enlightenment and the human rights movement, women all over the world learned to use their heads, to demand education and training, and to claim a new role in society and the church.

In the second women's movement, which began at the beginning of the 1970s, women learned to become aware of themselves as women and to advocate their self-determination and their totality physically, culturally and in religious terms. In contrast to the first women's movement, this second movement also presented a challenge to the religions, a challenge which has only just begun. As societies have developed into a technocratized world with the ideals of efficiency, achievement, technological thought and the profit motive, women have begun to exploit their education, their opportunities, and to work out their identity in this society. Applied to the religions, this means that women no longer put themselves in the niches which a particular religion has given them, no longer allow themselves to be comforted by the friendliness of a particular religion to women, but independently investigate their tradition, examine the way in which it is historially conditioned and look for traces of their own independent history. In so doing women free religions from pressures which hitherto had hardly been seen from the theological perspective.

Here are some examples:

Jewish women are beginning to experience their history anew, *Standing Again at Sinai*, to quote the title of the American Jewish theologian Judith Plaskow's book. They see the Jewish religion as dynamic, not as static, and are attempting to develop it further for women, to develop new rituals for women (e.g. Bar Mitzah, birth of a daughter, rituals for life-cycles, etc.). That is also giving rise to a new self-awareness over against Christianity, its claim to do most justice to women, and its hidden anti-Judaism, which puts the Jewish religion on a lower level than Christianity.

Christian women are discovering feminine symbols which were long concealed and hardly became visible in theology, liturgy and rituals: Sophia, Ruach, the feminine Holy Spirit, the femininity of God. Against a theology which persists in the revelation concluded in Christ, they are developing and practising the ideas of an ongoing revelation which includes the experiences of women. The relevance of other religions which fell victim to the Christian claim to absoluteness to women's culture is also being taken seriously.

Muslim women are interpreting anew the laws which discriminate against women. For example, the permission to strike a woman is retranslated 'keeping women in a restricted space', or is understood symbolically. The tradition of women's community is being given new life, specifically for an industrialized urban world in which individual women have few opportunities. The distinctive values developed in women's cultures are being stressed over against the Western life-style.

One thing unites Jewish, Christian and Muslim women, for all their difference: a shared concern to expose discrimination against women, whether open or hidden. Here is an example by way of illustration. In the Jewish-Christian-Muslim cultural sphere there is the image of the woman as Adam's rib. It was used in the second Hebrew creation story, entered deeply into Christianity and also appears as an Arabic proverb: 'Woman was created hard and crooked like a rib.' The image of the rib has become an expression of the dependence of the woman on the man, her second-class status and her deformity, and was already used in this sense in the mediaeval 'Hammer of the Witches': 'Because she (the woman) was formed from a crooked rib, i.e. from a bone in the chest, she is crooked and as it were disposed against the man. From this defect it also emerges that as the woman is an incomplete animal, she is always deceptive.'[12] In all three religions there are new interpretations by women who are learning to see this prejudiced image anew.

For the Jewish theologian Pnina Navé Levinson the 'rib' is a false translation: the term could equally well be translated 'side'. Thus God created a human being: Adam is one side and Eve the other, which God created, adorned and shaped in beauty.[13] For contemporary Christian exegetes

(Trible, Schüngel-Straumann) the rib represents the equality and solidarity of women and men. These exegetes also refer back to the mediaeval feminine exegesis of Christiane de Pisan, for whom Adam was created out of ugly mud and Eve out of finer material.[14]

For Muslim women this derogatory image of the rib is a discrepancy from the Qur'an, which has never regarded the woman as a second creation of God. For them, the myth of the rib is one of the texts of the Hadith literature, which infiltrated the Qura'nic statements about equality, and which needs to be looked at again.[15] These new interpretations are linguistically, logically and academically correct and can also be put forward from the male side. However, this has hardly happened.

The liberation of women through religion can ultimately come about only where women become subjects instead of objects, where in active shaping, thought and criticism they appropriate religion anew and translate it in their own particular society. If the religions become Sarah/Hagar/Abraham religions instead of just Abrahamic religions, they will also become humanized and make an active contribution to fulfilling their meaning: that of living out the equality of women and men before God on this earth.

Notes

1. As literature on the topic, in addition to the works cited below see G. Parrinder, *Sex in the World Religions*, London 1980; M. Wallach-Faller, 'Die Frau im Judentum – ein geschwisterlicher Überblick', *Fama* 6, 1990, no.4.
2. J. van Ess, in H. Küng et al., *Christianity and the World Religions*, 82.
3. Cf. B. Greenberg, 'Female Sexuality and Bodily Functions in the Jewish Tradition', in J. Becker (ed.), *Women, Religion and Sexuality*, Geneva 1991, 65.
4. N. Minai, *Schwestern unterm Halbmond*, Munich 1987, 203f.
5. R. de Tryon-Montalembert, 'Is das Judentum frauenfeindlich?', *Judaica* 3, 1985, 138.
6. M. Fander, 'Reinheit/Unreinheit', in *Wörterbuch feministische Theologie*, Gütersloh 1991.
7. Cf. P. Trummer, *Die blutende Frau*, Freiburg im Breisgau 1991, 87.
8. D. Wendebourg, 'Die alttestamentlichen Reinheitsgesetze in der frühen Kirche', *Zeitschrift für Kirchengeschichte* 95, 1984, Vol. 2.
9. F. Mernissi, *Geschlecht, Ideologie, Islam*, Munich 1987, 29.
10. Minai, *Schwestern unterm Halbmond* (n.4), 173.
11. Ibid., 245.
12. H. Schlüngel-Straumann, *Die Frau am Anfang. Eva und die Folgen*, Freiburg im Breisgau 1989, 17.
13. Cf. P.N. Levinson, *Was wurde aus Saras Töchtern?*, Gütersloh 1989, 36.
14. Schlüngel-Straumann, *Die Frau am Anfang* (n. 12), 14.

15. R. Hassan, 'An Islamic Perspective', in J. Becker (ed.), *Women, Religion and Sexuality* (n. 3), 75.

Masao Abe

'Dazzling Darkness'. The Understanding of 'Ultimate Reality' in Buddhism and Christianity

In his response 'God's Self-Renunciation and Buddhist Emptiness: A Christian Response to Masao Abe',[1] which is directed to my article 'Kenosis and Emptiness',[2] Hans Küng raises a number of crucial issues for the Buddhist-Christian dialogue. Due to the restriction of space, however, I would like to limit myself to answering the following three issues which I believe to be the most essential. First, is Abe's approach a true dialogical hermeneutic? Second, is the idea of the kenosis of God himself truly Christian? Third, is Sunyata the central concept of Buddhism?

I

In response to the first question, Hans Küng argues:

> There is no question: Masao Abe's basic intention is dialogic. He isolates key concepts from Christian texts which he then transplants into a Buddhist context, where the concept of kenosis is understood not simply as ethical, exemplary humiliation, but is recast as ontological emptying, an emptying of God, Himself, yes, ultimately as Emptiness in general, Sunyata. In this manner, as a Buddhist, he discovers his own world – even on the foreign, Christian soil. Just as the Christian authors earlier gave a Christian exegesis of Greek or Buddhist texts, so also Abe gives a Buddhist exegesis of the Christian texts.[3]

Hans Küng concludes that my interpretation of the kenotic passage in Philippians is 'a Buddhist exegesis of the Christian texts' in that it isolates key concepts from Christian texts and transplants them into a Buddhist context. Is this understanding of my interpretation of the hymn in Philippians and the subsequent discussion of the kenosis of God a fair and pertinent one? My basic intention in this regard is not to impose Buddhist categories upon the Christian context, then to give a 'Buddhist' exegesis of the Christian texts. Instead, I have tried to understand the Christian texts, in the present case the concept of kenosis, from within a Christian framework, as much as this is possible.

Nevertheless, I have offered a new interpretation that differs from the traditional orthodoxy, 1. because I cannot be completely satisfied with the traditional interpretation and 2. because, in order to cope with the challenge by contemporary anti-religious ideologies, a new interpretation is urgently needed today. In this connection, I have tried to understand the Christian notion of kenosis by deepening the spirituality of Christianity without at the same time distorting Christianity. Careful readers of my interpretation,[4] I hope, will not fail to recognize this intention.

Although I am a Buddhist, I hope my readers will dispel the presupposition that my discussion and interpretation of Christianity is a 'Buddhist' exegesis. I sincerely hope that my discussion of Christianity will be judged not in terms of whether it is Buddhistic or not, but in terms of whether or not it is in accord with Christian spirituality. The inter-religious dialogue may adequately and effectively take place if each side of the dialogue tries to grasp the other side's spirituality from within, without imposing its own ontological and axiological categories.

In my article 'Kenotic God and Dynamic Sunyata', which considers the Epistle to the Philippians (2.5–8), I emphasized that 'Christ's kenosis (self-emptying) signifies a transformation not only in appearance but in substance, and implies a radical and total self-negation of the Son of God'.[5] I also argued that 'in the kenosis of Christ, it is not that the Son of God *became* a person through the process of his self-emptying, but that fundamentally Christ *is* a true human being and true God at one and the same time in his dynamic activity of self-emptying'.[6]

Taking one step further, I insisted that if Christ the Son of God empties himself, should we not consider the possibility of the self-emptying of God – that is, the kenosis of God the Father? Is it not that the kenosis of Christ – that is, the self-emptying of the Son of God – has its origin in God 'the Father' – that is, the kenosis of God? Without the self-emptying of God 'the Father', the self-emptying of the Son of God is inconceivable. This is why I stated:

> In the case of Christ, kenosis is realized in the fact that one who was in the form of God emptied 'himself' and assumed the form of a servant. It originated in the Will of God and the love of God which is willing to forgive even the sinner who has rebelled against God. It was a deed that was accomplished on the basis of God's *will*. On the other hand, in the case of God kenosis is implied in the original *nature* of God, that is, 'love'.[7]

Criticizing Karl Rahner's understanding of the self-emptying of God as still leaving behind traces of dualism, I argued:

> If God is really unconditional love, the self-emptying must be total, not partial. It must not be that God *becomes something else* (Rahner's words) by partial self-giving, but that in and through total self-emptying God *is* something – or more precisely, God *is* each and every thing. This emphasis,

however, should not be taken to signify pantheism (see the following section). On the contrary, only through this total kenosis and God's self-sacrificial identification with everything in the world is God truly God. Here we fully realize the reality and actuality of God, which is entirely beyond conception and objectification. This kenotic God is the ground of the kenotic Christ. The God who does not cease to be God even in the self-emptying of the Son of God, that is, the kenosis of Christ, is not the true God.[8]

This is the point of my understanding of the kenotic God. Does this understanding indicate, as Hans Küng suggests, that I take the concept of kenosis 'not simply as ethical, exemplary humiliation, but as *ontological* emptying, an emptying of God, himself yes, ultimately as Emptiness in general, Sunyata'?[9] Since the *nature* of God is *love*, an emphasis on the self-emptying of God as his dynamic nature does not necessarily indicate an 'ontological' interpretation at the expense of the 'ethical' meaning of the Son of God's self-emptying. And, in my understanding, I am *not* trying to 'replace'[10] the kenotic God of Christianity 'by the all-inclusive (dynamic) Emptiness (Sunyata) of Buddhism',[11] as Hans Küng suggests.

Everything in my understanding and interpretation of the idea of kenosis is based on the most fundamental tenet of Christianity, namely that 'God is love' (1 John 4.8). If God is really all-loving, God does not have the Son of God emptying himself without God himself ceasing to be God the Father. Again, if God is really an all-loving God, he is not self-affirmative but self-negating, not self-assertive but self-emptying, and becomes *das Nichts* by completely identifying himself with everything in the universe, including the most sinful man. This understanding may not be the same as the traditional Christian understanding, but it is not correct to characterize it as a 'Buddhist' interpretation, as Hans Küng suggests, because my understanding arises from reflection on this central Christian definition, 'God is love.'

II

Second, is the kenosis of God himself truly Christian?

Rejecting the notion of the kenosis of God as unbiblical, Hans Küng strongly maintains that:

> In the entire New Testament ... nowhere is there mentioned an incarna-
> tion or a renunciation (kenosis) of God Himself; the Philippian hymn only
> speaks of a kenosis of Jesus Christ, the Son of God. Furthermore, this
> kenosis is not understood as a permanent status, position, relationship but
> as a humiliation occurring in a unique, historical life and death on the
> cross.[12]

It is clear that an explicit literal reference of kenosis can be found only in the Philippians passage. This does not, however, mean that the concept of kenosis is a limited or special one in the New Testament. II Corinthians 8.9 conveys the same idea as that of Philippians in its own words:

> For you know the grace of our Lord Jesus Christ, that though he was rich, yet for your sake he became poor, so that by his poverty you might become rich.

This idea of kenosis or condescension can also be found in John 3.13; 16.28; 17.5; and Romans 15.3. A New Testament scholar states: 'We should recognize that the *kenosis* motif is not confined to any one or two, or more passages, but is the underlying theme of the New Testament. The very incarnation assumes a condescension.'[13]

The crucial issue of our present dialogue is not, however, the kenosis of the Son of God, but the kenosis of God himself. In this regard, Hans Küng argues:

> Certainly, the self-sacrifice of the Son does not occur against the will of the Father. God desires the redemption of humanity and so also the self-sacrifice of Jesus. Still, God the Father does not give Himself up but His Son (the Church condemns the monophysitic 'patripassianism'), and so God the Father (*ho theos*) does not die upon the cross, but the man, Jesus of Nazareth, the Son of God. Only He, not God Himself, is (according to the dying words of Jesus quoting Psalm 22.1 [Vulgate 21.1]) forsaken by God! Jesus being forsaken by God is, according to the New Testament, no divine 'paradox', but human agony crying to heaven.[14]

Thus Hans Küng's attitude toward the kenosis of God is basically the same as that of the early church. With this understanding of God who is impassible and immutable, how does Hans Küng understand the problem of evil, especially the problem of the Holocaust at Auschwitz? Due to the contemporary human predicament, the theological climate has been considerably changed. In this regard we should not overlook the following remarks by Karl Rahner, a leading Catholic theologian of our time.

> If it is said that the incarnate Logos died only in his human reality, and if this is tacitly understood to mean that this death therefore did not affect God, only half the truth has been stated. The really Christian truth has been omitted ... Our 'possessing' God must repeatedly pass through the deathly abandonment by God (Matthew 27.46; Mark 15.4) in which alone God ultimately comes to us, because God has given himself in love and as love, and thus is realized, and manifested in his death. Jesus' death belongs to God's self-utterance.[15]

Through a uniquely trinitarian interpretation of the Christ event, Jürgen

Moltmann also emphasizes the death of God's Fatherhood in the death of the Son.

> When one considers the significance of the death of Jesus for God himself, one must enter into the inner-trinitarian tensions and relationships of God and speak of the Father, the Son and the Spirit.[16] The Christ event on the cross is a God event, and conversely, the God event takes place on the cross of the risen Christ. Here God has not just acted externally in his un-attainable glory and eternity. Here he has acted in himself and has gone on to suffer in himself. Here he himself is love with all his being. So the new christology which tries to think of the death of Jesus as the death of God must take up the elements of truth which are to be found in *kenoticism* (the doctrine of God's emptying of himself).[17] In the forsakenness of the Son the Father also forsakes himself, though not in the same way ... The Son suffers dying, the Father suffers the death of the Son. The grief of the Father here is just as important as the death of the Son. The fatherlessness of the Son is matched by the Sonlessness of the Father, and if God has constituted himself as the Father of Jesus Christ, then he also suffers the death of his Fatherhood in the death of the Son. Unless this were so, the doctrine of the Trinity would still have a monotheistic background.[18]

Though I have some disagreement with and criticisms of Karl Rahner's and Jürgen Moltmann's interpretation of the kenosis of God (cf. pp. 15–26 in *The Emptying God*), I deeply sympathize with them because to me the kenosis of God as understood by them deeply accords with the spirituality of Christianity.

I also find a strong statement of the kenosis of the Father in Hans Urs von Balthasar. In his work *Theodramatik 3: Die Handlung* (pp. 297–309), Balthasar explains trinitarian theology in its relation to the *kenosis* of Christ. He writes:

> We spoke of a first *kenosis* of the Father in his self-expropriation in the 'generation' of the consubstantial Son. This first *kenosis* extends itself, as if by itself, to the common trinitarian *kenosis*, since the Son could not be consubstantial with the Father other than in self-expropriation and since their 'We', the Spirit, likewise can only be God if he personally seals the self-expropriation which is identical in the Father and the Son in as much as he wants nothing 'for himself' but rather (as his revelation in the world shows) only wants to be pure proclamation and gift of the love between Father and Son (13.26; 16.13–15). With this original *kenosis* (*Ur-Kenose*), the other *kenoses* of God into the world are basically made possible and are mere consequences of it: the first 'self-limitation' of the trinitarian God on the basis of the freedom extended to creatures, the second deeper 'self-limitation' of the same trinitarian God through the covenant which from

the outset is indissoluble on God's part, regardless of what happens with Israel, and the third not only christological kenosis but that of the entire Trinity, on the basis of the incarnation of the Son alone who makes clear to the world from the outset his eucharistic disposition in the *'pro nobis'* of the cross and the resurrection (308).

In this regard, however, Hans Küng raises a very crucial question about the notion of the kenotic God, one which must be properly answered by a kenotic theologian.

The stumbling-block of a (Buddhist or Christian) Christology (and Trinitarian doctrine) which completely identifies Jesus with God and brazenly declares Jesus' death to be the death of God is made strikingly clear in the case of the resurrection: such a Christology cannot explain who brought this supposedly dead God back to life.[19]

The answer is dependent on how the notion of kenosis is to be understood. If kenosis is merely understood as a humiliation or condescension in terms of self-emptying, the question that Küng raises above is naturally inevitable and its answer must be negative, i.e., there is no living God who could have brought Christ back to life. But the Philippians hymn clearly shows that kenosis includes not only the humiliation of the Son of God but also the *exaltation* of the Son of God. Precisely as a result of his humiliation, Christ was raised to a place higher than before. Thus, quoting from *Interpreter's Bible*, 5, p. 50, 'The way he took was that of self-denial and entire obedience, and so acting he won his sovereignty,' I clearly recognized the inseparability of the state of humiliation and the state of exaltation in the event of Christ's death on the cross. Self-emptying is nothing but self-fulfilment. Thus my answer to the above question is affirmative: God the Father and God the Son glorify each other through an inverse correspondence, through an 'other-self affirmation via own-self negation'.

In this connection, we must not overlook the following passages in the book of Colossians: it is unclear how much attention Hans Küng pays to them in his current discussion.

For in him (Christ) all the fullness (*pleroma*) of God was pleased to dwell (1.19).

For in him the whole fullness (*pleroma*) of deity (*theotetos*) dwells bodily (2.9).

These passages clearly show the fullness of God dwells in Christ, especially in bodily form. It was God's pleasure that all of his fullness should dwell in Christ in order that through Christ, God might 'reconcile to himself all things, whether on earth or in a heaven, making peace by the blood of his cross' (1.20).

As I said earlier, in Jesus Christ the state of humiliation and the state of exaltation are inseparable; kenosis and pleroma are inseparable. Now the most crucial question is *how* they are inseparable. Does the state of humiliation come first and then the state of exaltation follow afterwards? Is kenosis a cause and pleroma an effect or result? Such a temporal or causal understanding of the inseparability of these twin sides of the same reality is nothing but a conceptualization or an objectification of the two sides without existentially and religiously committing oneself to the midst of the event. It is an outsider view, not an insider view. For an insider, committing one's self religiously to faith in Jesus Christ, the state of humiliation and the state of exaltation are not two different states but a single, dynamic one; that is, humiliation as it is is exaltation, and exaltation as it is is humiliation; kenosis as it is is pleroma, and pleroma as it is is kenosis. Each pair in these two sets of biconditional terms is dynamically non-dual through mutual and simultaneously reciprocal negation. How is this dynamic identity of the 'as-it-is-ness' of humiliation and exaltation, kenosis and pleroma, possible? It is possible because the dynamic identity is based on the kenotic God the Father, who is self-emptying and unconditional love, and ultimately on the Godhead who is neither *essentia* nor *substantia*, but *Nichts* or *Ungrund*.[20]

Thus in my article 'Kenotic God and Dynamic Sunyata', in concurrence with Moltmann, I stated as follows:

> The death of Jesus on the cross is not a divine-human event, but is most certainly a trinitarian event of the Father, the Son, and the Spirit. What is important in this regard is the total, personal aspect of the sonship of Jesus. The sonship of Jesus, however, is ultimately rooted in *Nichts* or *Ungrund* as the Godhead in 'the unity of three persons in one God'. Only here ... can we say with full justification – as Moltmann states – that 'in the Cross, Father and Son are most deeply separated in forsakenness and at the same time are most inwardly one in their surrender' (*The Crucified God*, 244). Again, only here – when the sonship of Jesus is understood to be ultimately rooted in *Nichts* as Godhead – can the event of the cross of Jesus be understood truly as the event of an unconditioned and boundless love fully activated for the Godless or the loveless in this law-oriented society.[21]

In this way I understand Godhead as *Nichts* or *Ungrund*, which is exemplified by Christian mystics such as Meister Eckhart and Jakob Böhme. Is my interpretation of God as *Nichts* 'a Buddhist exegesis of the Christian texts'[22] or 'the renunciation of God Himself in Buddhist Sunyata'[23] or a replacement of the kenotic God 'by the all-inclusive (dynamic) Emptiness (Sunyata) of Buddhism',[24] as Hans Küng suggests? (I also came to understand God as *Nichts* through my critique of Hans Küng's statement 'God in the Bible is subject and not predicate: it is not that the love is God, but that God is love – God is one who faces me, whom I can address' [cf. *The Emptying God*, 25–6].)

III

At this point we must turn to the third question, that is, is Sunyata the central concept of Buddhism? In this connection, Hans Küng raises (i) the question of Being and Nothingness, then (ii) the problem of Sunyata as Buddhism's ultimate Reality, and finally (iii) the issue of an Eastern-Western understanding of God.

(i) The question of Being and Nothingness. Referring to Hegel and Heidegger, Hans Küng points out an affinity and difference between them and Buddhism (cf. *Buddhist Emptiness and Christian Trinity*, 35–7). Unfortunately, his point of discussion is not so clear to me. So I would like to present my own view of this question as follows: as Hans Küng correctly points out, for Hegel neither pure Being nor pure Nothing is true, and only Becoming as their unity (*Einheit*) or unseparatedness (*Ungetrenntheit*) is their truth. In his *Science of Logic*, Hegel argues:

> The truth is not their lack of distinction, but they are not the same, that they are absolutely distinct, and yet unseparated and inseparable, each disappearing immediately in its opposite. Their truth is therefore this movement, this immediate disappearance of the one into the other, in a word, Becoming: a movement wherein both are distinct, but in virtue of a distinction which has equally immediately dissolved itself.[25]

This is strikingly similar to Buddhist understanding of Being and Nothing. However, as I pointed out elsewhere,[26]

> Despite Hegel's emphasis on the unseparatedness and material passing over (*übergehen*) of Being and Nothing, it cannot be overlooked that in his system Being is prior to Nothing. In Hegel the beginning (*Anfang*) of everything is Being as such, and his dialectical movement develops itself in terms of Being (thesis), Nothing (antithesis), and Becoming (synthesis). In this way, Being as such is the supreme principle of Hegel's metaphysical logic. In so far as Being is thus given priority over Nothing, however dialectical 'Becoming' as the unity may be, it is not a genuine Becoming but a quasi-Becoming which is after all reducible to Being because in Hegel Becoming is a synthesis of Being and Nothing in which 'Being' is always the thesis. In addition, by asserting that there is a final synthesis, his system cuts off all further development: it swallowed up the future and time itself. For all its dynamically fluid, dialectical character, his system is consistently formulated in an irreversible, one-directional line with Being as the beginning.

By contrast, in Buddhism Being has no priority over Nothingness; Nothingness has no priority over Being. There is no irreversible relation between Being and Nothingness. Thus 'Becoming' – to use this term – in Buddhism is not a *synthesis* which presupposes duality of Being and Nothingness with priority given to Being, but is instead a complete *inter*dependence and *inter*penetration among everything in the universe – that is, *pratītya-samutpāda* or dependent co-origination. 'Becoming' in Buddhism is grasped in terms of *pratītya-samutpāda* and, as such, is completely free from irreversibility and from any sort of priority of either contrary, being or non-being, over the other. Dependent co-origination is not *werden* in Hegel's sense, which is a synthesis of Being and its conceptual contrary, Nothing. Dependent co-origination is neither Being nor Nothing, nor even Becoming.

(ii) Hans Küng raises a very basic question which any Buddhist thinker must answer, that is, 'What is actually the highest truth, what is the ultimate Reality in Buddhism? Is it Sunyata for all schools of Buddhism?'[27] Then he points out various paradigm shifts in the history of Buddhism from the primitive Buddhism to Madhyamika and Yogacara schools in which such key notions as *Nirvana*, *Sunyata* and *Dharmakaya* have been interpreted differently. This historical fact makes the question 'What is the ultimate Reality in Buddhism?' difficult.

In this connection we must first clearly realize an essential difference between Christianity and Buddhism in understanding 'ultimate Reality'. Christianity also underwent various paradigm shifts in its history, but the ultimate Reality has always been believed to be 'God'. And as Paul emphasizes 'One God and Father of us all, who is above all and through all and in all' (Ephesians 4.6), God is believed to be 'one' absolute God. This monotheistic character of God is the underlying theme of all forms of Christianity regardless of their historical diversity. By contrast Buddhism is fundamentally free from the monotheistic character. Rejecting the age-old Vedantic notion of Brahman as the sole reality underlying the phenomenal world, Gautama Buddha advanced the teaching of *pratītya-samutpāda*, that is, dependent co-origination in which everything in and out of the universe, without exception, is interdependent, co-rising and co-ceasing. Nothing exists independently. Even the ultimate does not exist by itself. Rather, this complete interdependency itself among everything in the universe is understood as 'ultimate Reality' in Buddhism. It is often called 'not one, not two', because it is neither monotheistic nor dualistic. The diversity within Buddhism is bigger than that in Christianity, because Buddhism has no single volume of canon like the Bible in Christianity, and instead of talking about one absolute God, Buddhism takes *pratītya-samutpāda* and Sunyata, i.e. Emptiness, as the ultimate Reality. The diversity of understanding of ultimate Reality in Buddhism should not be judged by Christian standards. It is quite natural in Buddhism that even such key concepts as *pratītya-samutpāda*, Nirvana, Sunyata and *tathatā* (suchness) have been grasped differently.

Buddhism, and particularly Mahayana Buddhism, based on the idea of Sunyata or anatman, developed itself freely and richly according to the spiritual climate of the time and place into which it was introduced. Thus, throughout its long history in India, China and Japan, Buddhism produced many divergent forms which are radically different from the original form of Buddhism preached by Sakyamuni. Nevertheless, they were not driven out from the Buddhist world, but became spiritual foundations from which new forms of Buddhism emanated. In this connection it may be interesting to note that one Buddhist scholar regards the history of Buddhism as 'a history of heresy', meaning by this that Buddhism has developed itself by means of heresy and by continually embracing various heresies.

In the West, where Mahayana Buddhism in China and in Japan is relatively unknown, people are apt to judge the whole of Buddhism by taking the 'original' form of Buddhism preached by Sakyamuni as their standard. Such a static view fails to appreciate the dynamic development of Buddhism. The diversity and profundity of the history of Buddhism, especially of Mahayana, is no less rich than the whole history of Western philosophy and religion. It is a development coming out of the inexhaustible spring of Sunyata or *tathatā* (suchness). Yet, this 'history of heresy' in Buddhism has evolved without serious bloody inquisitions or religious wars. There is no equivalent to the European Crusades in the history of Buddhism.

Even though, as I said earlier, it is quite natural for Buddhists to employ such key concepts as *pratītya-samutpāda*, Nirvana, Sunyata and *tathatā* differently at different times in the history of Buddhist thought, we must fully realize with Hans Küng that,

> there is no stifling the critical question – what is a Buddhist supposed to make of talk about an Ultimate Reality, when each and every thing is 'empty' and emptiness is somehow everything? Can we talk concretely, or do we have to go around in circles?[28]

Hans Küng correctly emphasizes that 'sunyata has to be seen in the context of the macroparadigm changes'[29] of Buddhist thought. Thus he refers to Nagarjuna's *Madhyamaka-kārikā* and to the Yogacara doctrine as the two main trends in the history of Mahayana Buddhism. In this connection, Hans Küng severely criticizes my approach to the issue of the Buddhist ultimate Reality.

> If I am not mistaken, Masao Abe did not propose Buddhist Ultimate Reality as all Buddhists would understand the term, but as it is understood in a very specific Buddhist paradigm: in the Madhyamika as interpreted by a specific Zen philosophy.[30]

I admit the precision of his criticism and the limitation of my approach to the issue. I did not particularly pay due attention to the Yogacara doctrine and other schools of Buddhism when I discussed Sunyata as ultimate Reality in Buddhism. This is because I thought (and still think) that with respect to the

Buddhist-Christian dialogue in which we are now engaged, what is needed is not a detailed discussion of the doctrine of, say, Sunyata within the various schools of Buddhism, but 1. a self-critical view of Sunyata as the ultimate Reality underlying Mahayana Buddhism as a whole, 2. for each participant in the Buddhist-Christian dialogue to represent his or her own religion, not merely intellectually or doctrine based, but existentially as well. By doing so, each participant may spiritually clarify the essence of his/her religion through a personal existential commitment. Without speaking from such an existential commitment, the inter-faith dialogue may be apt to be merely conceptual and superficial. A self-critical existential commitment on the part of each dialogue partner is essentially necessary because interfaith dialogue today must take place not merely between the two religions in question, but in the face of challenge by the current anti-religious ideologies prevailing in our society which seriously questions the *raison d'être* of religion itself. My existential, and not merely intellectual, approach to interfaith dialogue probably gives Hans Küng the impression that 'Masao Abe did not propose Buddhist Ultimate Reality as all Buddhists would understand the term, but as it is understood in a very specific Buddhist paradigm: in the Madhyamika as interpreted by a specific Zen philosophy'.[31]

Now we must answer Hans Küng's basic question, what is ultimate Reality in Buddhism? Hans Küng himself rightly mentions two Buddhist options with regard to ultimate Reality. According to him, the first option is to understand 'Emptiness' with Nagarjuna and the Madhyamikas as primarily *negative*, whereas the second option is, with the Yogacara school, to interpret 'Emptiness' *positively*. It is true that Madhyamika and Yogacara understand 'Emptiness' differently, but I am afraid that it is an oversimplification to state, as Hans Küng does, that Madhyamika understands Emptiness negatively whereas Yogacara understands it positively.

In his book *Mādhyamika and Yogācārā*, Gadjin M. Nagao, a renowned Buddhologist of Japan today, states:

> Presently (by modern scholars) the Madhyamika philosophy ... is believed to be wholly inherited by Maitreyanātha, Asanga, and other Yogācāras. The Prajñāpāramita sūtras are equally revered as authentic by both schools, and further, the doctrine of emptiness occupies an important position in the Yogācārā school.[32]

Of course Nagao recognizes the difference between Madhyamika and Yogacara in their understanding of Sunyata:

> ... Is it proper to speak of the logical process involved in establishing śūnyatā as the same in both schools? Isn't it that, although the name śūnyatā is shared by both, what is intended by this name is entirely different in the two schools? For one thing, their points of departure differ: the

Mādhyamika starts from pratītya-samutpāda, while the Yogācāra starts from abhūta-parikalpa (unreal imagination). Another remarkable difference is that the Yogācāra speaks of the 'existence of non-existence' when defining śūnyatā. We must also pay attention to the fact that, although both the Mādhyamikas and the Yogācāras are thought to base their idea of śūnyatā on the Prajñāpāramitā sūtras, the Yogācāras also place importance on the *Cūlasuññata-sutta* of the Majjihima-nikāya.[33]

Before becoming involved in the detailed discussion of the difference between Madhyamika and Yogacara, it is important for our purpose of answering the question 'What is ultimate Reality in Buddhism?' to explore the true meaning of 'Sunyata' underlying both schools, Madhyamika and Yogacara, in contrast to the earlier Abhidharma's view of Sunyata, which the Mahayana Buddhists tried to overcome.

In early Buddhism, the theory of dependent co-origination and the idea of Emptiness were still naively undifferentiated. It was Abhidharma Buddhism which awakened to a particular philosophical understanding of Emptiness and set it up in the heart of Buddhism. But the method of its process of realization was to get rid of concepts of substantiality by analysing phenomenal things into diverse elements and thus advocating that everything is empty of any substantial reality. Accordingly, Abhidharma Buddhism's philosophy of Emptiness was based solely on *analytic* observation – hence it was later called the 'analytic view of emptiness'.[34] It did not have a total realization of the emptiness of phenomenal things. Thus the overcoming of the concept of substantial nature or 'being' was still not thoroughly carried through. Abhidharma fails to overcome the substantiality of the analysed elements themselves.

But beginning with the *Prajñāpāramitā-sūtra*, Mahayana Buddhist thinkers transcended Abhidharma Buddhism's analytic view of Emptiness, erecting the standpoint which was later called the 'view of substantial emptiness'.[35] This was a position which did not clarify the Emptiness of phenomena by analysing them into elements; rather, it insisted that all phenomena were themselves empty in principle and that the nature of phenomenal existence itself is empty of substantial, perduring content. With respect to everything that is, the *Prajñāpāramitā-sūtra* emphasizes: 'not being, and not not being'. 'Isness' is not to be equated with 'being', nor yet with the negation of 'being'. This sutra clarified not only the negation of being, but also the position of the double negation – the negation of non-being as the denial of being – or the negation of the negation. It thereby disclosed 'Emptiness' as free from both being and non-being. That is, it revealed *prajñā* – wisdom.

It was Nagarjuna who gave this standpoint of Emptiness as found in the *Prajñāpāramitā-sūtra* a thorough philosophical foundation by drawing out the implications of the mystical intuition seen therein and developing it into a complete philosophical realization. Nagarjuna criticized the proponents of substantial essence of his day who held that things really exist in a one-to-one correspondence with concepts. He said that they had lapsed into an illusory view which misconceived the real state of the phenomenal world. He insisted that with the transcendence of the illusory view of concepts, true Reality appears as *animitta* (no-form, or non-determinate entity). But Nagarjuna rejected as illusory not only this 'eternalist' view, which took the phenomena to be real just as they are, but also the opposite 'nihilistic' view that emptiness and non-being are true reality. Nagarjuna thereby took the standpoint of Mahayana Emptiness, an independent standpoint liberated from every illusory point of view connected with either affirmation or negation, being or non-being, and called that standpoint the *Middle Way*.[36]

Nagarjuna's idea of the Middle Path does not indicate a midpoint between the two extremes as the Aristotelian idea of *to meson* might suggest. Instead, it refers to the way which *transcends every possible duality* including that of being and non-being, affirmation and negation. Therefore, his idea of Emptiness is not a mere emptiness as opposed to fullness. Emptiness as Sunyata transcends and embraces both emptiness and fullness. It is really formless in the sense that it is liberated from both 'form' and 'formlessness'. Thus, in Sunyata, Emptiness as it is is Fullness and Fullness as it is is Emptiness, formlessness as it is is form and form as it is is formless.[37]

Hence, the well-known passage in the *Prajñāpāramita-hrdaya-sūtra* – the *Heart Sutra*:

> Form is emptiness and the very emptiness is form; emptiness does not differ from form; form does not differ from emptiness; whatever is form, that is emptiness; whatever is emptiness, that is form.[38]

As the *Heart Sutra* clearly indicates, the realization that 'form is emptiness', however important and necessary it may be, is not sufficient; it must be immediately accompanied with the realization that 'the very emptiness is form' and those two realizations are one, not two. In later Chinese Buddhism one encounters the saying 'True Emptiness is Wondrous Being'. This phrase indicates not only the dynamic identity of non-being and being, negation and affirmation, but also the recovery and re-establishment of being out of non-being.

In this connection, there are two more points which are important for adequately understanding the notion of Sunyata. First, although Sunyata is an ontological or metaphysical concept established by Nagarjuna to indicate the ultimate Reality, it is also unmistakably a practical and religious ideal. In Nagarjuna and Madhyamika, as in Buddhism in general, meditation is of cardinal importance, and Sunyata or Emptiness was recognized as an object of meditation. The same is the case with respect to Yogacara. As Nagao argues, 'The Yogacara who, as the name suggests, was greatly concerned with yoga-praxis, inherited the Nagarjunian notion of Emptiness, and, when they elucidated features of yoga-praxis such as the six pāramitās, the ten bhūmis, and so on, Emptiness seems to have been the basis of their theories.'[39] Second, although the realization of Emptiness is essential, one should not *cling to* Emptiness as Emptiness. This is why Mahayana Buddhism has throughout its long history rigorously rejected the attachment to Emptiness as a 'confused understanding of Emptiness', a 'rigid view of nothingness', or a 'view of annihilatory nothingness'. In order to attain true Emptiness, Emptiness must empty itself: Emptiness must become non-Emptiness (*asunyata*). Since Emptiness is non-Emptiness it is ultimate Emptiness (*atyanta-Sunyata*).[40]

Precisely because true Emptiness is Emptiness which 'empties' even itself, true Emptiness is absolute Reality which makes all phenomena, all existents, truly *be*, and stand forth. This is a Buddhist answer to the question. 'Why is there anything at all, rather than nothing?'[41]

The existential realization that true Emptiness 'empties' itself indicates that ultimate Reality is not a static state which is objectively observable but a dynamic activity of *emptying* in which everyone and everything is involved. Indeed, there exists nothing whatsoever outside of this dynamic whole of *emptying*. You and I are involved in this dynamic whole of *emptying*. You are Emptiness and Emptiness is you.

Although the term Sunyata or Emptiness sounds negative, the true meaning of Sunyata is positive and affirmative. So Sunyata is regarded as the synonym for *Madhyama pratipat* (The Middle Path), *Tathata* (Suchness), *Dharmakaya* (Body of Truth), and so forth. In the *Prajñāparamitā sūtra*, ultimate Reality is called *prabhāsvaram cittam* (the spotless, luminous, pure mind) and, in the latter Madhyamika and Yogacara schools, Sunyata is compared with *prabhāsvaram cittam*.[42] I myself use the term 'boundless openness'[43] to make the point that Sunyata is completely free from any kind of centrism – not only from egocentrism but also from anthropocentrism, cosmocentrism and even theocentrism.

Boundless openness is unobjectifiable; 'it' cannot be thought to have a centre that occupies a position relative to other points on a perimeter, for there is no perimeter, and therefore no centre relative to a perimeter. It is like a circle whose centre is everywhere but whose circumference is nowhere, to borrow a well-known metaphor from Christian mysticism. The state of boundless openness is the state of complete emptyingness. When realized existentially, this state or standpoint is a complete emancipation from any kind of bondage resulting from discrimination based on any kind of centrism.

IV

At the end of his response, 'God's Self-Renunciation and Buddhist Emptiness', Hans Küng seeks for a structural similarity between Buddhist

'Emptiness' and Christian 'pleroma' under the title 'An Eastern-Western Understanding of God'. I highly appreciate and share his *intention*, but I cannot completely agree with his *conclusions*.

Correctly understanding that Nirvana, Emptiness and Dharmakaya are parallel terms for the Buddhist conception of ultimate Reality, Hans Küng argues as follows:

> Their function is analogous to that of the term 'God'. Would it, then, be wholly impermissible to conclude that what Christians call 'God' is present, under very different names, in Buddhism, insofar as Buddhists do not refuse, on principle, to admit any positive statement?[44]

I have no objection to this argument and, because I do not refuse, on principle, to admit any positive statements, I fully admit that 'what Christians call "God" is present, under very different names, in Buddhism'. But I have some reservation with respect to the remainder of his argument:

> What is, according to Christianity, *the one infinite reality* (my emphasis) at the beginning, in the middle, and at the end of the world and humanity? ... If God is truly the 'Ultimate Reality', then God is *all these things in one*.[45]

Thus he mentions *Nirvana, Dharma, Emptiness* and *the primal Buddha* as Buddhistic parallels to the Christian notion of God. I must part from Hans Küng, however, when he talks about God as 'the one infinite reality at the beginning, in the middle, and at the end of world and humanity'. For it seems to me that Hans Küng believes that infinite or ultimate Reality must be *one*. (Elsewhere he talks about 'the question of the one true Ultimate Reality'.)[46] His Judaic-Christian understanding of ultimate Reality is monistic or monotheistic. In Buddhism, however, the ultimate does not begin with a conception of *one* infinite reality but rather with the *denial* of the conception of one infinite reality. This is clearly seen from the fact that Gautama Buddha did not accept the age-old Vedantic notion of *Brahman* as the sole reality underlying the phenomenal universe and which is identical with *Atman* as the unchangeable substantial Self. Instead, the Buddha advocated *pratītya-samutpāda* or dependent co-origination and *anatman* (no-self). The Buddha's doctrines constitute a rejection of monism or monotheism and imply an epistemic awakening to the boundless openness in which everything, including the one and the many, the divine and the human, is grasped as completely interdependent and interpenetrating. Because the Buddha was dissatisfied with monotheism as an expression of the nature of ultimate Reality, it is quite natural that the realization of Sunyata or Emptiness arose from this Buddhist context as the ultimate Reality beyond a monotheistic standpoint.

Buddhism is neither monistic nor monotheistic, neither polytheistic nor pantheistic. Buddhism may be called *panentheism*, however, because immanence and transcendence are dynamically and completely identical in

Buddhism. The key point in this respect is that immanence and transcendence are identical through the negation of negation, that is, the negation of immanence and the negation of transcendence. Transcendence and immanence, the one as opposed to the relative many, the finite and infinite, are diametrically opposed to each other and yet through the negation of negation they are realized as dynamically identical. Ultimate Reality relates to itself through the bottomless ground of its own ultimacy or unconditionality by negating itself from within itself, by emptying itself of its own infinite unrelatedness and embracing the form of its own self-negation. This dynamic identity of the finite and infinite, of the transcendent and immanent, etc., is realized through the function of ultimate Reality's relating to itself through its own boundless openness or *Ungrund*. This function is the principle of self-emptying of Emptiness itself, both within and through itself. It is this dynamic principle of the self-negation of the boundless Whole within itself that sets up an 'inverse correspondence' between the two faces of this self-interrelating Whole, between, namely, the finite and infinite, or the primal one and the relative many.

Inverse correspondence is not in any way a pantheistic concept; rather, it is a concept belonging to a functionalist ontology and takes its full meaning only alongside the notion of the principle of self-transcendence *via* internal self-negation, or self-affirmation through self-negation, of the unobjectifiable Whole itself. This is what is meant by *dynamic* Sunyata.

Quoting Nicholas of Cusa's notion of *coincidentia oppositorum*, Hans Küng suggests a structural similarity between the Buddhist 'Emptiness' and the Christian 'pleroma'.[47] However, unless the Christian notion of 'pleroma' is freed from the monotheistic structure, I do not see 'a structural similarity' between 'Emptiness' and 'pleroma', even though both concepts can be said to transcend and embrace all opposites in their respective manner. As I said before, 'Emptiness' as the ultimate Reality in Buddhism is not monotheistic, nor pluralistic, nor pantheistic. But the Buddhist notion of ultimate Reality is panentheistic in that immanence and transcendence are totally and dynamically identical through mutual negation. Through 'trans-descendence', ultimate Reality is at once inter-relational and boundlessly open in all directions. There is no single centre in any sense – even in the theocentric sense – and thus *'coincidentia oppositorum'* is fully and completely realized. 'Emptiness' is not the one infinite reality nor one absolute God but *Nichts* in the sense of the absolute No-thingness which is beyond and yet embraces both being and nothingness. It is right here that everything, including all of nature, human, non-human, and divine is realized just as it is, each in its individual and relational suchness.

In Christianity, the real 'pleroma' or 'fullness' of God should be identical with the real 'kenosis' or 'self-emptying' of God himself, a kenosis which is total, not partial. Only through the realization of the total kenosis of God himself is the real 'pleroma' of God fully realized. Only in the kenotic God can kenosis as-it-is be dynamically one with pleroma, and pleroma as-it-is be dynamically united with kenosis. Only in the kenotic God can humiliation as-it-is be exaltation, and exaltation as-it-is be humiliation. I believe that this dynamic identity of kenosis and pleroma indicates the ultimate Reality in Christianity.

However, if the notion of kenosis is applicable only to the Son of God, but not to God himself, that is to say, if God is understood *not* to empty himself even in the self-emptying of the Son of God, then the above dynamic identity of kenosis and pleroma, humiliation and exaltation, cannot be fully realized. 'Ultimate Reality' is then only realized in a limited sense. That is to say, 'ultimate Reality' still retains a monotheistic sense and is only one-sidedly transcendent. However, if one breaks through the monotheistic framework and realizes the kenosis of God himself, the ultimate Reality as the dynamic identity of kenosis and pleroma is fully realized. It is right here that the basic tenet of Christianity, 'God is love', is completely fulfilled. Once freed from its monotheistic and theocentric character, Christianity not only becomes more open to inter-faith dialogue and co-operation without the possibility of falling into exclusivism, but it also becomes compatible with the autonomous reason peculiar to modern humanity and will be able to cope with the challenge by Nietzschean nihilism and atheistic existentialism. The future task of Christianity is to open up the monotheistic framework through the full realization of the kenosis of God himself and to realize the ultimate Reality as the dynamic unity of kenosis and pleroma.

The dialectic identity of kenosis and pleroma, self-emptying and self-fulfilment, may be compared with 'dazzling darkness', a term employed by Pseudo-Dionysius the Areopagite.[48] It does not mean that God as the ultimate Reality is half dazzling and half dark. Instead, it indicates that God is fully dazzling and fully dark at one and the same time. That is to say, being dazzling as-it-is is darkness; being dark as-it-is is dazzling. This dialectical identity as the ultimate Reality is possible only when God is understood to be completely kenotic or self-emptying and not One as a monotheistic unity, nor one nor two nor three, but as *Nichts* or *Ungrund*.[49]

Now with respect to Buddhism, the traditional static view of Sunyata must also be broken through and interpreted dynamically – not as the static *state* of Emptiness, but as the dynamic *activity* of emptying everything, including itself. In Sunyata, form is ceaselessly emptied, turning into formless Emptiness, and formless Emptiness is ceaselessly emptied, and therefore for ever freely taking form. For this reason the *prajñāpāramitā sūtra* emphasizes:

Form is emptiness and the very emptiness is form.

Here we may also quote the Mahayana Buddhist expression: 'Samsara as-it-is is Nirvana; Nirvana as-it-is is samsara'. These statements are nothing but verbal expressions of the Buddhist ultimate Reality which may very well be compared with 'dazzling darkness'. Darkness (samsara) as-it-is is dazzling (nirvana); the dazzling (nirvana) as-it-is is darkness (samsara). Again, in order properly to understand the Buddhist ultimate Reality as 'dazzling darkness', one must clearly realize 'self-emptying Emptiness' by breaking through the traditional static view of Sunyata. The future task of Buddhism is to realize how this self-emptying Emptiness concentrates itself into a single centre in the boundless openness, a centre which is the locus of the real manifestation of personal deity and the ultimate criterion of ethical judgment and value judgment in general.[50]

As Hans Küng rightly states, 'every statement about Ultimate Reality would ... have to pass through the dialectic of negation and affirmation. Every experience of Ultimate Reality would have to survive the ambivalence of nonbeing and being, dark night and bright day.'[51] In full agreement with his statement, I would like to present the idea of 'dazzling darkness' as the common symbol of the ultimate Reality in Buddhism and Christianity, the meaning of which can be realized only by going beyond the traditional formulations of the doctrines and practices of both Buddhism and Christianity.

God is 'dazzling darkness'
because in God, who is the infinite love,
kenosis as-it-is is pleroma,
pleroma as-it-is is kenosis.

Sunyata is 'dazzling darkness'
because in Sunyata, which is boundless openness,
samsara as-it-is is nirvana,
nirvana as-it-is is samsara.

Notes

I am grateful to David Cockerham, who revised the manuscript and gave valuable suggestions at its final stage.

1. Hans Küng, 'God's Self-Renunciation and Buddhist Emptiness: A Christian Response to Masao Abe', in *Buddhist Emptiness and Christian Trinity*, ed. Roger Corless and Paul F. Knitter, New York 1990, 26–43.
2. Masao Abe, 'Kenosis and Emptiness', in *Buddhist Emptiness and Christian Trinity*, 5–25.
3. *Buddhist Emptiness and Christian Trinity*, 34.
4. 'Kenotic God and Dynamic Sunyata', in *The Emptying God, A Buddhist-Jewish-Christian Conversation*, ed. John Cobb and Christopher Ives, New York 1990, 9–

26. 'Kenotic God and Dynamic Sunyata' is a revised and expanded version of 'Kenosis and Emptiness'.

5. *The Emptying God*, 10.
6. Ibid.
7. Ibid., 14.
8. Ibid., 16.
9. *Buddhist Emptiness and Christian Trinity*, 34.
10. Ibid., 33.
11. Ibid.
12. Ibid.
13. Jennings B. Reid, *Jesus, God's Emptiness, God's Fullness: The Christology of St Paul*, New York 1990, 67.
14. *Buddhist Emptiness and Christian Trinity*, 33–4.
15. Karl Rahner, *Sacramentum Mundi*, Vol. 2, London 1969, 207f.
16. Jürgen Moltmann, *The Crucified God*, London and New York 1974, 204.
17. Ibid., 205.
18. Ibid., 243.
19. *Buddhist Emptiness and Christian Trinity*, 34.
20. *The Emptying God*, 26.
21. Ibid., 25.
22. *Buddhist Emptiness and Christian Trinity*, 34.
23. Ibid.
24. Ibid., 33.
25. *Science of Logic*, tr. W.H. Johnston and L.G. Struthers, London 1929, Vol. I, 95.
26. Masao Abe, *Zen and Western Thought*, Honolulu 1985, 53.
27. *Buddhist Emptiness and Christian Trinity*, 37.
28. Ibid., 39.
29. Ibid.
30. Ibid.
31. Ibid.
32. Gadjin M. Nagao, *Mādhyamika and Yogācāra*, SUNY, Series on Buddhist Studies, New York 1991, 189.
33. Ibid., 199.
34. In the T'ién-t'ai Sect, the view of emptiness of Hinayana Buddhism is called the 'analytic view of emptiness', and the view of emptiness in Mahayana Buddhism is called the 'view of substantial emptiness'.
35. See n. 34 above.
36. Pages 316–18 of the text are taken from Masao Abe, *Zen and Western Thought*, 93–4, with some adaptation.
37. *Zen and Western Thought*, 127.
38. *Prajñāpāramitā-hrdaya-sūtra*, Taisho 8.848.
39. *Madhyamika and Yogacara*, 51–2.
40. *Prajñāpāramitā-sūtra*, Taisho 8.250b.
41. *Buddhist Emptiness and Christian Trinity*, 40.
42. *Madhyānta vibhāga*, 1.22c.
43. *The Emptying God*, 30.
44. *Buddhist Emptiness and Christian Trinity*, 42.

45. Ibid.
46. Ibid., 41.
47. Ibid., 42–3.
48. *Pseudo-Dionysius, the Complete Works* tr. Colm Luibheid, New York 1987, 135–7; Evelyn Underhill, *Mysticism*, New York 1974, 347.
49. *The Emptying God*, 213–26, 162–9.
50. Masao Abe, 'Free Will and the Ultimate Criterion of Value Judgment in Sunyata', in *The Emptying God*, 55–9.
51. *Buddhist Emptiness and Christian Trinity*, 43.

Abdoldjavad Falaturi

Christian Theology and the Western Understanding of Islam

1. The unresolved problems

'The dialogue with Muslims has many advantages for us Christians,' remarked a Dutch colleague some years ago. He taught theology and religious studies and was giving a lecture at a conference in the Evangelische Akademie at Mülheim in the Ruhr. He continued enthusiastically: 'For example, we learn that Muslims do not esteem Muhammad as highly as we esteem Jesus, but only regard him' – and here he moved the palm of his hand downwards – 'as a human being down here. In any case Muhammad does not have as high a status as we thought and' – here he enthused his audience with further examples – 'these are gains that we have from dialogue with the Muslims.'

'So we can collar the Muslims and bring them in' – to Christian faith, of course – exulted an Austrian Islamic scholar and missionary at the Cusanus symposium held in Trier between 13 and 15 October 1982, referring to his book on Muhammad which had the same purpose.

'I've given up dialogue meetings,' a Catholic pastor who was very involved in dialogue with Turkish Muslims in the Cologne suburb of Mülheim told me, and he gave his reason: 'I've discovered that I couldn't get rid of my desire to missionize.' An honest answer from an honest heart.

The views quoted above are certainly not individual instances. But it is equally certain that they do not provide any generally valid criterion for Christian-Muslim dialogue. However, they do at least indicate problems which have their basis in the historical development of the dialogue; quite specifically also because the use of the term 'dialogue' has meanwhile been broadened to such a degree that its content and aim are almost limitless. This blurring of the term in particular requires of all partners in dialogue that before they enter into a conversation they should establish their standpoint in relation to the dialogue in question – what they understand by it and what they intend by it.

It is not my purpose at this point to open up a new dialogue, but to evaluate the indefatigable commitment of Hans Küng to a wide-ranging and serious dialogue with Islam. Regardless of the criticism which has constantly been expressed, that the part of his work *Christianity and the World Religions* which claims to be a 'dialogue with Islam' is not a dialogue with Islam but with Islamic scholars, I would like to conentrate on that: as a model example of both an apt Western understanding of Islam and a well-disposed Christian theological position on it. I am not concerned here to give a critique of the book or to quarrel pedantically with individual formulations and notions. My concern is rather – and I think that the author will approve of this – to limit myself to some basic questions of Islam as I understand and practise it. But a prerequisite for that is that I should first say something about my own position on Christian-Muslim dialogue after thirty-seven years experience of it, which I have had above all in dialogue with Christians before and since the new era of dialogue between the world religions.

2. Dialogue of the religions and cultures

I see 'dialogue of the religions and cultures' today as 'the attempt to understand and to be understood'; the attempt to understand conversation partners as they understand themselves; and the concern to be understood by others as we understand ourselves; and this with the aim of working together in a deliberate concern to combat the ongoing process of the reification of human beings as a consequence of the inexorable growth of materialism which has penetrated as far as our spiritual sphere.

Dialogue in this sense has as its indispensable presupposition partnership on an equal footing; mutual respect; a readiness to understand the positive values of the structure of the faith, culture and world-view of others as they understand themselves; a readiness to concede the problems and burdensome values of one's own view in order to avoid a one-sided encounter; the concern to put oneself in the position of the other in order to create the most fruitful basis possible for dialogue, which can be achieved on a religious level only if one is inwardly prepared to concede that the love and mercy of God is also to be found among those of other faiths and is not present only among those who share one's own beliefs. One thus has to be ready to surrender an egocentric, absolute claim to truth which runs counter to the divine Being and the creativity of that Being.

If none of this happens, the dialogue will remain fruitless. This happens wherever a negative attitude towards each other forms the starting point; wherever the superiority of the one to the other destroys equality in partnership; wherever mutual values and problems are not taken into account; wherever the conviction that one possesses an exclusive cultural value or religious truth leads to a belittling of the culture, faith and form of life of the other; wherever one or other party seeks to have their prejudices confirmed by the dialogue; wherever there is a concern (conscious or unconscious) to maintain the traditional images of hostility; wherever problematical prejudices form the basis of the encounter, with the ultimate aim of putting the other in the dock (and this often happens to Muslims in dialogue with Christians), presenting them with a list of charges, condemning them, and providing endorsement for the views of the prosecutor, even combined with the notion of missionizing (openly or in a concealed way) for one's own religion, culture or civilization and making a show for the benefit of one's own public.

Occasions of dialogue also remain unbalanced and unfruitful wherever the boundaries between different levels of discussion are blurred or confused, resulting in bewilderment, aggression and dissatisfaction. It is really quite obvious that neither a Christian nor a Muslim nor an adherent of any other religion is stamped by his or her religion alone. A series of other factors have their effect: these include predominantly cultural features; political and ideological views; basic historical and traditional values; ethnic and confessional characteristics; regional customs and usages, myths, popular belief and superstition, language and art; economic, social and legal conditions, philosophical schools; literature and poetry, etc. So it is these and other spiritual trends which in addition to the specifically religious norms, instructions and paradigms influence or determine action and being either positively or negatively. Whatever a Muslim or a Christian does here or elsewhere can never, ever, be apostrophized as Christian or Muslim.

The Christian-Muslim dialogue poses one particular set of problems on an academic and especially a theological level. In their *present* form and status the phenomenology of religion and comparative religion are a specifically Western achievement, and the scientific vocabulary developed to this end is not value-neutral. The necessary concepts, propositions and arguments have been derived predominantly from Christian theology and Western spiritual life or have been orientated on new forms of it.

The non-Christian religions and theologies have also been evaluated according to these criteria and still are, as though Christian and Islamic religious phenomena or the other religious were simply transferrable. This is where the main problem lies. The dialogue really needs to begin here. Unless that is done, those involved fail to hear what is being said to one another. In fact Christianity and Islam have two different models of faith, each of which has its own significant claim. It is impossible here to analyse these models and to demonstrate the meaning and inner logic of each of the two closed systems of faith. For this problem I refer to my brief article 'Are Christians and Muslims really listening to each other?'[1] Here I shall simply quote some conclusions:

The firm conviction that the revealed guidance corresponds as a light to that 'orientation on God' which God has given on their way to human beings, as the only vehicles of the divine Spirit, by their justly created nature (*fitra*), is of decisive significance for the Islamic system of faith; here is a consistent correspondence between creation and revelation. So guidance is not something which is forced on human beings from outside. Rather, within the framework of the divine mercy it is a necessity without which human beings will not be in a position to attain the highest goal, the presence of God; indeed (as becomes clear through the act of creation) parallel to their closest link with the divine, human beings are exposed to their innate tendency and to external deviations.

Guidance as God's mercy, or God's mercy in the form of guidance are the heart of the Islamic system of religion and belief, just as love, redemption and salvation are the heart of the Christian religion. Neither of these can be transferred to the other. Fundamental differences mean that (quite apart from the completely different christology of Islam and Christianity, which can never be bridged) other, even central, concepts like scripture, faith, religion, prophet, emissary take on a different meaning. Whereas, for example, scripture in Christian theology largely loses its significance in the shadow of Jesus, in Islam as the expression of the revelation of guidance for all human beings, accompanied by mercy, it represents the possibility of being addressed directly by God and thus of experiencing God consciously anew (i.e in addition to the connection with God offered to one).

As a consequence of this, scripture must be infallible and unassailable; otherwise it is unworthy of belief and fails to fulfil its purpose. The same is true in Islam of the bringers of guidance (the emissaries and prophets). Whereas in the framework of compelling faith in redemption these are, or must be, in need of redemption and carry the burden of sin, the Qur'an is resolutely opposed to such accusations. This fundamental rejection of the biblical accounts of prophecy on the part of the Qur'an should give a historian freed from the pressure of apologetics occasion to revise the ill-considered thesis that the Qur'an is written off by the Bible.

The Qur'an repeatedly confirms its connection with the Torah and the Gospel, but only through revelation. The historian or anyone who goes by concrete facts must, however, cope with the following question.

What is the origin of these fundamental and in no way fortuitous modifications of the biblical texts which fit consistently only into the Islamic structure of faith and completely contradict the biblical accounts, though the system of faith presented by Christian theology cannot continue to exist without these accounts? The Qur'an is more consistent in its conviction that it is only the 'orientation on God' which, as the content of the revealed guidance which the Qur'an calls 'Islam', can always and everywhere connect all human beings with their God – in other words a conviction to which Christian theology cannot assent without doing away with itself.[2]

Islamic theology has developed no vocabulary for a scientific assessment of other religions. It starts from its traditional terminology and its traditional understanding of Judaism and Christianity. But its criterion is absolute Islamic monotheism, and everything else is centred on this. Islamic theologians are seldom aware of the otherness of Christian theology, which to the present day has spread its wings into all the humanities. There is a failure to recognize the spiritual power of Christian theology, its scope, its active involvement and massive participation in the problems which the secular world has produced with an inexorable dynamic in a short space of time. Not only with a view to a fruitful dialogue but also in its own interest, Islamic theology will make a great gain and enter a new scientific phase if it familiarizes itself with Christian theology, even if only out of a purely academic interest. If this had happened, both Islamic and Chrisitan theologians would long since have discovered that they move within two different systems of faith and thought and that as a result they speak different languages; they would have recognized that this has also affected phenomena which – as I have indicated above – should long since have been accepted as being common to both.

3. An evaluation of 'Christianity and Islam'

Critics have repeatedly denied that Hans Küng's great work *Christianity and the World Religions* is a dialogue because there is no conversation in it with those who regard themselves as representatives of the particular religions. However, in my view, at least as far as Islam is concerned, this attempt has an attraction of its own: Islam – seen from outside – is presented in the categories of Western thought and there are reflections on it from the perspective of Christian theology. Despite all the resentment that Muslims may nurse at such an attempt, the achievement and significance of the work remains undisputed.

Against the background of a history of Western culture and theology stamped with the image of Islam as an enemy, the presentation of Islam by Josef van Ess, and Hans Küng's reflection on it, aim at a revision of the negative view of Islam which is so firmly rooted in the West. That can clearly be seen from the beginning of the presentation and the reflection on it. The following brief quotations may serve as evidence for this.

Van Ess introduces the account of Islam with a pragmatic reference: 'Interest in Islam goes back a long way, but it has not been supported by reliable information. What one can hear or read in the media about Islam, and what intellectuals generally say about it, is alarming. Alarming in a twofold sense: first, because of the biases and prejudices that these judgments betray, and secondly because of the demonizing accent in which they are presented.

No one is afraid of Buddhism or Hinduism, but anxiety is the normal attitude towards Islam. And this has not just been the case since the oil crisis and the Islamic Revolution; even in the Middle Ages and the early modern period, broad public interest in Islam flourished most when there was something to fear ...'[3]

Hans Küng's reflection ends in the recognition: 'Ultimately, in both Islam and Christianity there is a decision of faith for which one has to render a reasonable account to oneself and others. As a Christian, here I can be convinced that if I have chosen this Jesus as the Christ for my life and death, then along with him I have chosen his follower Muhammad, in so far as he appeals to one and the same God and to Jesus.'[4]

This is an honest and model example of a pioneer on the way to understanding among the nations through the reconciliation of their religions. That makes all the more regrettable remarks which give rise to misunderstanding, like this one: 'But let us admit that Islam continues to remain for us primarily alien, politically and economically more threatening than Hinduism or Buddhism, and at any rate a phenomenon which we find it difficult to understand.'[5]

How can a Hindu, a Buddhist, or in particular a Muslim dialogue partner carry on a serious dialogue when they know from the beginning that in the eyes of the Christian participant they are seen as 'threatening' or even very threatening? For what reason is the dialogue now being carried on? To diminish the threat? Is that an aim of the dialogue? And who is threatened and for what reasons? In this way, will not any basis for a dialogue on an equal footing be ruled out right from the start?

Similarly, the following remarks lead to misunderstanding and incomprehension: 'This Islamic restoration, known as "revolutionary popular Islam" (also akin to the Sunnite Muslim brotherhood) is actualizing the Qur'an's social critique ("justice") and threatening, very much more effectively than Marxism, to become the instrument of protest for the impoverished, oppressed masses from Pakistan to Morocco.'[6]

Here too the question arises as to where the threat emanates from and who is threatened. Does the danger emanate from the social criticism of the Qur'an, in other words from the Qur'anic ideal of justice? Or from the 'impoverished, oppressed masses' of the Muslims? For whom is the danger? For the oppressors? Or for a 'just' system of order? Does not the danger emanate neither from the Qura'nic ideal of justice nor from the oppressed masses but from the misuse and instrumentalization of an Islamic ideal in favour of an illegitimate policy?

We know – at least I am convinced of this – that the God of the Torah is the God of those who have been deprived of their rights and that the God of the Gospel is the God of the poor and oppressed, and that Moses and Jesus were to be found on the side of the oppressed and not on the side of the oppressors.

Rather, it is disjunctions related to the cultural situation of the Islamic countries which provoke most misunderstandings and displeasure.

The development going on in the various Islamic countries seems to be ending up in an either-or situation:

Either the attempt is made to emerge from pre-industrial culture through industrialization. But in that case scientific-technological culture has to be taken over willy-nilly. And the longer this appropriation goes on, the more a simple recourse to the Qur'an and Sunna or *shari'a* ceases to be enough to solve the complex problems of an industrial society ...

Or else the Islamic states try ... to block the further advance of Western scientific and technological culture. This is the great refusal – but in practice it is not carried out consistently. A standstill in the field of industrial and technological development would of course be tantamount to making the structural asymmetry of the gap between North and South a permanent feature and pre-programming the North-South conflict. But that means that the Third World would never, even in the longest term imaginable, enjoy equal rights with the industrialized countries. What do we do in this dilemma?[7]

This religious pointing of cultural phenomena disqualifies the dialogue partner.

Unavoidable though these disjunctions seem to be as laying the foundations for the subsequent outline of 'the third way: religion in secular society', they fail in their aim of describing the reality of the Islamic world. At any rate, the very differentiated attitudes of Muslims in the Islamic countries to the West as a complex power factor in respect of science and technology, in economics and politics, and in the military sphere – especially against the background of colonial experiences (which continue to make a clear impact at least among the people concerned) – cannot be pressed into a simple scheme.

Perhaps we can spare ourselves a long discussion by citing at this point the attitude of a country which Hans Küng always cites explicitly as a prototypical example of an anti-Western attitude: post-revolutionary Iran. According to the 'Constitution of the Islamic Republic of Iran',[8] the factors which further the Islamic Republic include: '(*a*) the use of science, technology and progress in human experiences and a concern to develop them further; (*b*) rejection of any suppression and subjection, any domination and slavery'.[9]

These two points are expanded by the postulate 'to secure independence in the areas of science, technology, agriculture, military affairs and the like'.[10]

Point (*a*) postulates precisely the framework which Hans Küng proposes as a third way, in other words not, say, a hopeless and anachronistic battle against science, technology, industry and progress. Unfortunately, no notice is taken in this Christian dialgoue with Islam of point (*b*) and the supplementary statement. Here it should be pointed out emphatically that it is not Islam as a religion which represents an anti-Western factor. It is (and this remains the case even today) rather the resistance deeply rooted in the psyche of each individual to 'oppression', 'subjection' and 'slavery' which moved the Reformers (both Sunni and Shi'ite) to achieve liberation from oppression by means of the revival of the universal values of Islam. These values are similarly directed against the 'pseudo-values of permissive Western culture'[11] which Küng himself describes as inappropriate both for Islam and for Christianity.

In the same way, the Qur'an, the Sunna and the brilliant period of Islamic history are used to propagate the move to science and technology as a religious duty of Islam. There are clear instances of this in the writings and lectures of significant Shi'ite reformers like Sayyid Gamladdin, known as al-Afghani (the revolutionary movement in Iran believes that it is implementing his ideas, among others), and in those of the Sunni reformers like Sheikh Muhammad 'Abduh. So we do not need to wait – as Hans Küng expects – for the 'effects of the many Islamic students who have studied in the West'. Quite apart from this, a development took place as early as the second half of the nineteenth century which *per se* and without including any ecumenical aim created the basis for 'a new ecumenical paradigm of secularity viewed against a religious background'[12] for which Küng pleads as a 'third way' between 'either' and 'or'. It is here that the 'common challenge for both Christian and Islamic theology'[13] lies.

This conclusion is not based on hearsay, nor in stating it am I relying on this author or that. Rather, it is the essence of my personal experience in intensive encounter with both cultures. After training in all branches of the Islamic sciences (of both the Shi'ite and Sunni trends) I derived my motivation to come to Germany in the winter semester of 1954/55 from it; similarly, it is for this reason that I have been intensively preoccupied with the Western humanities. Prompted by the same motivation and aim, shortly after my arrival I began to seek ecumenical dialogue: against this background I think that I can claim that I can evaluate Hans Küng's concern for dialogue more intensively than many others.

If one considers Küng's work against the cultural and historical background of the 'usual' Western understanding of Islam, beyond question it contributes to tearing down walls of misunderstanding and ignorance. It has contributed towards smoothing the way on which Christians and Muslims can meet each other for honest dialogue. That this dialogue also challenges us to criticize erroneous interpretations by our partners and to remove some prejudices and false judgments is a duty which is also grounded in the influence of Hans Küng and, as he would want, furthers understanding between Christianity and Islam on the basis of equal rights and the recognition of each side's self-understanding. It is along the lines of this enlightening criticism that – I am firmly convinced – even more intensive exchange and many more intensive *direct* conversations will be necessary and possible.

Notes

1. In 'Gemeinsam vor Gott. Religionen im Gespräch', *Jahrbuch für Interreligiöse Begegnungen* I, 1990/91, 128–34.
2. Ibid., 133f.
3. H.Küng et al., *Christianity and the World Religions*, 5 [the translation of the published text has been changed in places to avoid abrupt changes of style].
4. Ibid., 129.
5. Ibid., 19.
6. Ibid., 51.
7. Ibid., 53f.
8. A German translation was produced by the Embassy of the Islamic Republic of Iran, Bonn 1980; no such English translation seems to be available.
9. Ibid., 24.
10. Ibid., 26.
11. Küng et al., *Christianity and the World Religions*, 56.
12. Ibid.
13. Ibid., 57.

VII Effects

John Bowden

Dialogue between the Religions?
Questions from Great Britain

On the occasion of Hans Küng's sixty-fifth birthday this article offers a
discussion of part of the foundation of his programme 'The Religious
Situation of Our Time' from a British perspective. Since, for reasons which
will emerge, this perspective will inevitably be a personal one, I should begin
by saying that I am an Anglican priest and theologian and a professional
publisher and translator, living my life in an area where theology and the
churches communicate with a wider audience in a tangible and quantifiable
way. As a result of this experience my approach will at times lead beyond some
of the customary parameters of theological discussion. However, that in itself
would seem to be in keeping with the steadily widening appeal of Hans Küng's
work.

The *New Dictionary of Christian Theology*, published by a conservative-
evangelical press in England in 1988, contains a major article on Hans Küng.
'In general,' it tells its readers, 'Küng's theological approach results in an
ecumenical, rather than specifically Roman Catholic, theology.' It cites as
'twin principles' in his theology 'the normative priority of the historical Jesus
and the NT gospel over all subsequent developments of the tradition, and the
need to be open to the critical rationality and liberal attitudes of the modern
world', and concludes: 'Küng's radical, often polemical and provocative,
application of these principles makes him virtually a Protestant in conservative
eyes.'[1]

Here, if it were needed, is clear evidence that Hans Küng's self-confessed
concern to engage in 'critical, ecumenical theology' is acknowledged and
understood by the most demanding of audiences, and I can confirm that the
readership of his books in Great Britain is catholic in the widest of senses.
That was beginning to be the case during the 1970s; now, particularly after his
Global Responsibility and the programme which it heralds, there is a sense that
Hans Küng belongs to the world, to all of us, including those of other faiths.

So it can safely be said that Hans Küng is himself fulfilling many of the
criteria he laid down for the doing of theology today: lucidity for non-
believers; uncompromising efforts to reach the truth; fair, objective discussion; priority for the complex problems of today; language intelligible to
today's men and women.[2]

Hans Küng is being read and welcomed in Britain, but how is he being understood? That is a more difficult question to answer. The reception of theology in Britain is a complex matter, and those from abroad who judge theological understanding from what appears on the printed page often have a surprise when they encounter the more informal, often oral dialogue through which theological issues are discussed there. As Adrian Hastings pointed out in his *History of English Christianity*,[3] Christianity in England relies greatly on foreign theologians. However, his summary picture of the current situation shows how difficult it is to assess their impact.

> Not so much creative theology has been produced in Britain in these years. Attempts to dialogue with a decaying Marxism can still be intellectually demanding but have become culturally out of date and of quickly diminishing practical value; attempts to incorporate liberation theology may be socially appropriate but are often intellectually too simple; attempts to construct a convincing theology through the medium of story-telling or an explanation of contextualization and the relationship between gospel and culture are seldom sufficiently pressed to be quite satisfying either historically or theologically. None of this should be surprising. Society and the academic world as a whole have never enjoyed less of a sense of a shared convincing faith, ideology or philosophy. There is a great sense of suspended judgment about ultimates, including both the future and the meaning of the past. Theology could hardly be unaffected.[4]

There is theological concern, and deep questions are being asked, but because of the prevailing uncertainty they are often not framed coherently enough to become substantial articles, let alone books. Instead of writing, people think, talk and read. And that is important enough.

Since Hans Küng's writings range so widely, in a short space one can focus on one particular aspect for discussion. So I have chosen to consider his famous programme: 'No peace among the nations without peace among the religions. No peace among the religions without dialogue between the religions. No dialogue between the religions without investigation of the foundations of the religions.'[5] And because it is quite impossible to provide a well-documented account of an understanding of these theses as there is not the material available, I propose to indicate a likely British reaction by asking three questions which are also comments, illustrating them from evidence which is to hand. Finally, on this basis I shall put two further questions as part of a personal dialogue with Hans Küng.

So first: Who dialogues? What is the substance of the dialogue? How do we carry on the dialogue?

(a) Who dialogues?

The profile of British theology may not be high internationally, but Britain itself is an important country for theology, as for so many other aspects of Western culture, standing as it does between American culture on the one hand and European culture on the other, and often torn between the two. Moreover in the aftermath of its colonial empire it has cultural and therefore theological links with much of the rest of the world, particularly English-speaking Africa, Australasia and the Far East. So a British theological publisher acts so to speak as an import-export agent, a delicatessen. Britain is not cut off from what is going on around the world.

How far there is a concern to assimilate and think about what is available is, however, another matter. Interest is limited. To keep to publishing as an illustration, a serious theological publishing house cannot aspire to be a supermarket: the numbers of its customers are just not great enough. And that applies to any form of theological or inter-faith dialogue. The churches are declining and divided; the place of theology in British universities is becoming increasingly tenuous; the number of theological seminaries is small; there are only a handful of significant religious newspapers and journals; the interest of a wider audience has to be fought for, and even when it is gained, the level of knowledge in it is abysmally low. Despite its history and its established Church of England, Britain is now a very secular, pluralist country – perhaps even more so than statistics indicate. That may also indicate what will happen in other Western countries over the next decades. If it does, then the picture which follows is of much wider significance.

The most recent survey available of religious practice is for the whole of the United Kingdom (England, Wales, Scotland, Northern Ireland) and was carried out by Marc Europe in 1990.[6] Out of a total population of 57 million, church membership is now 6.8 million – 15% of the adult population. However, this proportion varies widely between the regions, from 11.4% in England, through 32.7% in Scotland, to 76.9% in Northern Ireland. Since 1980 church membership has declined by 10%. Despite their prominent public positions, neither the established Church of England nor the established Church of Scotland are the largest churches; that position is held by the Roman Catholic Church by a small majority. In fact the major churches have very similar memberships: there are 1.94 million Roman Catholics, 1.84 million Anglicans, and 1.8 million members of the older free churches (from the Methodist and Presbyterian traditions). In the last decade these churches have all experienced declines greater than the average, the Roman Catholics of 17% and the Anglicans of 15%. Their losses are offset by gains in the newer free churches, the Pentecostalists and Gospel churches, whose membership of nearly 1 million represents an increase of 67%, and the 'non-trinitarian churches', from Jehovah's Witnesses to scientologists, whose membership of 459,000 is an increase of 16%. The number of members of other faiths, at 1.85 million, is similar to that of the main churches; of this total about half are Muslim; Jews number just over 100,000.

Here is a complex group of believers who in all, Christian and non-Christian, amount to just over 15% of a predominantly secular population. And they prove even more complex when one moves behind the figures to reflect on what we know of the make-up of the groups. The effect of immigration is one important factor, which partly explains the vast rise in the membership of the 'new churches' and in the proportion of those of non-Christian faiths; it also goes some way towards explaining the numerical superiority of the Roman Catholic Church, whose numbers have been swelled by people coming to live in Britain from the Republic of Ireland or the Mediterranean countries, though the increased appeal of post-Vatican II Catholicism among the middle classes must not be ignored. At any rate, the contrast between immigrant working-class Catholics and new middle-class Catholics was sufficient to prompt the writing of a book on *The Two Catholic Churches*.[7] And one could also argue that in its decline the Church of England is splitting ever more clearly into two Anglican churches, one merging in with the evangelical movement in the free churches and the other closing ranks to preserve 'catholic' patterns, above all a male priesthood, with the less doctrinaire centre, concerned more to face the issues of the modern world, apparently almost ecclesiastically helpless in the face of dogged politicking.

Of all these, who dialogues? Two things stand out from this complex picture of many conflicting faiths in a secular society. First, for one reason or another many groups are just not prepared to engage in dialogue on matters of faith, and in fact cultivate a solidarity among their own ranks so fulfilling that there is thought to be no need for dialogue – only persuasion. This trait is particularly evident among those religious groups whose membership is increasing. Secondly, because this comparatively limited religious practice is set in a very secular society, those believers both aware of the issues posed by that society and prepared to engage in dialogue are so aware of their precarious position that they find it very difficult to achieve that quality to which Hans Küng attaches such importance and which he calls 'steadfastness'.[8] They would feel much more able to appropriate for themselves two of the headings from Dietrich Bonhoeffer's 1943 New Year's reckoning, taking stock of the previous decade: 'No ground under our feet', 'Who stands fast?'[9] Hans Küng seems to have an enviable firmness of conviction, a sense of belonging in a tradition, which is not easy to find in Britain, as is indicated by Adrian Hastings' remarks above. This is because what seems most evident to sensitive believers or 'half-believers' in Britain is the disintegration of the Christian tradition around them, as it either dissolves into the secular world or becomes distorted into new forms claiming to perpetuate a particular Christianity which in fact never was.[10]

Something more of the predicament of these would-be dialoguers will emerge if we move on to the second question.

(b) What is the substance of the dialogue?

British theological activity is, as I have said, difficult to chart. However, one thing is clear. Since the Second World War British theologians have been best at asking questions, rather than providing answers or constructing systems. It was Britain, not the United States, with its much greater theological activity, which sparked off the two major theological discussions of recent times. Bishop John Robinson's *Honest to God*, published in 1963,[11] rapidly sold well over one million copies worldwide (including more than 100,000 in Germany) and was translated into eighteen languages. *The Myth of God Incarnate*, a major questioning of the doctrine of the Incarnation by seven scholars led by John Hick,[12] in 1977 became the subject of a debate that extended to all the national newspapers and in the United States caused trouble for the American church publisher.

Perhaps the most distinctive feature of British theology in this questioning approach has been its extensive use of historical criticism, often beyond limits which theologians on the European continent have found acceptable. This was particularly evident in World Council of Churches discussions, in the 1960s and 1970s, when British biblical scholars found it hard to get a hearing for their views because their approach seemed to break 'the rules' of the debate.[13]

Examples of this radical questioning are not difficult to find. James Barr, then professor in Edinburgh, in his *The Semantics of Biblical Language*[14] launched a devastating attack on attempts to construct a 'biblical theology', particularly by offering biblical 'concepts'. Dennis Nineham, professor in Oxford, in his *The Use and Abuse of the Bible* introduced into discussions of biblical authority the spectre of 'cultural relativism', that problem which at the beginning of this century so haunted Ernst Troeltsch and is still a major issue today, and in a series of publications radically questioned how much we can in fact know of the historical Jesus.[15] C. F. Evans, professor in London, in *Is 'Holy Scripture' Christian?*[16] went so far as to question the status of the biblical canon. Professor Evans' questions give a good indication of the flavour of this British approach:

Is it, after all, obvious that the Christian church was meant to have a holy scripture in the sense of the Old Testament, which it succeeded in demoting but which it fatally took as a model? It should be granted that the written text is strong precisely where tradition is weak, and that as a fixed text it is less prone to corruption and more capable of acting as a purge, but these need be no more than debating points, as good in their way as the debating points from the other side, that it is the church which decided the canon and that scripture does not interpret itself. Is it necessary for them to be blown up into a doctrine of holy authoritative scripture? It is to be granted also that such a scripture has effected reform in the church, notably at the Reformation, though not without grave distortion, for the Reformation was nowhere more disastrous than in its belief that it had achieved a fixed doctrine of the position of scripture in the church. Is it to be assumed automatically that what scripture has done before it will necessarily do again, and that in its make-up it is fitted for this? Has not reform in our own time come from other sources, and included not only reform by the word of God but reform of the word of God?'[17]

Nor has such questioning stopped at the Bible. 'Doctrinal criticism' is an approach pioneered by George Woods, professor in London and taken further by Maurice Wiles, professor at Oxford, which has extended the approach of biblical criticism to the whole field of doctrine, to show, often with devastating results, the degree to which the formation of doctrine was historically conditioned. This approach was worked out most fully in Maurice Wiles, *The Making of Christian Doctrine*,[18] and it was the focussing of his approach on the doctrine of the Incarnation which produced the most explosive parts of *The Myth of God Incarnate*, mentioned above. Of course this approach has major consequences for any understanding of the doctrine of the Trinity, and these were brought out by James Mackey, professor in Edinburgh, in his *The Christian Experience of God as Trinity*.[19]

These critical studies have both reflected, and furthered, a widespread questioning among Christians in Britain which has been going on since the 1960s. The failure of German (and indeed American) theologians to take note of them has to be regarded as an unfortunate sign of a characteristic which is all too often associated, sometimes but not always with justification, with British thought, namely insularity. For here, whether they have been listened to and considered or not, radical and substantive questions have been asked which go to the very heart of Christianity, questions about the authority and truth of the Bible and Christian doctrine. These questions are certainly part of an 'investigation of the foundation of the religions', and they have been asked by scholars who for the most part are practising Christians, involved in the life of the churches and also, not least through their positions in the collegiate life of secular universities, in dialogue with the world. Once they have been asked, they cannot be un-asked, and if they are obviously ignored by a Christian tradition or church or theologian, there is a suspicion that this reluctance to respond to them is part of an approach which still has an element of ideology about it.[20]

Does the Bible still have a special, unique status? Are the doctrines of Incarnation and Trinity still viable? These are the issues here, raised by theologians who are not deliberately trying to undermine Christian belief, but taking further a line of questioning demanded of them simply by their role and context in a particular modern society. Where can Christian thinkers find 'steadfastness' if not only the context out of which they speak but also the spiritual, theological and intellectual tradition on which they reflect is becoming more and more fragmented? What if it increasingly looks as if that hope, still cherished in many quarters, that despite modern questioning the Christian tradition can still be rescued in its present form, is an illusory one? And there is yet a further problem.

(c) How do we carry on the dialogue?

'Dialogue' is a good, positive, comfortable word, and its use has become increasingly popular. But what is dialogue, and how is it carried on?

In practice, dialogue can be carried on between a group of people meeting together for a shorter or longer period of time, whether in their own personal capacity or as the representatives of an official body; it can be a collection of published papers with a more or less clear focus; it can be the overall impression given by a number of books from different perspectives on a specific topic; or it can be, quite generally, the sum total of a number of communications in different media and at different levels relating to a particular issue in a national, continental or even global context. Jewish-Christian or Christian-Muslim dialogue can be any of these things.

However, dialogue is not carried out by disembodied spirits, and for it to take place at all, people have to get together, papers have to be circulated, meetings have to be organized, books have to be published, space on radio and television has to be found, and so on. All this takes a great deal of effort, especially in a society when more and more people are becoming 'privatized', and consumption and spectatorship have widely taken the place of personal involvement. And it all costs money. Dialogue has an economic dimension. Who pays?

Dialogue at the local level, where those involved are active in their own personal capacity, poses few economic problems. But economic problems arise as soon as dialogue involves representation, the payment of expenses for travel, the expenditure of time. Who gets chosen? Who has the time to go? Who makes the choice? And are those chosen truly representative of those whom they are meant to represent? One has only to read the proceedings of any session of the General Synod of the Church of England to see the problems with which that church has burdened itself by opting for a parliamentarian style of government which of necessity excludes from its delegates most of those most typical of church membership and attracts the leisured and those with the financial means to participate.

As economic resources become scarcer, opportunities for personal meeting on a wide scale become fewer because of the cost of travel and accommodation, and communication through the various media becomes increasingly important. But here again there are difficulties. Opportunities for carrying on dialogue through the printed word are also shrinking. What is happening in Britain can again serve as an example of what may well become a worldwide problem.

For almost two centuries, many of the activities of the institutional churches and other movements have been supplemented and counterbalanced by a complex of organizations existing alongside, and as a supplement to, the churches. From the eighteenth century onwards in Britain, the foundations were laid for educational institutions and societies to 'promote Christian knowledge', 'to propagate the gospel', to engage in work at home and abroad in an effort to present Christian life and thought to the modern world. Some of these bodies were very partisan, but many were not, and the wide range of them guaranteed a certain number of checks and balances. Here was a broad context for dialogue. But these organizations are now in decline and most of the longer-standing ones are disappearing, to be replaced, if at all, by much narrower and more militant groups. And with them goes a wide network of journals, newspapers, newsletters and so on.

Furthermore, during the nineteenth century, great publishing houses believed that publishing religious books was part of the social commitment which went with their activity, so a substantial part of publishing output generally was devoted to books in this area, which were not hived off into a 'ghetto' of their own. However, changes in society, coupled with a wave of take-overs in publishing have severely reduced the scope for publishing theology. In these conditions there is a danger that theological publishing may be dominated on the one hand by commercial houses prepared to go on publishing only if it brings in a satisfactory financial return (with the danger of commercialism) and on the other by the publishing arms of religious organizations who subsidize their publishing programme (with the danger that much of this becomes one-sided propaganda).

Finally, in the past, when Christian traditions and Christian values were still so widely known, the national press and the radio could provide competent and responsible coverage of religious and theological issues. Now, however, not only do such issues have to compete for space along with other topics, but knowledge of the background to them is so limited that few journalists are capable of presenting them capably. The result is that everything tends to be reduced to 'the personality' and substantive issues are left out of account.

All this is hardly a promising background for the practice of dialogue.

Against such a pessimistic view it could be argued, rightly, that there has been an undoubted rise of interest in the nature and history of religious belief in our secular world, as witnessed by radio and television programmes, books from a variety of general publishing houses, and courses in many universities, and this might well be seen as a more positive parallel to Hans Küng's 'investigation of the foundations of the religions', 'fair, objective discussion', 'in language intelligible to today's men and women'. But there is a price to be paid. Here we must note the now established division that has grown up (in both Britain and America) between 'theology', the rational reflection by those of a particular faith on their beliefs, and 'religious studies', the almost scientific approach to a faith-community from outside, interest in it from the perspective of believing from within.[21] From the perspective of religious studies, 'believing' can seem virtually to amount to adopting an ideology (i.e. that particular set of ideas and practices which a group accepts to hold it together and give it cohesion), and once this assumption gains ground it need not be long before all groups of religious believers, Christians included, are regarded as groupings apart from 'the world', opting by choice for their own conventions of behaviour and beliefs. Each of these systems of behaviour and belief is seen as valid for a particular religious group in its own right but relative to other belief systems (the Christian community is active in one way, the Jewish in another).

Once this kind of relativity is accepted, the quest for meaning, for making sense of one world under one God, the search for truth, is in effect abandoned. Christian belief, in particular, suffers the severance of the links with the wider world which it has had from the start and is banished to its ghetto. And if that happens, the odds against the survival of a form of Christian belief which carries on the breadth, intellectual commitment and generosity of the best of past tradition are high.

So once again, in the face of the practical difficulties of dialogue, 'steadfast-ness' comes under threat. It can be had, but the price is excessively high. When old structures of communication are crumbling or ceasing to be economically viable, and there is so much pressure on those who still hold religious beliefs to interpret themselves in a new perspective, the very process of dialogue becomes questionable. Who is to initiate it, where are partners to be found, and what form is it to take?

(d) Conclusion

This set of three questions has not been intended to dispute the fundamental rightness and importance of Hans Küng's programme in 'The Religious Situation of our Time'. Its purpose has been, rather, to ask whether his three statements are not, viewed from a perspective like the British perspective, too simplistic. I end by focussing my comments in two further questions, this time addressed to Hans Küng himself:

1. Does the programme of 'The Religious Situation of Our Time' pay

sufficient attention to the *disintegration* of the Christian tradition in the modern world? Does it consider the possibility, so vividly exemplified in the British theology I have cited, that 'investigation of the foundations of the religions', particularly when carried out on the basis of modern historical criticism, might contribute further to that disintegration?

2. Do we not need more than just dialogue *between the religions*? And is steadfastness in one's own tradition the only possible stance? Indeed for many, is it a possible stance at all? Might it not be that more emphasis should be placed on dialogue between the religions and the secular world, and might not the secular world have much to offer as well as to gain? Some of those who find it difficult to maintain a Christian stance in a society like modern Britain attach a great deal of importance to the footholds offered by that secular humanism (in the widest sense) represented by historical criticism, and in the wider world by statements like the United Nations Universal Declaration of Human Rights. This tradition has done much to clarify priorities for religious belief in the past and may well do so in the future. If God acts anywhere in history, might God not be acting above all here?

Notes

1. *New Dictionary of Christian Theology*, edited by Sinclair B. Ferguson and David F. Wright, Leicester and Downers Grove, Ill. 1988, 373f.
2. See Hans Küng, *Theology for the Third Milennium*, 204f.
3. Adrian Hastings, *A History of English Christianity 1920–1985*, London and New York 1986, 663.
4. Adrian Hastings, *A History of English Christianity 1920–1990* (second edition), London and Philadelphia 1991, xxvi-xxvii (this passage was not in the first edition).
5. Hans Küng, *Judaism*, ii.
6. *Marc Europe UK Christian Handbook 1992–3*, London 1992, 26–30, 205–65.
7. Antony Archer, *The Two Catholic Churches*, London 1986.
8. See Hans Küng, *Global Responsibility*, 94f.
9. Dietrich Bonhoeffer, *Letters and Papers from Prison*, London and New York 1971, 3, 4.
10. I wonder whether Hans Küng has considered the notion of the 'pseudo-paradigm', something which looks as though it might be a continuation of a paradigm from the past, but which is in fact a modern construction made for ideological purposes? Much Christian 'fundamentalism' would seem to fall into this category.
11. John A.T. Robinson, *Honest to God*, London and Philadelphia 1963.
12. John Hick (ed.), *The Myth of God Incarnate*, London and Philadelphia 1977.
13. Because this point is an important one, I quote here at length the comments of one of those involved.

    'As the work went on, I became increasingly aware of certain assumptions on the part of many of my colleagues, assumptions which were important because they largely accounted for the zest and sense of urgency they brought to their exegetical work. They assumed, first of all, that when they had discovered the meaning of a passage, they were dealing with a word of God, part of God's self-disclosure to the situation in which the words were originally written or spoken. But more than that, they at least *started* with the assumption that that word of God would also prove to have a contemporary meaning, and that the exegete's task was not completed till he had discovered what it was. To put the distinction in a rough and ready way, the exegete has not only to answer the question: What it *meant*, but also the question: What it *means*. A lot of this did not seem to me self-evident' (Dennis Nineham, *Explorations in Theology* 1, London 1977, 94).

His discussion goes on for several more pages. *Mutatis mutandis*, I have the same feelings about some contemporary Roman Catholic theology also.

14. James Barr, *The Semantics of Biblical Language*, Oxford 1961 reissued London 1983.
15. Dennis Nineham, *The Use and Abuse of the Bible*, London 1976; see also his *Explorations in Theology* (n. 13 above); *The Gospel of St Mark*, Harmondsworth 1963, and above all 'Epilogue', in *The Myth of God Incarnate* (n. 12 above), 186–204.
16. C.F. Evans, *Is 'Holy Scripture' Christian?*, London 1971.
17. Ibid., 17f.
18. Maurice Wiles, *The Making of Christian Doctrine*, Cambridge 1967; see also *The Remaking of Christian Doctrine*, London 1976; the programme for 'doctrinal criticism' can be found concisely stated in his 'Looking into the Sun', *Working Papers in Doctrine*, London 1976, 148–63.
19. James P. Mackey, *The Christian Experience of God as Trinity*, London 1983.
20. For further discussion of ideology in this connection see my *Jesus – The Unanswered Questions*, London 1988, 18–20.
21. It is worth noting that American university presses are in the main prepared to publish only religious studies, not theology.

Ronald Modras

A Symbol of the Council: Influences in the United States of America

By any empirical measure, the impact of Hans Küng on the church in the United States has been powerful and pervasive – on laity as well as clergy and religious, on Protestant as well as Orthodox and Catholic Christians, on ordinary Sunday church-goers as well as students and academics. With the possible exception of Karl Rahner, no Catholic theologian in this century comes close to exerting his influence. Commanding the attention of Americans on the eve of the Second Vatican Council, he came to embody the ideals of Catholic self-criticism, dialogue, and reform. He generated an excitement able to fill not only lecture halls but convention centres. And when the highest echelons of power in the Catholic church sought to marginalize him and discredit his theology, they only succeeded in making him a symbol of the Council for hundreds of thousands of Catholics throughout the world but certainly in the United States.

It is no little nor enviable thing to become a symbol. If, as I believe, Küng, Paul Tillich and other analysts are correct in assessing ours as a time of transition in the history of the Christian church, it is necessarily an era of collapse and creation, decay and new birth. Pope John Paul II well represents the waning years of the second millennium of Western Christianity and all that Pope Gregory VII and his eleventh-century reform symbolizes: Roman centralism, imposed clerical celibacy, and claims to unlimited papal authority that ultimately led to schism. No one today better than Küng represents the countervailing forces threatening those Gregorian claims and structures. Nor does anyone better represent the willingness to confront the challenges already impinging on Christianity from its third millennium.

A symbol for the council

Although German-reading theologians already knew from his 1957 book, *Justification*, that he was someone worth watching, Küng came to widespread American consciousness in 1961, one year after Pope John XXIII announced his intention to convoke an ecumenical council. *The Council, Reform and*

Reunion, the first of Küng's books to be translated into English, appealed to an audience far beyond theologians. It appeared at a critical time for great numbers of American Catholics who were moving out of ethnic ghettos steeped in cultural Catholicism.[1] They required more intellectual substance from their church than their immigrant forebears or working-class parents did. College-educated and successful in their professions and careers, they chafed at being treated as children by their church leaders, whether at the parochial or papal levels. They looked for priests and theologians who took them and their questions seriously. With *The Council, Reform, and Reunion*, they knew they had found one.

For most laity, of course, as for most priests and religious, the one, true Catholic church seemed to be functioning quite adequately, so that the very idea of an ecumenical council came as something of a puzzlement. What would the bishops possibly talk about (a new Marian dogma)? To this group Küng's book came as a shock. Here was a Catholic theologian writing about reform as a word with a substantial Catholic pedigree long prior to Luther. (Yves Congar had done it with a book on church reform ten years before Küng's, but the Vatican had forbidden its translation.)[2] Here was a book endorsed by two Cardinals (König and Lienart) saying that, precisely out of loyalty, Catholics not only may but need to criticize their church. As for what needed reform, the litany included 'Roman centralism – episcopal bureaucracy ... moral theology especially on atom bombs and sex – Latin in the liturgy ... Thomism – rationalism – Marianism – the pilgrimage racket.'[3] Küng had not as yet called for ending mandatory celibacy for priests or the ordination of women, but readers still had reason to wonder at the book's *Imprimatur*.

It was also a critical time for American Catholic theologians. With other American Catholics they too regarded democracy as the future form of all civilized government. They believed that the American experience of church-state relations had something to teach the universal church. But the Vatican's (1899) censure of 'Americanism' (*Testem benevolentiae*) had been a rebuke of some very American ideals: religious liberty, separation of church and state, the compatibility of Catholicism with modernity, and a positive attitude towards Catholic cooperation with other religious bodies. A decade later the anti-modernist encyclical, *Lamentabili* (1907), unleashed a witch-hunt that was especially detrimental to creative theological thinking in the United States.

Only fifty years after *Testem benevolentiae* were the ideals of Americanism championed once again, this time by the Jesuits Gustave Weigel and John Courtney Murray. Weigel broke ground in ecclesiology and ecumenism by his willingness to judge theologians from other Christian traditions in their best light. Murray suffered silencing by the Vatican for writing on separation of church and state and for questioning the neo-scholastic thesis that 'error has no rights'. Murray argued that papal encyclicals criticizing religious liberty had to be read within the context of their origin, in this case with the church's struggle with the French Revolution and the laic laws of France's Third Republic. Murray's critical-historical interpretation of papal encyclicals not only won the day at the Second Vatican Council, but, as David Tracy has pointed out, helped pave the way for a favourable reception of Küng's method and theology by American Catholic theologians.[4]

Küng's books appealed compellingly for Catholic concern and active involvement in the movement for Christian unity. But his books were being read by more than Roman Catholics. American Protestant theologians were just as amazed as Karl Barth was to learn that the Council of Trent was susceptible of an authentic Catholic interpretation compatible with Reformation principles. If the very crux of sixteenth-century polemics required rethinking, what of the other classic areas of controversy? No longer was *catholica non leguntur* axiomatic for Protestant scholars. Even a cursory review of the periodical literature confirms the opinion that, ever since his book on justification, Küng has won a wide and respectful hearing from American Protestants.[5]

The early 1960s were watershed years for US Catholics. They had one of their own in the White House and a pope even atheists loved. Within this climate, early in 1963, the thirty-five-year-old Küng came to the United States for the first of numerous lecture tours. His topic, unprecedented at that time in Catholic circles, focused on the church and freedom. Audiences sat transfixed to hear Küng argue that Scripture was the judge of the church's leaders and that the decisive issue confronting Catholics was the biblical freedom of the children of God. Here was unvarnished Barthian neo-orthodoxy. To borrow a phrase from William Shea, my colleague at Saint Louis University, Küng was 'finding truth in alien texts'.[6] But American Catholics resonated with it because it corresponded to democratic principles Americans tend to cherish with visceral intensity. It was not by chance that Americans felt a greater affinity for this Swiss theologian than for most of his European counterparts. He came from a land with a strong tradition of democracy, where bishops were still elected in some dioceses and relative local autonomy was taken for granted even in the church.[7]

On the eve of Küng's 1963 lecture tour, a furore erupted when it accidentally came to light that he, along with three of the most highly respected theologians in America (Godfrey Diekmann, John Courtney Murray and Gustave Weigel), had been blacklisted from speaking at Catholic University in Washington, DC. The *cause célèbre* implicated not only the university administration but the Apostolic Delegate and aroused even more curiosity about what Küng had to say.[8] The effort by several bishops to prevent Catholics from hearing him in their dioceses only served to make him a symbol of the freedom about which he was lecturing. In recognition of his scholarly achievements, there began a long string of honorary doctorates (Saint Louis University, Pacific School of Religion, Loyola University of Chicago, the University of Michigan), of lectureships and professorships (Stanford, Union Theological Seminary, University of Chicago, University of Michigan).

Changing Catholic perceptions

From the very beginning of his career with his book on justification, Küng employed the historical-critical method in his theology. He was neither the first nor the only one to do so, as a whole generation of Catholic theologians began to profit from the ground-breaking work of Bernard Lonergan and Karl Rahner justifying the historical method. But when Vatican II put an end to the Counter-Reformation and the imposed monopoly of neo-scholasticism over Catholic theology, defensive manuals of an ahistorical Catholic theology were suddenly out of date. It was precisely at this time, in 1967, that the English translation of Küng's *The Church* appeared on the American scene.

Despite the fact Küng's *On Being a Christian* sold more copies, I would contend that *The Church* has thus far been his most influential book, at least in the United States. Almost immediately it became a standard textbook in both Catholic and Protestant seminaries, colleges and universities, and it has remained so for twenty-five years. The book was faulted by a variety of Catholic theologians for being too biblical (G. Baum), too Barthian (R. McBrien). But, *nolens volens*, Küng changed the way even conservative Catholics talk and therefore think about the church, particularly with regard to charisms and ministry.

Yves Congar explicitly credited Küng for the large place the subject of charisms has in the ecclesiology of Vatican II.[9] Küng developed this pneumatological aspect of Pauline theology in *The Church* as the basis for his theology of ministry as something to which all Christians are called. The Index to the 1966 American edition of the *Documents of Vatican II* contained the entry – 'Ministries: see Clergy; Priests; etc.'[10] 'Ministry' had been a Protestant word, rarely used by Catholics. Within fifteen years, the Jesuit sociologist John Coleman could speak of 'ministry' as a pervasive catchphrase among American Catholics, at least among the professionals who practised it and were the mediators of Catholic tradition at the local level.[11] Küng made popular a new ministerial language and vocabulary that helped change American Catholic perceptions. 'Ministry' came to describe an over-arching reality, of which priesthood and even the papacy had been reduced to sub-categories.

'Not a Catholic'?

As with *The Church*, so with his subsequent books on the priesthood, infallibility and christology, Küng was criticized for his theological method. Several American Catholic critics (R. Brown, A. Dulles, H. Egan) faulted him not only for making the New Testament canon the norm for later Christian tradition (*norma normans normata*) but for creating a virtual 'canon within the canon'. Küng was taking as a norm for critically assessing later New Testament developments the earlier traditions of Mark, Q and the proto-Pauline epistles, ultimately Jesus of Nazareth as we can know him from critical-historical research. (It is worth noting that in a recent document the Vatican did the same thing when it distinguished between the Jesus of history and Matthew's Gospel regarding Pharisees.)[12]

It was not Küng's historical-critical method but his radical and consistent use of it that aroused American criticism. The method itself has become virtually universal in American theology, Catholic and Protestant alike. Generally the only scholars who reject it are self-acknowledged fundamentalists. The christology of *On Being a Christian* may have shocked some German bishops, but it did not surprise the professors or students in American seminaries and universities who had already been doing the equivalent of Küng's christology from below for nearly a decade. In the United States of the 1970s, at least, it was not Küng's christology that made him exceptional, but his clarity and persuasiveness. These were also, apparently, the qualities that from a Vatican perspective made him dangerous.

After the devastating blow rendered to papal authority and credibility by Pope Paul VI's birth control encyclical, restoring the prestige of the papacy was manifestly part of the programme of Pope John Paul II. As never before possible, the international media and a genius for gesture were used to cultivate the image of the pope as universal bishop, visiting nations as he once visited parishes. One year into Pope John Paul II's pontificate, Küng wrote a lengthy article, published in the *New York Times* and elsewhere, acknowledging the pope's many virtues but setting forth too some critical questions about his theological and ecclesiastical agenda. Two months later Küng was declared 'no longer' a Catholic theologian, ostensibly for his opinions on infallibility.

In the United States as elsewhere, Küng's interpretation of infallibility – as a perseverance of the church in truth despite the possibility of individual error – was controversial. The issue, however, was not Küng's interpretation of infallibility but his encouragement for a further exploration of the topic by the church and its theologians. In light of Küng's influence, his advocacy of such a theological inquiry could not help but be alarming and intolerable to those in Vatican circles, for it impinged on the very ideology and mystique of the papacy.

If there had been any doubt as to the influence Hans Küng was having in the United States, it was now dispelled. Catholics and Protestants alike voiced anger and dismay. Küng had not been the first theologian since Vatican II to experience censure, nor would he be the last. But for no one else was the ground swell of support so widespread. According to the highly respected Jesuit weekly *America*, the Vatican declaration was 'for any one who loves the church ... a cause of profound sadness'. Its Protestant counterpart, *The Christian Century*, described the censure as 'a sad day for the church and a good day for its enemies'. A group of seventy-five American Catholic theologians declared that they might not always agree with Küng, nor any other scholar for that matter, but they had no doubt: 'Hans Küng is indeed a Catholic theologian.'[13]

Clearly, however, statements were no longer enough. The Vatican action against Küng was but the culmination of a series of restrictive measures in 1979, and it was now obvious that Rome was set upon a course of restoration. During the months of January and February, concerned Catholics all over the United States met to discuss whether and how to organize. In March 1980 a national convention was held in Milwaukee with representatives from ten metropolitan areas. The result was the establishment of the Association for the Rights of Catholics in the Church (ARCC), an organization committed to working for justice and structural change within the Catholic church. Since its inception ARCC has formulated a charter of rights which it has translated and disseminated throughout the United States and abroad. With a series of publications and conferences, ARCC works to keep the issue of human and Christian rights in the forefront of the American Catholic consciousness.

ARCC was a sponsoring agency of the 1989 'Call for Reform in the Catholic Church', initiated by the Chicago Call to Action, another Catholic reformist group representing another Küng success story. 'Call to Action' had been the name of a 1976 conference sponsored by the US bishops to promote justice in both the church and American society. Expecting no follow-up from their archbishop at the time, a group of Chicago Catholics decided to organize independently of church leadership. Their membership had been modest until 1981, when Küng agreed to be the principal speaker at their annual meeting. The Vatican had already declared him no longer a Catholic theologian, but one would not have known it from the 1,800 Chicago Catholics for whom he was obviously not only a spokesperson but a source of strength.

By October 1989, however, discouragement ran high throughout the United States, as the Vatican continued its restorationist course, systematically replacing pastoral bishops with more willing tools of its restrictive policies. Precisely to encourage flagging spirits, Küng was invited to be the keynote speaker at a conference in Washington, DC, on the future of the American church. The twenty-fifth anniversary of Vatican II was approaching, and to mark the event the Chicago Call to Action leadership drafted a

'Call for Reform'. They travelled to Washington to ask Küng for a critique. Instead, he gave it his ringing endorsement and made it the peroration of his address:

- a call for incorporating women into all levels of church ministry and decision-making;
- a call for discarding mandatory celibacy for priests;
- a call for widespread consultation of lay people for developing church teaching on human sexuality;
- a call for democratizing the selection process of bishops;
- a call for open dialogue, due process, and academic freedom in the church.

The audience was electrified. They wanted copies to take home with them for distribution. Priests, religious and laity lined up to sign their names to it, some of them at considerable risk to their church-related jobs. By the time it was published in the *New York Times* (Ash Wednesday 1990), the 'Call to Reform' had 4,500 signatories. As of this writing, the number is nearly twenty-five thousand.

The Catholic mainstream

There are any number and a wide variety of Catholic reformist organizations at work in the United States today. Some, like ARCC and Chicago Call to Action, have been directly influenced by Küng either in their origin or development. In others (Catholics Speak Out, Women's Ordination Conference, Coalition of Concerned Canadian Catholics, Corpus, Federation of Christian Ministries), the influence is more indirect but still quite real, as Küng gives the pre-eminent example of a critical Catholic who refuses to give up or go away. Taking heart from Küng's critical loyalty, reform-minded American Catholics work from within for the kind of Catholic Christianity he represents. The Americans who read Küng and belong to reformist organizations are obviously not garden-variety Catholics. But neither are they marginal. They have an influence far beyond their numbers. A 1992 survey indicates that they represent the views of the majority of US Catholics.[14]

From a perspective of twelve years after the fact, the 1979 attempt to marginalize Küng and his theology can be seen to have achieved only patchy success. Writers looking for an alternative Catholic authority to a present-day position of the official magisterium will often prefer to cite Karl Rahner rather than Küng. There is no doubt, however, that Küng's opinions still carry considerable weight, if not from his authority then from his arguments.[15] The members of the Catholic Theological Society of America and the College Theological Society do not agree with all of Küng's positions any more than they do with anyone else's, but they are certainly more sympathetic to Küng than to his foil at the Vatican's Congregation for the Doctrine of the Faith, Joseph Cardinal Ratzinger.[16] Numbering some two thousand Catholic theologians as members, these associations are obviously mainstream and representative of American Catholic theology. The same cannot be said for the avowedly conservative Fellowship of Christian Scholars, which, while partisan to Cardinal Ratzinger, numbers only some three hundred members, only a handful of whom are practising theologians.

Among the clergy, religious and lay leaders of the American church, the attempt to discredit Küng has been even more of a failure. On the contrary, it made him even more of a symbol of Vatican II by making him a victim of procedures widely regarded as antithetic to the Council. Küng has since been joined by Edward Schillebeeckx, Leonardo Boff, and several Americans, most prominently Archbishop Raymond Hunthausen and the moral theologian Charles Curran. These public censures and similar measures (loyalty oaths, prohibitions of public dissent) may have been intended to silence some troublesome individuals and intimidate others, but they have only served to alienate large segments of American Catholic society.

In 1986 Bishop James Malone, then outgoing president of the National Conference of Catholic Bishops, expressed grave concern at the 'developing estrangement' in the US church from the Holy See over issues like freedom and the perceived return to central control.[17] More recently, Archbishop Rembert Weakland of Milwaukee voiced similar alarm over a 'growing disaffection from Rome'. He perceives throughout the United States a palpable anger and animosity. An indifference to what Rome says is 'very pronounced' not only in academic circles but at 'all cultural levels'.[18] In the time-honoured practice of blaming the victims, some conservatives have tried to fault Küng and other 'dissenters' like him for the present declines being suffered by institutional Catholicism.[19] Empirical evidence indicates, however, that the Vatican has no one to blame but itself.[20] It is not by chance that Catholic donations to the church have declined in the last several years. Not allowed to voice their views any other way in their church, American Catholics are voting with their pocketbooks. What is remarkable is that more do not do so with their feet.

That more Catholics do not join other churches is, in my estimation, thanks to Küng and those like him. Küng, Curran, Schillebeeckx, Boff, and a score of lesser-knowns who remain doggedly Catholic in their allegiance give compelling witness to countless American Catholics that there is still a place for them in the Roman Catholic church. Küng's example of patient and persevering loyalty gives hope and courage that this too shall pass. A future pope may yet realize the grave consequences of the church's ban on artificial contraception (exploding populations, poverty, famine, ecological disasters). The promises offered by the Second Vatican Council (collegiality, church unity, reform) may yet be realized in the church's third millennium. It is with an eye on that third millennium that Küng has set out upon what may well be his most influential as well as ambitious 'project'.

The next hundred years

From the very beginning of his career, Küng has striven for greater understanding, mutual respect and unity among Christians through historical analysis, self-criticism and dialogue. His move from inter-Christian to inter-religious relationships and concerns represents a widening of scope that appeals to a far broader spectrum of Americans than Catholics. His search for an ecumenical theology for peace based on a world ethic speaks to secularist as well as religious Americans, activists as well as academics. It is too early to tell how successful he will be in his application of Thomas Kuhn's paradigm theory to present-day religious systems, particularly Judaism, Christianity, and Islam. His latest enterprise will find an interested and supportive hearing in the United States, however. Virtually every college and university in America, both secular and religious, has courses in world religions. Küng's work on the world religions in our contemporary situation will be sure to find its way into the bibliographies of required reading for the next generation of American students.

For us who are of an earlier generation, it is difficult to believe that Hans Küng is already sixty-five. We who experienced the Second Vatican Council as students still remember him as the *enfant terrible* of the early 1960s who inspired us to concern for Christian unity and taught us to think critically about the Catholic church while still loving it and calling it our own. We have grown, if not old then older together, and he keeps us thinking critically and caring about unity. If he enjoys long life, good health, and continued productivity in his already immensely fruitful career, there is no doubt but that his influence in the United States, as elsewhere, will grow as we all continue to learn both with him and from him.

In the United States on such happy occasions, we invariably sing the traditional but lacklustre Happy Birthday. Very much out of self-interest as well as good will, Küng's many friends and supporters may well find the words of the Polish equivalent more expressive of our sentiments: '*Sto lat niech żyje nam* – may he live for us a hundred years.'

Notes

1. See James J. Hennesey, *American Catholics: A History of the Roman Catholic Community in the United States*, New York and Oxford 1981, 307–31. See also

Ronald Modras, 'Eine Einwanderer Kirche wird erwachsen', *Herder Korrespondenz* 35, 1981, 460–6.

2. Yves Congar, *Vraie et fausse réforme dans l'Église*, Paris 1950.
3. *The Council, Reform, and Reunion*, 158.
4. David Tracy in *Gegenentwürfe: 24 Lebensläufe für eine andere Theologie*, ed. Hermann Häring und Karl-Josef Kuschel, Munich and Zurich 1988, 311–23.
5. John J. Carey, *Theology Today*, 30, 1973, 35.
6. William M. Shea, 'Dual Loyalties in Catholic Theology: Finding Truth in Alien Texts', *Commonweal*, 31 January 1992, 9–14.
7. The significance of Küng's Swiss background is correctly emphasized by Robert Nowell in *Passion for Truth: Hans Küng and His Theology*, London and New York 1981.
8. Leonard Swidler (ed.), *Küng in Conflict*, New York 1981, 5–6.
9. *The Jurist* 32, 1972, 175.
10. Walter Abbott S.J., *The Documents of Vatican II*, New York 1966, 775.
11. John Coleman, S.J., 'The Future of Ministry', *America*, 28 March 1981, 243–9.
12. *Notes on the Correct Way to Present the Jews and Judaism in Preaching and Catechesis of the Roman Catholic Church*, 1985.
13. For a lengthy but only illustrative index of American reaction, see Swidler, *Küng in Conflict* (n. 8), 552–85.
14. A May 1992 Gallup Survey revealed that 81% of US Catholics agree that 'it is possible to be a good Catholic and publicly disagree with Church teaching'. Three-quarters (75%) support expanding the priesthood to include married men, and 63% support the ordination of women (The Gallup Organization, Princeton, NJ 08542).
15. Demonstrative of the seriousness with which Küng's theology is regarded in the USA are the numerous dissertations already written on it: his methodology (C. LaCugna); christology (W. Buggart; J.G. Ramisch); apologetics (W.E. Gordon); criteria for orthodoxy (C.E. Espinoza); and his thinking on authority (J.M. King), infallibility (E.V. Mylonas), priesthood and ministry (T.P. Rausch).
16. To cite just a few leading representative voices: 'Küng is always admirable in the seriousness with which he wrestles with the New Testament' (Raymond Brown, *America* 126, 531). 'In his theological writings, Hans Küng has addressed in great depth and breadth the central questions of Christian belief today' (Charles Curran, Foreword to H. Küng, *Why I Am Still a Christian*, 1986, 11). 'Hans Küngs Theologie in den USA zustimmend aufgenommen wurde' (David Tracy, *Gegenentwürfe*, above n. 4, 311).
17. *Origins* 16, 1986, 396.
18. *National Catholic Reporter*, 29 May 1992, 20, 24.
19. Richard Malone in *New Oxford Review* 56, January 1989, 10.
20. See Andrew M. Greeley, *American Catholics since the Council: An Unauthorized Report*, Chicago 1985.

Evgeni Barabanov

On Being a Christian in the Underground: Russian Experiences

The topic of 'the theology of Hans Küng and Russia' is basically not so much one from the past as one for the future. But that does not mean that it has no past. Quite the contrary. These remarks, too, are primarily about a past event. But they should be understood less as a concluding evaluation than as a task for the future. And if one sets them against the wider horizon of the dialogue between the Christians of Russia and the West, they could be an important corrective to the problem of mutual understanding on which there is still too little reflection.

1. The time before perestroika

Before the time of *perestroika* the name of Hans Küng was mostly mentioned in a negative context. The theologian from Tübingen was a dangerous enemy in the context of incessant state atheistic propaganda and the ideological struggle with 'the remnants of religion'. He was an enemy because he insisted uncompromisingly on the truth of Christianity; he was dangerous because he did this in a talented, enthusiastic, honest way, without avoiding uncomfortable questions. He worked with historical precision and at the same time took into account the present state of scholarship, with great openness to the present difficult situation of church and society.

However, in the same anti-religious literature there was often mention of Küng's sharp, radical criticism of the mediaeval feudal orientation of the Roman Catholic church and its conservative institutions, and even of the doctrine of the 'one true church' and the 'infallibilty of the pope'. Such a criticism was welcomed and indeed often used by anti-religious propagandists for their own ends; here, however, it was regarded as an 'apt example of the general crisis of religion and especially of the Roman Catholic church' in the 'present period when Christianity is dying out'.

The official Russian Orthodox church also tried to ignore Küng's challenge. There were many reasons for this. The state ban on defending Christianity and Christian values allowed the church to avoid uncomfortable questions about its own deviations from the demands of the Christian message and – in contrast to Küng – to limit the significance of this message to the liturgical prayer-life of the faithful. On the other hand, the criticism of the feudalism of the Catholic church could be transferred directly to the Orthodox church, which persisted in Byzantine traditionalism and would not entertain any thoughts of the possibility of an epoch-making change in the church's doctrine, morals and discipline. Finally, Küng's theology also disturbed international church political diplomacy (primarily, of course, governed by state interests). Hypocritically concealed under the make-up of 'ecumenical dialogue' unknown to the simple believer, behind the scenes this diplomacy made common cause with the conservative circles of the Roman Curia.

The church dissidents also avoided Hans Küng's theology. In their battle against the arbitrariness of the princes of the church and their underhanded assent to the oppression of the faithful, and against the dual morality of the church which justified the direct collaboration of the supreme church government with the secret police and the Communist authorities, they relied for the most part on the old canon law of the Byzantine empire, on the dreams of a rebirth of the mediaeval theocracy, on the spiritual models of early Christian and old Russian holiness. The church dissidents allied their hopes for a religious renewal with the lost ideals and values of the past and not with programmes of reform.

2. On Being a Christian – *an event*

And nevertheless despite all these unfavourable conditions, Küng's ideas slowly but steadily began to penetrate into Russian discussions, discussions about the future of Christianity and the church, about the foundations of Christian faith, and about a Christian programme which could present the church to a sick society. In retrospect, one can say that for many people who were seriously reflecting on their Christian identity, the encounter with *On Being a Christian* – that *summa* of Christian faith, focussed on problems but balanced in its theology – became a central event of their spiritual life.

A detailed account of the fortunes of *On Being a Christian* in Russia is impossible without some autobiographical remarks: to acquaint the Russian reader with Küng's theology was and is the most important element in my own theological and cultural work. I discovered about Hans Küng, his books and his theology, in the middle of the 1970s, from an article in one of the German newspapers which were being brought to Moscow illegally. Just a brief account of Küng's basic positions led me to search for his books. But unfortunately I found them neither in the libraries (today we know that they were kept secret in the so-called 'restricted stacks' for professional propaganda people) nor in the possession of private individuals. It was only thanks to the help of a teacher friend from Munich who was herself interested in the development of Christian dialogue between Germany and Russia that I succeeded in laying hands on the important *On Being a Christian*.

The Table of Contents alone was riveting: 'The Challenge of Modern Humanism ... What is Special to Christianity?, The Real Christ, Christianity and Judaism, The Programme: God's Cause and Man's Cause, Community of Faith, The Praxis of the Church, Being Christian as Being Radically Human ...' Indeed, this was just what we needed to get out of the ghetto into which we had been forced and to reflect anew on the destiny of our church and of faith against the broad but unattainable horizon of the present.

Subsequent reading confirmed that I was right in supposing that this book was as necessary for Russian readers as it was for Western readers. And immediately we thought of translating it for the 'samisdat', the underground press. Books by Catholic theologians had also been translated previously by emigrés or by my friends in Russia. But these were books of theologians who had written before the Second Vatican Council: Romano Guardini, Jacques Maritain, Emile Gilson, Louis Bouyer and so on. Küng's theology was rather different: his writing combined the latest state of research, which included the gigantic work of exegetes, historians, theologians, philosophers and experts on religion, not only with a great openness to all the tormenting questions of present spiritual life, but also with a bold concern to give honest, constructive answers.

Nevertheless, paradoxical though it may seem, *On Being a Christian*, which – according to Küng – had been written in language that was easy to understand for 'Christians and atheists, Gnostics and agnostics, pietists and positivists, lukewarm and zealous Catholics, Protestants and Orthodox – in a word, for all those who, for any reason at all, honestly and sincerely want to know what Christianity, what being a Christian, really means', proved unusually difficult to translate.

Why? The difficulty did not of course lie in the language but in the topics with which Küng was concerned. And although the translation was checked by several German scholars who were at home in German culture, much remained obscure and inaccurate, above all in the sphere of the New Testament. Both the translators and later the readers lacked the real knowledge of the historical-exegetical, scientific theological foundation on which Hans Küng was building, or which he was using for constructing his edifice.

At least briefly, it is necessary here to recall the tragic situation of the Russian Orthodox theology of the last seventy years. This situation was radically different from that, for example, in the former German Democratic Republic. In Russia after the Revolution in the course of a few years almost all religious publication was discontinued, all places for training clergy were closed, many churches were destroyed and thousands of priests shot or deported to death camps. The clergy academies and seminaries which were opened after the Second World War in Moscow and Leningrad with Stalin's permission were artificially isolated from all that twentieth-century theology lives by: a scientific historical-exegetical basis; a connection with contemporary philosophical thought, with religious studies, psychology, sociology and so on. The main task of these seminaries and similar institutions was to prepare priests for their liturgical activity. Everything other than the 'cult' of the Russian Orthodox church – the religious instruction of children and adults, preaching, apologetics, mission, social activity, the publication of religious books and journals – was banned.

In this atmosphere a small number of theologians worked either for episcopal diplomats in the Department for Foreign Church Affairs or in church chancelleries, or occupied themselves with scholarly investigations of patristics. The exegetes, who for the most part relied on the legacy of the Holy Fathers, only partially used the works of nineteenth-century scholars. Not only was nothing to be heard in the academies and chancelleries of the problems of contemporary hermeneutics, but nothing was known even of what is accessible to any student in a German theological faculty: the 'synoptic problem', biblical criticism, form criticism, tradition criticism, redaction criticism and so on. Indeed even now Russian readers know nothing of such classic works as Schweitzer's *Quest of the Historical Jesus*, Dibelius' *From Tradition to Gospel*, or Bultmann's *History of the Synoptic Tradition* or *Theology of the New Testament*, not to mention the later works of Cullmann, Käsemann, Jeremias, Hahn, Bornkamm, Conzelmann, Braun, Blank, Zimmermann and so on.

Nor do they have access to basic lexicons like the *Theological Dictionary of the New Testament* or the *Lexikon für Theologie und Kirche* or the new German Ecumenical Commentary on the New Testament. Even today, unfortunately, the Russian Orthodox church does not trouble itself with the problems of more recent historical exegesis.

3. *Reactions to* On Being a Christian

Of course the appearance of *On Being a Christian* in the samisdat at the end of the 1970s (later the translation was printed abroad and brought illegally to Russia) provoked a lively discussion among readers which lasted more than a year. The initiator of this discussion was the remarkable Russian priest and original theologian Sergei Alexeivich Zeludkov (who died in 1984); with indefatigable enthusiasm he provided help with the translation work.

As there could be no question at this time of open discussion of banned themes, Zeludkov resorted to the form of a correspondence in which people from different cities took part. Sometimes they did not even know each other. About a dozen people took part in this discussion by letter, related to particular themes: theologians, philosophers, writers, historians, believers, doubters, free thinkers. Quite opposed positions over Küng's book emerged among them. The letters, which were typed and signed only with an initial, went from hand to hand and prompted new reactions, new questions, arguments and counter-arguments, and aroused the desire for a new correspondence.

A precise analysis of this discussion must be the subject of a separate work, but in general terms the following can be said about the position of the readers. For both Zeludkov and myself, as for many others, including non-believers, Küng's book became a cheering discovery of the great liberating power of Christianity which overcomes the tearing apart of past and present, scientific knowledge and church dogmatics, reason and faith, church and society, action and proclamation, loyalty to the challenge of Jesus and life in the church. This was a discovery of questions which cannot be avoided and answers in which one can steep oneself, of dangerous, admonitory invitations from the gospel and the demands of present and future.

The book opened up new perspectives, was a stimulus to an extended self-understanding, and provoked responsible criticism and self-criticism. And at the centre of it all was not a theory, a world-view or 'idea', but the firm ground of the gospel, the words, actions and person of Jesus Christ. 'Küng's book,' wrote one of those taking part in the discussion, 'is an attempt to read the documents of the New Testament canon afresh with the eyes of people today; if you like, to experience the events of the gospel anew and to give these old letters a spiritual, intellectual and emotional hearing among our contemporaries ... This wonderful book which is written just for us ...'

Another group of readers, which also included some liberally-minded priests, approached the book with caution – as a necessary help for a certain group of theologians, clergy and pastors who were concerned with the problem of pastoral care. But they resolutely refused to give the book to members of their congregations out of fear that it 'could shatter the childlike faith of these little ones'. They opposed open discussion of the Christian element of Christianity with their pastoral care in the patriarchal sense and loyalty to the traditional teaching of the Orthodox church.

Finally there was a third, quite significant group of readers, exclusively believers from the ranks of the strict Orthodox, whom in Küng's terminology one can describe as 'ideologically immunized Christians'. They regarded *On Being a Christian* as a vivid example of the 'fatal self-destruction of Christianity'. Their objections, which have now become an element in the widespread ideology of the Orthodox reaction to the post-communist democratization of society, were directed both at the general intention of the book and some of its individual features, which a Western person would take for granted.

The fire of their criticism was above all directed at the 'modern men and women' whom *On Being a Christian* addresses, the men and women representing the world-view from whose questions and demands Küng began. Of course none of the critics questioned the Copernican system or excluded the 'horizon of the present'. Nevertheless, a clearly negative judgment was passed on all radical changes, beginning from the time of the Renaissance and the Enlightenment and including the whole subsequent process of secularization with its predominant forces of science, technology, industry and democracy, either as 'new paganism' or 'a dangerous heresy within Christianity'. Both the view of life and the values, problems and goals of 'modern men and women' were regarded as 'pagan' or 'heretical' – and not only those of modern men and women, but of the whole of Western Christianity which was responsible for this phenomenon.

For example, a well-known priest from St Petersburg wrote: 'In contrast to Western Christians, the true children of Orthodoxy have never insisted on any "freedoms" in the modern sense of this word. We have always recognized for every human being a fundamental freedom which is truly bestowed by God – the freedom to choose betwen God and Satan, between good and evil, between moral purity and sin ...' The logic of the conclusions which follow is understandable; as 'anything that does not derive from Orthodox faith is sin', of course all these things are sinful: the suspect demand for any new freedoms and independence in judgment, criticism of the 'immutable foundations of doctrine, a 'free' study of texts of the New Testament which allows 'different strata of the tradition', the need for scientific historical research, which is meaningless for faith, and the dangerous christology 'from below', which is described as a 'new Arianism'.

This samisdat discussion of *On Being a Christian* expressed the fact that Küng's ideas were coming into contact with a culture in which the ideas of the Middle Ages and those of the nineteenth-century liberalism, modern technological knowledge and archaic mythological ideas, impulses to a rediscovery of the Christian character of Christianity and the need for an authoritarian and isolationist interpretation of church life (which is primarily grounded in humility, prayer and obedience) exist actively alongside one another and conflict with one another.

4. Reactions to problems of religion in modernity

The book *Does God Exist?*, again translated in Moscow and printed abroad in 1989, seemed to the majority of Russian readers to be 'too theoretical', 'élitist'. And that is understandable. The world-view of Soviet men and women has not been influenced by Schopenhauer, or by Nietzsche, Freud or Heidegger. The latter were simply unknown and inaccessible to them. Even Marx was not read in Soviet Russia: resistance to the imposition of Marxism-Leninism destroyed any need for critical analysis of the notions of the author of *Das*

Kapital. For the majority of Soviet men and women the question of belief in God was and is a matter of practical decision and not theoretical reflection. And the place of encounter with God is the church, which is concerned with prayer and hymns of praise and not with abstract reflections ... Evidently the topicality of *Does God Exist?* will emerge later, when Russian post-communist men and women enter into closer contact with modern Western culture and its spiritual heritage.

Equally typical were the reactions to Küng's lectures, like those on 'Religion and Science' and 'Religion at the End of an Era', which he gave in Moscow in May/June 1989 and which were later printed in Soviet newspapers (as before, in the church newspapers the ideology of an isolationist Orthodox triumphalism prevails). His theses of 'paradigm shift' in the history of Christianity, the reciprocal relationship between modernism and post-modernism, were regarded by some as the assertion of a religious and cultural polymorphism in the spirit of Spengler (who is known and popular in Russia) and by others as a dangerous relativization of the substance of Christianity (which is usually identified in an uncritical way with the allegedly 'universal' Hellenistic-Byzantine-Russian paradigm) and understood only by a few as a signal for reflection on the theme of the fundamental changes which are directly connected with the entry of post-totalitarian Russia and Russian Christianity into a polycentric, open information society.

By contrast, Küng's lecture on art and religion, which was given at a symposium held at the same time devoted to the extensive exhibition by Otto Herbert Hajek in Moscow, was received with great enthusiasm. That is also understandable: the hall did not contain any theologians but artists, art historians, real lovers of art, who are concerned with the same problems, but without dogmatic prejudices.

It would be completely inadequate to apply the categories of 'success' and 'failure' to the reception of Hans Küng's theology in Russia. For is it appropriate to talk of the 'success' of a theological questioning in a situation like that depicted above, where such questioning is illegal? Or in the situation of an information boom, violent political revolutions and severe economic changes which have done away with totalitarianism in society in an extremely painful way? One thing is evident: Hans Küng opened the way for Russian believers and non-Christians to have a contemporary understanding of Christianity and church; to a theology which is capable of listening to the tormenting questions of life, and responding to them without betraying the challenging truth of the message of the gospel of God's cause, which can and must be the human cause. And precisely for that reason, not only are dissertations being written about Küng (unfortunately by philosophers rather than by theologians), but increasingly frequently people of the younger generation are picking up his texts, a generation which is more open to the real challenges of modern life than its bankrupt ideological teachers.

This year a new edition of the books by Hans Küng mentioned above will appear from one of the most significant Moscow publishers. For numerous readers this will be their first encounter, their first acquaintance with them. And I am sure that they will be joyfully and gratefully received.

A Select Bibliography: 1955–1993

This bibliography contains details of all books by Hans Küng (original German and British/American editions) and all material published in English, in chronological order of original publication.

I Books

1. *Rechtfertigung. Die Lehre Karl Barths und eine katholische Besinnung*, Johannes Verlag, Einsiedeln 1957, extended edition [4]1964
British edition: *Justification. The Doctrine of Karl Barth and a Catholic Reflection*, Burns and Oates, London 1965
American edition: *Justification. The Doctrine of Karl Barth and a Catholic Reflection*, Thomas Nelson and Sons, New York 1964; paperback edition with a new introduction, Westminster Press 1981

2. *Konzil und Wiedervereinigung. Erneuerung als Ruf in die Einheit*, Herder Verlag, Freiburg, Basel and Vienna 1960
British edition: *The Council and Reunion*, Sheed & Ward, London 1961
American edition: *The Council, Reform and Reunion*, Sheed & Ward, New York 1961; paperback edition Image Books, Doubleday, New York 1965, with a new introduction

3. *Damit die Welt glaube. Briefe an junge Menschen*, J. Pfeiffer, Munich 1962
British edition: *That the World May Believe. Letters to Young People*, Sheed & Ward, London 1963
American edition: *That the World May Believe*, Sheed & Ward, New York 1963

4. *Strukturen der Kirche*, Quaestiones disputatae 17, Herder Verlag, Freiburg, Basel and Vienna 1962; pocket book edition with a new preface, Piper Verlag, Munich 1987
British edition: *Structures of the Church*, Burns & Oates, London 1965
American edition: *Structures of the Church*, Thomas Nelson and Sons, New York 1964, paperback edition with new foreword Crossroad Publishing Company, New York 1982

5. *Kirche im Konzil*, Herder-Bücherei 140, Freiburg, Basel and Vienna 1963, second enlarged edition 1964
British edition: *The Living Church. Reflections on the Second Vatican Council*, Sheed & Ward, London 1963; *The Changing Church. Reflections on the Progress of the Second Vatican Council*, Sheed & Ward, London 1965

American edition: *The Council in Action*, Sheed & Ward, New York 1963

6. *Freiheit in der Welt. Sir Thomas More*, Theologische Meditationen 1, Benziger Verlag, Einsiedeln 1964
British edition: *Freedom in the World: Sir Thomas More*, Theological Meditations 3, Sheed & Ward, London and New York 1965
American edition: see no. 17

7. *Theologie und Kirche*, Theologische Meditationen 3, Benziger Verlag, Einsiedeln 1964
British edition: *The Theologian and the Church*, Theological Meditations 1, Sheed & Ward, London and New York 1965
American edition: cf. no. 17

8. *Kirche in Freiheit*, Theologische Meditationen 3, Benziger, Einsiedeln 1964
British edition: *The Church and Freedom*, Theological Meditations 1, Sheed & Ward, London and New York 1965
American edition: cf. no. 17

9. *Christenheit als Minderheit. Die Kirche unter den Weltreligionen*, Theologische Meditationen 12, Benziger Verlag, Einsiedeln 1965
British edition in *Christian Revelation and World Religions. The World's Religions in God's Plan of Salvation*, ed. J. Neuner, Burns & Oates, London 1967, 25–66
American edition: cf. no. 17

10. *Gott und das Leid*, Theologische Meditationen 18, Benziger Verlag, Einsiedeln/Zurich and Cologne 1967

11. *Die Kirche*, Ökumenische Forschungen I.1, Herder, Freiburg, Basel and Vienna 1967; pocket book edition Piper Verlag, Munich 1977
British edition: *The Church*, Burns & Oates, London 1967; paperback edition Search Press, London 1971
American edition: *The Church*, Sheed & Ward, New York 1967; paperback edition Image Books, New York 1976

12. *Wahrhaftigkeit. Zur Zukunft der Kirche*, Kleine ökumenische Schriften 1, Herder Verlag, Freiburg, Basel and Vienna 1968, paperback edition 1971
British edition: *Truthfulness. The Future of the Church*, Sheed & Ward, London 1968
American edition: *Truthfulness. The Future of the Church*, Sheed & Ward, New York 1968

13. *Menschwerdung Gottes. Eine Einführung in Hegels theologisches Denken als Prolegomena zu einer künftigen Christologie*, Ökumenische Forschung II.1, Herder Verlag, Freiburg, Basel and Vienna 1970, pocket book edition Piper Verlag, Munich 1989, with a new preface

British edition: *The Incarnation of God. An Introduction to Hegel's Theological Thought as Prolegomena to a Future Christology*, T. & T. Clark, Edinburgh 1987

Unfehlbar? Eine Anfrage, Benziger Verlag, Zurich, Einsiedeln and Cologne 1970, expanded new edition *Unfehlbar? Eine unerledigte Anfrage*, Piper Verlag, Munich 1989, updated with a foreword by Herbert Haag
British edition: *Infallible? An Enquiry*, Collins, London 1971, paperback edition Fontana Library, London 1972, new edition 1980
American edition: *Infallible? An Inquiry*, Doubleday, New York 1971, paperback edition Image Books, New York 1972, reprinted with a new foreword 1983

15. *Was ist Kirche?*, Herder-Bücherei 376, Freiburg, Basel and Vienna 1970, pocket book edition Siebenstern Taschenbücher, Munich and Hamburg 1970

16. *Wozu Priester? Eine Hilfe*, Benziger Verlag, Zurich, Einsiedeln and Cologne 1971
British edition: *Why Priests? A Proposal for a New Church Ministry*, Collins, London 1972, paperback edition Fontana Library of Theology and Philosophy, London 1972
American edition: *Why Priests? A Proposal for a New Church Ministry*, Doubleday, New York 1972

17. *Freiheit des Christen* (see also nos 6–9), Buchclub Ex Libris, Zurich 1971, pocket book edition Siebenstern Taschenbücher, Hamburg 1972
American edition: *Freedom Today*, Theological Meditations 1, Sheed & Ward, New York 1966

18. *Was in der Kirche bleiben muss*, Theologische Meditationen 30, Benziger Verlag, Zurich, Einsiedeln and Cologne 1973
British edition: *What Must Remain in the Church*, Collins, London 1977

19. *Fehlbar? Eine Bilanz* (with contributions by A. Antweiler et al.), Benziger Verlag, Zurich, Einsiedeln and Cologne 1973

20. *Christ sein*, Piper Verlag, Munich 1974
British edition: *On Being a Christian*, Collins, London 1977, paperback edition Fount Paperbacks, London 1978, reissued SCM Press, London 1991
American edition: *On Being a Christian*, Doubleday, New York 1967, paperback edition Wallaby Books, New York 1978, Image Books, New York 1984

21. *20 Thesen zum Christsein*, Piper Verlag, Munich 1975
American edition: see no. 27

22. *Was ist Firmung?*, Theologische Meditationen 40, Benziger Verlag, Zurich, Einsiedeln and Cologne 1976

American edition: see no. 27

23. *Jesus im Widerstreit. Ein jüdisch–christlicher Dialog* (with Pinchas Lapide), Calwer Verlag, Stuttgart and Kösel Verlag, Munich 1976
British edition: *Brother or Lord? A Jew and a Christian Talk Together About Jesus*, Collins, London 1977
American edition: cf. no. 27

24. *Gottesdienst – warum?* Theologische Meditationen 43, Benziger Verlag, Zurich, Einsiedeln and Cologne 1976
American edition: see no. 27

25. *Heute noch an Gott glauben?* (with Walter Scheel, *Mut zu kritische Sympathie*), *Zwei Reden*, Piper Verlag, Munich 1977

26. *Existiert Gott? Antwort auf die Gottesfrage der Neuzeit*, Piper Verlag, Munich 1978, pocket book edition dtv-Taschenbücher, Munich 1981
British edition: *Does God Exist? An Answer for Today*, Collins, London 1980, paperback edition Fount Paperbacks, London 1980, reissued SCM Press 1991
American edition: *Does God Exist? An Answer for Today*, Doubleday, New York 1980, paperback edition, Vintage Books, New York 1981

Partially published in *Freud and the Problem of God*, Yale University Press, New Haven 1979 (see also no. 39)

27. *Wegzeichen in die Zukunft. Programmatisches für eine christlichere Kirche*, Rowohlt, Reinbek bei Hamburg 1980
American edition: *Signposts for the Future*, Doubleday, New York 1978

28. *Die Christliche Herausforderung* (a shortened version of *Christ Sein*), Piper Verlag, Munich 1980
British edition: *The Christian Challenge. A Shortened Version of On Being a Christian*, Collins, London 1979
American edition: *The Christian Challenge. A Shortened Version of On Being a Christian*, Doubleday, New York 1979

29. *Kirche – gehalten in der Wahrheit?*, Benziger Verlag, Zurich, Einsiedeln and Cologne 1979
British edition: *The Church – Maintained in Truth?*, SCM Press, London 1980
British edition: *The Church – Maintained in Truth?*, Seabury Press, New York 1980

30. *24 Thesen zur Gottesfrage*, Piper Verlag, Munich 1979

31. *Kunst und Sinnfrage*, Benziger Verlag, Zurich, Einsiedeln and Cologne 1980
British edition: *Art and the Question of Meaning*, SCM Press Ltd 1981

American edition: *Art and the Question of Meaning*, Crossroad Publishing Company 1981

32. *Glauben an Jesus Christus*, Theologische Meditationen 59, Benziger Verlag, Zurich, Einsiedeln and Cologne 1976

33. *Ewiges Leben?*, Piper Verlag, Munich 1982, pocket book edition Piper Verlage 1984
British edition: *Eternal Life?*, Collins, London 1984, paperback edition Fount Paperbacks, London 1985, reissued SCM Press, London 1991
American edition: *Eternal Life? Life after Death as a Medical, Philosophical, and Theological Problem*, Doubleday, New York 1984, paperback Image Books, New York 1985

34. *Christentum und Weltreligionen. Hinführung zum Dialog mit Islam, Hinduismus, Buddhismus* (with Josef van Ess, Heinrich von Stietencron, Heinz Bechert), Piper Verlag, Munich 1984, pocket book edition in three volumes, *Islam, Hinduismus, Buddhismus*, Gütersloher Verlagshaus Gerd Mohn, Gütersloh 1987
British edition: *Christianity and the World Relgions. Paths of Dialogue with Islam, Hinduism and Buddhism*, Collins, London 1987, paperback edition, Fount Paperbacks, London 1987, reissued with a new preface SCM Press, London 1993
American edition: *Christianity and the World Religions. Paths of Dialogue with Islam, Hinduism and Buddhism*, Doubleday, New York 1986, paperback edition, Doubleday, New York 1986, reissued with a new preface Orbis Books, Maryknoll 1993

35. *Woran man sich halten kann. Christliche Orientierung in orientierungsarmer Zeit*, Theologische Meditationen 59, Benziger Verlag, Zurich, Einsiedeln and Cologne 1976
British edition: *Why I am Still a Christian*, T. & T. Clark, Edinburgh 1987
American edition: *Why I am Still a Christian*, Abingdon Press, Nashville 1987

36. *Dichtung und Religion. Pascal, Gryphius, Lessing, Hölderlin, Novalis, Kierkegaard, Dostojewski, Kafka* (with Walter Jens), Kindler Verlag, Munich 1985, pocket book Piper Verlag, Munich 1988
British edition: *Literature and Religion. Pascal, Gryphius, Lessing, Hölderlin, Novalis, Kierkegaard, Dostoyewsky, Kafka*, Paragon House, New York 1991

37. *Church and Change. The Irish Experience*, Gill and Macmillan, Dublin 1986

38. *Theologie in Aufbruch. Eine ökumenische Grundlegung*, Piper Verlag, Munich 1987, pocket book edition Piper Verlag, Munich 1992
British edition: *Theology for the Third Millennium. An Ecumenical View*, Harper-Collins, London 1991

American edition: *Theology for the Third Millennium. An Ecumenical View*, Doubleday 1988, paperback edition, Doubleday, New York 1990

39. *Freud und die Zukunft der Religion*, Piper Verlag, Munich 1987
American edition: *Freud and the Problem of God*, Enlarged edition, Yale University Press 1990 (see also no. 26)

40. *Christentum und Chinesische Religion* (with Julia Ching), Piper Verlag, Munich 1988
American edition: *Christianity and Chinese Religions*, Doubleday, New York 1989
British edition: *Christianity and Chinese Religions*, SCM Press, London 1993

41. *Anwälte der Humanität. Thomas Mann, Hermann Hesse, Heinrich Böll* (with Walter Jens), Kindler Verlag, Munich 1989

42. *Die Hoffnung bewahren. Schriften zur Reform der Kirche*, Benziger Verlag, Zurich 1990
British edition: *Reforming the Church Today. Keeping Hope Alive*, T. & T. Clark, Edinburgh 1990
American edition: *Reforming the Church Today. Keeping Hope Alive*, Crossroad Publishing Company, New York 1990

43. *Projekt Weltethos*, Piper Verlag, Munich 1990, pocket book edition Piper Verlag, 1992
British edition: *Global Responsibility. In Search of a New World Ethic* (with a preface by HRH The Duke of Edinburgh, KG), SCM Press, London 1991
American edition: *Global Responsibility. In Search of a New World Ethic*, Crossroad Publishing Company 1991

44. *Das Judentum. Die religiöse Situation der Zeit*, Piper Verlag, Munich 1991
British edition: *Judaism. The Religious Situation of Our Time*, SCM Press, London 1992
American edition: *Judaism. Between Yesterday and Tomorrow*, Crossroad Publishing Company, New York 1992

45. *Mozart. Spuren der Transzendenz*, Piper Verlag, Munich 1991
British edition: *Mozart. Traces of Transcendence* (with a foreword by Sir Yehudi Menuhin), SCM Press, London 1992
American edition: *Mozart*, W.B. Eerdmans, Grand Rapids, Michigan 1992

46. *Die Schweiz ohne Orientierung? Europäische Perspektiven*, Benziger Verlag, Zurich, Einsiedeln and Cologne 1992

47. *Denkwege, Ein Lesebuch*, ed K.-J. Kuschel, Piper Verlag, Munich 1992

48. *Credo. Das Apostolische Glaubensbekenntnis – Zeitgenossen erklärt*, Piper Verlag, Munich 1992

British edition: *Credo. The Apostles' Creed explained for Today*, SCM Press, London 1993
American edition: *Credo. The Apostles' Creed explained for Today*, Doubleday, New York 1993

49. *Die grosse christliche Theologen*, Piper Verlag, Munich 1993
British edition: *The Great Christian Theologians*, SCM Press, London 1994

50. *Das Christentum* (in preparation)

51. *Der Islam* (in preparation)

II Lexicon articles

'Freedom, intellectual', in *New Catholic Encyclopedia*, Vol.VI, New York and London 1967, 100–2

'Justification', in *Encyclopedia Britannica* Vol.13, Chicago and London 1967, 162–3

III Contributions to volumes of essays

'Justification and Sanctification According to the New Testament', in *Christianity Divided. Protestant and Roman Catholic Theological Issues*, ed. D.J. Callahan, New York 1961, paperback edition London and New York 1962, 309–35

'Reunion and Doctrine on Justification', in *The Church. Readings in Theology*, ed. A. LaPierre, E. Wetterer, B. Verkamp and I. Zeitler, New York 1963, 101–11

'Theological Currents in Europe Today', in *A New Europe?*, ed. S.R. Graubard, Boston 1964, 560–80

'God's Free Spirit in the Church', in *Freedom and Man*, ed. J.C. Murray, New York 1965, 17–30

'Comment' (on no.25 of the Dogmatic Constitution), in *Church. Vatican II's Dogmatic Constitution on the Church*, New York 1969, 55

'The Freedom of Religions', in *Attitudes Towards Other Religions. Some Christian Interpretations*, ed. M.E. Marty, New York and London 1969

'Participation of the Laity in Church Leadership and in Church Elections', in *Bishops and People*, ed. L. and A. Swidler, Philadelphia 1970, 87–112, similarly in *A Democratic Catholic Church. The Reconstruction of Roman Catholicism*, ed. E.C. Bianchi and R.R. Ruether, New York 1992, 80–93

'What is the Essence of Apostolic Succession?', 'The Petrine Office', in *Readings in the Theology of the Church*, ed. E.J. Dirkswager Jr, Englewood Cliffs, New Jersey, USA 1970, 125–32, 142–67

'What is the Christian Message?', in *Mission Trends*, No. I, *Crucial Issues in Mission Today*, ed. G.H. Anderson and T.F. Stransky, New York 1974, 101–10

'Vatican III: Problems and Opportunities for the Future', in *Toward Vatican III. The Work That Needs to Be Done*, ed. D. Tracy, H. Küng and J.B. Metz, New York 1978, 67–90

'Toward a New Consensus in Catholic (and Ecumenical) Theology', in *Consensus in Theology? A Dialogue with Hans Küng and Edward Schillebeeckx*, ed. L. Swidler, Philadelphia 1980, 1–17

'Belief in a Son of God?', in *The Bible Now*, ed. P. Burns and J. Cumming, Dublin 1981, 143–51

'Catholic and Protestants: An Ecumenical Inventory', in *Vatican II by those Who Were There*, ed. A. Stacpoole, London 1986, 24–31

'Christianity and World Religions: Dialogue with Islam', in *Toward a Universal Theology of Religion*, ed. L. Swidler, Maryknoll 1987, 192–209, also in *Muslims in Dialogue. The Evolution of a Dialogue*, ed. L. Swidler, Lewiston, Queenston and Lampeter 1992, 249–72

'What is True Religion? Toward an Ecumenical Criteriology', in *Toward a Universal Theology of Religion*, ed. L. Swidler, Maryknoll 1987, 231–50

'Discovering God Anew', in *The Incarnate Imagination. Essays in Theology, The Arts and Social Sciences. In Honor of Andrew Greeley*, ed. I.H. Shafer, Bowling Green 1988, 256–69

'Paradigm Change in Theology', in *The Whirlwind in Culture. In Honor of Langdon Gilkey*, ed D.W. Musser and J.L. Price, Bloomington 1988, 67–105

'Paradigm Change in Theology: A Proposal for Discussion', and 'What does a Change of Paradigm Mean?', in Hans Küng and David Tracy (eds.), *Paradigm Change in Theology*, Edinburgh and New York 1989, 3–33, 212–19

'Spero contra spem', in *Living Philosophies. The Reflections of Some Eminent Men and Women of Our Time*, ed. C. Fädeman, New York 1990, 40–6

'God's Self-Renunciation and Buddhist Emptiness: A Christian Response to Masao Abe', in *Buddhist Emptiness and Christian Trinity. Essays and Explorations*, ed. R. Corless and P.F. Knitter, New York 1990, 26–43

'God: The Last Taboo? Science, God and the University', in *Theology and the*

University. Essays in Honor of John B. Cobb, Jr, ed D.R. Griffin and J.C. Hough Jr, Albany 1991, 51–66

'The Meaning of Life', in *The Meaning of Life. Reflections in Words and Pictures on Why We Are Here*, ed. D. Friend and the Editors of *Life*, Boston, Toronto and London 1991, 105

'Christianity and Judaism', in *Jesus' Jewishness. Exploring the Place of Jesus in Early Judaism*, ed. J.H. Charlesworth, New York 1991, 259–69

'No Peace in the World Without Peace Among Religions. An Ecumenical Way Between Fanaticism and Forgetfulness of Truth', in *Proceedings, 27th IARF World Congress, Europe 1990*, ed. The International Association for Religious Freedom, Frankfurt am Main 1991, 71–83

IV Articles in newspapers and journals

'The Pope with the Bishops', *Prism* 6.1, 1962, 7–14

'The Ecumenical Council in Theological Perspective', *Dialog* I, 1962, 40–9; also in *Theology Digest* 11, 1963, 135–9

'Does a Catholic Have to Defend Everything?', *The Sign*, February 1963, 11–12

'Can the Council Fail?', *The Furrow* 13, 1962, 53–5, also in *Cross Currents* 12, 1962, 269–76

'Is Criticism Enough?', *The Sign*, February 1963, 12–13

'Venerating Mary. Difficulties in the Way of Reunion', *Pax Romana Journal* 6, 1961, 13–14

'Pope John as a Good Shepherd', *The Catholic World* 195, 1962, 7–13

'Objections to the Council', *Jubilee* 9, April 1962, 16–19

'Ecumenical Orientations', *Worship* 37, December 1962, 83–94

'One Flock, One Shepherd', *Catholic Digest*, November 1962, 31–5

'The Free Church' (letters page), *The Sunday Times*, 26 Mary 1963

'Reflections on the Council' (letter to Father Van Ackeren), *Theology Digest* 11, 1963, 65

'A Word of Thanks' (after his first lecture tour of America), *America* 108, 1963, 826–9

'Servus Servorum Dei. Why Pope John Was Great', *The Tablet* 217, 1963, 630–2, 645–6, also *Our Sunday Visitor*, 30 June 1963

'The Missions in the Ecumenical Age', *African Ecclesiastical Review* 5, 1963, 97–108

'Reunion and the Jews. An Answer to Rabbi Arnold Jacob Wolf', *The Christian Century* 80, 1963, 829

'The Mass of the Future', *The Sign* 41, 1963, 18–21

'What Christians Expect of Vatican II', *Christianity and Crisis* 23, 1963, 156–60

'Latin: The Church's Mother Tongue', *Harper's Magazine* 227, 1963, 604

'The Council So Far', *The Catholic Layman* 77, 1963, 6–13

'The Church and Freedom', *Commonweal* 78, 1963, 343–53

'The Council – End or Beginning?', *Commonweal* 81, 1965, 631–7

'The Charismatic Structure of the Church', *Concilium* 1.4, 1965, 23–33, also in *The Catholic World* 201, 1965, 302–6

'And After the Council?', *Commonweal* 82, 1965, 619–23

'The World Religions and God's Plan of Salvation', *Indian Eccleisastical Studies* 4, 1965, 182–222

'The Reform of the Roman Church, Reform Towards Other Christian Churches, Reform Towards Other Religions, and Reform Towards the World', *The Sunday Times*, 12 December 1965

'What Has the Council Done?', *Commonweal* 83, 1966, 461–8

'A Question to the Church', *The Month* 224, 1967, 259–61

'Holland Shows the Way', *The Tablet* 221, 1967, 1250

'What is the Essence of Apostolic Succession?', *Concilium* 4.4, 1968, 16–19

'With Windows Open to the Street', *Union Seminary Quarterly Review* 23, 1968, 147–57

'Intercommunion', *Journal of Ecumenical Studies* 5, 1968, 576–8

'Blame Everything on the Council', *The Critic* 27, 1969, 38–41

'Tribute to Karl Barth', *Journal of Ecumenical Studies* 6, 1969, 233–6

'Dissent May Be a Duty', *The Voice* 1.11, Washington 1969, 3

'Participation of the Laity in Church Leadership and in Church Elections', *Journal of Ecumenical Studies* 6, 1969, 511–33

'Mixed Marriages: What is to be Done?', *The Tablet* 224, 1970, 518–20

'The Extent of Convergence', *Concilium* 6.4, 1970, 54–7

'Mixed Marriages: A Rejoinder' (letter to Yves Congar), *The Tablet* 224, 1970, 782–3

'Breakthrough on Mixed Marriages', ibid., 1136–8

'Towards a Discussion of Infallibility', *Worship* 45, 1971, 287–9

'Statement' (on what is the Christian message), *Japan Missionary Bulletin*, December 1970, also in *Catholic Worker*, Australia, November 1975, 9–12

'To Get to the Heart of the Matter. Answer to Karl Rahner', *Homiletic and Pastoral Review* 71, 1971, 9–21, 27–32, 49–50

'Who Shall Choose the Bishops?', *The New York Times*, 28 January 1971

'Why I am Staying in the Church', *America* 124, 1971, 281–3, also in *The Tablet* 225, 1971, 433–6; *Catholic Worker*, Australia, June 1971, 4–6; *Catholic Herald*, 17 August 1973

'Why Infallibility?', *The New York Times*, 3 June 1971

'What is the Criterion for a Critical Theology? Reply to Gregory Baum', *Commonweal* 94, 1971, 326–30

'Response' (to A. Dulles, 'The Theology of Hans Küng: A Comment'), *Union Seminary Quarterly Review* 27, 1972, 143–7

'Letter to the Vatican' (dated 24 January 1972), *Origins, NC Documentary Service*, 16 March 1972

'A Short Balance Sheet of the Debate on Infallibility', *Concilium* 9.3, 1973, 129–36

'Authority in the Church. An Exchange Between Hans Küng and Karl Rahner', *The Tablet* 227, 1973, 597–8; also in *America* 129, 1974, 9–11

'Papal Fallibility: O Felix Error!', *Journal of Ecumenical Studies* 10, 1973, 361–2

'The Case is Open', *The Tablet* 227, 1973, 670–1, also in *America* 129, 1973, 133–46

'Confirmation as the Completion of Baptism', *Colloquium*, Australia and New

Zealand, 8.1, 1975/6, 33–40, and 2, 5–13; also in *US Catholic* 40, July 1975, 19–22 (in abbreviated form)

'The Origin of Resurrection Belief', *Theology Digest* 23, 1975, 136–42

'The Infallibility Issue', *The Tablet* 228, 1974, 662–3, also in *National Catholic Reporter*, 19 July 1974

'From Anti-Semitism to Theological Dialogue', *Concilium* 10.7/8, 1974, 103–10

'Being a Christian (Text of the Press Conference on *Christ Sein*)', *The Tablet* 228, 1974, 1021–2

'Statement on Women Priests: Theology No Barrier', *National Catholic Reporter*, 12 December 1975

'Religious Service Today – Why?', *Accent* 10, Adelaide 1977, 4–14

'Feminism a New Reformation (16 theses)', *The New York Times Magazine*, 23 May 1976

'Rome Must Find a Way to Cope With the Growing Conflict Within the Church', *The Times*, 28 August 1976

'Christianity, Faith and Hope", *The Catholic Connection* 1, Alexandria, Virginia 1976, no.6, 1, 3

'Christ and Change', ibid., no.7, 3, 6

'Jews and Gentiles', ibid., no.8, 3, 6

'On Being a Christian' (press conference on the English and American edition on *On Being a Christian*), *America* 136, 1977, 1–2; also in *The Tablet* 231, 1977, 79–80

'Answer to Bishop B.C. Butler', *Catholic Herald*, 25 February 1977

'What Must Remain in the Church I–IV', *New Citizen*, New Zealand, 1 and 20 October, 3 and 17 November 1977, and 23 February, 9 and 23 March 1978

'Is Jesus a Bond or Barrier? A Jewish Christian Dialogue' (with Pinchas Lapide), *Journal of Ecumenical Studies* 14, 1977, 466–83

'Catholics and Protestants Today', *Theology Digest* 27, 1979, 255–9

'The Pope who Held His Hand Over Me', *The German Tribune*, Hamburg, 20 August 1978

'Pope John Paul II: His First Year', *The New York Times*, 19 October 1979, also in *Chicago Tribune*, 25 October 1979, *The Age*, Melbourne, 3 January 1980; *Magill*, Dublin, November 1979, 22–4

'How Should We Speak Today about the Holy Spirit', *Concilium* 128, 1979, 114–17

'My Deep Sorrow', *The Universe*, 4 January 1980

'Why I Remain a Catholic', *The Times*, 28 January 1980, also in *The New York Times*, 28 January 1980; *The Irish Times*, 20 January 1980; also in *Consensus in Theology? A Dialogue with Hans Küng and Edward Schillebeeckx*, ed. L. Swidler, Philadelphia 1980, 159–65

'Open Letter', *The Tablet* 224, 1980, 303; also in *National Catholic Reporter*, 28 March 1980

'Rebel Theologian and the Catholic Conflict', *The Times*, 15 April 1980

'A Letter on Christology and Infallibility', *Concilium* 138, 1980, 85–97

'Hans Küng writes to the Pope about Clerical Celibacy', *National Catholic Reporter*, 16 May 1980; also as 'The Human Right to Marriage', *The Observer*, 7 September 1980, and 'A Rebel's Open Letter to Pope John Paul', *The Age*, Melbourne, 22 September 1980

'The Freedom of the Election of the Bishop in Basel', *Concilium* 137, 1980, 95–8

'Does God Exist? An Answer for Today', *Horizons* 7.2, Villanova, Pa 1980, 299–320

'To What We Can Still Cling. Humanizing America's Iconic Book', *Society of Biblical Literature Centennial Addresses*, Chico 1980, 39–56

'Where I Stand', *Bulletin of Pacific School of Religion*, Berkeley 1981, 1, also in *Christianity and Crisis* 2, February 1981, 3–11; *United Presbyterian AD*, March 1981, 23–5

'Church from Above – Church from Below', *Renewal Information, Opinions, Comments* No.2, London 1985, 3–14

'"Consistency" Key to Preach Gospel Credibly', *National Catholic Reporter*, 6 November 1981

'Science and the Problem of God', *The Journal of the Interdenominational Theological Center*, Atlanta 1982/3, 95–107

'Will the Pope Win over Women?', *The New York Times*, 16 November 1983

'Rome Fears US Renewal', *National Catholic Reporter*, 30 December 1983

'Twenty Years of Ecumenical Theology – What For?', *Concilium* 170, 45–52

'*Concilium* in Faith with the Council: 1985 and After', *Concilium* 170, 1983, 90–2

'Dying with Christian Dignity', *Commonweal*, 27 January 1984

'Parsifal, A Theology for Our Time', *Michigan Quarterly Review* 23, 1984, 311–33

'Christianity and World Religions: The Dialogue with Islam as One Model', *Harvard Divinity Bulletin* 15, December 1984–January 1985, 2, 4–8

'A Christian Scholar's Dialogue with Muslims', *The Christian Century*, 9 October 1985

'Fear of Freedom at the Vatican', *The Globe and Mail*, Toronto, 4/5 October 1986, also as 'Speaking Out After a Long Silence', in *National Catholic Reporter*, 11 October 1985, 9–10, 23–26; *Church in Anguish. Has the Vatican Betrayed Vatican II?*, ed. H. Küng and L. Swidler, New York 1987, 58–74

'What is the True Religion? Toward an Ecumenical Criteriology', *Journal of Religion for Southern Africa* 56, 1986, 4–12; *Ching Feng* 3, Hong Kong 1987, 95–122; and as 'Ecumenism and Truth: The Wider Dialogue', *The Tablet* 233, 1989, 92–3

'Christianity and Islam', *Indo Asia* 2, Sachsenheim 1986/7, 6–16

'Introduction: The Debate on the Word "Religion"', *Concilium* 183, 1986, XI–XV

'Towards an Ecumenical Theology of Religions: Some Theses for Clarification', ibid., 119–15

'Freedom for Truth – Peace among Religions', *Dialogue. A Quarterly Journal Exploring the Implications of the Baha'i Faith for our Time*, Los Angeles 1986, No.2, 8

'Christianity and World Religions: The Dialogue with Islam as One Model', *The Muslim World* 77.2, 1987, 80–95

'Is the Christ's Table Divided?', *International Christian Digest* 1.7, September 1987, 37–9

'Geneva Forum: What is the Church?' (with P. Webb, P. Potter, I. Sook Chung, G. Priestland), *International Christian Digest* 1.2, Nashville 1987, 12–14

'On Being a Christian Theologian', *The Critic* 42.4, Chicago 1987, 11–16

'The Hour of Truth for South Africa', *Concilium* 189, 1987, XI–XII

'Ecumenism and Truth: The Wider Dialogue', *The Tablet* 233, 1989

'No Peace in the World without Peace Among Religions. An Ecumenical Way between Fanaticism and Forgetfulness of Truth', *World Faith Insight* 21.2, 1989, 3–22; also in *Dharma World* 18, 1991, 10–16

'My Personal Spero', *Seeds of Peace* 6.1, Bangkok 1990, 28–31

'What Comes after Götterdämmerung? Downfall and Redemption in the Late Work of Richard Wagner', in *Parsifal, Bayreuth Festival Programme* 1, 1989, 59–82

'Seven Foundations for the Future', *The Times*, 28 July 1989

'Under Rome's Displeasure', *The Tablet* 234, 1990, 125–6

'He That is not Against Us is For Us', *Perspectives* 5.2, Grand Rapids 1990, 4–5

'Response to Francis Cook: Is It Just This? Different Paradigms of Ultimate Reality in Buddhism', *Buddhist Christian Studies* 9, Hawaii 1989, 143–56

'Rediscovering God', *Concilium* 1990/1, 86–102

'Towards a World Ethic of World Religions', *Concilium* 1990/2, 102–19

'Prayer of the Religions in the New World Context', *Concilium* 1990/6, xi–xiii

'Redefining our Fundamental Values', *Word Link* 11/12, Lausanne 1990, 76–7

'Faith in the Future', *The Guardian*, 15 February 1991

'All Children of Abraham', *The Church Times*, 22 February 1991, also *The Tablet* 235, 1991, 260–4, 294–5

'From Three Faiths, One Reconciliation', *Los Angeles Times*, 31 March 1991; also as 'Religious Reconciliation is the Key To Peace', *Kansas City Star*, 1 April 1991

'Two Flags Over Jerusalem? There Can be No Peace Among the Nations Without Peace Among the Religions', *European Affairs* 5.1, 1991, 68–73

'In Search of a New World Ethic', *The World* 5.3, 1991, 14–16

'World Religions and World Ethos', *Universitas* 34.2, 1992, 79–85

'Book Meant as Service to Judaism', *The Church Times*, 3 April 1992

'Toward a Universal Declaration of Global Ethos', *Journal of Ecumenical Studies* 28.1, 1991, 123–5

'Against Contemporary Roman Catholic Fundamentalism', *Concilium* 1992/3, 116–25

V Interviews

Only published interviews and conversations are listed here; titles were usually provided by the newspaper or journal concerned.

Interview with J.B. Sheerin, *The Catholic World* 197, 1963, 159–63

'A Brotherly Approach from Both Sides', interview with T. de Quénétain, in *Steps to Christian Unity*, ed. J.A. O'Brien, New York 1964, 74–85

Interview with D. O'Grady, *The Way* 20, 1964, 11–13

'Conversation at the Council' (with J.C. Murray, G. Weigel, G. Diekmann and V.A. Yzermans), *The American Benedictine Review* 15, 1964, 341–51

'The Church and the Council', interview with D. Fisher, *The Catholic Herald*, 18 June 1965; *St Louis Review*, 25 June 1965

'The Spirit of Change in the Church', interview with P. Granfield, *The Homiletic and Pastoral Review* 66, October 1965, 17–21

Interview in *Listening. Current Studies in Dialog* 1, 1966, 172–82

'The Roman Curia Must Be Reformed', interview with J. Horgan, *The Irish Times*, 18 November 1967; also in *St Louis Review*, 8 December 1967; *The Advocate*, Melbourne, 25 January 1968

Interview with A. MacLeod, *The New Zealand Listener*, 18 October 1971

Interview with R. Murray, *The Month* 232, 1971, 117–21

Interview with J. O'Connor, *Intellectual Digest* 2, New York, March 1972, 19–22

'Mysterium Ecclesiae', *The Tablet* 227, 1973, 835–9

'Sermon on the Mount. Will it Play in Peoria?', *US Catholic* 43.1, January 1978, 30–4

Interview with John Wilkins, *The Tablet* 229, 1975, 381–2 (with a correction on p.414)

'A Catholic Maverick', interview with W.F. Willoughby, *Washington Star*, 28 February 1972

'We Can't Go Backward', interview with A.M. Kerr, *The Catholic Connection* 2.5, Alexandria, Va, 1977, 3

'On Being a Catholic Christian', *US Catholic* 44.5, May 1979, 12–16

'The Inquisition and Doctor Küng', conversation with P.P. Read, *The Observer Review*, 9 November 1980

'The Teacher the Pope has Banned for "Heresy"', interview with I. Rowan, *The Sunday Telegraph*, 9 November 1980

'A Conversation with Hans Küng', *The University of Chicago Magazine* 74.4, 1982, 20–1

'The Vatican is a Totalitarian State', interview with M. Westerman, *Newsweek*, 8 August 1983

'Religion Should Never be Ignored', interview with K. Masud and T. Ahsan, *The Muslim Magazine*, Islamabad, 24 February 1984

'Speaks Out on the Church in Africa', interview with P. Byrne, *Speak Out! A Christian Magazine for Youth*, Ndola/Zambia, March/April 1986, 8–9, 15–16

'Father Hans Küng Speaks on Life Issues', conversation with P. Lefevre, *East Texas Catholic*, 22 November 1985, 10

'Hans Küng's Theological Pilgrimage to Iran', interview with A. Swidler, *National Catholic Reporter*, 30 December 1988

'The Church in China. An Interview with Professor Julia Ching and the Rev. Hans Küng', by P.H. Samway, *America*, 22 April 1989

'The New Ethic: Global Responsibility', interview with N. Gardels, *New Perspective Quarterly* 8.2, 1991, 44–51

'The Christian Thing to Do', interview with B. Ivry, *Newsweek*, 8 July 1991

'Discussing Anti-Judaism in the New Testament with Hans Küng', *Explorations* 6.2, Philadelphia 1992, 1–4

VI Prefaces and editorials

Introduction to V.A. Yzermans, *A New Pentecost, Vatican Council II, Session 1*, Westminster, Maryland 1963, xix–x

Foreword to L. Swidler, *The Ecumenical Vanguard. The History of the Una Sancta Movement*, Pittsburgh, PA 1966, ix–xi

Preface to J. Müller, H. Haag and G. Hasenhüttl, *The Unknown God?*, New York 1966, 7–9

Foreword to R. Modras, *Paul Tillich's Theology of the Church. A Catholic Appraisal*, Detroit 1976, 11–13

Preface to A.B. Hasler, *How the Pope Became Infallible*, New York 1981, 1–26

Editorial, 'Conflicting Ways of Interpreting the Bible', *Concilium* 138, 1980, vii

Editorial, 'Who Has the Say in the Church?', *Concilium* 148, 1981, vii–ix

Editorial, 'The Right to Dissent', *Concilium* 158, 1982, vii–viii

Editorial (with Jürgen Moltmann), 'Mary in the Churches', *Concilium* 168, 1982, vii–ix

Foreword, 'Notulae on the Buddist–Christian Encounter', to Takeuchi Yishnoriu, *The Heart of Buddhism. In Search of the Timeless Spirit of Primitive Buddhism*, edited and translated by J.W. Heisig, New York 1983, vii–xii

Preface to W.G. Oxtoby, *The Meaning of Other Faiths*, Philadelphia 1983, 9–10

Editorial, 'Christianity Among the World Religions', *Concilium* 183, 1986, ix–x

Preface to *The Peace Bible. Words from the Great Traditions*, ed. S. Scholl, Los Angeles 1986, vii–ix

Editorial, 'An Ecumenical Assembly for Peace', *Concilium* 195, 1986, xvii–xviii

Editorial, 'Ethics of World Religions and Human Rights', *Concilium* 1990/2, vii–viii

Editorial, 'Fundamentalism as an Ecumenical Challenge', *Concilium* 1992/3, vii–viii

Preface to K.J. Kuschel, *Born Before All Time? The Dispute over Christ's Origins*, London and New York 1992, xvii–xix

VII Tapes

'The Infallibility of the Church', lecture and discussion at the University of Glasgow (1 cassette), Peter Okell Sound Features, Salford, Great Britain 1970

'Five Lectures and Two Discussions at the University of Melbourne 1971' (2 cassettes), Clarion Enterprises Pty Ltd, South Melbourne, Australia 1971

'Jesus: Challenge to the Church', lecture in Chicago 1971 (2 cassettes), The Thomas More Association, Chicago, Illinois 1971

VIII Documentation

Hans Küng, *His Work and His Way*, ed. H. Häring and K.J. Kuschel, Collins, London 1979, and Doubleday, New York 1980

Küng in Conflict, ed. L. Swidler, Doubleday, New York 1981

Robert Nowell, *A Passion for Truth. Hans Küng: A Biography* (US subtitle *Hans Küng and his Theology*), Collins, London, and Crossroad Publishing Company, New York 1981

IX Special editions

J.P. Frank, *Conversation with Küng*, Phoenix, Arizona 1984

'Is There One True Religion – Or Are There Many?', Ninth Annual Lecture, St George's House, Windsor Castle 1986

Appendix: Documentation

Editors' Preface

On Tuesday 18 December 1979 a statement by the Congregation for the Doctrine of Faith was delivered to Hans Küng in Tübingen by a courier of the Bonn nunciature. It contained the charge that in his writings Küng deviated 'from the complete truth of the Catholic faith'. The consequence: 'Therefore he cannot be regarded as a Catholic theologian or teach as such.' This withdrawal of the church's licence (*missio canonica*) had been agreed in advance with German church circles, especially with Cardinal Höffner, the then President of the German Conference of Bishops, and Georg Moser, the then Bishop of Rottenburg, and co-ordinated down to the smallest detail. So similar statements were issued from Cologne and Rottenburg.

There were various protests in Tübingen during 18 December and above all on Wednesday 19 December, particularly by the faculty and the students. Faced with them, the Bishop of Rottenburg telephoned Hans Küng on 19 December. He suggested that they should meet as soon as possible for a conversation, and this was arranged for that very evening, at Küng's house. Bishop Moser was accompanied by Vicar General Dr Karl Knaupp and Dean Alfred Weitmann, and Küng had asked his two colleagues Norbert Greinacher and Walter Kasper to be present. During this conversation, which lasted around three hours, Bishop Moser offered to mediate personally with the Pope if Küng would further clarify his theological position on the questions in dispute in a letter for the attention of the Pope, at Moser's suggestion taking up a statement of the German Conference of Bishops on *Infallible?* of 4 February 1971, which had avoided the term infallibility.

The next day Küng telephoned the bishop, agreeing to write such a document on condition that, if it were to be published, the bishop's letter to Cardinal Šeper with the reservations it contained should be published at the same time. Subsequently the bishop did not keep to this agreement. On the evening of 19 December, at the end of the conversation in Küng's house, the following press release was agreed: 'On the evening of Wednesday 19 December 1979, Bishop Dr Georg Moser and Professor Dr Hans Küng met in Tübingen for a conversation on the content and effects of the statement by the Congregation for the Doctrine of Faith. An attempt was made to come to an agreement in this difficult situation.'

Hans Küng worked the whole of Thursday 20 December on his letter for the attention of the Pope; it was ready towards midnight and immediately taken to the bishop in Rottenburg. Walter Kasper also had this letter and telephoned expressing his agreement. The document had a further covering letter to the bishop, which was meant to clarify Küng's basic intention:

Dear Bishop,

The enclosed statement is made in response to your express wish that I should contribute to making possible a way out of a situation which seems almost hopeless. It has proved extremely difficult for me to produce in such a short time, on top of all my other duties, a text in which I can make a responsible theological reply. But I hope with all my heart that this statement can serve to ward off incalculable damage to our church.

May the Spirit of God and Jesus Christ guide you on your difficult journey to Rome!

Best wishes,
Yours sincerely,
Hans Küng

Hans Küng

Statement for the attention of the Pope, 20 December 1979

I have always understood myself to be a Catholic theologian and I shall continue to do so. I still regard myself as a priest of the *Ecclesia catholica*. As a Catholic theologian I have been and am particularly concerned for the 'Catholic', that is, the 'whole, universal, comprehensive, total' church. So I have been and am constantly concerned to teach the Christian truth in Catholic breadth and depth. Thus all my life I have been occupied with the continuity of faith and the community of faith which is maintained through all disruptions: Catholicity in time. I have also been occupied with the universality of faith and the community of faith which embraces all groups: Catholicity in space. In this spirit I would like to continue to present Catholic doctrine as a Catholic theologian. In this I know that I am at one with countless theologians, pastors, teachers of religion and lay people. I venture to make the following remarks on the most recent statements by the Congregation of Faith; I begin with some general remarks.

In my most recent publications on the question of infallibility I have not been concerned to sharpen the question but to clarify it in a constructive way – without any *pertinacia*. In my preface to Hasler's book (in addition to reporting his findings) I merely brought together thoughts from my 'balance sheet' on the infallibility debate which was published in 1973. The theological meditation *The Church – Maintained in Truth?*, written in parallel, also states explicitly: 'This meditation is not intended to provoke any new dispute over infallibility.' It was not, and is not, my concern to make accusations but to ask questions; I am ready to subject my views to a new examination. To this end both in the preface and in the meditation I took up the French theologian Yves Congar's request that Rome should appoint an ecumenical commission of internationally recognized experts in the various disciplines. My theological work so far has not been governed by 'contempt for the *magisterium* of the church' – I must energetically reject this charge – but by the concern that the church's *magisterium* should have new credibility in the church and the world. Nor have I in any way 'put my own judgment first as a norm of truth' – even in opposition to 'the church's sense of faith' – but in scholarly honesty and loyalty to the church I have orientated the whole of my theological work on the gospel of Jesus Christ and on the Catholic tradition. I may not conceal the fact that I still have severe reservations about the way in which the Congregation goes about its work. It seems particularly incomprehensible to me that the Congregation did not even allow me the possibility of stating and justifying my position before its more recent and serious step. Moreover, the procedure is offensive in that the Congregation in its statement also raises serious charges against my view of 'some main items of Catholic faith' (christology and mariology), although these questions were never the subject of Roman proceedings against me.

And now after these general remarks, some comments on the central question at issue. My view of the *magisterium* and infallibility is seen in a one-sided and negative way in the statement by the Congregation of Faith. By way of clarification I would like to state the following – taking up remarks made by the German Conference of Bishops on 4 February 1971:

Already in my earlier publications on the question of infallibility I never expressed any doubts that there are church statements which are true and can be recognized as being true; in changing historical modes of thought and forms of expression they remain the same; they remain irrevocable, and call for an unmistakable yes or no.

I equally acknowledge that the church has the duty and the task to proclaim the Christian message attested by scripture and to do so in a clear and binding way. Here, however, the statements made in the Declaration *Mysterium Ecclesiae* of 1973 on the historical conditioning of all expressions of faith must be taken seriously.

I have also always affirmed that those holding office have a specific responsibility to see that the church abides in the truth and that it states the Christian truth in a binding form, demarcating it in particular situations from that which is not Christian (definitions of faith or dogmas). In this connection the ecumenical councils have special authority as a representation of the whole church, the college of bishops with the Bishop of Rome as its head. In respect of this special significance of the ecumenical councils I too, also and particularly on questions of christology, in principle stand on the same ground as the councils of the early church, and have therefore paid particular attention to making them comprehensible to people of today.

As for the First Vatican Council, it was never my purpose to deny its definitions of faith, to put the authority of the Petrine office in question, or even to make my own view the criterion of theology and disturb Catholic people in their faith. On the contrary! I have merely asked how, in view of the well known theological difficulties, the possibility of infallibly true statements as understood by Vatican I can be grounded in scripture and tradition. That is not a trumped-up question as far as I am concerned but an authentic one, and the debate on infallibility which followed, in a wide international framework, had at least one result: a great many theologians whose Catholicity is quite beyond dispute have conceded the necessity and justification for this enquiry.

I therefore ask you seriously to believe that in doing this – while recognizing my own personal risk very well – I wanted to perform a service for our church in order to clarify, in a spirit of Christian responsibility, this question which burdens so many people inside and outside the Catholic church. The question is of particular importance for an understanding with the Eastern churches, towards which Pope John Paul II has given a new and hopeful impulse by setting up a special commission. A new discussion of the question is also important from an ecumenical perspective.

This statement is made in the trust that the present difficult controversy, the consequences of which are unforeseeable, can be brought to a positive solution in a spirit of true Catholicity.

(from N. Greinacher and H. Haag, eds, *Der Fall Küng. Eine Dokumentation*, Munich 1980, 122–5)

Karl Rahner

Letter to the Pope, 7 December 1981

Professor Dr Karl Rahner,
Sillgasse 6,
A 6020 Innsbruck

7 December 1981

Holy Father,

We theologians who are the signatories to this letter see ourselves as church theologians who are devoted to this our Catholic Church, who are loyal to the church's ministry, and understand their task as service to the orthodoxy of church teaching. In this conviction we address Your Holiness with a petition coming from both mind and heart, that the Holy See should do everything possible to see that the efforts towards peace between the church's *magisterium* and Hans Küng do not flag and run into the sand, but continue and find a satisfactory solution. We are convinced that Küng's own inner disposition justifies this hope for agreement. It is further our opinion that in this concrete situation the *magisterium* in the church should of its own accord declare itself ready for new joint reflections and should set these in motion.

In our view, in the present situation it would be good if the Holy See were to encourage some of the theologians whose signatures are below to hold a conversation with Hans Küng on the questions in dispute. Here we presuppose that the Holy See, too, is convinced that there are substantive matters which have not been clarified in every respect and which cannot wait to be pursued further only after a 'submission' on Küng's part.

Furthermore we would find it extremely helpful if you yourself, Holy Father, were to have a conversation with Hans Küng so that he can describe his basic intentions to you. As you know, Hans Küng himself has already asked for such a conversation on many occasions – most recently in a personal letter of 25 August 1980.

Your Pentecost Letter to the German Bishops last year suggests such a conversation, and so above all do your words about the place and significance of theology in the church on the occasion of your visit to Cologne and Altötting in Germany. Of course Hans Küng, too, would have a new contribution to make to such a conversation.

We do not think that there was merely hopeless dissent in the Küng case. Efforts at agreement and reconciliation must continue. Nor must one think that the matter has been settled in the meantime.

It is now almost two years since the decision of the Congregation of Faith of 18 December 1979. But the disagreement among Catholics continues; confidence in the church's ministry continues to suffer hurt; and the silent exodus from the church is supposed to be because of this conflict between the church and Küng. We theologians cannot give up hope, so we are communicating these requests to Your Holiness.

We have deliberately avoided involving a larger number of professors of theology in this step, not least to guarantee its confidentiality.

With respectful greetings

Prof. Dr Marie-Dominique Chenu (Paris)
Prof. Dr Heinrich Fries (Munich)
Prof. Dr Alexandre Ganoczy (Würzburg)
Prof. Dr Joseph Lescrauwet (Louvain)
Prof. Dr Rudolf Schnackenburg (Würzburg)

On behalf of all signatories:

Karl Rahner*

*The agreement of all living signatories to the publication of this letter has been obtained.

Norbert Greinacher and Herbert Haag

Appeal to the Pope, 24 April 1980

Autumn 1980 saw the appearance of a documentation on 'the Küng case' (*Der Fall Küng*), edited by the Tübingen Catholic theologians Greinacher and Haag. On the basis of 163 documents this volume told the story leading up to the withdrawal of Hans Küng's licence, reconstructed the process of its withdrawal, and reflected the attitudes of groups and institutions, theological faculties and individuals, in Germany and abroad. The volume ended with an analysis by the two theologians and a personal 'Appeal to the Pope'. The analysis made here is of such fundamental significance that we are reprinting it once more as a third document. Like many other initiatives with the same intent, the appeal to the Pope has still not met with any response, either public or personal.

1. Pastoral dimension

The great concern of countless people, above all in the churches, cannot be overlooked. Teachers of religion who based their instruction on publications by Hans Küng are asking themselves what they should do in the future. Priests who used Küng's theology as a guideline for their preaching are refusing to read out the pulpit statement by the German bishops. Pastoral workers, who are encouraged by Küng's proposals for reform, are deeply disturbed in their work. Theologians all over the world feel affected by Küng's condemnation. Students and candidates for the priesthood doubt whether it makes sense to go on studying theology. Catholic academics, artists, intellectuals to whom Küng has shown a way of believing with intellectual honesty are asking themselves whether there is still a place for them in this church. Although the authorities have attempted to impose their view with a tremendous amount of expensive publicity, even the so-called 'ordinary people' who unfortunately could not have a voice in this book have protested with thousands of letters to the bishops and messages of sympathy to Hans Küng in opposition to the measures of the Roman Congregation of Faith and the Bishop of Rottenburg.

In all Christian freedom, the bishops and the Pope must be asked a question of conscience: do you still represent the sense of faith of the whole church? In whose name and for whom do you speak in condemning Hans Küng? Are you not disowning those very people who by conviction share in the church's thought and work? Are you really doing justice to your task of witnessing to the

Christian message in a credible way today? Are you aware of your responsibility for the faith of all members of this church?

There can be no doubt that the credibility of the Catholic church has been deeply shaken. The supreme representative of this church cannot get away with pleading vehemently for human rights in today's society while on the same day violating the rights of a Christian through the abuse of the church's legal system. The credibility that many women and men have built up and regained for the church through their own laborious and sacrificial work and their testimony in the service of the church has been impaired, and indeed partly destroyed. The Pope and the bishops must be led to ask themselves, 'How do you explain this?'

2. Theological dimension

It is our conviction that there is no meaningful alternative to a theology which is consistently related to scripture and historically responsible, which without reservation takes up the questions of our time and orientates itself solely on Jesus Christ. Of course we would not be theologians and professors if on a whole series of points we did not have our critical questions to put to our colleague Hans Küng. But anyone who has read Hans Küng's hermeneutical principles, i.e. the normative perspectives for his theological work ... can hardly avoid noting that only with this vision can theology be done seriously and fruitfully today. Here there is also a welcome accord between Hans Küng and Edward Schillebeeckx, which Küng puts like this: 'The first "source", the first pole, the first norm of Christian theology is God's language of revelation in the history of Israel and the history of Jesus ... The second "source", the second pole of Christian theology, is the world of our own human experience.'

What has been said above about the general orientation of theology applies in particular to christology. If things were as the statement by the Congregation for the Doctrine of Faith of 15 December 1979 describes them, then the theologian would have only to repeat previous formulations by the church's *magisterium* and provide justification after the event for new formulations by the *magisterium*. No theologian who stands in the Christian tradition and at the same time is aware of his obligation to critical rationality can accept that. So in the central sphere of the Christian message, in credible witness to the person and cause of Jesus, with good reasons, Hans Küng has taken new ways by exploring the field of tension between God's revelatory language in history and our own modern world of experience. In so doing he has opened up new access to Jesus Christ for countless people.

3. Ecumenical dimension

One should also have no illusions: the Roman measure has struck the ecumenical movement a real blow. The response from the World Council of Churches, from Protestant theologians and churches is clear. Once the classic controversial theological questions like justification, scripture and tradition, the nature of the church, word and sacrament had been worked through theologically – not least by means of the works of Hans Küng – the obstacle to a reconciliation of the churches remained the question of ministry and especially the Petrine service. Despite all the questions that can be put to Hans Küng here as well, there can be no doubt that once again a solution is possible only in the direction which he, along with many others, has taken. The door to ecumenical understanding has been shut for the foreseeable future. Here too, the Pope and the bishops must be led to ask themselves, 'How do you explain this?'

4. Political dimension

Küng's Professorship in Ecumenical Theology and his Institute for Ecumenical Research have been put directly under the University President, and are not part of any faculty. This compromise with the law relating to church and state must not disguise the fact that considerable cause for conflict remains. This is shown above all by the debate in the Baden-Württemberg Landtag and Professor Küng's letter to Minister Engler of 21 January 1980. How long will a faculty and a university allow appointments and dismissals, indeed even details of university practice, to be decided formally by the local bishop but in reality directly by the Roman Curia, without any basis in the law relating to state and church? For how long will the political public allow the church, by an increasing number of decisions to deprive professors of their licences, to compel the state to set up more and more new professorships? For how long will the state governments simply make themselves an extension of the Roman claims to power, without testing whether the church is observing its own legal ordinances? For how long will the church be allowed to interpret the regulations of the Concordat quite one-sidedly in its favour with the aid of the 'prevalent doctrine of the law of church and state' – and also be given the state's sanction ... Can the Catholic hierarchy constantly on the one hand call on the state to settle conflicts within the church and on the other get round state laws when these prove inconvenient to it?

The church side will have to decide. *Either* it continues to interpret the legal clauses about church and state completely one-sidedly in its favour and compels the state to constantly new concessions. In that case it must not be surprised if within the foreseeable future all the stipulations of the Concordat (incuding the church tax) are increasingly put in question by the public. *Or* it keeps strictly to the Concordat and avoids of its own accord anything that could strain regulations which have become anachronistic. For as the problem of confessional schools shows, in the long run even the prevalent opinion of constitutional lawyers will not be much use to the church.

The public will then have to ask whether in the present situation concordats with the Vatican can still be a meaningful basis for ordering the complex relationship of state, society and church in Germany.

5. Church–historical dimension

Time and again in church history there have been phases of critical decision which have been of the utmost significance for the church's further development. There was such a juncture when Paul fought for the right of non-Jews in the church, not without conflicts with Peter. Further changes are associated with the names of Constantine, Charlemagne and Gregory VII. The decisions of the church had an ominous effect at the time of the Reformation: at that time the Roman supporter of an understanding, Cardinal Contarini, who was suspected of heresy, died; the central Roman Inquisition (the predecessor of today's Congregation of Faith) and the Index of prohibited books were set up; and many concerned for reform were in despair. It was a historical disaster of world magnitude when in the 'Rites Dispute' of the seventeenth century the same Inquisition vitiated missionary efforts towards an integration of the Christian message into Asian thought and life by a narrow-minded and short-sighted decision.

Today the church is once again at a fatal turning point in its history. Here Hans Küng must be right. *Either* it develops the openness which came about through Pope John XXIII and the Second Vatican Council, attempts to integrate interpretations and expressions of Christian faith which have multiplied over history or recently come into being, like the theology of liberation, and thus becomes a truly Catholic, plural, conciliar church. Or it retreats into the ghetto, absolutizes a historically conditioned Roman interpretation and form of life as the only Catholic one, and thus increasingly becomes a major sect. The Küng case and countless other indications seem to suggest that the authorities are tending towards the second possibility.

In the name of all those, named and unnamed, whose protest is expressed in this document, we resolutely and passionately oppose such a momentous mistake. We call on all members of the church, whether or not their voices are heard in this book, not to resign and leave the field to others, but, trusting in the workings of the Spirit of Jesus Christ, to continue to devote themselves indefatigably to a comprehensive reform of the church in the service of all men and women.

6. Procedural dimension

The accusation will probably be made that the documentation presented here is also 'anything but a documentation of understanding', that rather it 'shows no readiness for reconciliation but rather a resolve for open confrontation'. But we are convinced that this documentation was necessary, indeed called for. Anyone who studies it without prejudice from beginning to end cannot avoid finding that an injustice has been done to Hans Küng by his church. The laws of the church have been flagrantly violated. The procedure scorns the principles of Christian brotherliness. The substantive questions raised by Küng have either not been perceived or have been answered in a know-it-all tone ... In view of this, as teachers of theology and priests of the church we make ourselves the spokesmen of the protest articulated in this book and throughout the world, and address the Pope directly:

Holy Father! Take up the case again without delay! Appoint an unprejudiced commission of bishops and theologians to examine properly and not under the pressure of time the theological questions which have been raised! We appeal to your responsibility and your conscience: make good a wrong that has been done! Do not leave the rehabilitation of Küng to history! Make your personal action a blessing for the church!

Tübingen, 24 April 1980

(from N. Greinacher and H. Haag, eds., *Der Fall Küng. Eine Dokumentation*, Munich 1980, 540–6)

Contributors

Masao Abe is Professor of Buddhist Philosophy in the Department of Philosophy at Perdue University, West Lafayette, Indiana.

Evgeni Barabanov contributes to the Moscow paper *Voprosy Filosofi* as a historian of art, philosopher and theologian.

Tony Bayfield is a rabbi and Director of the Sternberg Centre for Judaism in London.

Shalom Ben-Chorin is a freelance writer and theological journalist in Jerusalem.

Leonardo Boff is Professor of Systematic and Ecumenical Theology at the Instituto Theologico Franciscano in Petropolis, Brazil.

John Bowden is an Anglican priest and theologian and Managing Director of SCM Press in London.

Kenneth W. Brewer is a Methodist pastor and doctoral student in systematic theology at the Department for Theological and Religious Studies of Drew University, USA.

Johannes Brosseder is Professor of Systematic Theology in the Pädagogische Hochschule in Bonn.

John B. Cobb is Emeritus Professor of Systematic Theology in the School of Theology in Claremont, California.

Abdoldjavad Falaturi is Professor of Islamic Studies and Director of the Islamic Scientific Institute in Cologne.

Albert H. Friedlander is a rabbi in Kensington, London.

Norbert Greinacher is Professor of Practical Theology in the Catholic Faculty of Theology at the University of Tübingen.

Hermann Häring is Professor of Systematic Theology in the Theological Faculty of the Catholic University of Nijmegen, The Netherlands.

Peter Hebblethwaite is a journalist on theological and church affairs and lives in Oxford, England. He contributes regularly to *The Tablet* and the *National Catholic Reporter*.

Werner Jeanrond is Professor at the School of Hebrew, Biblical and Theological Studies in the University of Dublin.

Kurt Koch is Professor of Dogmatics in the Theological Faculty in Lucerne.

Karl-Joseph Kuschel lectures in Ecumenical Theology and Theological Aesthetics at the Catholic Theological Faculty of the University of Tübingen and is Deputy Director of the Institute for Ecumenical Research there.

Charles Middleburgh is a rabbi and teaches at Leo Baeck College, London.

Ronald Modras is Professor of Theological Studies at St Louis University, St Louis, USA.

Elisabeth Moltmann-Wendel is a Protestant theologian and freelance journalist who lives in Tübingen.

Sir Nevill Mott is Emeritus Professor of Physics in the University of Cambridge. He worked at the Cavendish Laboratory and was awarded the Nobel Prize for Physics.

David Tracy is Professor of Systematic Theology in the University of Chicago.

Lukas Vischer is Professor of Ecumenical Theology in the Protestant Faculty of Theology, University of Bern.